BROADMOOR MEMORIES

MEMORIES

THE HISTORY OF THE BROADMOOR

Architectural rendering of the Broadmoor Hotel by Warren & Wetmore of New York. 1917. El Pomar Foundation

BROADMOOR
MEMORIES

THE HISTORY OF THE BROADMOOR

BY ELENA BERTOZZI-VILLA

Published for the Broadmoor by Pictorial Histories Publishing Company, Inc.,
713 South Third Street West, Missoula, Montana 59801.
Publishing Coordinator, Stan Cohen.

THE BROADMOOR HOTEL has a long and glorious history of providing the very best in dining and accommodations in surroundings that combine the refinement and flair of European design with the raw beauty of the American West. Generations of travelers from all over the globe have come here to have the times of their lives in this unique setting.

This book is a token of our respect for the staff members who have been a part of the Broadmoor's history and our deep appreciation for the guests who have stayed with us over the decades. We guide the Broadmoor's future with a clear mission: to hand it down in pristine condition and good health for yet another generation of employees and guests to enjoy.

The story that follows will take you from the early days when Pikes Peak and its foothills overlooked the empty plains, to the present, where they provide the backdrop for one of the world's finest resorts. The Broadmoor Hotel invites you to step into our past. I am sure you will want to stay.

STEPHEN BARTOLIN JR.
President, Broadmoor Hotel

Spencer and Julie Penrose, 1937. Courtesy Hermine Weber

To Spencer and Julie Penrose, may their dream live on.

Riders on horseback behind the Broadmoor, circa 1924.
The wooden bridge leads to the island in the center of Cheyenne Lake. Courtesy Richard L. Goudie

Contents

Romancing The Plains

WHEN THE BROADMOOR hotel was completed in June of 1918 it blossomed on the barren prairie like an exotic Italian lily. Unlike most resort hotels, which spring up in the midst of wealth and glamour, the Broadmoor was conceived and constructed in an economically depressed area and time. This mecca for those seeking pleasure and repose in the dramatic beauty of the Colorado foothills was the product of the imagination and impetuous will of the hotel's founder, Spencer Penrose. His creativity and business acumen, combined with the refinement and artistic sense of his wife, Julie, brought prosperity, culture, and one of the world's finest hostelries to the region they had adopted as their own.

Spencer Penrose was the epitome of the American success story. Although born of an aristocratic Philadelphia family, he left his inherited wealth and prestige to go West and make his fortune with his own two hands. A large and imposing man, he had no qualms about using the strength of his character or his fists to attain his goal of great wealth. By 1906 he had become a multimillionaire, and the storminess of his nature was tempered by his marriage to a vivacious, charming widow named Julie who matched his atheism with her devout Catholicism, his brashness with her delicacy and love of beauty, and his egotism with her altruism and generosity. Spencer Penrose had reached a point in his life where he wanted to expend his energies to create something beautiful and lasting, and Julie was the perfect partner for such an endeavor. Together they created the Broadmoor Hotel, a place where beauty found its expression in every detail and where visitors could enjoy all of the best things in life in a setting as nearly perfect as could be created by almost unlimited funds and exquisite taste.

The story of the Broadmoor Hotel begins in 1918, but to understand its setting we must go a little farther back. As far as anthropologists have been able to determine, the plains around the base of Pikes Peak show few signs of settlement by human beings before the Spanish, French and

Julie and Spencer Penrose created a thing of lasting beauty on Colorado's Front Range.

AT LEFT: The Broadmoor on a summer afternoon in 1993. One way to live the Good Life in Colorado.

American colonists arrived. No Native American tribes made their homes here, although tribes of nomadic plains Indians such as the Utes, Cheyennes and the Sioux often passed through. The mineral springs in the foothills, later called Manitou Springs, were used for their medicinal properties and the towering mountain was revered. Farther south the Anasazi made their homes in the cliffs and the Navaho and Pueblo Indians had permanent settlements in southern Colorado and New Mexico.

In the 1700s the whole southwest was laid claim to by the Spanish conquistadors led by Coronado in search of gold and other riches. Little did they realize that the gold they were seeking lay under their horses hooves and was to become a magnet for generations of future fortune seekers. The land later became the property of France and was sold to the United States as part of the Louisiana Purchase.

Until the mid-1800s, this area still had no permanent residents. Trappers, traders, explorers and especially mineral assayers came and went until the great mineral riches that underlay large portions of the West were identified and streams of people began to cross the country in search of gold. As the forty-niners moved through Colorado, some stayed on. In 1858 the first settlers attempted to establish a town at the base of Ute Pass, but as their search for gold was unsuccessful, they soon left. Miners who arrived in 1859 had better luck because the town served as a trail stop for those trying their luck in settlements higher up in the mountains. By 1860 the small cluster of homes and businesses called itself Colorado City and boasted a number of handsome buildings. The location seemed ideal, for in addition to the possibility of gold, the land was fertile, lumber was abundant and the possibilities seemed bright.

Unfortunately for the town founders, gold was not discovered in sufficient quantities to hold the population who had that as their single purpose. Although the Colorado legislature chose Colorado City as the capital for

the territory in 1861, as soon as they realized that the town was losing its lifeblood they moved it to Denver. Colorado City then suffered a number of crippling setbacks which rendered its future quite dim. In 1863 Fountain Creek flooded, decimating the crops; what was left was eaten by a plague of grasshoppers. These natural disasters were followed by the onset of violence between the Native American populations who had encampments nearby and the white settlers who had more or less peacefully co-existed up to this point. Once the cycle of violence had begun, the whites lived in fear of attack and set up what defenses they could, but there were deaths on both sides which further soured the possibilities for the city's growth.

In 1864 Colonel Chivington and his group of militia men attacked a Cheyenne and Arapaho Indian encampment at Sand Creek and massacred all, mostly women and children. This quelled the "Indian menace" for a period until the U.S. government made a treaty which recompensed the tribe and acknowledged the government's fault. By the late 1860s hostilities had ceased and the stage was set for the arrival of the man who first realized the potential of the location.

General William Jackson Palmer was a Philadelphian[1] of Quaker ancestry who had come West to make his fortune. He first saw the area as a scout for the Kansas-Pacific Railway while attempting to determine the best path for extending the Kansas-Pacific from Denver to the Pacific Coast. He was Managing Director and Superintendent of the Railway, a job he

---

1. Curiously enough, a number of the people associated with the history of the region and the Broadmoor area came from Philadelphia.

had accepted after commanding the 15th Pennsylvania Cavalry during the Civil War. Riding through the area on his way to Colorado City he was struck by the incredible panorama that unfolded around him: the perpendicular grandeur of Pikes Peak, which vividly contrasted with the flatness of the plain, the sculpted green foothills watered by cascades such as Seven Falls, and the eerie beauty of the Garden of the Gods. While bathing in the soda springs the next day, he began to imagine a resort city where the sick could take the waters and breathe the clear mountain air and the well could disport themselves among the area's natural wonders. Though, at that time, founding cities was not one of his plans for the future, events conspired to make his vision a reality.

His experiences as the commander of a daring and highly successful group of cavalrymen during the Civil War had taught him that the seemingly impossible could be achieved if enough determination was brought to bear on the task. The war had brought together large numbers of young men from all over the country and showed them that by working together they could accomplish great things. Palmer's 15th Pennsylvania Cavalry was an extremely close-knit, loyal group of young men who respected their leader and who were to be essential to his new project in the West. The end of the Civil War spurred movement to the West by several groups of these men who were disgusted by the carnage and vicissitudes of war. They wished to create new colonies where people could start afresh without the strife and corruption of the East Coast. This was certainly an idealistic dream, but the purity and starkness of the Rocky Mountains inspired them to think that a better world was possible. Palmer shared this ideal, along with the more practical desire to make money by promoting the development of the vast lands along the Rocky Mountains.

BELOW: This map was designed to encourage less-experienced forty-niners to try their luck around Colorado City. Notice the arrows indicating likely gold sites and good campgrounds.

Starsmore Center for Local History, Colorado Springs Pioneers Museum

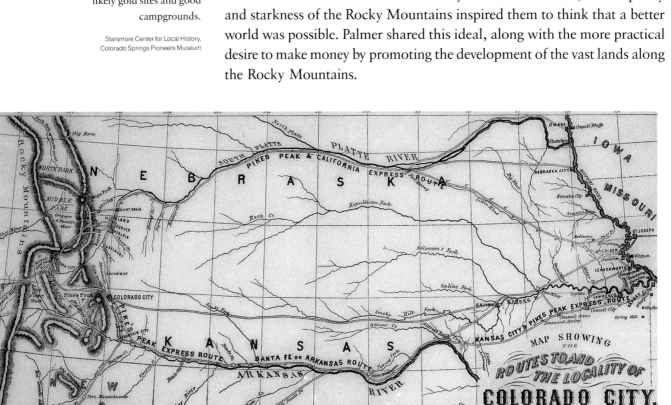

When the Kansas-Pacific Railway decided to use a route other than the one Palmer had recommended, he left the company with his head full of ideas for the land that he had scouted. General Palmer decided to build his own railroad which would extend south from the stopping point of the Kansas-Pacific in Denver down into Mexico. Being a well-traveled man and familiar with European sources of capital, he knew that he could find investors for his project despite the difficult economic situation in America in the aftermath of the Civil War. He began by purchasing large tracts of land, including the Pikes Peak region, where he intended to create the city he had imagined. The attractive settlement would both promote his new railway and be rendered accessible by it. The city he had in mind, however, was not just any city, but a city worthy of the grandeur of its surroundings and the woman that he wanted to bring there. For, in the process of planning the railroad and finding funding for it, he had met his Queen. She was a fascinating, delicate beauty who distracted his attention from his desire to build a railroad and a fine city. After meeting her, his heart demanded that he create an environment where she would be happy. Unfortunately, his vision of an ideal environment did not coincide with hers.

Palmer met Queen Mellen while negotiating a partnership in his railroad and real estate investments with her father, William Proctor Mellen, a New York lawyer. His serious soldierly demeanor dissolved at the sight of the petite, dark-haired beauty, and from that moment on he was torn between his Rio Grande Railroad and his role as an assiduous and dutiful lover. He attempted to combine his two passions by envisioning a city which would serve his purpose while providing a perfect setting for his new-found love. He personally had found the answer to his needs in the West and thought of it as a place to retreat from all of the ills that afflicted the East. He imagined a city where alcohol and debauchery would be illegal and the citizens could pursue health, culture and happiness under the serene auspices of Pikes Peak. Queen, however, unlike Palmer's image of her as a woman who would be content in a strict moral and temperate climate, was happy in large cities, surrounded by ample opportunities for social engagements and the comfortable life of her class. Though she came to Colorado Springs and tried to live here in order to please her husband,

ABOVE: The trail leading up Ute Pass was a hazardous one and only wide enough for one wagon. Wagon trains such as this one taking supplies into higher settlements had to alternate with the traffic coming down.

Starsmore Center for Local History, Colorado Springs Pioneers Museum

AT RIGHT: The vivid colors and unusual shapes of the rock formations in the Garden of the Gods have inspired awe and a sense of mysticism since they were first viewed by human eyes.

Bob McIntyre photo

BELOW: The center of Manitou Springs with the Navajo Springhouse in the foreground, the bathhouse on the left and the Manitou Cliffhouse Hotel in the background, circa 1880.

Photo by Fredrick Stehr
Starsmore Center for Local History,
Colorado Springs Pioneers Museum

she never liked it. The unpaved streets and rugged lifestyle were too much for her and she finally settled permanently in England with her three daughters leaving her husband alone and unhappy in the beautiful surroundings that he had chosen for her.

Although unappreciated by Queen, Colorado Springs came into its own under the guiding hand of its founder. When General Palmer founded the city in 1871, he set aside land for a university and for extensive city parks. He also established legislation banning the sale of liquor within the city limits and attempted to promote a climate of strong moral standards. To this day, downtown Colorado Springs has broad beautiful streets lined with trees that center around Pikes Peak Avenue, lovely parks, and a clause in all property deeds which prohibits the selling of alcoholic beverages (which is no longer enforced). Despite this clause, which was not agreed to by all, Palmer and his associates successfully created a city where the rich and enterprising would feel comfortable and want to come to live.

AT RIGHT: Colorado Springs in the early days, circa 1890. It was not the bustling metropolis Palmer had optimistically described to Queen.

Starsmore Center for Local History,
Colorado Springs Pioneers Museum

THE MAN WHO HELPED ORGANIZE and coordinate the investors that Palmer had been able to woo in England was Dr. William Bell. Bell had accompanied Palmer on the scouting party for the Kansas-Pacific Railroad and they had become close friends. He also saw to it that Colorado Springs was well-publicized in England and many Britons came to see and experience the American West. In the early days the town was called "Little London" due to the large number of British settlers and visitors. Dr. Bell set the tone for the budding community by entertaining lavishly in the lovely stone manor he had built in Manitou[2] Springs. It was furnished with exquisite materials from Europe. Beautiful scenery and high society alone however, were not enough to spur the growth of the new city. General Palmer had built a bath house at the soda springs in Manitou, but he had not really capitalized on the idea that the Pikes Peak region could be considered a place to attain health. But by 1872 people had already begun to visit the dry alpine climate of Colorado Springs in the hopes that their tuberculosis and other lung

ABOVE: The trip up the canyon to see Seven Falls was usually undertaken by burro, a frequent sight in the streets of Colorado Springs. Adventurous visitors climbed the rickety wooden ladder to the top of the falls.

Starsmore Center for Local History,
Colorado Springs Pioneers Museum

2. Manitou was given its name by another stockholder in Palmer's companies, William Blackmore who had been reading Longfellow's poem "Hiawatha" and associated it with the Ute Indians he saw in town. The springs had first been named "La Font," but upon Blackmore's insistence the name was changed to that of the Algonquin deity in the poem.

AT RIGHT: Queen Palmer and her youngest daughter, Elsie, at the manse in England, which she much preferred to Colorado Springs. A frequent guest in Queen's house was John Singer Sargent whose haunting portrait of Elsie is on display at the Colorado Springs Fine Arts Center.

Starsmore Center for Local History, Colorado Springs Pioneers Museum

BELOW: General William Jackson Palmer with his dogs at Glen Eyrie in 1900.

Starsmore Center for Local History, Colorado Springs Pioneers Museum

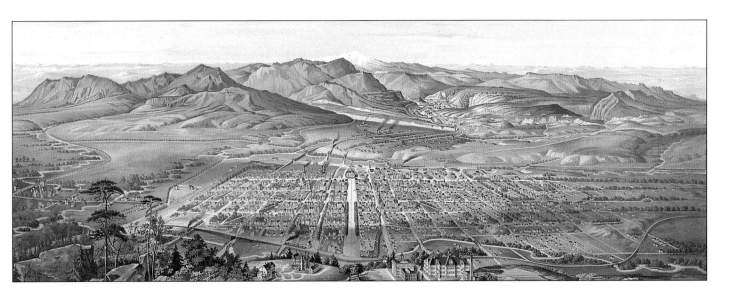

ailments would improve. Capitalizing on this trend, in 1874 two young doctors began to circulate rumors that the springs at Manitou could actually cure a wide range of disorders. One of the two, Dr. Solly, published a pamphlet which outlined how each of the springs caused improvements in different parts of the body. Surprisingly enough, sufferers discovered that they did improve and word of the new spa spread to the East Coast and Europe.

Thus began one of Colorado Springs most successful industries. Consumptives began to come to the city in great number, and Sanatoria and hospitals were built to accommodate them. There was no known cause or cure for tuberculosis at the time. It was a mysterious disease which seemed to pick its victims at random from all walks of life. Though "cures" of all sorts and natures were inflicted upon patients of tuberculosis, the only recognized treatment was to send the afflicted to dry mountain climates where they were given high protein diets and encouraged to rest and sleep outside in the cold air. Many homes and hotels, including the Broadmoor, were built with open sleeping porches so that tuberculosis patients could be exposed to the healing air at all times.

A number of Colorado Springs' most illustrious residents came here initially seeking a cure. Some, like Artus Van Briggle, the renowned Art Deco potter (although he later succumbed to tuberculosis), came and improved long enough to establish a business. Others, such as author and champion of Native American civil rights Helen Hunt Jackson, who suffered from bronchial catarrh, were completely cured. The influx of consumptives and their families as well as other factors brought good economic times to Colorado Springs. Growth attracted more settlers, including several of the principal actors in the history of the Broadmoor area, who also found their way here guided by the hope of improved health and economic prosperity.

ABOVE: The city of Colorado Springs as Palmer envisioned it—lush, green and orderly. Drawing entitled "Pikes Peak Panorama," circa 1898.

Starsmore Center for Local History, Colorado Springs Pioneers Museum

In 1880, another Philadelphian arrived in Colorado Springs. William J. Willcox, accompanied by his wife and children, came hoping to find a cure for his tuberculosis and to improve the family's lot. His father was a very wealthy paper and cement manufacturer in Philadelphia, but after his second marriage he insisted that his son accomplish something on his own. Despite the fact that he had little experience in agriculture, Willcox purchased fifteen hundred acres of land on the mesa at the base of Cheyenne Mountain and established a small dairy. Though the origin of the name is not known, he called it the Broadmoor Dairy Farm.

The dairy was not the first enterprise on the land which is now the Broadmoor Hotel. In the late 1860s the Myers brothers had a ranch where they grew corn for making brooms which they sold in their shop in Colorado City. The land to the west of what is now Mesa Avenue was owned by William F. Dixon, who purchased it in 1875. His house stood on Mesa Road, next to the present location of El Pomar Center and he collected toll from the few residents of Colorado Springs who ventured up into the Canon to view the unusual falls and sculpted rocks.

Willie Willcox purchased the land that had been the Myers farm and additional land extending south and east. Dixon remained in possession of his land until he sold it to Stratton and later Penrose in the 1900s. The Willcoxes built a beautiful stone house with sixteen rooms and central heating. There were three small cottages for the milkers, and cow and hay barns for the animals. An ice house and spring house were built near Spring Creek,[3] which ran through the

---

3. This creek now runs through the Broadmoor golf course and the pond is part of the Colorado Springs School, four blocks down Broadmoor Ave.

property and formed a small lake near the house. The dairy had the tranquil and prosperous air of a Pennsylvania farm. Despite appearances however, Willcox's inexperience with animal husbandry soon began to take its toll. The cows became ill and produced such little milk and poor quality butter, that he was ready to abandon the project and return to Philadelphia. He realized that without expert advice and significant capital investments his Colorado project could not be a success and began negotiations to sell the farm.

The Broadmoor project was not destined to fail however, for yet another young man had come West to seek his fortune — this time all the way from Prussia and when he saw what the inexperienced American had called a "dairy" his Teutonic pride demanded that he set things right. Count James Pourtales first saw the lovely mesa that would anchor his heart and much of his money to a remote spot on the Colorado front range when Dr. Solly (of Manitou miracle water fame) took him to the Broadmoor Dairy to introduce him to Willy Willcox in December of 1885. The two men immediately liked each other and began a friendship which would end only with Willcox's death in a riding accident after many years of business and social partnership. Pourtales had his own reasons for wanting to stay in Colorado Springs, and he couldn't resist the opportunity to show the Americans what a little German scientific farming could do for Willcox's ailing dairy herd. Willcox, instead of going back to Philadelphia, threw in his lot with the genial Count.

Pourtales was a Prussian Count, whose estates in Glumbowitz (in an area that is now Poland) were undergoing hard times due to environmental and economic difficulties. He came to the United States in 1884 and 1885 to seek opportunities for investment so that he could raise enough capital for the improvement of his European estate and to study American agricultural methods. These methods, however, he found far inferior to those practiced in Germany where he had studied. He had heard that one of the soundest investments in the United States was mortgages which paid at least eight percent and he researched the opportunities for obtaining these in various parts of the country. Despite the fact that eight percent mortgages did not abound in the Pikes Peak region, Pourtales came to Colorado Springs often. Like Palmer before him, he was interested in more than making money, and the city held great attraction for his romantic half.

Countess Berthe de Pourtales (who was James' first cousin from the French branch of the family) had come to Colorado Springs earlier with her two young daughters to distract herself from the failure of her first marriage to wealthy Bostonian, Sebastian Schlesinger, and to visit her brother, Louis Otto Pourtales, who had a ranch in Florissant, Colorado. Otto divided his time between Florissant and Colorado Springs where he led a busy social life (including a brief infatuation with Queen Palmer). His sister set up house in a cottage downtown and decided to stay for a while. Their father had emigrated from France years before and Berthe had been born in Washington, and then moved to Cambridge when her father began working at Harvard. She, like Queen Palmer, was possessed of uncommon beauty and refinement. Her lissome figure and cultured ways were much appreciated by Colorado Springs' high society. Count James Pourtales had long been interested in his lovely cousin. Once she had freed herself from her first marriage, he began an extensive courtship which involved numerous visits to the city that harbored her.

James Pourtales came to America not only to seek romance and fortune, but also to expand and enrich his experience beyond that of the German landed nobility from which he came. Had he been like other young men of his class he would have stayed in Germany, leased out his estates to a caretaker, and lived as well as possible off of the income in the drawing rooms of Europe. He believed, however, that everyone should have some practical knowledge of the world in which he lives and some direct experience of work. Shortly before coming to America he had personally taken over the management of his estates so that he could improve the income they produced. He studied agriculture and was familiar with the latest

ABOVE: Hand-tinted photo of Williams Canon by Gustav Sandahl, circa 1910.

Colorado Springs Pioneers Museum

LEFT: This early view of Cascade Avenue in downtown Colorado Springs shows the magnificent buildings constructed by the principles in the town's development. General Palmer's Antlers Hotel and the fine residences of Dr. Solly and Count James Pourtales inhabit an otherwise empty plain, 1887.

Starsmore Center for Local History, Colorado Springs Pioneers Museum

RIGHT: Count James Pourtales'
affable appearance combined
with his considerable charm and
purportedly large fortune made
him one of the Springs' most
popular citizens. Circa 1885.

Starsmore Center for Local History,
Colorado Springs Pioneers Museum

methods for optimizing yield and improving stock. Pourtales wanted to be in touch with the source of his wealth, and the land and people that produced it. The principles that he would live his life by were ". . . do not overestimate yourself; listen for you can learn something from everyone; do not steal; be polite, generous, but not weak; be an aristocrat by breeding and not false pride."[4] His experiences in the Colorado Springs area reflect that he lived his life according to these principles, though he found that those with whom he did business did not have the same high moral standards that he had. This is, perhaps, one explanation of why his business undertakings did not do particularly well, though the strength of his character increased his worth in his cousin's eyes.

BERTHE, THOUGH ATTRACTED by the Count's charisma, was not easily convinced to formally join her destiny to his, and the Count had to be assiduous in his attentions. Before he was able to win Berthe, the charms of the Broadmoor mesa had begun to bewitch him. His plans for investment in lucrative mortgages were derailed by his partnership with

4. Count James Pourtales in his autobiography, *Lessons Learned from Experience*, U.S. copyright 1955, The Colorado College.

Willcox which demanded his personal involvement as well as his capital. Making the Broadmoor Dairy into a profitable enterprise would require a great deal of time and effort, something he could little afford given the condition of his estates in Prussia. Love, however, blinds even the most well-intentioned and in 1886 he began researching the possibilities for the new business.

He began by analyzing the market, which had a great deal of potential. The wealthy residents of Colorado Springs were certainly willing to pay for good quality butter and milk, but none was available. Pourtales determined that the dairy herds west of the Mississippi had only the sparse plains grass as fodder which did not provide them with enough calories to produce milk high in butterfat. He began conducting experiments in Colorado Springs, studying those cows which produced well and augmenting their diet to produce more and better milk. Pourtales agreed to become Willcox's partner if he met the conditions which Pourtales felt would turn the business around. The money that he contributed to the project must be spent the following way: firstly, to buy a large amount of adjoining land with good water rights so that alfalfa hay could be produced, secondly to sell most of the original herd and purchase eighty head of sound cattle, thirdly to purchase a milk separator and enlarge the barns. It was clear to Pourtales that water was the most precious resource on the arid mountain plain and he saw to it that the dairy acquired enough new land with water rights to ensure the production of high quality hay. Towards the end of 1886, when the dairy seemed to be well established on the road to profitability, the Count returned to Prussia to tend to his estates there, without the benefit of profits from American investments. This long commute between Colorado Springs and Glumbowitz was to be the downfall of his business dealings in Colorado. Time and again he would leave his affairs in good condition only to have them ruined by poor management in his absence.

Once again under the unaided direction of Willcox, the Broadmoor Dairy began to encounter serious difficulties. The quality of the milk and butter were much improved and were selling well, but competing dairies irritated by the Broadmoor's success tried to sabotage the business. They went so far as to pour gasoline into the milk cans and spread rumors that Broadmoor products were inferior. The well-bred Willcox had no idea how to counter such unethical practices. Many of the cows then became infected with brucellosis and had to be put down. In 1887 Willcox informed Pourtales that the

ABOVE: The Countess Berthe de Pourtales was not easily won, but after she married the Count she was a loyal partner in his quixotic ventures.

Broadmoor Historical Collection

business was no longer making a profit and Pourtales returned to Colorado Springs in a fury.

Throwing all caution to the winds, Pourtales decided that the dairy could be profitable only if it were much larger and better able to provide good fodder and water to the cows. He bought more land and more cows. Under the amused gaze of Berthe and worried frowns from Willcox he went personally to barns in Colorado Springs and Denver to witness the milk production of exceptional cows and when he found a cow that produced well he bought it. He also purchased a beautiful Swiss bull named William Tell to improve the bloodlines of the stock. To avoid fluctuations in the butter and milk markets he set up a cheese factory and brought in an expert to run it. By 1889 his efforts had paid off and the dairy produced such high quality butter, milk and cheese that Broadmoor products were sold as far away as Denver and Leadville. At this point, his investments in the Broadmoor Dairy far exceeded Willcox's and the terms of their original agreement. Pourtales became the owner and principal shareholder in the dairy thus further enmeshing himself in the destiny of Colorado Springs despite all of his plans to the contrary!

Although the Broadmoor Dairy was doing well, Pourtales realized that the dairy business would never provide a large enough return on his investment and his estate in Prussia was in dire need of capital. He needed to come up with a more lucrative business or his interests at home would suffer serious setbacks. He began to look at the land which made up the dairy in a new light. Perhaps some of the land that he had accumulated for hay farming could be used for speculation in real estate. During the period that he had been concentrating on the dairy, Colorado Springs had been growing rapidly, primarily to the north and east, but Pourtales thought that he could convince people to move south and he just happened to have a great deal of land on a beautiful mesa. Pourtales decided that the only

BELOW LEFT: Pourtales's sense of humor was evident in all areas of the business.

Starsmore Center for Local History, Colorado Springs Pioneers Museum

BELOW RIGHT: This advertisement appeared in the local papers as part of the bitterly fought war between competing dairies.

Broadmoor Historical Collection

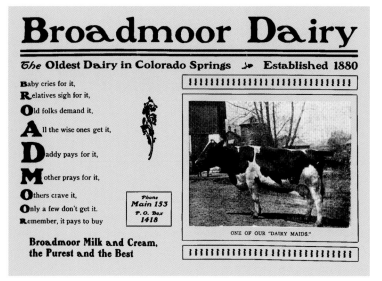

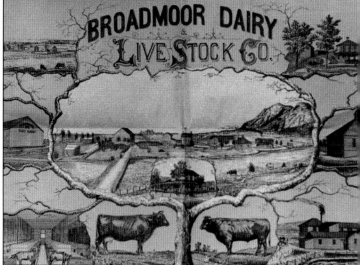

way to make a good profit from the land was to create an upper-class suburb of Colorado Springs with numerous amenities which would greatly increase its value as home sites. Then he would have to convince the wealthy and prestigious to build homes on the lots. Needless to say, transforming hay fields into an exclusive suburb was no small task, but the thin mountain air had apparently stripped Pourtales of prudence and caution and he attacked this new proposition with enthusiasm.

In the latter part of 1888, Pourtales formed the Cheyenne Lake, Land and Improvement Company, investing two hundred and forty acres of dairy farm land and nine thousand dollars in the enterprise. Willcox became a partner with the investment of three thousand dollars, and they were obliged to include Judge E.A. Colburn who was the guardian for three children who owned eighty acres of land right in the middle of the proposed suburb. Recognizing that land values were skyrocketing, the Judge refused to sell the land to anyone except himself. The company's intent was to promote and sell lots of land and to supply the residents with water from a yet-to-be-constructed lake. Pourtales's close attention to the procurement of land with water rights for the farm served him well, for an adequate water supply would be essential to the establishment of a new residential district.

Given the importance of the lake, Pourtales placed it in a central location on the mesa and platted the suburb's main avenues radiating out from it. The mesa's four percent slope down towards the east necessitated the building of a dam along part of its eastern edge which had to be a minimum

of fourteen feet high. After he determined the size of the lake, three hundred feet long by fifteen hundred feet wide, he decided to build a twenty-foot dam with a one hundred and ten-foot thick foundation. The excavation of the earth was accomplished using teams of horses which pulled huge shovels known as "wheel scrapers." At rest the shovel was tipped up and balanced on two wheels. When the horses started to pull, the lip of the shovel was forced under the earth until the shovel was filled, at which point the load was tipped back on the wheels and hauled away. When the excavation was finished, water was diverted from Cheyenne Creek and the lake was filled.

True to Pourtales' design, the lake greatly enhanced the beauty of the land. Cheyenne Mountain was reflected in its glassy mirror and the edges soon grew green with grass that would hopefully spread to encompass the homes that he envisioned. With a plow, he had the avenues scraped

Cottage at Broadmoor by Douglas & Hetherington ARCHITECTS

and planted tree seedlings along both sides. On paper, the suburb was a marvel, all it needed was buyers. The Count, however, could not devote himself entirely to the project because his beloved Berthe had finally agreed to marry him and wished to have his full attention which she had been sharing with numerous dairy cows and plat maps. Berthe wished to marry in the East so her family could attend, therefore the Count had to make arrangements for management of the property in his absence once again. Pourtales hired a reputable manager for the dairy, the Scotsman Duncan Chisholm. He also made agreements with his two partners in the Cheyenne Company that they would be very industrious in the selling of lots, as well as in the construction of their own homes in the Broadmoor which they had promised to build. Confident that this time all would be properly taken care of, the Count and Countess set off for Glumbowitz, stopping briefly in New York to marry before they returned to Europe for their honeymoon. Pourtales' vision of a trouble-free honeymoon disappeared as quickly as the water in his new lake, which mysteriously emptied itself fourteen days after it had been filled. Pourtales barely had time to return to Glumbowitz before bad news reached him there.

Willcox's son had become ill and the family had to go back and forth to Philadelphia for medical care, leaving the promotion of Broadmoor lots to Colburn. Colburn declined to build a house in the Broadmoor because Willcox had reneged on building the first one. Once again, competition for dairy goods became fierce, for one of the new residents of Colorado Springs was a dairyman, Louis Ehrich. He convinced one of the Broadmoor Dairy's employees to turn traitor and bribe cooks and maids of Broadmoor Dairy customers to ruin the products. The introduction of oleomargarine during this period also dealt a blow to the dairy business. Despite these troubles, Chisholm did his best, but there was little that he could do to combat the vagaries of nature. 1889 was a drought year for Colorado Springs. After months passed with no rain and the city's yards and gardens were drying up, city government officials decided that they

ABOVE: Broadmoor Cottages were actually large villas equipped with all of the latest conveniences. Pourtales described his prospective suburb in the most effusive terms to tempt the wealthy to build homes on the Broadmoor plain.

Investigate "BROADMOOR" For Fine Villa Sites: Before deciding where to purchase, rent or build, see this most desirable suburb of Colorado Springs, adjoining famed Cheyenne Mountain and Canons. Investigate the many unquestioned advantages it presents for the health or home-seeker, removed as it is from smoke, dust and bustle, yet within a few minutes, by electric cars, of business, pleasure and markets as offered by the most prosperous city in the West . . .
Money to Loan: In large or small sums at 6 per cent. To parties wishing to build at Broadmoor. Sites for sale from $8.00 per foot frontage, according to location. Information cheerfully furnished at the Company's office at Broadmoor. BROADMOOR LAND CO. D. Chisholm, Manager. Telephone 167

Broadmoor Historical Collection

would claim the water in Cheyenne Creek to alleviate the needs of the citizens. The city stated that it was obligated to take this step and that any damage to crops would be repaid later. Chisholm and Colburn watched in despair as Pourtales' seedling trees died and the alfalfa harvest was severely damaged.

Once again Pourtales returned to Colorado Springs seething. He now had upwards of $160,000 invested in the Broadmoor and every time he left something happened to place the whole in serious peril. The Count immediately started litigation against the City of Colorado Springs to protect his water rights, and won the case; forcing the city to establish expensive reservoirs up on the slopes of Pikes Peak. He then negotiated with his new rival in the dairy business so that both of them could operate profitably. Once again, however, he came to the realization that the dairy alone would not be enough and he had to find some way to make his planned suburb become a reality. This involved, of course, the investment of even more money and time.

First of all, he had to address the problem of the lake which was no more. He had spent most of the $12,000 capital of the Cheyenne Land, Lake and Improvement Company just to excavate the hole and build the dam. Though the bottom of the lake had appeared sound when the excavation was completed, it was peppered with tunnels that were the only remnants of a once-extensive prairie dog colony. The pressure of the water had reopened the burrows and the water drained away. At great expense, the burrows were filled with clay with only partial success. Finally a herd of sheep was led into the dry lake and fed at various points until the sheep dung, along with additional clay sealed the bottom. The lake, lovely as it was and is, cost Pourtales $25,000 before it was finished.

The cost of rebuilding the lake forced Pourtales to consider the sanity of his project once again, but he stood to lose so much that he did not

RIGHT: The scope of Pourtales' dream is evident in this circa 1891 photograph. The Cheyenne Mountain Country Club and the tram tracks are in the foreground, the Broadmoor Casino in the background and numerous seedling trees struggle to survive on the arid mesa.

Cheyenne Mountain Country Club

want to give up yet. Ever-increasing land speculation and his control of water rights convinced him that there was a fortune to be made if only he could attract the right kind of people to the Broadmoor. He replanted tree seedlings and kept his hopes high. This was accomplished by engaging in ever-more speculative mathematics. He calculated that he would need two hundred and fifty thousand dollars for the construction of what he called "Broadmoor City." Pourtales composed a prospectus outlining all of the beauties and advantages of the area. His "City" had spacious avenues lined with trees, plentiful water supplies, its own power plant and, most importantly, a Casino in the best European tradition on the east side of the lake. His plans also included a luxury hotel on the west side, but he realized that it would be impossible to build it immediately. In order to have enough land for this "City" he combined the assets of the Broadmoor Dairy and the Cheyenne Lake, Land and Improvement Company to create the Broadmoor Land and Investment Company, which controlled twenty-four hundred fourteen acres and a very expensive lake.

The population of "Broadmoor City" then took on primary importance in Pourtales' mind. Colorado Springs was a town with a higher than usual population of active, well-to-do young men. They came, as Palmer and Pourtales had, to test their manhood and find their fortunes and they found ample opportunity to do both in the Springs. Pourtales recognized that the support of this group was essential to his project and one day while chatting at El Paso Club (the best men's club in the city to which all the up and coming belonged), he had a marvelous idea. He would establish a country club out in Broadmoor City where these young bloods could play any number of sports, associate, negotiate and, most importantly, drink! For Colorado Springs was a dry town and there was nowhere within the city limits that a man could legally buy his friends an alcoholic beverage. Thus was born the Cheyenne Mountain Country Club which is presently

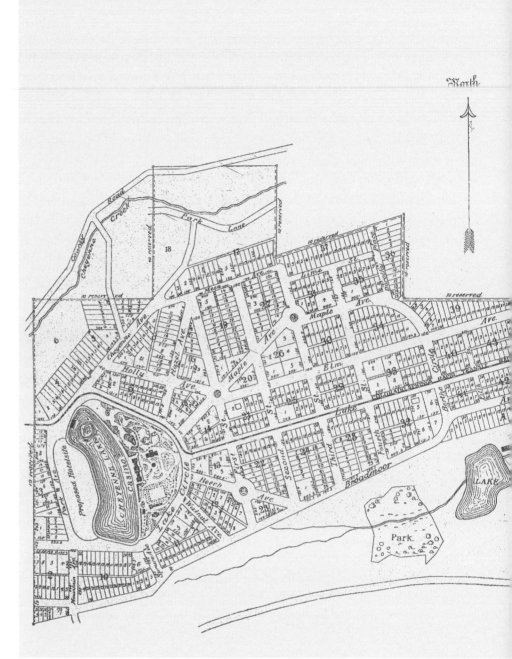

RIGHT: This drawing of the "Broaodmoor City" envisioned by Count James Pourtales was taken from the endpapers of his autobiography, *Lessons Learned From Experience*. Note the proposed hotel site across the lake from the Casino.

The Colorado College

situated just a few blocks down Lake Avenue from the Broadmoor Hotel. William J. Willcox was one of the three men who signed the articles of incorporation and Pourtales, the club's Vice President, sold them the land at a very reasonable rate. Thirty of Colorado Springs' finest joined the club. The clubhouse was inaugurated on the Fourth of July, 1891, with the first of many memorable parties to be held there. The club was extremely successful from its inception and attracted the attention of many to the Broadmoor area. The Cheyenne Mountain Country Club is an example of Pourtales' innovative mind, for it was the second country club to be established in the United States.

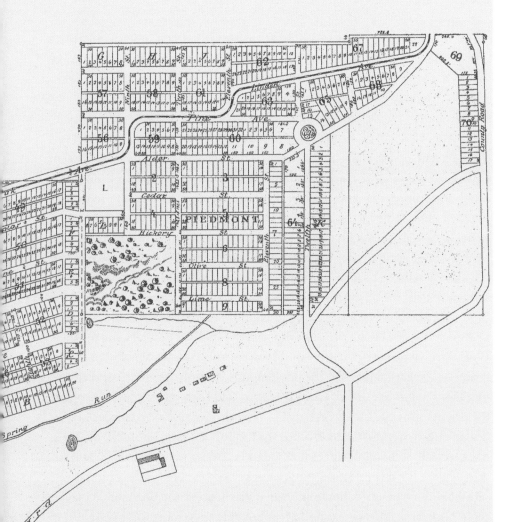

BROADMOOR

Scale: 400 ft = 1 inch.

Pourtales then began negotiations with the company that was replacing horse-drawn trams in downtown Colorado Springs with electric streetcars. Providing safe and adequate transportation to his suburb was a principal concern, because the train tracks that crossed Nevada Ave. before the intersection with the Broadmoor road were unprotected and several people had been killed there. These accidents concerned people who might otherwise have been interested in relocating to the suburb. After weeks of discussion and compromise, the Count obtained a contract stating that the streetcar network would include the four English miles of the Broadmoor suburb if Pourtales gave them twenty thousand dollars upon completion of the route.

T HIS DONE, POURTALES' need for cash was dire and he was obliged to go to Chicago and New York in search of investors. In New York, he made an agreement with the London and New York Investment Company for a loan of two hundred and fifty thousand dollars with the stipulations that the money be used for the improvements outlined in the Broadmoor City prospectus, that half of the income received from the sale of each lot go towards the payment of the loan, and that the London and New York Investment Company be given one thousand of the five thousand shares of the Broadmoor Land and Improvement Company. Pourtales calculated that the initial six hundred acres of land to be sold would bring in at least nine hundred thousand dollars, more than enough to pay off the loan, and this figure did not include the income from the water and electrical plants. Having not completely lost his sense of reason, he gave himself several months before assuming this large burden of debt for an empty plain thousands of miles from his home. From New York, Pourtales continued on to Glumbowitz where he found his lands and stock in a declining state of health and ever more in need of capital. When Chisholm wired him that the son-in-law of the famous Mr. Pullman was seriously considering buying the Broadmoor Company for three hundred and fifty thousand dollars, Pourtales was ecstatic and encouraged him to complete the negotiations as quickly as possible. The two parties were concluding the deal in mid-November of 1890 when the English banking house Baring Bros. unexpectedly went bankrupt. The English economy went into shock and the waves had a terrible effect on the American West where English capital was very heavily invested. Pullman immediately canceled the deal and Pourtales came back from Europe as quickly as possible to salvage what he could in Colorado Springs. He had no choice but to assume the loan from the London and New York Investment Company, and they had no choice but to give him the money though they would have gladly avoided it.

Once again in Colorado Springs, Pourtales found an architect for the crown-

BELOW: The Broadmoor Casino was a lovely building. Its wide porches and elegant columns set the tone for the atmosphere its builder wanted to create, circa 1892.

Starsmore Center for Local History, Colorado Springs Pioneers Museum

ing glory of Broadmoor City. He wanted a beautiful, European-style casino on the edge of the lake where the elite of Colorado Springs could dance, drink, watch the sun set behind the mountains and think about building houses on the surrounding plains. He hired an architect named Lindley Johnson from a Philadelphia firm, who drew up plans for a long elegant building which stretched along the east side of the lake and faced directly down Lake Avenue. The building was a two-story wooden structure with a white colonnade across the front and handsome arched windows to let in plenty of light. The porches which encircled the top floor created a covered walkway on the ground floor where guests could promenade and view the dramatic scenery to the east. The back of the top floor faced out over the lake where the lovely building was reflected. The boathouse opposite the island housed small sculls for trips out onto the water.

The interior was designed with simple elegance. The large entrance hall was paneled with dark oak. Two staircases led to the second floor. The bar and gaming rooms were to the left of the entrance along with a spacious area for billiards. The ladies salon and kitchens were to the right of the entrance. On the upper floor the stairways opened directly into the ballroom where concerts could also be held. The ballroom had French doors which opened onto a wide balcony beside the lake. The upper floor also contained dining rooms, reading rooms and another ladies salon.

Pourtales was delighted with the design and construction began in February of 1891. The news of the impressive building excited a great deal of interest and the Broadmoor Land and Investment Company finally began to receive offers for lots. The Count became extremely busy as he had to oversee the running of the diary, the operations of the Broadmoor Company, and the construction of the Casino. Just as his luck seemed to be turning, he fell ill with tuberculosis and was bedridden for weeks. He had hoped to sell many lots during the critical period when enthusiasm about the casino was high and before the effects of the Baring failure hit the economy of Colorado Springs, but this was not to be.

Although his illness was causing him to miss real estate opportunities, he was determined to open the Casino for business on the first of June and he had to find an orchestra and a staff. This he accomplished by sending Willcox to New York and a young music professor from Colorado College to San Francisco. Professor Pearson engaged Rossner's Hungarian Orchestra and Willcox found a manager and a French chef from prestigious establishments in New York. Pourtales worked from his bed, frantically ordering supplies and furniture and determining how all of the staff could be housed and fed. When he was finally allowed to get up and attend to things personally, there were innumerable problems to address. The urban staff was disoriented and incapacitated by the stark prairie surroundings and the unavailability of their traditional resources. A great deal of time and money was required to make things right for them. Pourtales had to personally oversee all of the landscaping necessary to make the exterior of the building attractive as well as ensure that all of the interior details were done correctly and up to standard. In the process of outfitting the Casino he came to the conclusion that setting up an enterprise of the quality he desired was an enormous undertaking and one that he had not been prepared for. But in the end it all paid off, when the Casino first opened its doors on the first July of 1891 it was a marvel.

People flocked to see the little palace with its orchestra, fine French wines and roulette wheels. The new electric street cars came up Lake Avenue and left the patrons at the foot of the oval park just before the building. Flower beds and grass carpeted the grounds, the lake was stocked with trout and strains of music floated out from the ballroom to entertain even the boaters on the lake. Liquor flowed in streams, for Pourtales had stocked the bar with the best that Europe and America had to offer. The quality of the food was much appreciated and the restaurant had to turn away diners because the staff could not meet the demands of so many.

Unfortunately for Pourtales, the great success of the Casino masked a number of irregular business practices among the newly assembled staff. Food, liquor, cigars and furnishings mysteriously disappeared and the cash box did not accurately reflect purchases. Pourtales found that he had to fire much of the original staff and find less prestigious, but more honest replacements. After only a few months of operation the Casino was twenty-five thousand dollars in debt and Pourtales had to scramble to find more cash for the company. His attempts on the East Coast to find funding did not succeed as money was still in short supply, but he was able to get twenty-five thousand dollars from a multimillionaire in Colorado Springs who had made his fortune mining gold in Aspen.

The search for capital for the Broadmoor company led Pourtales in a new direction. The economic situation on the East Coast was grim, but

LEFT: Interiors of the Casino
were simple but of top quality
workmanship. This is the
staircase that led to the music
room on the upper floor, circa
1895.

THE CASINO

recent gold strikes in Colorado had created an unexpected and extremely liquid source of funds very close to home. Gold had, in fact, been discovered in a cow pasture called Cripple Creek on the slopes of Pikes Peak not far from the Broadmoor mesa. Though still in a preoccupied fog worrying about the destiny of the Broadmoor Land and Investment Company, Pourtales had not lost sight of his initial goal to make enough money to retire in comfort to a rejuvenated Glumbowitz. These rumors of gold proved to be so tempting that in the latter months of 1891 the Count visited the budding camp with his friend Tom Parrish. The pair spent several days scouting the area and discussing the results of ore assays with the prospectors that had already staked claims. By the time they descended into Colorado Springs the Count had been infected with gold fever and it was the beginning of the end of his involvement with the Broadmoor.

The news that a foreign investor was considering investing in Cripple Creek sparked a great deal of interest in the area and land values began to climb exponentially. Good quantities of ore with high levels of gold were discovered and excitement in Colorado Springs reached a fever pitch. Pourtales was less and less inclined to expend his energies in the Broadmoor company especially given that land sales were almost non-existent and he could see no other way of encouraging sales. In 1892 he began making plans for bailing out, even if it meant losing the almost two hundred thousand dollars he had invested, at least he would lose no more. He was able to interest a small group of Colorado Springs investors in the project based on the success of the Casino, which was breaking even under the direction of the new staff. These partners took the burden of the second mortgage off of his shoulders and optimistically looked into building the planned hotel on the other side of the lake.

With the Casino on a relatively even keel and high hopes for Cripple Creek the Count and Countess returned to Europe for the first months of 1893. Then, in June of that same year, the Panic of '93 began when the mints in India stopped mining silver. The ensuing financial crisis wreaked havoc in the American economy, especially given that the Baring Bank crisis three years earlier (which had undermined his sale to Pullman) had already weakened the financial community. Numerous banks failed and money was not available at any cost. The five new shareholders in the Broadmoor were decimated by the blow and could provide no assistance. Pourtales had no option but to call the London and New York Investment Company and allow the Broadmoor to go into receivership.

Pourtales' contribution to the history of Colorado Springs was not yet at an end, for he went on to involve himself deeply in the booming gold camp of Cripple Creek. Even in Cripple Creek he seemed dogged by bad luck; he was never able to invest in a profitable endeavor. His luck finally and permanently changed for the better when he met a young geologist named R.A.F. Penrose, brother of Spencer, the man who was to bring great prosperity to his Broadmoor project years later. On the advice of Dick Penrose, Count James Pourtales, his wife, Berthe, and two others invested in the Common Wealth mine in Arizona, about forty miles from the Mexican border. The mine became profitable within a few months after the shaft was sunk and Pourtales was finally able to restore his estates in Prussia, which had become more and more dilapidated with each failed venture in Colorado. He and Berthe lived in comfort off the income for the remainder of their lives. The Count died at Glumbowitz in 1908 at the age of fifty-five. He did not live to see another daring entrepreneur finish the project that he had undertaken, but surely he would be delighted with what the Broadmoor has become today.

And what became of the Broadmoor Land and Investment Company? Duncan Chisholm was appointed manager of the property and the Casino continued to operate under the ownership of the receiver though it was never wildly successful. A small hotel was built next to the Casino in 1897, but it was a plain building and not the elegant complement to the Casino that Pourtales had envisioned. Shortly after the construction of the hotel, the Casino was consumed by fire. But all was not lost, for by that time a number of Colorado Springs residents had chosen to build homes under the promise of Pourtales' seedling trees. The streetcar line to the lake was a popular weekend outing for families and though the area was not growing by leaps and bounds, it was quietly prosperous. Before the end of the year, the London and New York Investment Company built a new casino in the same location. They hired a Colorado Springs architect named Thomas MacLaren, whose building was smaller and more modest, but quite as appealing in its particulars.

While the Broadmoor area was slumbering in its period of dormancy, the man who was to change it forever arrived in Colorado Springs. Summoned by his brother's stories of fortunes being made in Colorado gold and the recommendation of his friend Charles L. Tutt, Spencer Penrose came to see what the magic of Pikes Peak could do for him.

Penrose
finds himself,
his destiny
and his own
true love in
Colorado
Springs.

Minerals and Millionaires

After Count Pourtales had given up on the Broadmoor area it seemed that the glittering future he had foreseen for the beautiful mesa was never to become a reality. As time passed, the trees grew taller around the buildings that clustered by Cheyenne Lake, but few enjoyed their shade. Lacking the elegance of the previous structure and the charisma of its creator, neither the hotel nor the new Casino prospered, and in 1909 the London and New York Investment Company sold the buildings and the unsold Broadmoor lots (of which there were many) to a local organization. The Casino was leased out for church and social functions, but the crowds that had thronged up Lake Avenue in electric streetcars and carriages

BELOW: The Cripple Creek area as Bob Womack knew it. Before he discovered the ore-laden rock, it was just another mountain pasture. Circa 1885.

to marvel at Pourtales' achievements were a thing of the past. Spencer Penrose's arrival in Colorado Springs eighteen years earlier, however, had initiated the chain of events which would culminate in the fulfillment of Pourtales's dream.

Spencer Penrose was born in Philadelphia on November 2, 1865, and was the fifth of seven children, all boys, born of Sarah Hannah Boise and Dr. Richard A.F. Penrose. Both Richard Penrose and Sarah Boise could trace their ancestry back through a number of noteworthy individuals who were significant in the history of the United States. R.A.F. Penrose was a descendant of Bartholomew Penrose who had been a partner of William Penn's in the mid 1600s. Since that time the Penroses had intermarried with the most prestigious Pennsylvania families, and included generals, public officials and reverends among their numbers. The sons of R.A.F. and Sarah followed in their forefathers' footsteps.

The first son died in infancy, but the following four were all exceptional in their accomplishments. The eldest, Boise, graduated second in his class from Harvard and went on to become a Senator from Pennsylvania, an office which he held from 1897 until his death in 1921. He is remembered as heading the Republican political machine that controlled Pennsylvania for years and for being less than scrupulous in the methods that he used to exercise his power. Boise was followed by Charles Bingham, who graduated first in his class from Harvard at age nineteen and became a very successful physician. Richard A.F. Jr. graduated from Harvard *summa cum laude* and subsequently earned an M.A. and Ph.D. in geology. These degrees would serve both him and his brother Spencer well in their endeavors in the West.

Spencer's father lived to see his boys become great men, but Sarah Hannah Boise Penrose died at the age of forty-seven under circumstances that would affect her fifth son for the rest of his life. Spencer was fifteen years old and alone in the house with his mother when, with no warning, Sarah died. Spencer remained with the body until the rest of the family returned. For the rest of his life he was wary of being alone, and the mere mention of his mother's name was enough to make him relive the trauma and desperation of those hours. The loss of Sarah caused Dr. Penrose to become a dominating presence in the children's lives and strengthened the bonds among the Penrose brothers. They supported each other in times of need and celebrated each others' victories. Spencer attained his goal of wealth with the assistance of R.A.F., and Boise's political career was made possible in part by the financial support of his brother Speck.[1] In innumerable ways, the strength of the family unit made it possible for each of them to attain their goals.

As a young man, however, being the next in such an illustrious chain of sons was no easy task, and Spencer did not manage to come up to scratch in any of the areas where his brothers had been so successful. He went to Harvard, but barely managed to graduate in 1886 with a B.A. After obtaining his degree he came West with the desire to prove himself, and to prove to his father that he too would amount to something. He stayed in Las Cruces, New Mexico, operating a small business for four fruitless years before rumors of gold reached him and he decided to go and find some for himself. His brother Richard, who had often worked as a mining consultant in Colorado Springs, had told him of the numerous possibilities for entertainment and wealth to be found there. Another drawing point was one of his childhood friends, Charles Leaming Tutt, who had a fledgling real estate business that was starting to boom.

The Tutt connection with the Penrose family began in the mid-1800s in Philadelphia. Penrose's father, Dr. Richard A.F. Penrose, had known Charles Tutt's father, while they were studying medicine at the University of Pennsylvania. Spencer and Charley were childhood friends and maintained contact although their ways parted in adolescence. Penrose went

ABOVE: Charles Leaming Tutt Sr. was Penrose's friend and business associate. They had known each other since childhood in Pennsylvania. Circa 1907.

Courtesy R. Thayer Tutt Jr.

BELOW: "Mr. Tutt's Coach and Six on an excursion to General Palmer's Glen Eyrie, 1903. Mr. Charles Leaming Tutt and coachman on box; on top, right to left, Mrs. C. L. Tutt (dark hat), Mr. & Mrs. Benjamin C. Allen, Mr. Butler Williamson, Varina Davis Hayes and companions." (Webb family scrapbook) Varina Davis Hayes, Dr. Gerald Webb's wife, was Jefferson Davis' granddaughter.

Special Collections, Colorado College Library

---

1. This was Spencer's childhood nickname, and what he was called by his friends.

on to Harvard, but young Charley Tutt was forced to leave high school and go to work due to his father's early death.

Charles Tutt came to Colorado Springs in 1884 at the age of twenty to join a relative of his, Dr. Williamson, in a cattle business in the northern part of Colorado Springs known as Black Forest. When this proved successful, he built a home on the prairie for his prospective bride and returned to Philadelphia to marry Josephine Thayer, daughter of Judge Thayer, a respected jurist. When the couple returned to Colorado Springs, Tutt established his own real estate and insurance business. Thus, when whispers of gold once again swept through Colorado Springs, he was in an excellent position to begin investing. By the time Spencer Penrose arrived in Colorado Springs in spring of 1891, Tutt was speculating in real estate and mining claims in Cripple Creek.

When Speck arrived, his old friend met him at the railroad station. Penrose immediately expressed the need for a libation of the stronger sort and Charles drove him out to the Cheyenne Mountain Country Club, still one of the few places in the area where a man could drink legally and in peace. Tutt's choice of bar, just a few blocks from where the Broadmoor Hotel would arise twenty-two years later, foretold the bond which was to

The Glory That Was Cripple Creek

Although the Pikes Peak region had long held out the promise of gold, no significant gold strikes had been made in the area prior to 1891. Most of the residents of Colorado Springs had resigned themselves to the fact that the city would have to find alternate sources of income, such as invalids and tourists. Others, however, found this frustrating, given that fortunes were being made mining gold and silver in many other parts of Colorado such as Leadville, Aspen, and Central City. A number of prospectors doggedly continued to search the surrounding area for likely pieces of rock and brought them in to be assayed.

One such prospector was Bob Womack, who had a small cattle ranch on the lower slopes of Pikes Peak. There was a log cabin on the property next to a spring and spring house, during the building of which a man had almost been crippled. The settlers who had built the cabin, the Welty's, had named the land "Cripple Creek" prior to selling it to the Womack family. (There

be forged between Spencer Penrose and the mesa which had so enchanted Count James Pourtales.

Spencer Penrose's arrival was a fortuitous event for both himself and Charles. The four years that Spencer had spent in the West had not been profitable, and when he reached Colorado Springs he also reached the bottom of his pockets. Charley Tutt made him an offer of half of his real estate business for five hundred dollars if Spencer would live in Cripple Creek and manage the business there. Spencer agreed immediately, promising to pay later, given that his pride prevented him from wiring home for money. Charley accepted, knowing that the Penrose family had excellent credit, but in the years that followed the two made so much money that the $500.00 was never officially repaid. The Tutt and Penrose real estate business continued to grow as they invested in properties in Colorado Springs, Cripple Creek, Pueblo and even Denver. They also branched out into mining. Charles Tutt had purchased the Cash On Delivery mine in 1891 although its previous owners had had no luck with it and Dick Penrose assured him that there was no gold in it. He offered a third share in the mine to Spencer. Spencer had not yet built up much capital, but he could not pass up the opportunity and he reluctantly asked his brother Boise for

are several other explanations of how Cripple Creek got its name. Some old-timers say that the rocky creek bed lamed the cows that went to drink there and thus the name.) Bob Womack did not have much luck at raising cattle; primarily because he spent most of his time prospecting and the rest of it gambling and drinking in the saloons of Colorado City. He sold the land, which passed through several hands until it became the property of the Bennett & Myers Real Estate Co., but he stayed on as caretaker which allowed him to continue his habit of testing the area for gold.

The rocks appeared to tease him, several times he found loose pieces of rock with high gold content, but he was unable to find the vein from

LEFT: Just a few years after gold was discovered, Cripple Creek was thronged with people and hastily built wooden structures. This is Bennett Avenue before the first of Cripple Creek's major fires. Circa 1893.

Starsmore Center for Local History, Colorado Springs Pioneers Museum

money. Legend has it that his brother sent him $150.00 and told him to buy a train ticket home. Penrose invested the money in the mine and later gave his brother back $10,000 to repay the debt.

The two friends did not spend all of their time working. Both Charley Tutt and Spencer Penrose were extremely attractive men, over six feet tall with flashing eyes and impressive mustaches. Although they worked during the day, the nights were reserved for the almost unlimited opportunities for entertainment that Cripple Creek offered. Speck, in particular, was having the time of his life in the lawless, "anything goes" atmosphere of Cripple Creek, which was far removed from the straitlaced high society of Philadelphia and his stern father. According to Marshall Sprague, author of *Newport in the Rockies* and close personal friend of Julie Penrose, Speck's most significant dalliance was with a young woman of ill repute named Sally whose "gentle hobby was breaking mean horses." When Dr. Penrose heard of Speck's entanglement, he immediately sent R.A.F., Jr. to the scene to ensure that the family's black sheep did not stray too far from acceptable behavior. Sally was not heard from again.

Penrose drank enormously, as he was to do all his life, gambled and generally entertained himself with a group of young men who called them-

which the chunks had broken off. Bob Womack staked several claims, but gained nothing but the derision of the habitués of the Colorado City saloons for his efforts. But in October of 1890, he hit a patch of gold ore, some of which assayed out as high as $250.00 per ton. Enthusiastic, Bob returned to Colorado Springs to find investors so that the ore could be mined, but nobody believed him. Finally, Ed De LaVergne, a man with a good understanding of geology and a great deal of practical experience in mining, took an interest in the ore. He met with Bob Womack and his friend Professor Lamb from Colorado College.

Professor Lamb explained that gold comes to the surface of the earth during volcanic explosions and can be captured by cracks in the ground, rather than being swept off with the flow of lava. Lamb's research demonstrated that there had been considerable volcanic activity in the Pikes Peak area. A volcanic explosion at the Cripple Creek site had removed the crust of granite that covers

the mountains in the area and created a pocket. This depression trapped the precious minerals. De LaVergne noticed that the ore resembled sylvanite, a gold-silver tellurium. He knew that sylvanite was often associated with calaverite, a compound of gold and tellurium. After hearing Womack's stories of numerous finds of gold-bearing rocks De LaVergne began to suspect that gold veins underlay the entire basin which made up Cripple Creek. When he had confirmed his belief to his own satisfaction, he and a group of miners took

selves the "Socialites." This group contained several young men who were to become his associates and business partners in the years to come. The "Socialites" included Horace Devereaux, a Princeton football hero and exceptional polo player who played for the Glenwood Springs team. He became very good friends with Speck and spent most of his later years at the Broadmoor Hotel. One of the hotel's historic suites bears his name,

action. On April 5, 1891, the "Cripple Creek Mining District" was officially established. De LaVergne laid out the boundaries for the district which was six miles square and contained 23,000 acres.

Although interest was slow to develop, pros-pectors began coming to Cripple Creek and laying out claims. Count Pourtales' visit to the area in August was a great boost and sparked the interest of both prospectors and investors, though none of the mines were producing vast quantities

LEFT: Numerous pamphlets were printed to lure investors to the area. These describe the most productive mines and the men who profited from them.

Starsmore Center for Local History, Colorado Springs Pioneers Museum

RIGHT: Gold King Mine, the site of Womack's first strike, was a fairly typical shaft.

W.H. Jackson photo. Starsmore Center for Local History, Colorado Springs Pioneers Museum

ABOVE: The two partners anxiously supervise operations in the Cash On Delivery mine. Charles Tutt is seated on barrel at far right, Spencer Penrose on stacked lumber at far left. 1893.

Broadmoor Historical Collection

and he is buried at Will Rogers Shrine on the slopes of Cheyenne Mountain with the Penroses. Other members of the group were Charles MacNeill and Albert E. Carlton, both of whom were involved in the Broadmoor Hotel and Land Company and for whom two other suites are named.

The C.O.D. mine did, contrary to the expectations of many, start producing gold in adequate if not enormous quantities. But Penrose and Tutt, realized that looking for and mining gold was too risky a proposition. The miners strike in Cripple Creek in 1894 had almost turned into a civil war. Mine owners and striking miners battled each other with weapons and explosives and many lives were lost. It was much smarter and less dangerous to make money from the people that had already found the gold and gotten it out of the ground. Thereupon the partners sold the C.O.D. for $250,000 and then Tutt and Penrose looked for

of ore. Winfield Scott Stratton was a carpenter who worked in Colorado Springs for three dollars a day, just long enough to come up with a grubstake, and then he went back to prospecting until his money ran out. He had prospected in vain for years until he came to Cripple Creek in 1891 and staked a claim called the Independence. In 1893 Stratton hit a vein in the Independence mine. When he had the ore assayed he realized that his vein contained a minimum of three million dollars worth of gold. After Stratton's discovery, prospectors flooded the mining camp and other veins were found. In 1893 alone, two million dollars worth of gold was extracted from Cripple Creek mines. When Stratton sold the Independence in 1899, his total profit from the mine exceeded sixteen million dollars.

The population of Cripple Creek reached its peak in 1900 when fifty thousand people lived in the gold camp. Between 1897 and 1917 gold production was never less than ten million dollars

per year. By 1917, total production to date had grown to $294,000,000. After this point, production began to decline, and though gold was still being extracted from the ground, mining was controlled by large corporations and the era of the one-man mining operation was over. By 1920, only about five thousand people remained in Cripple Creek.

While it lasted, the phenomenon of Cripple Creek drew flocks of people seeking fortune and opportunity. One of the town's best sources of

FAR RIGHT: Penrose (2nd from left) and Tutt (far right) outside their first ore processing business in 1894. This company was dissolved when they became partners with Charles MacNeill.

Broadmoor Historical Collection

RIGHT: Three years after the founding of the Cripple Creek Mining District, the valley teemed with activity. 1894.

Starsmore Center for Local History, Colorado Springs Pioneers Museum

other likely prospects. Just about that time, Charles MacNeill had lost his ore processing mill to fire (a very common hazard in town built entirely of wood with less than responsible citizens). The three decided to collaborate and quickly became a force to be reckoned with in the Cripple Creek economy.

Processing the ore that was mined in Cripple Creek had been a problem from the beginning. Traditional mills required large quantities of water, which was lacking in Cripple Creek. Prior to the construction of functional mills in the mining town, all the gold ore mined in the high basin had been hauled to Colorado Springs or even Denver for processing. When chemical processes supplanted the crushing mills, some like MacNeill, built mills in Cripple Creek although all of the coal to run them had to be brought up the mountain. After his mill burnt, he formed a partnership with Penrose and Tutt and their company, the Colorado-Philadelphia Reduction Company, built a mill on the west side of Colorado Springs. At that point it was cheaper to transport the gold ore down the mountain than it was to ship coal up, and the danger of fire was somewhat less. MacNeill, Tutt and Penrose's plant began to earn large and sustained profits soon after it opened in 1896. In 1900, the trio went to New York and established

revenue (apart from actually finding gold) was fleecing the tenderfeet that arrived in Cripple Creek with money in their pockets seeking a good proposition. If the money wasn't lost to an able con man, there were numerous gaming houses, bordellos and other opportunities for losing it all. Only a few of those who came managed to avoid the pitfalls and derive great wealth from the gold-filled volcanic cavity on the slopes of Pikes Peak from which more gold had been extracted per square mile than any other place on earth.

the United States Reduction and Refining Company, a mill trust which
subsequently built and managed mills all around Cripple Creek.

WHILE THEY WERE organizing their company, fellow Socialite,
Albert Carlton, was tightening his control of the entire transportation network around Cripple Creek. Carlton had collaborated
with William Blackmer of Denver to control the Midland Terminal Railway,
which was the only railroad up to the mining town. At that point the group
of friends had a virtual monopoly on the transporting and processing of
Cripple Creek ore and they squeezed the market for as much as they could
get out of it. These men were respected by some as savvy businessmen,
while despised by others as cold-blooded capitalists. The tactics worked,
however, and profits accumulated.

By the year 1902, Tutt, Penrose and MacNeill had each earned enough
money to be quite comfortable, and Charley Tutt was ready to relax and
enjoy the fruits of his labors. Spencer Penrose's ambition, however, was
not just to be rich, but to be enormously wealthy and he continued to seek
out profitable avenues of investment. He was still very involved in Cripple

Creek, but he had more opportunity to devote himself to the pursuit of pleasurable entertainment in Colorado Springs. He spent time at the Cheyenne Mountain Country Club, El Paso Club and the Mining Exchange Building (where his offices were located) waiting for opportunity to knock.

In 1902 Daniel C. Jackling, a young geologist who had worked for Charlie MacNeill at his first mill in Cripple Creek, returned to Colorado Springs. He had gone to Utah and designed and built a large mill for DeLamar's Mercur Mine. In the process of building the mill, Jackling had come up with a new method for extracting copper from low grade copper ore. Jackling had researched the possibility of applying his new process in Bingham Canyon, Utah, a site where mineral deposits of high grade ore had been almost entirely mined out, but enormous quantities of low grade ore remained. When Jackling had failed to interest DeLamar in his Bingham Canyon idea he returned to the Springs and went to work for the mill trust. The mill trust, on Jackling's recommendation, bought the Bartlett copper-zinc smelter in Canon City and put Jackling in charge, but he wasn't happy.

Jackling knew that his idea for processing the low grade copper ore remaining in Bingham Canyon would work, and he told MacNeill about it as often as he could get him to listen. His technique would make it possible to process huge quantities of low grade ore cheaply and profitably. The problem was that a great deal of capital was required to set the project in motion. Jackling made no secret of his proposal, offering it to a number of mining magnates, including the Guggenheim family, all of whom turned him down. Initially, Penrose too dismissed Jackling's idea as impossible, but the lanky taciturn young man had a sound background as a mining engineer and Penrose began to look at his proposal more seriously.

Spencer's most trusted consultant, his brother Dick, said that theoretically the idea was a viable one and he encouraged his brother to think about how the market for minerals would change with the advent of electrical appliances, cars and similar small mechanical items in every home. Though the price of copper seemed too low to make Jackling's idea a profitable one at that time, R.A.F. believed that the price would rise dramatically when copper's essential role in these new industries was recognized. On the basis of these reports, Spencer and Charlie MacNeill were ready to gamble on Jackling. In February of 1903, MacNeill recommended that the mill trust provide Jackling with the financial backing for his project. Charley Tutt was reluctant to risk his hard-earned Cripple Creek fortune on something that was universally considered a lost cause. Tutt had a family as well, and had interests other than his own to consider. But soon his loyalty to his friends won out over practical concerns and he declared himself ready to walk the tightrope once again.

ABOVE: Albert E. Carlton, one of the dashing young men of Cripple Creek, later became a close friend and business associate of Penrose.

Special Collections, Colorado College Library

Speck had one more resource that he could appeal to for backing: his family. Boise, Charles, Dick, and Dr. Penrose had more faith in their black sheep now that he had produced such remarkable results in Cripple Creek and they announced that they would be willing to go along with the deal. In spring of 1903 the three partners and Dick Penrose went to Utah with Daniel Jackling. There they acquired Bingham Canyon and set up the Utah Copper Company. They raised capital by selling 500,000 shares at one dollar per share. Each of the partners purchased 83,333 shares and the mill trust took 50,000 shares in return for equipment and supplies. Almost all of the remaining two hundred thousand shares were purchased by Penrose's father and brothers.

Jackling began building his pilot mill immediately. The project was an immense one, for the mill had to be able to process an unheard-of volume of low grade ore in order to be successful. All of the industry experts said that it couldn't be done, and the eyes of the world were on the young engineer as he worked feverishly to finish the mill before the money ran out. As 1903 progressed Tutt, MacNeill and Penrose lived through a period of great strain and anxiety. This time, they could do nothing but watch and wait as their fortunes hung in the balance.

In the latter part of 1904, Jackling finished the mill and began processing ore. To the amazement of all, the mill refined ore at a profit its first day of operation. The skeptics acclaimed Jackling as a genius and revolutionary thinker. As the process produced sustained profits, Utah Copper Company shares first doubled and then tripled in value. The shareholders breathed collective sighs of relief and sat back to enjoy their profits and the admiration of those who had doubted them. Daniel Jackling was recognized as having made mining history. Today his statue stands in the Utah State Capitol building.

Charles Tutt, having helped his friends through their latest venture, was ready to retire and save his nerves from any more of Penrose's high risk projects. Speck bought Tutt's shares in Utah Copper on the open market for three times what Tutt had paid for them in 1903, thus becoming the primary shareholder of Utah Copper. Tutt officially announced his retire-

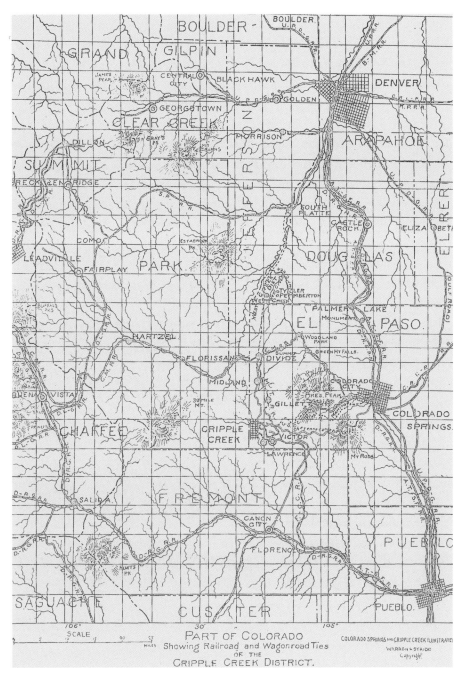

LEFT: This map, taken from a pamphlet promoting Cripple Creek, shows the relationship of the town to Colorado Springs. Mining activity was intense in the entire area following the big strikes.

Starsmore Center for Local History, Colorado Springs Pioneers Museum

ABOVE: Daniel C. Jackling revolutionized the copper mining industry and made wealthy men of those who had believed in him.

Utah State Historical Society

RIGHT: The Colorado-Philadelphia Reduction Plant was Tutt, Penrose and MacNeill's first highly successful business venture. This advertisement appeared in local newspapers in the early 1900s.

Broadmoor Historical Collection

ment from the Penrose-MacNeill interests in December of 1905, and limited his business activities to real estate. He had earlier purchased an island in Puget Sound where he had a summer house. Upon retirement, at the age of forty-one, he devoted himself to yachting and the enjoyment of the money that he had struggled to accumulate. Ironically, Tutt died of a heart attack in New York City only four years after retiring.

Back in Utah, Penrose and MacNeill were faced with the pleasant task of selecting partners for the expansion of Utah Copper. The Guggenheims, who had originally rejected Jackling's proposal, enthusiastically joined Penrose and by 1906 Utah Copper was expanding rapidly and was the most profitable of the copper companies backed by the Guggenheim family. Penrose had finally achieved everything that he had dreamed as a young man. He was rich, extremely rich, admired by many and, most importantly he had proven himself to his father. He might have been at a loss for what to do with himself, but someone else had taken an interest in his life and now that the great copper anxiety was over she wanted some attention.

Unlike Palmer and Pourtales, Penrose had absolutely no plans for sharing his life with a woman. He, Boise, and Dick considered themselves confirmed bachelors who thought that wives were just fine, as long as they were somebody else's. Speck was especially cautious after his narrow escape from Sally. He had never risked an intimate association with someone of his own class until a young widow, Julie Villiers Lewis McMillan, began to take an interest in him.

Julie had come to Colorado Springs in 1901 with her husband James Mc-Millan, who was suffering from tuberculosis, and their two children. She was one of the thirteen children born to the Honorable Alexander Lewis, mayor of Detroit and Elizabeth Ingersoll, also of Detroit. The son of Frenchman Louis Villiers, Alexander Lewis instilled a love of French culture in his children, especially Julie, his favorite. Julie was born in 1870 and grew up with all of the accouterments of wealth and luxury combined with the humor and joie de vivre of her father. Her education was that of

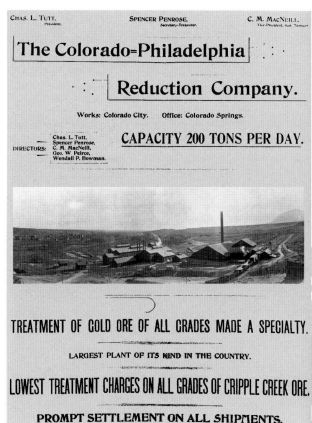

CHAS. L. TUTT, President. SPENCER PENROSE, Secretary-Treasurer. C. M. MacNEILL, Vice-President, Gen. Manager.

The Colorado-Philadelphia Reduction Company.

Works: Colorado City. Office: Colorado Springs.

CAPACITY 200 TONS PER DAY.

DIRECTORS:
Chas. L. Tutt,
Spencer Penrose,
C. M. MacNeill,
Geo. W. Peirce,
Wendall P. Bowman.

TREATMENT OF GOLD ORE OF ALL GRADES MADE A SPECIALTY.

LARGEST PLANT OF ITS KIND IN THE COUNTRY.

LOWEST TREATMENT CHARGES ON ALL GRADES OF CRIPPLE CREEK ORE.

PROMPT SETTLEMENT ON ALL SHIPMENTS.

many young girls in American high society and it culminated with a Grand Tour of Europe when she was seventeen. The tour confirmed her love of art and music, especially opera; interests that she was to ardently maintain for the rest of her life.

Upon her return from Europe, she married the boy-next-door, Jim McMillan, who had graduated from Yale with a degree in law and was the son of multi-millionaire Michigan Senator James McMillan. They wed in Detroit on June 18, 1890. In the ensuing decade, Julie had two children, young Jimmy and Gladys, her husband pursued his passion for yachting and golf and all seemed well. Then Jim went off to Cuba during the Spanish-American War and contracted tuberculosis. Upon his return they decided to move to Colorado Springs and hope for a cure. For Julie, Colorado Springs was to be the site of her greatest tragedies and greatest triumphs, during the more than five decades of her residence here she became interwoven into the very fabric of the city and will never be forgotten.

The McMillan's took up residence in a large and elegant home at 30 West Dale Street in downtown Colorado Springs. Like Queen Palmer, Julie McMillan was used to having all of the pleasures and entertainments that money could provide, but Julie's exile to Colorado Springs was a far cry from what Queen had encountered thirty years earlier. Downtown Colorado Springs was thickly populated with stately homes, built with Cripple Creek gold and by well-to-do consumptives like her husband who were flocking to Colorado. There was an opera house, a lovely theater and a number of cultural and artistic organizations. Julie not only tolerated Colorado Springs, she fell in love with it.

In return, Colorado Springs fell in love with her. Although her husband's illness confined him to the house, Julie's exuberant personality and penchant for social interaction made her a popular member of Colorado Springs' party life despite her lack of an escort. Julie's plight was not an unusual one, for there were several young women in Colorado Springs whose husbands were not well enough to leave their sickbeds. One of these, Edith Field, became Julie's close friend and they often went to parties together. On January 11, 1901, Spencer Penrose and Clarence Edsall gave one of their notoriously extravagant parties at the Cheyenne Mountain Country Club. Despite the fact that Colorado Springs was more than a thousand miles from the nearest ocean, the bon ton of the city determined that the

ABOVE: By 1903, Speck had plenty of time to enjoy himself. Hunting, fishing and mountaineering with his brothers numbered among his favorite activities. Speck, with brother Boise (right), on top of Mt. Penrose, British Columbia, 1903.

Local History Collection, Pikes Peak Library District

best way to liven up a frozen January in the Rockies was a clambake. Penrose and Edsall had the clams packed in ice in Rockland, Maine, and shipped by rail for the delectation of their guests. Spencer and Julie met for the first time at this affair, but Penrose was not unduly affected by the encounter. This lack of response piqued the curiosity of the petite, blond-haired, blue-eyed Mrs. McMillan who was not used to passing unnoticed, and she thoroughly informed herself about the nature of one of Colorado Springs' most legendary figures.

JULIE'S LIFE OF lighthearted socializing came to an end abruptly in April of the same year, when her son, Jimmy, died of a ruptured appendix. The blow was too much for James McMillan. Already weakened by tuberculosis, he died on May 9, 1902. Julie's experiences as a popular society matron had not prepared her for such a trauma. After the deaths of her son and husband she became a more serious and mature individual who was very attuned to the suffering of others. Although baptized a Catholic and raised an Episcopalian, Julie had not been particularly zealous in her practice of religion prior to losing half of her small family. These events caused her to turn back to the church, an institution which was to become very important to her later in life. Julie's daughter, Gladys, was another source of solace. The two developed an extremely close relationship, which allowed them to survive the blow that fortune had dealt them.

During the period of her mourning Julie solidified her friendship with Edith Field, who had also been widowed, and as time passed, the two began to rejoin the life of the town. Edith Field began a romance with a gentleman from Detroit and Julie, though she had vowed that she would never marry again, found her thoughts drifting to that handsome gentleman who had paid her no attention at the clambake. She knew that he lived a bachelor's life, with no permanent home and no servants to care for him. Speck's lifestyle had been glamorous and exciting during the mad days of Cripple Creek when he spent all of his time in mines, ramshackle offices and saloons, but those days were past. He rented rooms at El Paso Club, or lived with his friend Horace Devereaux, and his digestion was subject to the abuses inflicted upon it by a part-time cook and the whims of local eating establishments. Julie McMillan began sending her servants to do his laundry and clean up his quarters. She often invited him to the light-filled house perched on the edge of Monument Valley Park and plied him with delicacies. Spencer found himself becoming inordinately fond of the gracious and companionable young widow, but his father's warnings echoed in his ears and he successfully resisted any formalizing of the relationship.

Penrose, in the meanwhile, was managing his interests in the copper business with great success. Utah Copper merged with the Guggenheim's

Kennecott Copper, but Penrose remained one of the top shareholders. Speck then organized Chino Copper, which was also sold to the Guggenheims and then Ray Consolidated. When Jackling believed that his process could be applied to gold as well, they founded the Alaska Gold Company. Penrose's track record attracted many investors and the price per share went from twenty-five cents a share to twenty-seven dollars per share. At that point, Speck sold all of his shares, and when the stock collapsed shortly thereafter he left all of the others holding the bag.

Penrose was now an immensely wealthy man. Unlike many of those who made great fortunes in mining during this period he did not squander his wealth, but carefully invested it and personally saw to its management. This activity did not, however, occupy a great deal of his time. He had plenty of opportunity to engage in his favorite activities: big game hunting, visiting his brothers, and sampling excellent food and drink in the many clubs of which he was member on the East Coast. Speck now had the freedom to go anywhere and do anything he liked, but something called him back to Colorado Springs. Perhaps the clear dry climate of the mountains and the almost constant sunshine had become essential to him, or perhaps the West had changed him into a man who could no longer feel comfortable anywhere else. Julie Villers Lewis McMillan believed that the reason was possibly her charming self and was ever more determined to convince him of it. On the one hand, Spencer realized that he had a great deal of time and money and no one to share

ABOVE LEFT: Julie Villiers Lewis McMillan graced the ballrooms and promenades of Detroit's high society before moving to Colorado Springs. Circa 1888.
RIGHT: Julie, widowed at the age of 32, retained her beauty and spirited nature.

Local History Collection,
Pikes Peak Library District

it with, on the other he had his childhood memory of pain connected to the only woman he had ever loved and his father's warnings about scheming females. Although he knew that Julie had more than enough money in her own right and that if she was pursuing him it was because she genuinely loved him, Penrose could not resolve the situation. He decided instead to run away from temptation and booked a passage to Europe on the ship *Kaiser Wilhelm der Grosse* leaving New York in February of 1906.

While touring the decks of the departing vessel with his brother R.A.F. Jr., who was on his way to the gold fields of South Africa, Speck ran into a familiar looking group. Julie McMillan, her daughter, Gladys, and Edith Fields were on their way to Europe supposedly to place Gladys in a Swiss school. The coincidence proved to be too much for Spencer and before the crossing was completed he had consented to accompany the three women on a tour of France. Knowing that he was soon to succumb to Julie's wiles he had his brother Dick write his father a letter explaining his situation. In the letter the elder Penrose brother tells their father that Spencer has done everything that he could to rid himself of this infatuation including going away for months at a time, but that "separation had no effect on his affection for her."[2] While Spencer waited for his father's

ABOVE: Following his marriage, Penrose devoted himself to the economic prosperity and growth of Colorado Springs. This pamphlet, among many others of its kind, hoped to attract tourists and residents to the city.

Starsmore Center for Local History,
Colorado Springs Pioneers Museum

RIGHT: The McMillan (later Penrose) home, which later became the Broadmoor Art Academy, at 30 West Dale Street overlooking Monument Valley Park, was a mansion that included a greenhouse, music room and large terraces for entertaining.

Colorado Springs Fine Arts Center

---

2. As quoted in *Newport in the Rockies* by Marshall Sprague from Dick's letter to his father, Dr. Penrose.

reply, the party from Colorado Springs stayed at the Hotel Ruhl in Nice, enjoying the French Riviera. When the letter arrived from Philadelphia containing his father's approval for the match, Penrose decided to take the momentous step. His nature, so bold and decisive in the world of business, was not up to the task of asking for a lady's hand in marriage. He proposed to Julie by throwing the letter in her lap while she took the sun on the beach.

They married at St. George's Church in London on April 26, 1906. Edith Field was the maid of honor and a cousin of the McMillan family was Speck's best man. After the wedding the couple spent their honeymoon touring England and France by automobile. When they returned to Colorado Springs, Penrose moved into the large house on Dale Street and took up the domestic tranquillity of wedded life. Needless to say, however, life with Julie was anything but tranquil. Between 1906 and 1911 the Penroses traveled all over the world. They went to India, Egypt, Siam and to Europe again and again. Their frequent visits to Europe were partially due to the budding romance between Julie's daughter, Gladys, and the Count Cornet de Ways Ruart of Belgium.

Although Spencer spent much of their time abroad analyzing markets and assessing economies and business opportunities, Julie managed to divert his attention once in a while to enjoy the beauty and art of the lands through which they traveled. If nothing else, Penrose began to appreciate the value of art as an investment and a means of communication, a realization which would serve him well later on. Penrose was a firm believer in technological innovation and "progress," as had been evidenced by his willingness to back Jackling's highly unusual idea. His tours of the world and of the United States had exposed him to a number of gadgets and machinery that interested him greatly, and he was especially taken by the progress being made in automotive technology.

U PON THEIR RETURN to Colorado Springs in 1911, Penrose decided to buy a ranch south of the city so that he could experiment with technological advances in the breeding and feeding of livestock. Coincidentally, he chose to experiment with dairy Holsteins, as Pourtales had before him. Turkey Creek Ranch held his interest for a while, and it later became a place that he was extremely fond of, but it really wasn't enough to occupy the mind of a man who was used to making great things happen. He had been interested in automotive tourism since his honeymoon in Europe and he realized that the vast areas of the western United States were the perfect destination for such travelers. He fueled his interest in cars by purchasing four canary yellow Loziers and installing them in the garage at Dale Street. Although they entertained him, he continued

to live the quiet life of a millionaire in Colorado Springs. But things were bound to change, for the bubbling personality of his wife and the exposure to a whole world of innovation were exerting no small force on the man whose notoriously poker face masked the tumultuous changes occurring within.

By marrying Julie Lewis McMillan, Spencer Penrose had taken a step that was to radically change his personality and the way in which he lived his life. Until the age of forty-one he had dedicated himself to the rigorous pursuit of personal wealth and had adhered to the guidelines set by his strict, domineering father. Marriage to Julie in 1906 gave Spencer Penrose the license to start enjoying life, to start having fun. The first signs of his emerging flamboyant nature were apparent in his purchase of four bright yellow automobiles (sure to be considered vulgar by some) and his increasing willingness to do as his or his wife's fancy dictated. Julie, though occasionally capricious and self-centered, was essentially a charitable and generous individual. She nurtured and guided Spencer's new-found character traits into positive avenues of development. Her influence encouraged him to direct his time, energy and money to projects that would help people and improve the quality of life for the inhabitants of Colorado Springs. As their marriage developed into a partnership, he came up with a new project: to turn the entire Pikes Peak region into the most interesting, multi-faceted resort area that could be conceived of in his imagination — and he had the money to do it.

LEFT: Both Spencer and Julie loved to travel and spent long periods of each year away from Colorado Springs. Despite his frequent absences, Speck remained very much in charge of all of his business affairs and his staff had orders to forward all papers and communications to the forthcoming port of call. 1924.

Penrose Puts City On Map

WITHIN THREE YEARS of his marriage in 1906, Spencer Penrose had undergone a transformation. He was no longer the reserved, ambitious young man who had stepped off the train in Colorado Springs in December of 1892 anxious to make his fortune. By 1914, Speck was ready to change things, to make a difference in the part of the world where he had found a home. Speck had come to love the West and Colorado Springs in particular. The land had given him the opportunity to make something of himself and now he was ready to give back to the land.

He had established a reputation as an impetuous and astute business-man whose income, after taxes, was more than a million dollars a year. A beautiful, intelligent and cultured woman had consented to become his bride, and the effect of love on his character was quite surprising to those who knew him well. The man who had been suspended from the member-ship of the Cheyenne Mountain Country Club for engaging in fist fights in the commons room and who had ruthlessly battled with all of the resources at his disposal to break the Cripple Creek miner's strike was seen nuzzling his wife at parties and taking long walks hand-in-hand across the mesas. Penrose's intelligence and resourcefulness, previously focused exclusively on personal gain, began to be put, at least partially, at the service of the public good. In doing so, Penrose was aware that he was following in the footsteps of the city's founder, General William Jackson Palmer, with whom he had had an almost infinite number of differences of opinion. The serious, temperance-minded General strongly disapproved of Penrose's colorful lifestyle and his obvious devotion to the very best in fermented beverages. Speck's charitable impulses were certainly mingled with his incli-nation towards irony. His first gift to the City of Colorado Springs was a large outdoor swimming pool and a hacienda-style bathhouse with pink stucco walls and a tile roof. The pool, which opened in 1914, was con-structed in the middle of Monument Valley Park, the finest of the many

The Pikes Peak Auto Highway, Hill Climb, and the magnificent Broadmoor Hotel make the city of Colorado Springs known to millions.

AT LEFT: The cover drawing of this circa 1926 pamphlet imaginatively describes the routes of the Pikes Peak High-way and the Manitou and Pikes Peak Cog Railway. Penrose chose to use color advertising whenever possible to demon-strate the extraordinary qualities of light and color on the front range of the Rocky Mountains.

El Pomar Foundation

parks which had been donated to the citizens of Colorado Springs by General Palmer in 1907. Given that General Palmer died in March of 1909, we can only guess at how he would have reacted.

Several of the projects that Penrose was to undertake in his later years did, to some degree, mirror those of General Palmer: transportation networks, hotel construction and the promotion of Colorado Springs. Although Spencer Penrose was not anywhere near as altruistic or community-minded as Palmer, he succeeded in laying an economic foundation upon which the city is still building today. He began, in 1915, by recognizing how the automobile was changing America, and especially American tourism. If Colorado Springs was to prosper in the face of declining revenues from Cripple Creek, it could no longer depend exclusively on the very wealthy who came to pass their summers or the invalids who came seeking health. Colorado Springs needed to widen its appeal and its network of highways and roads so that the new breed of American who spent the summer motoring would want to make the city a stopping point.

The most visible and dramatic asset of Colorado Springs is Pikes Peak. And thus it was to Pikes Peak that Penrose turned when he began his campaign to make Colorado Springs a household word. Pikes Peak, although the area's highest mountain with an elevation of 14,110 feet, has slopes gradual enough to permit the building of a road to the summit. A carriage road had been carved from the sides of the mountain for adventure-seeking tourists in 1889, but it had fallen into disrepair from lack of use. The Manitou and Pikes Peak Cog Railway Company which completed a railway to the summit of Pikes Peak in 1890 had, for all intents and purposes, supplanted the need for a road.

Charles Noble, a railroad man who had worked on the Cripple Creek Short Line and other railways before coming to work for the Penrose-MacNeill interests, had been interested in building a road up the Peak for some time and had gone so far as to travel to Washington to ask the Department of Agriculture for permission to build it. Penrose decided to back

BELOW: The entrance to the Penrose Pavillion faces one of the park's duckponds, the pool extends to the north on the far side of the building. 1920.

Starsmore Center for Local History, Colorado Springs Pioneers Museum

Noble's idea and come up with the more than $100,000 that the road was estimated to cost. The road, he believed, would publicize the Pikes Peak region while eventually paying for itself with the revenues generated from the toll paid by the tourists who used it. While considering the best way to make the road a success, Penrose came up with the first of many ideas which demonstrated that his apparently conservative facade disguised the mind of an advertising genius: The summer following the completion of the Pikes Peak Auto Highway there would be a road race from the toll gate to the top of Pikes Peak featuring the most famous drivers that Penrose could find as well as the fastest cars the automobile industry had to offer. Penrose, supremely confident as usual, announced the race before the Pikes Peak Highway Co. had even obtained permission from the government to build the road, but the idea was extremely well-received both by the public

Carriages and mules at top of Pikes Peak, 1889.

It was no small feat to climb the carriage road up Pikes Peak before Penrose's road was built. The trail was rough and the altitude caused problems for both passengers and beasts of burden. Mules were used rather than horses, as is evident in the photograph above, because they tolerate the lack of oxygen better.

and by the budding automobile industry and the completion of the auto highway was enthusiastically awaited by car aficionados.

Articles of Incorporation were filed by the Pikes Peak Auto Highway Company on April 29, 1915, after permission had been granted by the Department of Agriculture for the construction of a toll road to the summit of Pikes Peak. The approval was not unconditional, the Department of Agriculture stipulated that construction be supervised and approved by the City of Colorado Springs and the federal government and that Penrose's contract for ownership of the road would expire after twenty years. The company was capitalized at $200,000. Penrose knew that he would have to provide most of the financial resources for the road, but he managed to convince Charlie MacNeill and A.E. Carlton to take up a share as well. Carlton was more than willing to get involved in Penrose's latest scheme, even though he was unlikely to turn a profit. Carlton had remained in Cripple Creek after the others had pulled out and was responsible for the Roosevelt Deep Drainage tunnel which drained the watershed down to below 8,800 feet, making it possible to mine gold at much deeper levels

LEFT: When the Pikes Peak Highway opened, virtually everyone who had a car took the sinuous route to the top. 1915.

Starsmore Center for Local History, Colorado Springs Pioneers Museum

than had been attainable before. When Carlton's interests were threatened by millionaire John T. Milliken's attempts to control Cripple Creek, Speck's monetary assistance allowed him to turn the tables and take over corporate control of the town's production. From that point on, Carlton and Penrose remained close friends and partners, a relationship that also developed between their wives. Ethel Carlton was one of Julie's best friends and after they had both been widowed they lived in neighboring suites at the Broadmoor Hotel and traveled all over the world together.

Construction began on the auto highway just a week after the papers were filed and work progressed rapidly, though at much higher cost than expected. While the highway was being built, Speck began accumulating and rejuvenating as many tourist venues as he could. In that same April of 1915 he set up the Pikes Peak Automobile Company, which maintained a fleet of passenger touring cars to transport those who did not wish to drive their own cars to the summit. Penrose's interests later expanded to include touring services all over the Pikes Peak region, a rent-a-car company and the Gray Line tours company. Although in 1915 Penrose couldn't purchase the railroad up Pikes Peak (he acquired it later, in 1925) he did purchase the adjacent Mount Manitou Incline, a very steep track up the mountain behind Manitou Springs.

The tracks up the mountain had originally been built to haul materials for a hydro-electric power plant in the early 1900s. When the power plant was completed, ca. 1907, Dr. N.N. Brumbach and his son Chester decided to transform the machinery into a tourist attraction. They made some modifications to the track and installed open-air cars that hauled those who dared up the 68% grade to a wonderful view at the top of the mountain, after which they precipitated back down again. Despite its rigors (which must have been considerable judging from the expressions captured in many of the photographs taken at the summit), the trip was a popular attraction for both tourists and locals.

The fact that Penrose took on these financial obligations, which showed no immediate signs of becoming profitable, demonstrated that his outlook and priorities had changed. He had no intention of throwing his money away or of giving it away outright, but he was investing in the future of Colorado Springs. He may have had some second thoughts about the feasibility of the Pikes Peak highway, as its construction consumed more and more money and his partners refused to increase their contributions accordingly; nevertheless the road went on.

The auto highway reached the summit of Pikes Peak in October of 1915. Costs had far exceeded the estimates and each consecutive mile cost more that the one that preceded it. The first mile leading out of Cascade cost almost six thousand dollars, five times the estimated price. Mile fourteen cost upwards of twenty-one thousand, and after mile seventeen had been completed the total cost of construction was more than a quarter of a million dollars. But it was beautiful! The highway was twenty feet wide, allowing the passage of two cars at any point, and the curves were even wider. The maximum grade was ten percent and the average grade six percent. The highway's surface was a parabolic curve, being four inches higher at the outer edge of the tangents and a quarter foot on the curves to maximize driving safety. The directors of the company took touring cars full of prestigious guests and representatives from the media up the landmark highway. The films and newscasts showed the world the incredible sights to be seen from the top of Pikes Peak.

The advertising success spilled over into 1916, which was an excellent year for the tourist industry in Colorado Springs. The season peaked in August for the first Pikes Peak Hill Climb, or as it later became known, the Race to the Clouds. Speck had engaged the widely known and respected race car driver, Barney Oldfield to participate in the race: Oldfield's face, as well as the sixty-pound gold and silver Penrose Trophy that Speck commissioned for the event, appeared in newspapers across the country. Penrose's organizers further added to the excitement by inducing as many teams from automobile factories to participate as possible. The teams included representatives from Cadillac, Stutz, Buick, Chalmers, Hudson, Grant, Maxwell, Studebaker, Mercer, Saxon and Delage.

The trip up the Manitou Incline was a rather harrowing one and, judging from their faces, some of the passengers faced the trip back down with even less equanimity. 1920.

Starsmore Center for Local History, Colorado Springs Pioneers Museum

After Penrose bought the Mt. Manitou Incline, he made major improvements in the physical plant and began an aggressive advertising campaign, including flyers like this one. 1916.

El Pomar Foundation

By race day, Colorado Springs was in an uproar. All of the hotels and boarding houses were full and the city was jammed with cars belonging to participants and spectators alike. The race lasted three days with the motorcycle events on the first day and various automobile events on the second and third. The final and most important race was the Non-Stock Free-For-All, held on the morning of August 12, 1916. The winner would take home the Penrose Cup and two thousand dollars in prize money. Despite the presence of all the famous drivers and cars, the race was won by Rea Lentz from Spokane, Washington, who drove a small homemade car outfitted with a Curtiss airplane engine. The winning time was 20:55:40. The whole event was a huge success and Penrose was delighted with the results of his first foray into the world of public relations.

At the time of this writing the Pikes Peak Hill Climb is still an extremely popular event that draws cars, drivers and devotees from all over the world. Lentz's record time long ago succumbed to a new, faster breed of automobiles and the current record is 10:47:22, held by Ari Vatanen and established in 1988 in a Peugeot Talbot Sports car. For the duration of his lifetime, Spencer Penrose was an avid personal and financial supporter of the race and his "Yellow Devil" Pierce-Arrow piloted by Henry McMillen was a familiar fixture in many editions of the "Race to the Clouds."[1]

---

1. For a complete history of the race see *Pikes Peak is Unser Mountain* by Stanley L. DeGeer, Peak Publishing Company, Albuquerque, New Mexico.

Pikes Peak and its many attractions were not, however, the only things on Penrose's mind in 1916. His years of traveling and love of excellent cuisine had made him a connoisseur of hotels, restaurants and quality of service. Though he loved the American West he had frequent cause to complain about the accommodations provided by western hotels, the food he was served and the way in which it was presented. Speck's knowledge of haute cuisine was part of his father's rigorous training. The Penrose family scions were members of the Rabbit Club, a gourmet cooking club frequented by

The Cog

The Manitou and Pikes Peak Cog Railway, constructed in 1890 and purchased by Penrose in 1925 is still under the same ownership as the Broadmoor Hotel, and is prospering. This unusual rail system, which was devised to handle the steep grades up and down from the summit of Pikes Peak, has two side rails which bear the weight of the cars and guide the wheels while a notched center rail engages the cog wheel which pushes the cars up the mountain. The design was copied from similar cog railways in Switzerland, but was adapted for the higher altitude and steeper grades of Pikes Peak.[2] The train leaves from its depot on the west side of Manitou Springs and transports its passengers to the summit in about two hours. The locomotives are Swiss made and utilize diesel engines. The railway has a perfect safety record.

2. For more information see *The Pikes Peak Cog Road* by Morris W. Abbot.

The Manitou Incline track up the mountain is visible from miles away. Notice the Cog Railway station at the lower left. 1915.

the culinary elite of Philadelphia. There, the Penrose boys learned not only how to eat the best food in the world, but also how to prepare it.

Speck, along with his friend and fellow gourmet Chester Alan Arthur II (son of President Arthur), decided to start a similar club in Colorado Springs in 1911 to instruct the natives in the art of culinary pleasures. Club meetings were dinners, prepared and served by those members who hosted the event and were held in various homes until Spencer Penrose built a clubhouse on the side of Cheyenne Mountain in 1914. The location was propitious. While dining on the succulent repasts prepared in the Cooking Club kitchen, Penrose looked out over the beautiful Broadmoor mesa and the dilapidated buildings that had once been the site of Pourtales' successes. He began to consider building a hotel which would be the culmination of his expertise as a businessman, lover of the good life, and promoter of Colorado Springs.

From its very beginnings, Colorado Springs had been in need of a world-class hostelry to cater to the wealthy tourists that came to the city in large numbers. Palmer had answered this need in 1883 by building the first Antlers Hotel designed by the multi-talented Dr. Solly. It was a lovely English-style

Penrose's 1918 Pierce Arrow, fondly known as the "Yellow Devil," is on exhibit at the Carriage House Museum on the Broadmoor Hotel grounds.

Photo: David Beightol, 1993.

building; the bottom three floors finished with gray stone and the upper floors with gables and other architectural flairs fashioned out of dark wood. The building had a great deal of character and style and graced the end of Pikes Peak Avenue until a fire that started on the nearby railroad tracks consumed it in 1898. Palmer immediately hired Fredrick Sterner, a New York architect who had remodeled his manor, Glen Eyrie in the north part of town, to design and construct a new hotel.

The second Antlers was even more European in both its exterior and interior design and reflected a general trend in the hotel industry to reassure tourists who were overwhelmed by the vastness and wildness of the landscape by building hotels that recreated Europe in America's backyard. Sterner's Antler's hotel was very similar in design to the popular Hotel Colorado in Glenwood Springs built by Walter Devereaux (brother of Spencer's good friend Horace) which was modeled after the Villa Medici in Rome. The Hotel Colorado boasted a huge hot springs pool and promised that guests would find themselves at least as or more at home than they would in the finest European spas.

The Pikes Peak Auto Highway

The Pikes Peak Highway itself remained under Penrose's control until the twenty-year contract expired in 1936. At that point it was taken over by the Department of Agriculture Forest Service and operated as a free road until 1948. Costs for maintaining the road were (and still are) high. When the Forest Service was no longer able to maintain it properly, the City of Colorado Springs assumed ownership. From 1948 to the present it has been operated as a toll road. Ever since Speck's contract expired, both the road and the race have been hotly debated by the city's citizens. Some feel that the road should be paved in order to save on maintenance costs, but this would probably signal the end of the race. Fortunately Spencer Penrose was better able to ensure the future upkeep of most of his other endeavors.

Penrose's first idea was to purchase the Antlers and turn it into the kind of hotel that he was imagining, but Palmer's heirs refused to sell the property to Penrose for the amount of money that he wanted to pay for it. Inspired by his own vision, and perhaps encouraged by Devereaux's success at creating an entire resort complex in the Rocky Mountains, Penrose decided that he would build his own hotel and that it would be the finest anyone had ever seen.

Speck was quite familiar with the area between the Cheyenne Mountain Country Club and the Cooking Club, two of his favorite haunts. The lake, with the boathouse on one side and the remains of the Casino on the other, was an enchanting spot and was situated in an area with enough free land around it so that a hotel would have plenty of space to expand and provide a wide range of possibilities for guests' recreation. The Broadmoor area had passed into the hands of Winfred Scott Stratton's estate in 1909 when the trustees purchased the land from Pourtales' receiver, the London and New York Investment Co. Stratton (the carpenter who made a fortune in Cripple Creek and then died in 1902) had made provisions in his will for a home that would care for the elderly and orphans in need of financial assistance. The Stratton home had been built on the eastern edge of the tract and the estate leased the buildings on the lake to several entrepreneurs over the years. In 1915, a Mr. Bergy reopened the hotel and casino, but met with such limited success that the property was for lease again in April of 1916. After some consideration, Penrose decided that the mesa was the perfect spot for his dream hotel.

The Penroses had already decided that they wanted to come and live in the Broadmoor area. In January of 1916, after leasing their downtown home, they purchased an elaborate Spanish-style villa slightly northwest of Pourtales' lake. Spencer and Julie were quite familiar with the house, because the previous owners, Ashton Potter and his wife Grace Goodyear Potter had held many glamorous parties at their home prior to their deaths in 1915. The Potters had named their home El Pomar (apple orchard in Spanish) because the house was constructed in the apple orchard of the Dixon toll house on Mesa Road. The house was perfectly situated for keeping an eye on whatever was to transpire on the shores of Cheyenne Lake.

Cooking Club group photo from the Webb collection including: Charlie MacNeill (standing, farthest on left), Duncan Chisholm (with beard), Eugene P. Shove (next to Chisholm) and Horace Devereaux (next to Shove). Penrose is seated third from the left. The chalkboard menu indicates which member is responsible for cooking and serving each course.

Once again, Speck was burning with enthusiasm for his new project and made the rounds of his friends, encouraging them to support him. They were, perhaps, slightly less enthusiastic this time, having recently been tapped for the Pikes Peak Auto Highway and not entirely convinced that a resort hotel situated on an almost empty plain four miles from downtown Colorado Springs was likely to be an overwhelming success. Despite their reservations however, Charlie MacNeill and Albert E. Carlton rose to the occasion and backed Penrose's latest flight into fancy. In April of 1916, Penrose and MacNeill began negotiations with the Stratton estate for the sale of the circa eighteen acres around Cheyenne Lake as well as an additional four hundred acres to the south for a golf course. The Stratton estate, concerned primarily with the building and operation of the Stratton Home,

The first Antlers Hotel, circa 1885. Dr. Edmund Solly's English-style designs were translated into reality by a firm of Boston architects. General Palmer called it the Antlers because of the numerous hunting trophies that adorned it. It was one of the finest buildings in Colorado Springs until it burned in 1898.

The second Antlers Hotel, designed by Fredrick Sterner, was completed in 1901. This building was torn down in the 1960s by Chase Stone and Russell and Thayer Tutt (of El Pomar Foundation) when the third Antlers Hotel and the Holly Sugar building were constructed on the site. Circa 1939.

had not sold a great deal of real estate and Penrose was able to negotiate the price of the land to his advantage. He demanded and obtained the water rights which were to be essential to the greening of the then barren plain, and also insisted that a reservoir be built in Cheyenne Canon for additional water.

In May, the Broadmoor Hotel and Land Company closed with the Stratton estate for the sum of $90,000. Penrose had rallied his friends and public opinion with his announcement that he was going to build "the finest hotel in the United States." He estimated that it would cost one million dollars

and in characteristic fashion, he wanted it built immediately. He lost no time in organizing his partners and starting the search for an architect and construction company. The Broadmoor Hotel and Land Company officers were Spencer Penrose, President and Clarence Carpenter, Vice-President (Carpenter was Speck's brother-in-law, having married Julie's sister Josie). The directors were: C.M. MacNeill, A.E. Carleton, Bernie H. Hopkins and Eugene P. Shove (Shove was a friend from Cripple Creek and was Carlton and Penrose's partner in the battle against Milliken). The company's secretary was Charles L. Tutt Jr., the son of Spec's old mining friend and partner Charles Tutt Sr. Speck had hired Charles Jr. as an apprentice after his father's death. Each of the partners had contributed to Speck's new project in varying amounts ranging from MacNeill's $350,000 to Tutt's $15,000. To this investment Charles Tutt was to add not only his own life's work, but also that of his sons.

Charles Tutt Jr. became President of the Broadmoor Hotel after Penrose's death in 1939. His son William Thayer became President after his father's death. Russell Tutt, Charles third son, served in many positions including President after Wm. Thayer.

Later in May, once again following in Palmer's footsteps, Penrose hired the architect Fredrick Sterner to design what was to become the Broadmoor Hotel. After having completed the second Antlers Hotel in Colorado Springs, Sterner had worked on several other hotels, the most impressive of which, the Greenbrier at White Sulfur Springs, West Virginia, opened in 1913. Sterner was known for his ability to design European-style hotels which gratified the American public's desire to have hotels of the same appearance and quality as those in Europe on their own continent. Initially this desire to imitate Europe was a result of Americans' feelings of inferiority. The American upper class looked to Italy, France, England and Germany for the standards by which to judge American art and architecture. The onset of World War I in Europe in 1914 forced the moneyed class of Americans who had always spent their summers on the French Riviera, in Bath, or in one of the many other pleasure spots on the continent, to stay on this side of the Atlantic. These Americans, who normally traveled by ocean liner and train with an entourage of servants, children and mountains of steamer trunks, found themselves crossing the country rather than the ocean and passing the summer in elegant hotels like the Greenbrier and the Hotel del Coronado in San Diego. This experience opened their eyes to the unique beauty of the American interior and the art and architecture that blended with and sprang from the American landscape.

PENROSE WAS FARSIGHTED enough to see that the European war offered an unhoped-for opportunity for American hotels to capture this profitable group of clients and seduce them permanently away from Europe. With this in mind, he rejected Sterner's design for an elaborate Italian palazzo-type structure, with two towers and an imposing rectangular shape. He sought an architect who could design a building which incorporated some of the spirit and architecture of America as well as the best of Europe. Penrose wanted a hotel that looked as though it belonged on the plains at the base of Cheyenne Mountain rather than on one of the seven hills of Rome. He wanted something that expressed the essence of the American spirit, over and above what had come from Europe.

He considered plans from several other firms before choosing those of Warren and Wetmore of New York. This firm was highly respected, having built some of the most impressive buildings in New York including Grand Central Station, the Ritz-Carlton and the Vanderbilt hotels among others. C.L. Wetmore came to Colorado Springs with preliminary plans in January of 1917. The plans called for a white tiered building of rather unconventional design. Rather than utilizing a large rectangular building and varying the facade, as was the style of most major hotels, the Wetmore plan proposed a building that decreased in size from the lower to the upper stories. This effect mirrored the surrounding mountains and gave the structure enough height to be striking without being overwhelming. A single tower, slightly off center, was another unusual feature which added to the building's charm. Wetmore took maximum advantage of the lake by extending two-story wings around its beaches. These wings had sleeping porches for the benefit of consumptives or guests who wished to immerse themselves in the surrounding park. The buildings were completed by red ceramic roof tiles which echoed the design of some of the local buildings including the Penrose's own home, El Pomar, on the other side of the lake.

The directors of the Broadmoor Hotel and Land Company approved Warren and Wetmore's plans for the hotel building in the last week of January 1917, but they had not been idle during the previous months. Penrose knew that he had to create a hotel with exceptional facilities in order to attract world-class travelers to the relatively unknown Pikes Peak region. The hotel's grounds and entertainment facilities were almost as important as the hotel itself. Golf, a sport which was just starting to become popular in the U.S. in 1891 when the Cheyenne Mountain Country Club laid out a rudimentary course that numbered among the first in the nation (it was described as being "just one hazard from start to finish"[3]), had steadily increased in popularity over the intervening years. Penrose wanted the Broadmoor to have a top-notch course which would be ready the day the hotel opened.

BROADMOOR HOTEL, INC.
COLORADO SPRINGS, COLORADO

In summer of 1916 he hired Donald Ross, one of the best-known golf course designers of his day. The second Broadmoor Casino was moved from its position by the lake down to the edge of the golf course where its original architect, Thomas MacLaren, adapted it for use as a golf clubhouse. As Ross prepared the plans for the course, Penrose purchased as much surrounding land as possible, both to protect the hotel's views and secure enough water to keep the grounds green. The Broadmoor Hotel and Land Company acquired nine hundred acres of land around the initial hotel grounds including the face and "horns" (the projecting rocks at the summit) of Cheyenne Mountain. Here Penrose planned to have a network of bridle trails and hiking paths for the hotel's guests. The directors also concerned themselves with the problem of the hotel's name. Given that the Broadmoor name had been in use since the late 1800s, it could not be copyrighted. The difficulty was resolved by raising the "a" thus rendering the name unique.

Julie Penrose, in the meantime, was evolving the design for the interiors. Her taste dictated that the hotel be furnished with discreet elegance utilizing the finest materials available. Although the exterior was intended to blend into its American surroundings, the interiors were rigorously European and she was extremely well-informed about the best possible suppliers and decorators both in the United States and abroad.

---

3. Percy Hagerman in his privately published pamphlet, *The Cheyenne Mountain County Club — The First Twenty-five Years.*

It was a difficult time for Julie emotionally, because her daughter, Gladys, was in Belgium in the thick of the Great War. Gladys McMillan had married the Count Paul Cornet de Ways Ruart early in 1914 and had taken up residence in his castle in Belgium. Their first and only child, Pauline, was born the same year. Shortly thereafter, the family was put under house arrest by the German Army. Julie Penrose lived in fear for their lives and vowed that if they were spared she would build a church. After Gladys' marriage into a Catholic family, Julie had returned to the religion of her childhood, Catholicism, with unprecedented zeal.

While Spencer was building the Broadmoor Hotel, she was consulting with Thomas MacLaren about a small church which would be located on the far side of the lake. The church, which Julie named the Pauline Chapel for her granddaughter, matched the style of El Pomar and the Broadmoor on the

Building the Broadmoor

These images were taken from the photograph album documenting the construction of the Broadmoor Hotel by James Stewart & Co. 1917–1918.

Local History Collection,
Pikes Peak Library District

Clearing the area after the Casino had been moved and before construction began.

This back view shows the lack of vegetation around the lake. The Olmstead Brothers landscaping project was a large one.

This view demonstrates how the decorative plaster mouldings on the hotel's exteriors were built into the walls.

The tram tracks that Pourtales had lobbied so hard to have installed were put to good use during the hotel's construction. Many materials arrived by train downtown and then went out to the Broadmoor in tram cars.

The south face of the hotel. The ballroom promenade is visible between the two wings. French doors surrounded the ballroom on all sides. The building to the far right is the first Broadmoor Hotel, which was renamed the Colonial Club.

Laying out the circular driveway was the final touch before the doors opened June 1, 1918.

exterior and was furnished with exquisite antiques, linens and paintings. The Pauline Chapel was the first church built in the Broadmoor area and was supported economically by Julie Penrose for the duration of her life. The Catholic church became increasingly important to her over time, and was the channel for a great deal of her beneficence to the Colorado Springs community. In this sense, Julie was at odds with her husband who despised religious organizations and refused to support projects in any way connected with churches, but this difference of opinion did not get in the way of their marriage.

The Broadmoor Hotel and Land Company sent out Wetmore's plans to several building contractors in April of 1917. The bids were opened on the 23rd and were all much higher than the $650,000 that the company had planned to spend. In May, after some debate and negotiation, the contract was awarded to the James Stewart Company of New York on an eight percent cost-plus basis. The Stewart Company's bid was for $900,000 and James Stewart estimated that he could complete the structure in three hundred and fifty days. This seems very little time in which to build a luxury hotel, especially during a war, and the reason for Penrose's haste is not known. Those who knew him well said that he was a man who played his hunches, and nine times out of ten his intuition led him to profits and glory. Penrose's intuition often led him to bet on what the outcome of situations might be, and as soon as James Stewart stated the figure 350 days, Speck placed a bet on it. Penrose bet one thousand dollars each against three of the architects and one of the builders that the hotel would be ready for occupancy by May 15, 1918.

ONE OF THE WELL-KNOWN, but unsubstantiated stories about Penrose relates that the $100,000 that he had initially used to back Jackling was money that he had won from a bet with Stratton. Speck bet that the Republican McKinley would beat Stratton's choice, the Democrat William Jennings Bryan, in the 1896 presidential election. McKinley won by a very small margin.

Construction began on the Broadmoor Hotel at the end of May, 1917. The main structure of the hotel was built of steel and concrete, a response to the public's well-justified fear of hotel fires. The hotel was to boast that its buildings actually incorporated Cripple Creek gold because the concrete was made from ore tailings from the gold mills. Despite the war, the supply of steel was adequate and work progressed rapidly. The Penroses involved themselves in every phase of construction and adaptations of the

LEFT: Decorative frieze across the front of the Hotel, just above the mezzanine terrace.

David Beightol photo, 1993

original design. Speck demanded to see examples of fixtures and other details before they were installed, and his tendency to change his mind at the last minute caused some turmoil in his relationship with the Stewart Company. Julie chose all of the furnishings, the artwork, the carpets and the china. The Penrose commitment to nothing but the very best for their hotel is evident in her choice of Rosenthal china for the dining room service.

BELOW: The Broadmoor's signature colors, blue and gold, appear on all of the early logos and china. The large plate with the deep blue rim is Rosenthal China from 1918.

John Gair photo, 1993

This willingness to spend money for the very best, was not shared by the other members of the board of directors who refused to invest any more than the initial amount agreed upon into the hotel. Penrose unconcernedly continued to pour money into the little details which he understood would make up the grand whole. After the first million dollars was gone, he put up another million, and then later, yet another million. The Broadmoor Hotel became increasingly important to him. It was not to be one of the many little projects with which he had entertained himself with over the years, but rather his crowning glory. The hotel was to be his palace, his showcase, the achievement for which he would be most respected.

As the construction of the buildings progressed the Penroses concerned themselves with the artistic details which so richly decorate the exterior and the first two floors of the Broadmoor. In March of 1918, work began on the outside walls. The artwork that adorns the outside of the main building just below the roof and above the balcony was applied by Paul S. Deneville, the artist of the Panama-Pacific exposition, whose graffito process was recognized as outstanding by many architects and builders. Deneville had perfected a process of applying designs in plastic clay to the walls of buildings and then baking them on with intense heat. A temporary wall was constructed around the main tower of the hotel so that the temperature could be raised

TOP AND MIDDLE PHOTOS: In the final months of construction, a virtual army of artists and craftsmen worked to complete the interior decorative details. Note the swan motif in the wallcoverings; swans appear in the decor of almost all of the public rooms.

Emery photo, 1918

BOTTOM PHOTO: Mattresses were piled in the mezzanine lounge as painters put the last touches on the window frames. This lounge no longer looks directly out onto the lake as it does in this picture. 1918.

Broadmoor Historical Collection

to the necessary degree. The process has proved itself over time, for the ornamentation is as impressive today as it was then and requires only occasional re-painting.

The design of the interiors was the work of the interior decorators Schleich and Smoraldi of New York, the firm responsible for the Crystal Room at the New York Ritz-Carlton. Schleich and Smoraldi decided that the walls and ceilings of the hotel would have intricately molded and painted plaster decorations, the style of which would vary depending on the decor of the room. The contract for the decorative moldings was granted to Rochett and Partzini of New York.

In the final stages of construction, the decoration of the mezzanine and first floors was undertaken by an army of over 100 Italian artists brought in from New York and Italy. The colored cement and plaster work designs are typical of Italian artisans, but different rooms were executed in different styles. The dining room is in the English style, the main lounge in the French style and the Palm Court in the Italian style. Most impressive of all is the elevator foyer which was arched and decorated to resemble the ceiling of the Villa Madama in Rome. The heavy circular pieces in the lobby are in the style of Luca Della Robbia (a fifteenth-century Italian artist), but incorporate whimsical references to the hotel's location. The putto in the molding over the elevator for example, is brandishing a tomahawk and wearing an Indian headdress. The lobby beams are painted with motifs from classical mythology, but incorporate small landscapes of local scenery such as the Garden of the Gods and the Mount of the Holy Cross.

The chandeliers and lighting fixtures which were suspended from these ceilings were and are themselves works of art. The most dramatic is the glittering crystal globe which now hangs in the elevator foyer at the top of the spiral staircase. Originally, this chandelier was the centerpiece of the ballroom, but as its light alone was not adequate, it was replaced with several larger ones. The lighting fixtures throughout the building are exquisite and exemplify Julie Penrose's penchant for beauty in every detail. The ornate decoration of the building itself was offset by the simplicity of the furnishings provided by Westing, Evans and Egmore of Philadelphia. The furnishings were of the best European manufacture, but were designed not to be ostentatious or draw the eye away from their surroundings. There was some concern that the war might interfere with the arrival of the materials from Europe and make it impossible to complete the interiors, but Charles Westing, of Schleich and Smoraldi stated that work would begin on time provided that the ships were not sunk or otherwise delayed (and they were not).

Penrose, though not a dancer himself, was insistent that the ballroom floor be as conducive as possible to comfortable dancing. He ordered the construction of a floor which consisted of three layers of wood laid on springs with resilient material between the layers so that the floor provided a springy foundation to inspire and support the dancers. The ballroom was originally surrounded on three sides by windows. Flooded with light during the day and surrounded by stars at night, it was one of the most romantic rooms in the building. In later years, the French doors and balconies which girded the ballroom were closed off as construction around the hotel blocked the views.

This Della Robbia-style molding over the elevator door in the Lobby incorporates the flavor of the Old West. The putto on the right is wearing an Indian headdress and brandishing a tomahawk.

David Beightol photo, 1993

The exceptional nature of the hotel's furnishings extended to the service areas of the hotel. Speck loved technology and progress and wanted his hotel to be equipped with the latest in everything. The kitchens and food storage areas were supplied with the most advanced machinery available. The Colorado Springs *Gazette* reported that a vegetable cellar described as a "scientific marvel" was constructed in the basement of the Broadmoor Hotel service building by P.B. Tallman, mechanical engineer for the construction company James Stewart & Co. The environment was controlled by a device which maintained the level of humidity and changed the air twice every hour. The incoming air was washed through brine which served as a germicide. The cellar was constructed to maintain the supply of finest quality fruits and vegetables which the hotel planned to offer to its guests.

Penrose saw to it that the array of opportunities for guests' entertainment were unmatched by any other resort hotel in the country, or perhaps the world. A spacious indoor swimming pool occupied the area where the drugstore is currently situated. The pool contained 100,000 gallons of pure mountain water. Each drop was purified and made bacteria-proof by the system of violet ray filters through which it passed. Turkish baths, saunas and massages were provided as well. The lake was seeded with more than ten thousand rainbow trout to provide

RIGHT: Chandelier in Ballroom.

David Beightol photo, 1993

fishing opportunities for the guests, and there was a fleet of canoes and rowboats for excursions onto the lake or to the island.

Golf, on a rugged, semi-mountainous course, was to be one of the hotel's main attractions. The course's designer, Donald Ross, had completed the Pinehurst, North Carolina, course earlier, to rave reviews. When Penrose hired him, he instructed him to build the finest course in the country and set no limit on its cost. The construction of the greens was a monumental task. The arid prairie soil had to be transformed into an evenly napped, lush green carpet. Penrose hired agronomists and experts to study the prob-

Large ceiling detail of main mezzanine.

David Beightol photo, 1993

Details, details.

LEFT: Ceiling detail of mezzanine lounge.

BOTTOM LEFT: Ceiling detail of lobby.

BOTTOM RIGHT: Ceiling detail of elevator foyer.

David Beightol photos, 1993

ABOVE LEFT: The ballroom had a very different aspect in 1918, when it was surrounded by windows on three sides. The chandelier has since been moved to the foyer at the head of the spiral staircase.

Emery photo

ABOVE RIGHT: This 1950 photograph of the indoor swimming pool is little changed (except for the ceilings) from its appearance in 1918. Local children loved the murals at the end of the pool for their artistic and educational value. The pool was covered and the Drugstore moved on top of it in 1961 as part of the hotel's modernization.

Bob McIntyre photo

lem, determine which kinds of seed were most appropriate, and to actually prepare the course. Lake Moraine peat, humus and soil were ground together in a carefully calculated mixture for the seed beds. Golf course turf generally takes several years to mature, but the resulting course was touted as being exceptional the day of its opening, July 1, 1918. At the time it was the only championship golf course in the world above 6,000 feet in altitude.

For those who preferred equestrian sports, the stables and polo fields lay just across Lake Circle (where the Broadmoor garage is now located) and riders could take advantage of an extensive network of trails to the west of the hotel and up into Cheyenne Canon. Penrose already had a fleet of touring cars and busses from his Pikes Peak business which he adapted so that hotel guests could easily obtain access to the many attractions of the region. Guides were available for hiking, hunting or fishing excursions into the "Wild West" which lingered just beyond the hotel grounds.

The less daring could avail themselves of the tennis courts and lawn bowling greens near the golf course, or simply tour the grounds and admire the gardens. Penrose had addressed the problem of providing plants and flowers for the hotel and grounds in early 1917 by purchasing the Broadmoor Greenhouse from William Foster. The greenhouse had been in existence since 1902 and had provided flowers and plants to the few homes in the Broadmoor suburb as well as clients downtown. The business had done quite well under Foster's direction and continued its expansion into wholesale as well as retail markets. Foster was retained as manager and the business was divided into two sections: the Broadmoor Hotel Greenhouse Company which provided all of the shrubs, flowers and plants for the hotel and the Cheyenne Mountain Floral Company which maintained

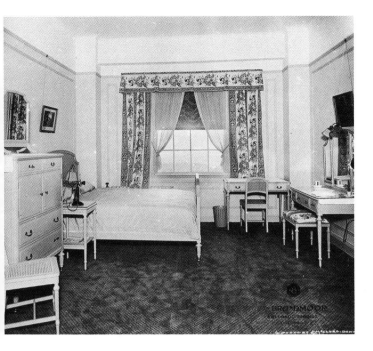

ABOVE LEFT: Simple elegance was Julie's dictum for the design of the bedrooms. The caption for this photograph reads "A Chamber—Taupe carpet—Furniture of gray enamelled—Drapes, yellow and black—Yellow silk spread—Walls gray and paneled—Ceiling, cream white." 1919.

Broadmoor Historical Collection

ABOVE RIGHT: The kitchens were organized to Chef Louis Stratta's specifications and he presided over them for decades. 1918.

Broadmoor Historical Collection

LEFT: Cover of an early brochure advertising the hotel. The porte cochere, which now covers the front of the loggia but is missing in this picture, was added in 1935.

El Pomar Foundation

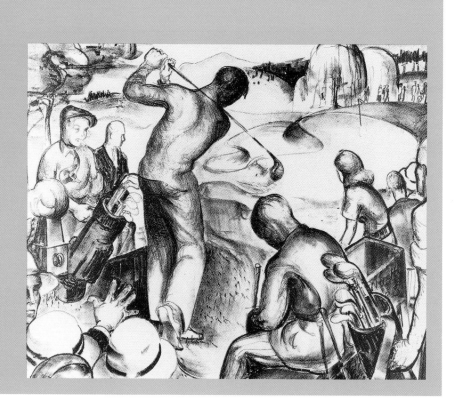

Larry Heller (Broadmoor Art Academy artist) lithograph of "Teeing Off at the Broadmoor" commissioned by Spencer Penrose.

Courtesy of Tracy and Su Felix, Bill Bowers photo

the original wholesale and retail business. The extensive landscaping of the hotel grounds was designed and executed by the renowned Olmstead Brothers of Brookline, Massachusetts who returned often to the Broadmoor in later years for other projects.

The Penroses did not neglect their guests' need for divertissement during the evening hours. A small theater was located on the north side of the first floor. The latest films were purchased in readiness to be shown, and the stage prepared for theatrical productions as well. Julie Penrose's passion was opera and fine music. She listened to music constantly in her home and engaged a fine orchestra so that the hotel could provide music at meals and for dancing. Guyla Boxhorn, a Rumanian, and his six piece London Society Orchestra were engaged for the 1918 summer season. They had played at many select social events in the States and court functions in Europe.

As 1918 progressed and the opening date approached, Penrose had to organize a skilled team of professionals so that the quality of the hotel's service would meet his rigorous standards. He already had a general manager, W.S. Dunning, who had been involved with the Broadmoor project since its inception. Mr. Edward Burke was hired as his assistant. Both of these men had previously worked at the Antlers in the same capacities. One of the many stories about the origin of Speck's idea for a hotel relates that one of Penrose's partners had a suite at the Antlers Hotel. Penrose and his friends were notorious for their loud parties and one of the Antlers Hotel guests complained to the manager about the noise. When this did not appear to have any effect, the guest complained to the hotel's owners and Dunning was fired. Penrose purportedly told Dunning not to worry about finding work because he would build his own hotel and Dunning would be the manager. This story may have some basis in fact because Penrose also wooed his executive chef, Louis Stratta, away from the Antlers (it also might explain why Palmer's heirs were reluctant to sell a controlling interest to Penrose). Penrose was much assisted in the hiring of the rest of his staff by the many hotel men that he knew in the East. On May 20, 1918, the first Maître d'hôtel arrived with 25 waiters selected from the best hotels on the East Coast. His name was Fred Pellegrini and his assistant was E.E. Gallotti.

Good public relations and advertising were to be key to the success of the Broadmoor Hotel, in order to attract clients to a location not formerly known as a luxury resort. W. E. Frenaye was hired as the advertising manager and he began a campaign to educate the elite of America about the existence of a new resort destination. Frenaye designed a small booklet which was sent to travel agents and clubs all over the country. The *Preliminary Opening Announcement* provided a nutshell description of the hotel which was particularly apt: "Architecturally designed to conform to the landscape of the Pikes Peak region, it includes the best features of many famous European resort hotels, and affords every convenience and luxury that could be desired by the most fastidious. Yet, size and prodigality were not the objects sought. Rather, the owners have planned to make the Broadmoor quiet and home-like, rich in little touches of refinement and beauty."

BELOW: Cover of the *Preliminary Opening Announcement*, 1918.

Broadmoor Historical Collection

THE PENROSES TOOK trips to the East Coast where Penrose made the round of his clubs publicizing the hotel and waxing enthusiastic about the joys of the West. He frequently recited his favorite poem to explain his feelings for the land:

"Out Where The West Begins" by Arthur Chapman

Out where the handclasp's a little stronger,
Out where the smile dwells a little longer,
That's where the West begins;
Out where the sun is a little brighter,
Where the snows that fall are a trifle whiter,
Where the bonds of home are a wee bit tighter,—
That's where the West begins.

Out where the skies are a trifle bluer,
Out where the friendship's a little truer,
That's where the West begins;
Out where a fresher breeze is blowing,
Where there's laughter in every streamlet flowing,
Where there's more of reaping and less of sowing,—
That's where the West begins.

Out where the world is in the making,
Where fewer hearts in despair are aching,
That's where the West begins;
Where there's more of singing and less of sighing,
Where there's more of giving and less of buying,
And a man makes friends without half trying—
That's where the West begins.

ABOVE: Centerfold of the
*Preliminary Opening
Announcement* depicts
the features of the soon-to-be
completed Broadmoor
Hotel, 1918.

Broadmoor Historical Collection

Penrose attracted as much media attention as he could, which was not
difficult given his notoriety as a mining millionaire and organizer of the
Pikes Peak Auto Race. He saw to it that Americans began to associate the
Pikes Peak region with spectacular events, beauty and luxury. He "put Colorado Springs on the map" as a local newspaper reported.

By the end of May, 1918, Penrose decided that the hotel could host
a preliminary opening on the first of June. The wings, Northlake, Southlake,
Northmoor and Southmoor were not completed, but the main building
was almost ready for occupancy. The architects and builders would not
manage to collect on their bet, but they had misjudged by a mere fifteen
days. The Olmstead Brothers Company had armies of men laying out the
gravel circular driveway and setting plants and trees on the grounds. The
high probability of late frosts had made it impossible for them to prepare
the plants in advance and Penrose insisted that it all be in place for the
first of June. Final touches, including a last coat of paint on the bedroom
walls, were carried out at top speed so that all would be ready for the
scrutiny of the press and the Colorado Springs and Denver dignitaries who
had been invited to view the Penroses' masterpiece.

Envision, if you can, the Broadmoor Hotel on the eve of its opening.
The freshly painted white[4] exterior with the frescos in bold relief was
reflected in the lake to the rear and provided a stunning vista down Lake

---

4. The hotel buildings were not painted pink until several years after the opening.

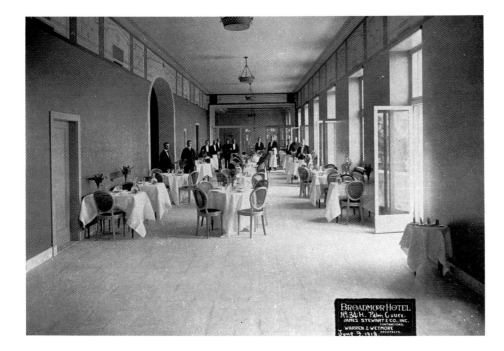

The Palm Court was frequently pressed into service as a dining room until another room was added on the Lake Terrace in 1924.

Broadmoor Historical Collection

Avenue. The streets surrounding the hotel and continuing down to Colorado Springs were unpaved and lined with much smaller versions of the trees that now somewhat obscure it. The hotel positively seemed to shimmer like a mirage, like an enchanted castle in the middle of a deserted plain. But it was real, and its charm and loveliness were to attract multitudes and instill a great sense of pride in the people of Colorado Springs. Penrose had given the city a gem, an heirloom which to this day enriches the city both emotionally and financially. On June 1, 1918, the doors opened and the party began.

BELOW: Penrose was not above altering nature to serve the public relations department. He encouraged Maxfield Parrish to put the lake in front of the hotel in his painting and blithely put the mountains in front of it in this composite photograph. Circa 1925.

Broadmoor Historical Collection

Broadmoor Opens to Raves

T HE FIRST OF innumerable parties to be held at the Broadmoor Hotel began the evening of June 1, 1918. Frantic preparations continued until the last minute, but when the doors opened to the public the main building was a showcase. The Penroses led their guests through rooms where chandeliers blazed and champagne corks popped; they celebrated the culmination of a year and a half of intense, but gratifying labor. This party was not yet the formal opening, for many of the guest rooms, wing buildings and recreational areas were not completed, but the Penroses wanted to show the locals what they had wrought at the base of Cheyenne Mountain. Speck was extremely proud of his accomplishment, but also somewhat anxious for its success.

While the Broadmoor Hotel and Land Company was in the process of building the Broadmoor Hotel, the United States was just beginning its involvement in World War I. American soldiers joined Allied forces after the sinking of the *Lusitania* in April of 1917, and the war raged on until the Armistice was signed on November 11, 1918. Penrose was in the politically delicate position of having built a luxury resort in a period of suffering, sacrifice and hard times for many Americans. He was very sensitive to the possible repercussions of his project and did much to publicly demonstrate his patriotism and willingness to assist the war effort during the planning and construction phases of the hotel. His business-oriented mind, however, saw to it that his public acts of patriotism also attracted attention to the hotel. On March 7, 1918, the *Denver Post* reported that Spencer Penrose, multimillionaire builder of the Broadmoor Hotel, had announced that he was donating his 30 West Dale Street home to the War Department as an army hospital for sick and wounded soldiers. The home had been rented by W.F. Moore, a Philadelphia multimillionaire, since the Penroses had vacated it to move to El Pomar. The offer was never accepted by the War Department, but it certainly made good press.

Penrose initiated a broad range of events and entertainments to publicize his new hotel and the world came to enjoy them.

AT LEFT: The Broadmoor Tavern opened in 1939 with this menu. A multi-course luncheon could be had for $1.50.

Courtesy John N. McCarty, Bill Bowers photo

Penrose combined support for the war effort and publicity even more successfully with his choice of a golf pro for the Broadmoor Golf Club. Again stating that nothing but the best would do, he hired Jim Barnes of the Whitemarsh Valley Country Club in Penrose's home city of Philadelphia. Barnes was rated the best pro in the country in 1917, and Penrose ensured that the press would take note of his engagement by offering him double the salary he had been earning at the Whitemarsh, $15,000 a year. Barnes was hired on the first of April, 1918, but since the opening of the Broadmoor course was not until the first of June, Penrose sent him on a two-month tour of the country to raise money for the Red Cross. The tournaments were extremely popular, raised a great deal of money, and pitted Jim Barnes against the best professional and amateur players in the country.

Jim Barnes' tour coincided with a massive advertising campaign. Just before the hotel opened, the Broadmoor Hotel and Land Company closed a deal with the Erwin and Wasey Advertising Company of Chicago. The contract called for $45,000 worth of advertising in the nation's best periodicals. The sum was the largest amount ever spent to advertise anything in the Pikes Peak region. The ads did not stress lavish expenditure, but rather the beauty and healthful nature of the hotel's surroundings. The magazines which carried the ads included the *Saturday Evening Post, Cosmopolitan,* and *Vanity Fair* in addition to all major newspapers. All of these promotional activities ensured that the media's eyes were on Colorado Springs for the formal opening, which was held June 29, 1918. To record the event, Penrose invited several well-known artists so that their representations of the hotel could be used as advertising. The Russian landscape artist James Marchesi, a specialist in black and white sketches had come before the opening to make a series of drawings of the hotel and the surrounding landscape, and these images were supplemented by those of Jonas Lie, who executed two oil paintings of the hotel, and Vernon Howe Bailey. Bailey's sketches were used in the Broadmoor's first brochure and some of the originals still hang in the hotel's lobby and lounges. High society from all over the United States attended the opening and spread the word of their satisfaction with America's new resort throughout the country.

Although Spencer Penrose was not a lover of the fine arts, he recognized

A Land of Pine-spiced Air and Golden Sunshine

SAWING the turquoise sky far overhead, Colorado's pine-clad Rockies smile down on BROADMOOR. Here, at Colorado Springs, in its beautiful mountain-park of 2,000 acres, nestles America's finest hostelry.

¶ Differing from mere "resort" hotels, THE BROADMOOR is open all the year. Here summer days are cool, sunny days that lure one out-of-doors to golf, to ride—to unravel entrancing mountain paths. Autumn brings glorious Indian Summer that flames with vivid color and lingers until January.

¶ At THE BROADMOOR, should he choose, one may dine *al fresco* on an open terrace that overlooks a trout-stocked lake, or at one of the stone fireplaces high on Mt. Cheyenne prepare a camper's meal.

¶ With the added advantages of indoor swimming, two Turkish bath parlors and a little theatre, THE BROADMOOR offers every distinction of cuisine, service and appointment of the finest metropolitan hotel.

The BROADMOOR
COLORADO SPRINGS
BUILT OF STONE, STEEL AND CONCRETE
NATURALLY IT IS FIREPROOF

Write for illustrated booklet

Hundred Million Dollar Hotel Group.
Guests of Spencer Penrose
Broadmoor Hotel - Sept - 1920.

art's ability to portray and enrich his hotel. He wanted to engage an artist of acknowledged renown to depict the Broadmoor the way that he saw it — as a magical place, redolent with romance and possibilities. On a more practical level, he was frustrated by the fact that a photograph could not incorporate all of the essential assets of the hotel: the lake, the mountains, the entrance and the intense colors of the whole, into one picture. In 1919 he began a lengthy correspondence with Maxfield Parrish, an artist known for his use of intense colors and Art Deco style, and encouraged him to use artistic license in such a way as to combine all of these elements into one painting. Parrish seemed reluctant to come and only after much wooing and raising of the fee did he consent to come and view the hotel in person.

In 1920 he visited the Broadmoor and did some initial studies of the hotel. He shipped the painting to Penrose in spring of 1921. The painting was, and is, a delight to behold. The lake, which Parrish placed in front of the hotel, shimmers and reflects the hotel's pink embracing arms. The red and purple mountains and the indigo blue sky provide a dramatic backdrop for the elegant building in their midst. Penrose loved the painting and used reproductions of it on posters, menus, matchbooks and numerous other small items which publicized the hotel.

Penrose did not limit his advertising campaign to the public. He was a newcomer to the hotel business, and felt that he had to make a serious effort to meet and fraternize with his new colleagues. He knew the owners and managers of the best hotels in the country from a client's perspective, but he needed to establish a relationship of cooperation and shared business interests so that the Broadmoor Hotel could become part of the hotel brotherhood. His idea was a novel one at that time, and quite well-received by a group of men who were used to providing the very best for others and not necessarily enjoying it themselves.

In the fall of 1920 Spencer Penrose invited sixty men from prominent East Coast hotels for two all-expenses-paid weeks at the Broadmoor. He hired private railroad cars to transport them to Colorado Springs, and upon their arrival treated them like kings. They watched and participated in races up Pike Peak, polo tournaments, airplane races from Colorado Springs to Denver and around Pikes Peak, a golf tournament, dances and visits to the attractions of the Pikes Peak area. He treated them to a dinner at the Cooking Club and assigned them the title "The Hundred Million Dollar

Hotel Group." The week was not solely for pleasure. Penrose proposed the creation of a system of standardization for rating hotels, as well as the election of a board of hotel experts to do the actual ratings. Penrose felt that guests would be protected from profiteers and unethical business practices by such a system. His advice was well taken and appreciated as much as the fine wine that accompanied it.

The members of the group did not forget Penrose's gesture. To express their appreciation, the following year they presented Spencer Penrose with a silver replica of the Broadmoor at a dinner at the Hotel Commodore in New York. The plaque was made by Black, Starr & Frost Jewelers of New York, and cost two thousand dollars. The

ABOVE: The Maxfield Parrish version of the Broadmoor Hotel incorporated all of the elements Penrose had requested: hotel, lake, mountains, and the dramatic intensity of color. The oil painting was completed in 1921 at the artist's studio in Vermont.

El Pomar Foundation

AT LEFT: Penrose loved the Parrish painting and used the image on menus, lipstick blotters, advertisements and brochures like this one. Circa 1924.

Broadmoor Historical Collection

The members of the "Hundred Million Dollar Hotel Group" gave Penrose this silver plaque at the Hotel Commodore in New York in 1921. It hung in the lobby of the hotel for many years and is now in El Pomar Foundation building.

inscription on the plaque reads *"An Appreciation—The subscribers here to present this tablet to Mr. Spencer Penrose of Colorado Springs, Colorado as an appropriate memento of their sincere appreciation of the generosity and hospitality so sumptuously bestowed upon them as his honored guests at the beautiful Broadmoor Hotel. The special private train from New York and return September 1st to 14th 1920, so graciously provided by Mr. Penrose will ever remain as a connecting link in the chain of fraternity and mark an epoch in the annals of hoteldom that shall shine resplendent in the memories of all of us who were so cordially favored by the friendship of our host, whom we joyously acclaim as a Prince of Entertainers and a Bon Vivant of rare accomplishments. Our Gratitude is no less sincere than our esteem is exalted."*[1]

The hotel's completion and opening did not diminish Penrose's interest in the project; he seemed, rather, to become more and more involved in the Broadmoor and Colorado Springs' well-being. The opening party was only the beginning of a series of parties, sporting events and business endeavors of many kinds which kept the Broadmoor Hotel and Spencer Penrose in a whirlwind of activity for the next two decades. In retrospect it seems incredible that one man could have been the motivating force behind such a diverse array of initiatives, but his stamp is on them all.

---

1. The New York members of this group founded the Tavern Club of New York in 1922 to maintain the spirit of convivality that the trip had fostered. Penrose was named a charter member and visited the club regularly.

Motoring Mania

PENROSE'S PERSONAL PASSION for automobiles had not diminished since his first purchase of four Loziers at one time shortly after his marriage. He had a fleet of cars of his own, the Pikes Peak Automobile Company cars for tourist transport up Pikes Peak, and in addition the cars that he purchased explicitly for the use of guests at the hotel. During the years that followed he organized the Gray Line Tours Company, a local taxi service and a "drive-it-yourself" car service (a predecessor of rent-a-car companies). Given the quantity of his vehicles (in the 1920s the hotel maintained a fleet of thirty-eight Pierce-Arrow touring cars) and his passion for implementing the latest technology, Speck experimented in the "oiling" of many roads around the Broadmoor. When these proved successful, he requested that the City of Colorado Springs pave Lake Avenue, from the end of Nevada Avenue to the Broadmoor. This was done, primarily because Penrose contributed $50,000 to the $150,000 cost of the roadway.

ABOVE: Gray Line cars took guests and tourists to scenic attractions in numerous locations. This car is parked beside the bridge at Royal Gorge, about seventy miles from Colorado Springs.

Broadmoor Historical Collection

The road, completed in 1920, was three miles long and constituted the longest stretch of pavement in southern Colorado. The "Broadmoor Boulevard" was inaugurated by breaking a bottle of champagne over the hood of one of Penrose's cars, followed by a large party at which Governor Oliver Shoup (one of Penrose's friends from Cripple Creek) gave a speech extolling the virtues of progress. Penrose even had a news reporter named Fred Parrish fly over the scene in an airplane and film the event. In 1928, the road between Denver and Colorado Springs was finally completely paved, something Penrose had been advocating for years, and Denverites could arrive at social events at the Broadmoor Hotel without the thick coating of dust that had accompanied them prior to the road's paving.

Broadmoor cars and guest vehicles were housed in the garage which faced the power plant on the other side of Lake Circle. In the first years it was unusual for guests to arrive by car. Most arrived by train. Colorado Springs was accessible from Palmer's Denver and Rio Grande Railway, a branch line from the Denver, Texas and Fort Worth Railway, the Santa Fe and Missouri Pacific Railway and the Chicago, Rock Island and Pacific Railway. But Penrose had built his Pikes Peak Highway secure in the knowledge that America would turn to cars for its preferred form of transport, and when they came he was ready.

Flying Machines

THE LEGENDARY AIRFIGHTS between English and German aces during World War I had transformed airplanes into objects of respect and adulation. Penrose wanted one for himself and envisioned the day that Broadmoor guests would arrive by air. He lobbied to convince the City of Colorado Springs and the Stratton estate to put aside a field where planes could take off and land and which could also be used as a polo or sports field. Penrose felt that an airfield was essential to ensuring that Colorado Springs remained in the forefront of amusement and sports centers in the country. In 1919 Penrose ordered a Curtiss Oriole from England and trained his chauffeur Harry MacMillan to be a pilot (Harry was used to a life of adventure, he was also Penrose's race car driver for the Hill Climb).

The official Broadmoor airplane was used for hotel business and for charitable purposes and figured in some of Penrose's wilder publicity ideas. Although Penrose's vision of large numbers of flying guests never materialized in his lifetime, he continued to promote aviation and when Alexander Aviation built a field slightly north of Colorado Springs he built a Broadmoor Hangar so that guests who did arrive by air would have adequate parking. The first guest to use the hangar was a most illustrious one. Charles Lindbergh made an unannounced, unexpected stop in Colorado Springs on September 18, 1928. Lindy and his associate, the W.W. I flyer Viscount Eric de Stroelbergh, came as guests of Spencer and Julie Penrose and stayed at the Broadmoor Hotel. Lindbergh's vehicle, a Ryan monoplane, remained in the hangar overnight and took off the following morning at dawn.

This memorable event was not Speck's first venture into airborne publicity. In 1922, Colorado Springs hosted an air circus whose purpose was to encourage interest in the air force reserves. The show consisted of thirteen big DeHaviland airplanes piloted by crack army flyers and featured races to and from Denver and around Pikes Peak as well as parachute drops. After the exhibition the aviators were the guests of honor at a dinner and dance at the Broadmoor Hotel. This air race from Denver to Pikes Peak became an annual event and Penrose invited top flyers to participate in it. In 1934, Colonel Roscoe Turner, the well-known flying ace, starred in the event.

Polo Ponies and Bucking Broncos

PENROSE'S VERY SUCCESSFUL advertising campaign stressed the unique panorama of divertissements available at a luxury hotel which happened to be in the middle of the "Wild" West. He saw to it, therefore, that the Broadmoor provided not only the finest of polo facilities, but also a rodeo complete with bucking broncos and roping steers; not only miles of well-tended bridle paths, but also grueling endurance races through rough terrain. In short, it was the best of both worlds.

The stables were constructed on Hazel Avenue just adjacent to the Broadmoor Garage (the garage was later extended to occupy this space as well). They were built of wood with beautifully carved details and housed horses that could be hired for the day, or the polo ponies that accompanied the guests of the hotel.[2] The land that the Broadmoor Hotel and Land

ABOVE LEFT: Speck always got into the spirit of the events that he organized. He and Governor Oliver Shoup donned western regalia for the 1921 Broadmoor Roundup.

Broadmoor Historical Collection

ABOVE RIGHT: Ogallala Sioux Indians initiate Penrose as an honorary member of the tribe at the annual Broadmoor Roundup. 1921.

Broadmoor Historical Collection

---

2. These stables burned and were replaced in 1958 with a concrete structure on the far side of the Penrose stadium.

Company had acquired up and around Cheyenne Mountain was laced with trails of varying degrees of difficulty and length to suit the style of any rider. The number of trails continued to grow for friends of Spencer's provided money to have trails named after them (and perhaps because they had lost a bet and that was the stake).

The first Broadmoor Roundup was held in the summer of 1920. The event was a combination of cowboy events and Native American demonstrations. Given that the Springs did not have any local Indians, Spencer Penrose invited twenty-five members of a tribe of Ogallala Sioux from their reservation in South Dakota. The Indians performed a ceremony in the ballroom of the hotel initiating Spencer Penrose into their tribe and assigning him the name "Chief White Eagle." After the ceremony and a dinner, at which the Sioux were the guests of honor, the young men surprised the crowd by inviting ladies to dance and proved to be excellent ballroom dancers. The entourage, including the Indian's

ponies, descended from the train that brought them from South Dakota at the station in downtown Colorado Springs, and then rode to the Broadmoor. The event was recorded in many of the nation's newspapers.

The Round-up was extremely popular with hotel guests and increased in size and variety every year. In order to provide an arena for this and other sporting events, the Broadmoor Riding Arena was built on the west side of the lake in 1930 (it was later transformed into the World Arena skating facility). The structure was 100 feet wide by 300 feet long, with no poles, columns or other supports within the arena. A raised platform at one end could accommodate up to five hundred spectators. The building was used for horse shows, dog shows, indoor tennis and polo and many other events until it was determined that an even larger arena was necessary.

An outdoor stadium was built next to the Riding Academy in 1938. The stadium was moved to another location in the early 1970s when construction began for Broadmoor West. Upon completion of what Penrose called the Will Rogers' Stadium the roundup became the Will Rogers Rodeo. After Penrose died in 1939 and the City of Colorado Springs took over the yearly event the stadium's name was changed to the Penrose Stadium and the rodeo became the Colorado Springs Rodeo. The event is now the Pikes Peak or Bust Rodeo, and is still held each year in Penrose Stadium.

Polo had been played in the Broadmoor area since the Cheyenne Mountain Country Club's membership of young aristocrats first started batting a ball around on the open plain. In 1892 a polo committee was organized and a reasonable field built shortly thereafter. The local team battled the Devereaux team from Glenwood Springs on many a memorable occasion and quite a number of handsome cups changed hands in awards ceremonies over the years. After Penrose built the Broadmoor, he established the Broadmoor Polo Association, which was incorporated in 1924. This association absorbed the Cheyenne Mountain team (not without some complaint on their part) and leased their field. Given that a strong contingent of polo lovers and players was already established in the Springs and was augmented by the patrons of the Broadmoor Hotel, the association achieved immediate success both economically and socially.

By 1928 things were going so well that Penrose built a new Broadmoor polo field and a Moorish-style grandstand just east of the stables. Polo was extremely popular during this period and was the focal point of many social events. Dinners, dances and parties were held at the Broadmoor both before and after the games. The games themselves provided entertainment for the Hotel's guests and for the people of Colorado Springs. The Broadmoor Women's Polo team was organized that same year. Reflecting women's changing position in society, women participated in all of the athletic opportunities that the Broadmoor Hotel offered. The media, however, was somewhat less enthusiastic. The *Denver Post* announced the team's formation with the following headline "Women Invade . . . Another Domain . . . Now It's Polo." Underneath this headline were pictures of the team members interspersed with cartoons of a rather uncomposed woman on a horse trying to hit a ball with the captions: "If the polo pony gets rough there won't be too much to do about it. What, with hairpins falling out and a little ball to hit, they'll have plenty to do."

ABOVE: The *Polo Annual* provided spectators with epigrams such as this one: "The click of the ball and a merry call / From a pal in the thick of the fray. / A pony quick and a bamboo stick / Are the best of all, I say."

Bill Bowers photo, Broadmoor Historical Collection

During the twenties, polo was supplemented with yearly endurance remount races sponsored by the American Remount Association and the United States Army Remount Service. These two groups had been set up by the government after World War I. When Europeans had come to the States to buy horses needed for cavalry, artillery and wagon trains they had been sorely disappointed by the quality of horses produced by the United States, and the Remount organization was the government's attempt to remedy the situation.

The Remount Association had set up a network of Government Remount Stallions across the country which were available to farmers and ranchers who wished to improve the quality of their horse stock. The Remount races tested the different breeds of horse against each other to determine which were the fastest and strongest across long distances. Each horse was ridden sixty miles a day for five consecutive days on five different courses. The horses were judged by their condition (60 points) and fleetness (40 points) each day. The western headquarters for these events was the Broadmoor Hotel where contestants started and finished each day. Spencer Penrose bore the expense for the competitions and provided the Broadmoor Cup which was taken home by the winner. This cup had been purchased by Spencer Penrose in England, where, for over a century, it was handed down to the winner of competitions at old Epsom Downs.

As cars increasingly supplanted carriages in Colorado Springs, Penrose felt that their passing should be recorded and, if possible, delayed. He went around to his friends who were divesting themselves of their carriages in favor of automobiles and purchased them. He hoped to revive coaching as a sport, or at least take the Broadmoor's guests on carriage rides. He purchased or was given carriages from several prominent families including the Webbs and Arthurs. He acquired Chester Alan Arthur II's (Speck's Cooking Club partner) entire collection and had them driven or carried through the streets of downtown out to the Broadmoor where they were stored in the carriage house at El Pomar. For many years the carriages were

used to transport guests and notable visitors at the Broadmoor Hotel. In the forties, Julie decided that they had become artifacts and should be kept in a museum. She engaged her friend, the architect Jan Ruhtenberg, to design a building for them. The carriages can still be seen in the Carriage Museum just in front of the hotel on Lake Circle.

Golf, Pugilists and Dancing in the Club

THE GOLF COURSE, as designed by Donald Ross, was an essential part of the Broadmoor Hotel's success. The course was an unusual one for the time, given its altitude and level of technical difficulty. Ross, who had designed courses for several of the top golf clubs in the country, declared the Broadmoor course his best work. The original links were 6,617 yards in length with a 74 par; every green was undulating. Jim Barnes established himself at the Broadmoor upon completion of his tour for the Red Cross and attracted many quality players to the roster of the Broadmoor Golf Club. Chick Evans, the holder of the National Amateur and National Open titles, became a non-resident member of the club as soon as it was built and played often on the course.

ABOVE: Awards Ceremony for the 1923 Remount endurance race. Governor Sweet (in front) awarded the $5,000 gold cup to Capt. E. Watkins and Norfolk Star (far left). Mrs. Penrose's entry, Chief, ridden by Jack Hall (far right) took seventh place.

Courtesy Richard L. Goudie

Once the course at the Broadmoor had opened Barnes participated in tournaments with locally and nationally known opponents on a regular basis, and the club began hosting noteworthy tournaments. The first important tourney was another Red Cross match. Jim Barnes and Chick Evans teamed up against Warren Wood and Jock Hutchinson on the fourth of July, 1918. In an expression of patriotic fervor, more than $10,000 was raised on that day alone. The Broadmoor Invitational Golf Tournament was held for the first time in 1921, and has been an honored annual event ever since.

Speck demanded a great deal from his professionals, but in return had great faith in their abilities. He was fiercely competitive especially when the competitor was another institution similar to his own. He was not above betting on the performance of his staff and frequently pitted his professionals against those of other clubs. On one occasion in 1921 he bet H.M. Blackmer, a Denver businessman (and Carlton's old partner from Cripple Creek), that Broadmoor pro Jim Gullane could beat the Denver Country Club's representative, Ralph Smith, a second time after Mr. Blackmer's affirmation that Gullane's first win had been a fluke. Each of the men put up five hundred dollars which was the highest purse ever contested in the West at the time. The winner is not recorded in the annals of Broadmoor history, which we might take to mean that Gullane lost, or could be the reason that the Blackmer Trail around Cheyenne Mountain was laid out shortly thereafter.

The golf clubhouse, previously the second Broadmoor Casino, also served several other functions. In the evening, the upstairs rooms became a nightclub where bands and singers performed livelier music than that enjoyed by guests in the hotel dining rooms. During the twenties, prior to the construction of the Riding Academy, Penrose utilized the upper floor of the club for Monday night boxing bouts. These events were attended by men and women from high society, both locals and guests, and were considered social "events." The *Denver Post* wrote: "These weekly bouts at the Broadmoor Golf Club are patronized by the elite of Boston, New York, Chicago, Detroit, Cleveland and many other cities . . ." The boxers could not be paid officially to fight, so they obtained their monetary reward as the spectators threw money into the ring in proportion to how much they enjoyed the fight. On one of the semi-final nights more than 350 spectators jammed the club. The club was expanded with a new wing in 1929 to better accommodate the large crowds that attended Broadmoor functions.

Penrose's love of boxing included sending invitations to boxing greats for appearances at the hotel. Jack Dempsey came to the Broadmoor in 1926, supposedly to train for an upcoming bout with Gene Tunney. He was subject to such a rigorous schedule of publicity events for the hotel, however, that he ended up leaving in order to be able to get into shape. He frequently returned as a guest at the hotel with his lovely wife, Estelle Taylor, a Hollywood actress. During these visits he occasionally consented to referee the boxing events at the hotel and provided the press with numerous photo opportunities.

When the Riding Academy was completed in 1930, events such as boxing bouts moved to that location. This freed the second floor of the golf club for social functions. In 1935 the nightclub area was transformed into the "Jungle Room." The room

BELOW: First match played on the Broadmoor golf links, July 4, 1918. The Red Cross benefit pitted Jim Barnes and Chick Evans against Jock Hutchinson and Warren Wood.

was decorated with African artifacts that the Penroses had brought home from one of their trips and exotic murals were painted on the walls. Bob Mc-Grew and his orchestra began playing in the club in that year and became a fixture in the years to come. The roof of the new wing provided an area for outdoor dancing and dining and proved extremely popular among the hotel's guests.

ABOVE: Crowd watching tournament play, from an early Broadmoor promotional brochure. Circa 1924.

El Pomar Foundation

Animals Wild and Domestic

BOTH SPENCER AND JULIE Penrose loved animals and made them an important part of their lives. They always had a house full of dogs, and a variety of wilder animals in the gardens of El Pomar. As a boy, Spencer enjoyed the Philadelphia Zoo and had many fond memories of trips there. His interest in animals became more scientific when he built Turkey Creek Ranch in 1912. The ranch included technologically equipped stables for Penrose's prize Holstein herd and his flock of rare sheep, both of which he was attempting to improve using scientific methods of breeding. To these animals he added Prince Albert, an elk, and a few other unusual animals that had come his way. After the hotel was built in 1918 he transferred the more interesting animals to the hotel grounds for the amusement of the guests, but the smell and noise were offensive to many, and close encounters with the animals were not always pleasant. In the early twenties the Broadmoor Hotel was ordered to pay $10,000 in damages to a boy, a guest at the Broadmoor Hotel, who was bitten by one of Penrose's monkeys. The jury found in favor of Mrs. McConnell from New York and Penrose decided that he had to come up with an alternate location.

He obtained the plans for the St. Louis Zoo, which he admired and in 1926 he began constructing buildings to hold the collection up on the slopes of Cheyenne Mountain where they wouldn't bother anyone yet still be accessible to the hotel guests. The Cheyenne Mountain Zoo was officially organized by Spencer Penrose in 1926, the most notable guest was Tessie the Elephant, who according to Penrose was a gift from the Rajah of Najpur in India, but was in fact obtained from a circus that could no longer keep her. The collection continued to grow because Penrose's friends gave him

gifts of animals that they thought suited his character. In October of 1927 Spencer Penrose was given a Bactrian camel by his friend Ed Ballard of the Sells-Floto Circus. The camel's name was "Ethel Volstead" and was intended as a joke, for Penrose was notoriously anti-Prohibition and Volstead was responsible for the legislation enforcing the ban on the sale of alcoholic beverages.

Many of the other animals that ended up in the zoo were initially kept as pets on the grounds of El Pomar. When wild animals were found by locals or the local authorities they were given to the Penroses. These included a mountain lion cub and black bear cub who had to be caged as they grew up and assumed their wild nature. By 1928 the collection included: 2 polar bears, 3 black bears, 1 boa constrictor, 1 elephant (Tessie), 1 camel (Ethel Volstead), monkeys, buffalo, elk, deer, Mexican goats, bobcats, mountain lions, seals, badgers, coyotes, pheasants, and eagles among others. The zoo was also possessed of a live gila monster (a rare find at the time) which lived in the Cheyenne Lodge on top of Cheyenne Mountain where it could be kept warm during the winter. An elephant house was constructed in 1928 for more elephants. The buffalo roamed forty acres on the slopes of Cheyenne Mountain. As the zoo grew in size and importance, Penrose handed over its direction to Robert Menary. Menary, who had come from Hawaii for his health, managed the zoo from 1939 to 1963 and made it into one of the finest privately owned small zoos in the world. Penrose's last gift to the zoo was a miniature railway (modeled after the Manitou and Pikes Peak Cog Railway) which departed from the

west side of the lake and transported hotel guests up the mountain to the zoo. The train, called the "Zoo Special" was completed just before Penrose's death in 1939.

Although Spencer Penrose left us few glimpses of the very private person hidden inside the public self, one of the only stories that has survived demonstrates the emotional importance that zoos had for him. Spencer and Julie Penrose went to Philadelphia so that Speck's throat condition could be diagnosed by Chevalier Jackson, one of the top specialists in the country. The appointment had been set up by Dr. Gerald Webb (a renowned Colorado Springs specialist in lung disease who was also on the Broadmoor Hotel's board of directors and had been associated with Penrose for many years). When Dr. Webb and Speck returned from Chevalier's office to the hotel room where Julie and Marka (Dr. Webb's daughter) waited, Webb stated flatly, "it's cancer."

ABOVE: Spencer Penrose with Ethel Volstead (the camel!) and monkey. 1927.

BELOW: Spencer Penrose and employees of the Manitou and Pikes Peak Cog Railway pose for a publicity shot in the new Zoo Special, built in Manitou Springs. It ferried guests from the lakeside station at the Broadmoor to the Zoo until it was replaced by a sleek Cadillac engine in 1950. 1939.

Broadmoor Art Academy artist Larry Heller painted this imaginative scene of nymphs in the Broadmoor Fountain in 1955.

Courtesy Dorothy Heller

Julie collapsed into Marka's arms. After she had been revived, Speck announced that they were all going to spend the rest of the afternoon at the Philadelphia Zoo, which terminated any further discussion of his condition.

The Broadmoor Art Academy

WHILE SPECK WAS entertaining himself entertaining the world, Julie had time to return to one of her overriding interests: the promotion of art and culture in Colorado Springs. The city, due to the educated and wealthy nature of its first inhabitants, had long fostered art and artists, but this feeling had no organization or center. When the War Department refused the Penroses' offer of their Dale Street home for a war hospital, Julie decided that the building was perfect for an art academy which could include facilities for music, dance and theater. The house and the accompanying garage were quite spacious with a splendid view of Monument Valley Park and were easily transformed into easel painting classrooms, studios and practice rooms. Spencer agreed to donate the $250,000 building on the condition that the academy be called the Broadmoor Art Academy, and so it was. The Penroses also provided a one thousand dollar yearly stipend for the first five years until the Academy was able to mobilize community support.

The Broadmoor Art Academy became Julie Penrose's "baby" much as the hotel had become Spencer's, and she devoted lavish amounts of her time and support to ensure its success. One of the few citations from Julie Penrose that has endured, is a statement about the academy reported in the *New York Telegraph*, in February of 1922: "The phase of the school in which I am especially interested is the industrial one. So few people realize that American industrial arts are in danger of degenerating until they disappear altogether. What we need in our homes today is more beauty in such simple things as wallpaper and fabric designs. Through them a hundred percent more beauty could be brought into our everyday lives." The Broadmoor Hotel remains a testament to how able she was to bring beauty into every aspect of a building.

In the years following its establishment, the Academy became extremely successful and gained a nationwide reputation as an art school and as the center for a new group of American artists. The images of the American frontier which the Pikes Peak region provided allowed these artists to break away from European schools of painting and lay the foundation for a "distinctly American school."[3] The Broadmoor Art Academy staff included such artists as John Carlson, Robert Reid, Randall Davey and Boardman Robinson. Students and associated artists included Larry Heller, Doris Lee, Peppino Mangravite, Eduardo Chavez and Edgar Britton. Mrs. Penrose purchased many works of art from artists at the Academy and during her lifetime they were often displayed on the walls of the Broadmoor Hotel's Little Theater and in the lobby.

AT RIGHT: Life drawing class in one of the greenhouse studios at the Broadmoor Art Academy.

Laura Gilpin photo
Starsmore Center for Local History,
Colorado Springs Pioneers Museum

By 1935 the Academy's success was such that it had outgrown the confines of the Dale Street house and had acquired additional wealthy patrons. Elizabeth Sage Hare, a New York cognoscenti of modern trends in art and architecture became friends with Julie Penrose and Alice Bemis Taylor, a Colorado Springs collector of Native American art and artifacts. The three women collaborated, with Alice Beamis Taylor providing most of the funding, and the idea for the Colorado Springs Fine Arts Center was born.

3. Stanley L. Cuba with Elizabeth Cunningham, *Pikes Peak Vision: The Broadmoor Art Academy, 1919–1945.* The Colorado Springs Fine Arts Center. 1989.

The modern building, designed by New Mexico architect John Gaw Meem, replaced the original Academy building and greatly expanded the possibilities for its growth. Although Julie did not contribute in any significant financial way to the new organization, she provided her enthusiasm and experience. Later, through El Pomar Foundation, she donated many works of art to the collection.

The influence of such a concentrated group of artists on Colorado Springs society was considerable. The Roaring Twenties and the more depressing thirties were rendered even more memorable by the presence of some of the artists' extroverted personalities. An annual costume ball was held at the Broadmoor Hotel to raise money for the Academy which attracted the elite of society in the most outrageous of costumes. Spencer and Julie Penrose both loved living life to the fullest and the combination of the Broadmoor's resources with the artists' imaginations ensured that there was never a dull moment.

ABOVE: Detail from beams in lobby, 1993.

David Beightol photo

EVENTS AT THE ACADEMY did not keep Julie from the Broadmoor Hotel. The hotel provided her with the perfect opportunity for living out two of her own personal passions: classical music and high fashion. World-class musicians were often invited to visit the lovely resort and provided the Broadmoor's guests and Colorado Springs residents with concerts that couldn't be matched outside of New York City. By 1935, the Hotel had hosted Vladimir Horowitz, Serge Rachmaninoff, Ignace Paderewski, and many noted opera singers. Julie was also a supporter of the Colorado Springs Symphony and did much to raise the level of musical performances in the city.

Julie also managed to provide the hotel guests and local citizens with her beloved haute couture. In the early twenties, Julie and her friends Ethel Carlton and Mrs. Doughtery, opened the Broadmoor Sports Shop on the basement level of Southmoor. The three women took trips to Paris and purchased the latest fashions, which were then offered for sale at the shop. Mrs. Carlton enjoyed the business and worked in the shop a great deal. Although Julie's interest was not quite as sustained, the shop was successful and a high fashion clothing shop has continued to occupy the same location. The Broadmoor Hotel's shop is now named "Posh" and offers the best in European and American designs.

While Julie was happily pursuing her interests, Speck was having some difficulty with his. Managing to keep social life lively without the benefit of alcoholic substances was one of the few things that soured Penrose's mood during this period of growth and well-being. Penrose was outraged when, in late 1918, politicians began seriously discussing the possibility of making his favorite sport, the enjoyment of fine liquors and wines, illegal.

HELP REPEAL THE
18th AMENDMENT

The timing was terrible. He had just opened a glamorous resort hotel that provided the absolute best of the world's cellars to the weary traveler in the heart of the United States, and the government was trying to make him serve water and lemonade. Despite Penrose's extremely loud protests on Capitol Hill, the Volstead act was enacted in 1919, and Prohibition began.

Spencer Penrose did everything he could to fight Prohibition. This included becoming President of the Colorado Chapter of the Association Against the Prohibition Amendment and attending protests in person, usually in a small carriage pulled by a llama to attract the most possible attention. He also hosted noted speakers and campaigners who opposed the law, such as Dudley Field Malone, at the Broadmoor Hotel. He was enraged by the hypocrisy of politicians who espoused Prohibition in public and then went home to a good bottle of bourbon. Given that he knew personally many of the nation's top politicians he was quite familiar with their habits. He was so angered by the behavior of his own beloved Republican Party that in 1928 he announced that he would vote for Al Smith, the Democratic candidate for President, rather than for Herbert Hoover because Hoover supported the Volstead Act.

Penrose's own personal war against Prohibition involved the taking of some precautionary measures. Before the law went into effect, Penrose bought as much top quality liquor and wine as he could find. He purchased entire cellars in New York and Philadelphia. Some of this cache remained in the East, and the rest was shipped to Colorado Springs in freight cars. The bottles were stored in the basement of his home, El Pomar, and the Broadmoor Hotel. What was stored in his home, he tapped as often as necessary during the fourteen dry years that followed. The collection in the hotel's basement was opened in 1933 and did a great deal for popularizing the hotel in the years after Prohibition had been repealed. To minimize his economic losses, Penrose purchased the Manitou Mineral Water Company so that he could sell sparkling water and ginger champagne to his guests instead of the real thing.

Despite Prohibition, business at the Broadmoor Hotel increased continuously throughout the twenties, necessitating the enlargement and adaptation of many areas of the hotel. This is not to say that the hotel was financially profitable, for it was not. Penrose's lavishness and desire to provide the very best for his clients caused him to spend more on his clientele than he charged

In 1921 the lake was still used for skating in the winter, the Sun Lounge was still a glass-enclosed veranda and the Lanai Suites had not yet been added to the upper stories.

Special Collections, Colorado College Library

them in return. In the hotel's first decade a room with a private bath and twin beds could be had during high season for $14 per day. This sum included three meals a day with live music at lunch and dinner and access to many of the hotel's facilities at no extra charge.

Penrose's personal fortune, however, allowed him not only to maintain the hotel, but also to embellish it. The mezzanine floor of the hotel was originally much smaller than it is today. The area that is now the Sun Lounge, which overlooks the lake, was actually outside, but covered with a glass ceiling and awnings. The dining area was limited to the one large room just north of the lounges. In 1922 the dining room was extended out onto the terrace so that the guests, most of whom were on the American Plan (which included meals as opposed to the European Plan which did not) could all be accommodated. The Colonial Club, a building which was already on the property when the Broadmoor Hotel was built,[4] was modified and adapted to provide less costly accommodations for additional guests.

The Broadmoor Florist and Greenhouse was expanded, first in 1924 and then again in 1926 when two new greenhouses tripled flower production. The greenhouse did operate at a profit, primarily because its market included more than just the hotel. Penrose liked

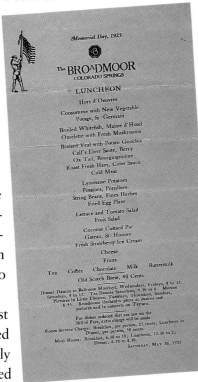

ABOVE: All meals were included on the American Plan and guests could partake of any and all of the items on the menu at each meal. 1925.

Broadmoor Historical Collection

---

4. This building was, in fact, the first Broadmoor Hotel. It had been built by the London and New York Investment Co. to attempt to attract business to the Broadmoor Casino after Pourtales had deserted the project. When the Casino burned, so did any chances of the hotel's success. The building was rented to various tenants with the second Casino until it was purchased by Penrose.

ABOVE: 1945 aerial view of the Broadmoor. The Colonial Club is at the bottom left and the stadium across the lake.

George Pearson photo, Broadmoor Historical Collection

to be surrounded by well-tended gardens and interested himself personally in the floral decoration of the hotel grounds. The gardens of the Penrose home, El Pomar, were extensive and maintained in the Italian tradition of sculpted greenery and flower beds carefully planned for their artistic effect.

While new developments were progressing within the hotel, Speck was looking around for ways to further develop the surrounding area. Given the success of the toll road up Pikes Peak, he decided to build a toll road to the top of Cheyenne Mountain so that visitors could gaze down on the Broadmoor Hotel from three thousand feet above it. The road was constructed in 1925, and rather than being another publicity success, aroused the anger of the entire community. Whereas the road up Pikes Peak brought fame and fortune to the city, citizens believed that the Cheyenne Mountain Road defaced the front of the mountain with its uneven switchbacks and served no real purpose. Despite, or perhaps to calm, these protests, Penrose built a beautiful, Pueblo-style lodge at the top of the mountain which provided simple meals and accommodations for those who climbed the winding road to the summit. The lodge became popular with honeymooners and tourists, while the large central room, decorated with Native American artifacts and hunting trophies, was often used for parties.

To publicize the lodge and road Penrose held another of his notorious sporting events. He decided to organize a marathon from the toll gate just after the Cooking Club to the Cheyenne Mountain Lodge. The course was shortened slightly to make it an even five miles. This race, dubbed the "International Mountain Marathon," was itself publicized by having Tessie the elephant parade through the streets of downtown Colorado Springs bearing six Indians of the Hopi, Zuni and Acoma tribes who were to be contestants in the race. The race was much publicized and succeeded in attracting the best male runners from the state of Colorado. The race was won by Pho-quaptewa, a member of the Hopi tribe who completed the course from just after the toll gate to the top of the mountain in thirty-five minutes and forty-nine seconds. The first Caucasian to finish the race was Jack Philpson who finished in forty-six minutes and fifty seconds.

In 1928 more land around the base of Cheyenne Mountain was purchased and platted into residential districts. Count Pourtales, Polo Park and the Dixon Heights areas were planned at this time and several reser-

voirs were also constructed to ensure adequate water for both the hotel and the new residents. Pourtales' vision of soaring real estate values had finally come true. The construction and success of the Broadmoor Hotel attracted many well-to-do residents, both locally and from out of state, who decided to build homes near the hotel and its elegant aura.

Depression and Renaissance

THE STOCK MARKET crash in October of 1929 signaled the end of an era, especially for the class of people that had so happily flocked to the gilded mountain resort in Colorado. Polo ponies, luxury automobiles providing motor tours to the pleasure spots of the country, and lengthy golfing vacations lost their place in reality and became unattainable dreams for those who had lived so well during the post-war period in America. The Penroses, not having speculated wildly in the market, and with secure investments in real estate and minerals, were not personally in crisis. The Broadmoor Hotel, however, immediately felt the impact of the economic crisis that was to rock the country during the thirties.

As the 1930–31 season progressed, it was clear that things would have to change radically at the hotel. The days of superabundance were over,

ABOVE: Perched atop Cheyenne Mountain the honeymoon lodge commanded spectacular views, but maintenance and supplies proved difficult and costly to provide and the lodge was torn down soon after Julie's death in 1956.

Broadmoor Historical Collection

BELOW: The main room of the Cheyenne Lodge, decorated with Native American artifacts and hunting trophies, was often used for parties and receptions. Circa 1940.

Courtesy Hermine Weber

and services and staff were drastically reduced. The employees who were in direct contact with the clients began working for tips only, and were called to work only when needed. During this period in American history, many of the country's great hotels ceased to be owned by single individuals or families. Many either failed entirely or became part of corporate conglomerates. Penrose, due to the size of his personal fortune, was able to keep the hotel, and given the times, felt that he should have complete control of it.

At the time, the hotel had numerous shareholders because when Penrose had initially raised money for the hotel he had involved as many investors and friends as possible. Penrose's personal investment in the property had far exceeded that of any other investor before the hotel was even half built. He had, however, never called in the company's debt and the amount continued to grow each year as Penrose personally supplied funds to cover the operating deficit.[5] In 1932 the company that represented Penrose's personal interests, El Pomar Investment Company, filed suit against the Broadmoor Hotel Inc. The hotel went into receivership; Penrose bought it back and became sole owner. At the sale he expressed the fervent wish that the "new" hotel would prove more profitable than the "old."

During the early thirties the hotel continued to function, albeit on a much smaller scale and with a primarily local clientele. Only the main building and the Colonial Club were available for occupancy and the rooms were by no means filled. This era, though not a profitable one economically, cemented the hotel firmly in the hearts of Colorado Springs residents. Many local social events were held in the elegant surroundings of the mezzanine and the cafe was a popular location for family outings. The bathing beaches on the lake were open to the public during the summers and many came to watch and participate in the swimming marathons and Acquapades which marked the opening of the bathing season. Penrose did his part to bolster public spirit during the hard times. The 1932 New Year's Eve Dinner Dance, which was attended by six hundred and fifty people, provided the menu shown here for $3.00 per person.

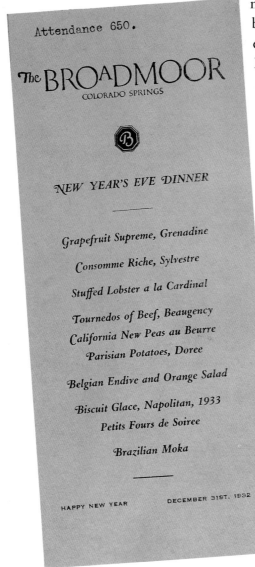

Attendance 650.

The BROADMOOR
COLORADO SPRINGS

Ⓑ

NEW YEAR'S EVE DINNER

———

Grapefruit Supreme, Grenadine

Consomme Riche, Sylvestre

Stuffed Lobster a la Cardinal

Tournedos of Beef, Beaugency
California New Peas au Beurre
Parisian Potatoes, Doree

Belgian Endive and Orange Salad

Biscuit Glace, Napolitan, 1933
Petits Fours de Soiree

Brazilian Moka

———

HAPPY NEW YEAR   DECEMBER 31ST, 1932

ABOVE: Dining at the Broadmoor Hotel, even during the Depression, was a sublime experience. This menu was served to guests at the 1932 New Year's Eve Dinner Dance.

El Pomar Foundation

———

5. Penrose contributed between $75,000 and $150,000 annually to the hotel to make up the deficit between operating costs and profits since the hotel opened in 1918.

Although things did not improve on the national scene, 1933 was a landmark year for Spencer Penrose because it signaled the end of the "Noble Experiment" as Prohibition was called by its supporters. He had his liquor from New York and Philadelphia sent out to Colorado Springs and celebrated with a "Victory Dinner and Dance" on December 5, 1933. The Broadmoor's liquor cache was opened amid much rejoicing and it was immediately made accessible to the public. The Broadmoor Drug Store had two lists from which customers could choose: "Popular Priced Wines and Liquors" or "Pre-War Liquors, Wines and Cordials." The prices of the latter were such that their supply was ensured for quite some time.

Broadmoor Pottery mustard pot produced for the hotel.

Courtesy Jim and Carol Carlton
John Gair photo

THE HOTEL REACHED its nadir in fall of 1935 when business was so bad that Penrose decided to close the hotel for the winter; only the Broadmoor Laundry, Greenhouses, Drug Store and Golf Club remained open. This was a very serious step because the core of the staff upon which the hotel depended had to find alternative employment. Executive chef, Louis Stratta and Maître d'hôtel, John Altrichter who had become legends in the hotel's standard of service, left the city until the following summer when the hotel re-opened on the first of June 1936. The hotel never closed again.

While things were quiet at the Broadmoor, Spencer became involved in one of the few purely altruistic endeavors of his life. As a multi-millionaire, he was often asked to donate money or participate in charitable organizations or activities for the betterment of humankind, but he was not a willing participant. He felt that stimulating the economy and providing employment were much better avenues for his time and money than simply supplying funding. These endeavors were not always successful, as was the case with the Broadmoor Pottery Company. When Penrose was approached by Paul Genter, who wanted to start a pottery company to compete against the successful Van Briggle Pottery, Speck agreed to fund it. Broadmoor Pottery never did very well, but it did bear the Broadmoor name and fostered private enterprise, two causes always foremost in his mind. One of the few exceptions that he made to his rule of not funding nonprofit organizations was his contribution to the Fountain Valley School for Boys on the plains to the south of Colorado Springs.

Cup from the 1940s Broadmoor service with the "City of Sunshine" logo, which also appears on the silver.

John Gair photo

The school's founder, Elizabeth Sage Hare (the same woman who worked with Julie Penrose on the Fine Arts Center), had come to Colorado Springs so that her husband Meredith could be put under the care of Dr. Gerald Webb. The Penroses had no children of their own, but Betty Hare managed to convince Speck that hers was a worthwhile cause. At the school's incorporation on December 30, 1929, he donated $7,500 towards the purchase of land and buildings. During the following ten years,

Julie & Speck
Honolulu

Speck and Julie sent their friends this photograph as their Christmas card for 1938. When they returned to the Broadmoor they brought Hawaii back with them.

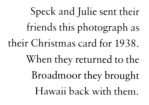

Courtesy Hermine Weber

BELOW: Dress rehearsal for the 1932 show, "Trial By Jury" in the Broadmoor Theater. The Fountain Valley School drama department put on numerous productions which were well attended by the general public due to the level of community involvement and advertisements like the one on the facing page.

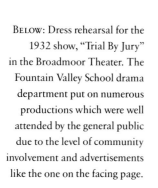

Fountain Valley School

Penrose donated a great deal of money for the school's operating expenses and built a large dormitory in memory of his brother, Senator Boise Penrose, designed by the architect of the Colorado Springs Fine Arts Center, John Gaw Meem.

Penrose also made the Broadmoor and its facilities available to both the students and faculty of the school. Students used the sports facilities at various times and also gave theatrical performances in the hotel's Little Theater. Penrose was on the school's board of directors from the day of its incorporation until his death in 1939. Julie Penrose took his place and maintained similar levels of involvement in the school's activities until her death in 1956. The Penroses' involvement in the school was especially critical in the early years when the Depression made it very difficult to find funding and an adequate number of students for the school.

As the Depression began to wane, Penrose was ready to rejuvenate the hotel and prepare it for the better times that he sensed were coming. He knew that the time left for himself was, at best, limited. In 1931 he had been diagnosed as having an early form of cancer in his throat. It was not serious and he continued to live the life that he always had, but perhaps a sense of his own mortality caused him to make changes in the hotel that would carry it forward after he was gone. Internal renovations needed to be made so that the hotel would be ready for the post-Depression boom that was sure to come.

In the meantime, the Penroses continued to travel a great deal. They went to Palestine, Egypt, the

Orient, New Zealand, and many times to Europe to visit Gladys and Pauline. Hawaii had become one of their favorite destinations. The Penroses rented a home there for several years and then made plans to build one of their own. Hawaii was to have quite an influence on the Broadmoor Hotel's entertainment and decor. Speck and Julie engaged Hawaiian singers and musicians for the nightclub and placed Hawaiian-style wicker furniture on the covered mezzanine. When business began to improve, the area between the two wings on the back of the building was filled in with suites that boasted dramatic views of the mountains and Hawaiian decor. These suites were named the Lanai Suites, lanai being a Hawaiian word for a covered verandah. The Golf Club was not spared the Pacific influence either. The "Jungle" nightclub became the "Hawaiian Village" in 1939 complete with thatch wall coverings and hanging lanterns. The season opened with bandleader Harry Owens and his Royal Hawaiians and the show featured several scantily clad young dancers.

To fully commemorate the demise of Prohibition, Penrose felt that there should be a comfortable and attractive place where liquor could be served on the first floor of the hotel as well. He began making plans for a large bar and grille room where serious drinkers like himself would feel at home and welcome. In the hotel's original plans the area to the right of the main lobby had been occupied by a broker's ticker tape room. Just after this room was a small café known as the "Rendezvous" and later as the "Indian Grille." This room was so named because a series of Charles Craig murals depicting the history of Native Americans adorned the walls.[6]

Penrose wanted a larger room, a cross between a gentleman's club and a hunting lodge, where guests could sample his newly opened liquor supply while dining on more traditionally American fare than the European Cuisine served in the dining rooms. Grilled meats, especially wild game carried back from hunts in the mountains, were a specialty. The new restaurant, called the "Tavern," was one of the few areas inside the hotel to have a distinctively western flair. The decor included furniture and paneling of local knotty pine and antique copper utensils displayed around the walls. The chandeliers were fashioned of large copper trays which contained bottles that had been transformed into lamps. Julie contributed a small Toulouse-Lautrec print entitled "Jane Avril," which hangs near the bar. The Tavern's decor now includes bottles from Penrose's collection of

ABOVE: Advertisement for "Trial by Jury," 1932.

Fountain Valley School

---

6. These are displayed on the walls of the Carriage Museum.

empties, which he had shared with many of America's most noted citizens. When the Tavern opened, however, the walls were lined with full bottles of the excellent quality beverages that he had obtained before the war. There they could be admired by those who had long missed them prior to being reverently consumed.

The Penroses had ambitious plans for the other side of the lake as well. During a trip to Europe in 1937, they had seen Sonja Henje ice skating in St. Moritz. They were delighted with both the athlete and the sport, and Spencer felt that both would soon become popular in the United States. The covered riding arena, constructed in 1929, had not been an overwhelming success because the fine weather in the Pikes Peak Region made it possible and preferable to hold most events outside. Penrose decided to transform the Broadmoor Riding Arena into an Ice Palace and then construct an ample outdoor stadium beside it.

The conversion was easily accomplished; refrigeration units were put into place to form a central oval on the arena floor and grandstand style seating was constructed all around it. The "Broadmoor Ice Palace" opened on

TOP: Decor in the Lanai Suites was quite a contrast to Julie's usually understated taste, but the rooms were extremely popular with guests and added an exotic flair to the hotel. Circa 1940. Broadmoor Historical Collection

MIDDLE: The lattice-ceilinged mezzanine lounge with Hawaiian furniture. The ballroom is visible through the French doors in the background. Circa 1940.
Broadmoor Historical Collection

BOTTOM: The Tavern Restaurant was another distinctly American note in the hotel's European-style decor. Its charm and less formal atmosphere made it an instant success. Julie dined often in the Tavern with her closest friends and it was considered quite an honor to be asked to join her at her corner booth, just outside of the frame of the photograph on the bottom left. Circa 1960.
Broadmoor Historical Collection

THE
RAVEN
PRINCE

E L I Z A B E T H   H O Y T

WARNER
FOREVER

NEW YORK   BOSTON

Warner Forever and the Warner Forever logo are trademarks of Time Warner Inc. or an affiliated company. Used under license by Hachette Book Group, which is not affiliated with Time Warner Inc.

Cover design by Diane Luger
Cover illustration by Franco Accornero
Book design by Stratford Publishing Services

Warner Books
Hachette Book Group USA
1271 Avenue of the Americas
New York, NY 10020
ISBN 978-0-7394-7625-3

Printed in the United States of America

*For my husband, FRED, my own wild blueberry pie—
sweet, tart, and always comforting.*

Acknowledgments

Thank you to my agent,
SUSANNAH TAYLOR, for her good humor
and staunch support; to my editor,
DEVI PILLAI, for her wonderful enthusiasm
and excellent taste; and to my critique partner,
JADE LEE, who plied me with chocolates at
crucial moments and persistently repeated,
"Believe!"

Chapter One

Once upon a time, in a land far away, there lived an
impoverished duke and his three daughters. . . .
—from *The Raven Prince*

LITTLE BATTLEFORD, ENGLAND
MARCH, 1760

The combination of a horse galloping far too fast, a
muddy lane with a curve, and a lady pedestrian is never a
good one. Even in the best of circumstances, the odds of
a positive outcome are depressingly low. But add a dog—
a very big dog—and, Anna Wren reflected, disaster be-
comes inescapable.

The horse in question made a sudden sideways jump at
the sight of Anna in its path. The mastiff, jogging beside
the horse, responded by running under its nose, which, in
turn, made the horse rear. Saucer-sized hooves flailed the
air. And inevitably, the enormous rider on the horse's
back came unseated. The man went down at her feet like a
hawk shot from the sky, if less gracefully. His long limbs
sprawled as he fell, he lost his crop and tricorn, and he

landed with a spectacular splash in a mud puddle. A wall of filthy water sprang up to drench her.

Everyone, including the dog, paused.

Idiot, Anna thought, but that was not what she said. Respectable widows of a certain age—one and thirty in two months—do not hurl epithets, however apt, at gentlemen. No, indeed.

"I do hope you are not damaged by your fall," she said instead. "May I assist you to rise?" She smiled through gritted teeth at the sodden man.

He did not return her pleasantry. "What the hell were you doing in the middle of the road, you silly woman?"

The man heaved himself out of the mud puddle to loom over her in that irritating way gentlemen had of trying to look important when they'd just been foolish. The dirty water beading on his pale, pockmarked face made him an awful sight. Black eyelashes clumped together lushly around obsidian eyes, but that hardly offset the large nose and chin and the thin, bloodless lips.

"I am so sorry." Anna's smile did not falter. "I was walking home. Naturally, had I known you would be needing the entire width of the throughway—"

But apparently his question had been rhetorical. The man stomped away, dismissing her and her explanation. He ignored his hat and crop to stalk the horse, cursing it in a low, oddly soothing monotone.

The dog sat down to watch the show.

The horse, a bony bay, had peculiar light patches on its coat that gave it an unfortunate piebald appearance. It rolled its eyes at the man and sidled a few steps away.

"That's right. Dance around like a virgin at the first squeeze of a tit, you revolting lump of maggot-eaten hide," the man crooned to the animal. "When I get hold of you, you misbegotten result of a diseased camel humping a sway-backed ass, I'll wring your cretinous neck, I will."

The horse swiveled its mismatched ears to better hear the caressing baritone voice and took an uncertain step forward. Anna sympathized with the animal. The ugly man's voice was like a feather run along the sole of her foot: irritating and tantalizing at the same time. She wondered if he sounded like that when he made love to a woman. One would hope he changed the words.

The man got close enough to the bemused horse to catch its bridle. He stood for a minute, murmuring obscenities; then he mounted the animal in one lithe movement. His muscular thighs, indecently revealed in wet buckskins, tightened about the horse's barrel as he turned its nose.

He inclined his bare head at Anna. "Madam, good day." And without a backward glance, he cantered off down the lane, the dog racing beside him. In a moment, he was out of sight. In another, the sound of hoofbeats had died.

Anna looked down.

Her basket lay in the puddle, its contents—her morning shopping—spilled in the road. She must've dropped it when she dodged the oncoming horse. Now, a half-dozen eggs oozed yellow yolks into the muddy water, and a single herring eyed her balefully as if blaming her for its undignified landing. She picked up the fish and brushed it off. It, at least, could be saved. Her gray dress, however, drooped pitifully, although the actual color wasn't much different from the mud that caked it. She plucked at the skirts to separate them from her legs before sighing and dropping them. She scanned the road in both directions. The bare branches of the trees overhead rattled in the wind. The little lane stood deserted.

Anna took a breath and said the forbidden word out loud in front of God and her eternal soul: "Bastard!" She held her breath, waiting for a thunderbolt or, more likely, a twinge of guilt to hit her. Neither happened, which ought to have made her uneasy. After all, ladies do not curse gentlemen, no matter what the provocation.

And she was, above all things, a respectable lady, wasn't she?

By the time she limped up the front walk to her cottage, Anna's skirts were dried into a stiff mess. In summer, the exuberant flowers that filled the tiny front garden made it cheerful, but at this time of year, the garden was mostly mud. Before she could reach it, the door opened. A small woman with dove-gray ringlets bobbing at her temples peered around the jamb.

"Oh, there you are." The woman waved a gravy-smeared wooden spoon, inadvertently flinging drops on her cheek. "Fanny and I have been making mutton stew, and I do think her sauce is improved. Why, you can hardly see the lumps." She leaned forward to whisper, "But we are still working on dumpling making. I'm afraid they have a rather unusual texture."

Anna smiled wearily at her mother-in-law. "I'm sure the stew will be wonderful." She stepped inside the cramped hall and put the basket down.

The other woman beamed, but then her nose wrinkled as Anna moved past her. "Dear, there's a peculiar odor coming from . . ." She trailed off and stared at the top of Anna's head. "Why are you wearing wet leaves in your hat?"

Anna grimaced and reached up to feel. "I'm afraid I had a slight mishap on the high road."

"A mishap?" Mother Wren dropped the spoon in her agitation. "Are you hurt? Why, your gown looks as if you've wallowed in a pigsty."

"I'm quite all right; just a bit damp."

"Well, we must get you into dry clothes at once, dear. And your hair—Fanny!" Mother Wren interrupted herself to call in the general direction of the kitchen. "We'll have to wash it. Your hair, I mean. Here, let me help you up the stairs. Fanny!"

A girl, all elbows, reddened hands, and topped by a mass of carroty hair, sidled into the hall. "Wot?"

Mother Wren paused on the stairs behind Anna and leaned over the rail. "How many times have I told you to say, 'Yes, ma'am'? You'll never become a maid in a big house if you don't speak properly."

Fanny stood blinking up at the two women. Her mouth was slightly ajar.

Mother Wren sighed. "Go put a pot of water on to heat. Miss Anna will be washing her hair."

The girl scurried into the kitchen, then popped her head back out. "Yes, mum."

The top of the steep stairs opened onto a miniscule landing. To the left was the elder woman's room; to the right, Anna's. She entered her small room and went straight to the mirror hanging over the dresser.

"I don't know what the town is coming to," her mother-in-law panted behind her. "Were you splashed by a carriage? Some of these mail-coach drivers are simply irresponsible. They think the entire road is theirs alone."

"I couldn't agree with you more," Anna replied as she peered at her reflection. A faded wreath of dried apple blossoms was draped over the edge of the mirror, a memento from her wedding. "But it was a single horseman in this case." Her hair was a rat's nest, and there were still spots of mud on her forehead.

"Even worse, these gentlemen on horses," the older woman muttered. "Why, I don't think they're able to control their animals, some of them. Terribly dangerous. They're a menace to woman and child."

"Mmm." Anna took off her shawl, bumping her shin against a chair as she moved. She glanced around the tiny room. This was where she and Peter had spent all four years of their marriage. She hung her shawl and hat on the hook where Peter's coat used to be. The chair where he once piled his heavy law books now served as her bedside table. Even his hairbrush with the few red hairs caught in its bristles had long ago been packed away.

"At least you saved the herring." Mother Wren was still fretting. "Although I don't think a dunking in mud will have improved its flavor."

"No doubt," Anna replied absently. Her eyes returned to the wreath. It was crumbling. No wonder, since she had been widowed six years. Nasty thing. It would be better in the garden rubbish pile. She tossed it aside to take down later.

"Here, dear, let me help you." Mother Wren began unhooking the dress from the bottom. "We'll have to sponge this right away. There's quite a bit of mud around the hem. Perhaps if I applied a new trim . . ." Her voice was muffled as she bent over. "Oh, that reminds me, did you sell my lace to the milliner?"

Anna pushed the dress down and stepped out of it. "Yes, she quite liked the lace. She said it was the finest she'd seen in a while."

"Well, I have been making lace for almost forty years." Mother Wren tried to look modest. She cleared her throat. "How much did she give you for it?"

Anna winced. "A shilling sixpence." She reached for a threadbare wrap.

"But I worked five months on it," Mother Wren gasped.

"I know." Anna sighed and took down her hair. "And, as I said, the milliner considered your work to be of the finest quality. It's just that lace doesn't fetch very much."

"It does once she puts it on a bonnet or a dress," Mother Wren muttered.

Anna grimaced sympathetically. She took a bathing cloth off a hook under the eaves, and the two women descended the stairs in silence.

In the kitchen, Fanny hovered over a kettle of water. Bunches of dried herbs hung from the black beams, scenting the air. The old brick fireplace took up one whole wall. Opposite was a curtain-framed window that overlooked the back garden. Lettuce marched in a frilled chartreuse row down the tiny plot, and the radishes and turnips had been ready for a week now.

Mother Wren set a chipped basin on the kitchen table. Worn smooth by many years of daily scrubbing, the table took pride of place in the middle of the room. At night they pushed it to the wall so that the little maid could unroll a pallet in front of the fire.

Fanny brought the kettle of water. Anna bent over the basin, and Mother Wren poured the water on her head. It was lukewarm.

Anna soaped her hair and took a deep breath. "I'm afraid we will have to do something about our financial situation."

"Oh, don't say there will be more economies, dear," Mother Wren moaned. "We've already given up fresh meat except for mutton on Tuesdays and Thursdays. And it's been ages since either of us has had a new gown."

Anna noticed that her mother-in-law didn't mention Fanny's upkeep. Although the girl was supposedly their maid-cum-cook, in reality she was a charitable impulse on both their parts. Fanny's only relative, her grandfather, had died when she was ten. At the time, there'd been talk in the village of sending the girl to a poorhouse, but Anna had moved to intervene, and Fanny had been with them ever since. Mother Wren had hopes of training her to work in a large household, but so far her progress was slow.

"You've been very good about the economies we've made," Anna said now as she worked the thin lather into her scalp. "But the investments Peter left us aren't doing as well as they used to. Our income has decreased steadily since he passed away."

"It's such a shame he left us so little to live on," Mother Wren said.

Anna sighed. "He didn't mean to leave such a small sum. He was a young man when the fever took him. I'm sure had he lived, he would've built up the savings substantially."

In fact, Peter had improved their finances since his own father's death shortly before their marriage. The older man had been a solicitor, but several ill-advised investments had landed him deeply in debt. After the wedding, Peter had sold the house he had grown up in to pay off the debts and moved his new bride and widowed mother into the much-smaller cottage. He had been working as a solicitor when he'd become ill and died within the fortnight.

Leaving Anna to manage the little household on her own. "Rinse, please."

A stream of chilly water poured over her nape and head. She felt to make sure no soap remained, then squeezed the excess water from her hair. She wrapped a cloth around her head and glanced up. "I think I should find a position."

"Oh, dear, surely not that." Mother Wren plopped down on a kitchen chair. "Ladies don't work."

Anna felt her mouth twitch. "Would you prefer I remain a lady and let us both starve?"

Mother Wren hesitated. She appeared to actually debate the question.

"Don't answer that," Anna said. "It won't come to starvation anyway. However, we do need to find a way to bring some income into the household."

"Perhaps if I were to produce more lace. Or, or I could give up meat entirely," her mother-in-law said a little wildly.

"I don't want you to have to do that. Besides, Father made sure I had a good education."

Mother Wren brightened. "Your father was the best vicar Little Battleford ever had, God rest his soul. He *did* let everyone know his views on the education of children."

"Mmm." Anna took the cloth off her head and began combing out her wet hair. "He made sure I learned to read and write and do figures. I even have a little Latin and Greek. I thought I'd look tomorrow for a position as a governess or companion."

"Old Mrs. Lester is almost blind. Surely her son-in-law would hire you to read—" Mother Wren stopped.

Anna became aware at the same time of an acrid scent in the air. "Fanny!"

The little maid, who had been watching the exchange between her employers, yelped and ran to the pot of stew over the fire. Anna groaned.

Another burned supper.

FELIX HOPPLE PAUSED before the Earl of Swartingham's library door to take stock of his appearance. His wig, with two tight sausage curls on either side, was freshly powdered in a becoming lavender shade. His figure—quite svelte for a man of his years—was highlighted by a puce waistcoat edged with vining yellow leaves. And his hose had alternating green and orange stripes, handsome without being ostentatious. His toilet was perfection itself. There was really no reason for him to hesitate outside the door.

He sighed. The earl had a disconcerting tendency to growl. As estate manager of Ravenhill Abbey, Felix had heard that worrisome growl quite a bit in the last two weeks. It'd made him feel like one of those unfortunate native gentlemen one read about in travelogues who lived in the shadows of large, ominous volcanoes. The kind that might erupt at any moment. Why Lord Swartingham had chosen to take up residence at the Abbey after years of blissful absence, Felix couldn't fathom, but he had the sinking feeling that the earl intended to remain for a very, very long time.

The steward ran a hand down the front of his waistcoat. He reminded himself that although the matter he was about to bring to the earl's attention was not pleasant, it could in no way be construed as his own fault. Thus prepared, he nodded and tapped at the library door.

There was a pause and then a deep, sure voice rasped, "Come."

The library stood on the west side of the manor house, and the late-afternoon sun streamed through the large windows that took up nearly the entire outside wall. One might think this would make the library a sunny, welcoming room, but somehow the sunlight was swallowed by the cavernous space soon after it entered, leaving most of the room to the domain of the shadows. The ceiling—two stories high—was wreathed in gloom.

The earl sat behind a massive, baroque desk that would've dwarfed a smaller man. Nearby, a fire attempted to be cheerful and failed dismally. A gigantic, brindled dog sprawled before the hearth as if dead. Felix winced. The dog was a mongrel mix that included a good deal of mastiff and perhaps some wolfhound. The result was an ugly, mean-looking canine he tried hard to avoid.

He cleared his throat. "If I could have a moment, my lord?"

Lord Swartingham glanced up from the paper in his hand. "What is it now, Hopple? Come in, come in, man. Sit down while I finish this. I'll give you my attention in a minute."

Felix crossed to one of the armchairs before the mahogany desk and sank into it, keeping an eye on the dog. He used the reprieve to study his employer for an idea of his mood. The earl scowled at the page in front of him, his pockmarks making the expression especially unattractive. Of course, this was not necessarily a bad sign. The earl habitually scowled.

Lord Swartingham tossed aside the paper. He took off his half-moon reading glasses and threw his considerable weight back in his chair, making it squeak. Felix flinched in sympathy.

"Well, Hopple?"

"My lord, I have some unpleasant news that I hope you will not take too badly." He smiled tentatively.

The earl stared down his big nose without comment.

Felix tugged at his shirt cuffs. "The new secretary, Mr. Tootleham, had word of a family emergency that forced him to hand in his resignation rather quickly."

There was still no change of expression on the earl's face, although he did begin to drum his fingers on the chair arm.

Felix spoke more rapidly. "It seems Mr. Tootleham's parents in London have become bedridden by a fever and require his assistance. It is a very virulent illness with sweating and purging, qu-quite contagious."

The earl raised one black eyebrow.

"I-in fact, Mr. Tootleham's two brothers, three sisters, his elderly grandmother, an aunt, and the family cat have all caught the contagion and are utterly unable to fend for themselves." Felix stopped and looked at the earl.

Silence.

Felix wrestled valiantly to keep from babbling.

"The cat?" Lord Swartingham snarled softly.

Felix started to stutter a reply but was interrupted by a bellowed obscenity. He ducked with newly practiced ease as the earl picked up a pottery jar and flung it over Felix's head at the door. It hit with a tremendous crash and a tinkle of falling shards. The dog, apparently long used to the odd manner in which Lord Swartingham vented his spleen, merely sighed.

Lord Swartingham breathed heavily and pinned Felix with his coal-black eyes. "I trust you have found a replacement."

Felix's neckcloth felt suddenly tight. He ran a finger around the upper edge. "Er, actually, my lord, although, of course, I've searched qu-quite diligently, and indeed, all the nearby villages have been almost scoured, I haven't—" He gulped and courageously met his employer's eye. "I'm afraid I haven't found a new secretary yet."

Lord Swartingham didn't move. "I need a secretary to transcribe my manuscript for the series of lectures given by the Agrarian Society in four weeks," he enunciated awfully. "Preferably one who will stay more than two days. Find one." He snatched up another sheet of paper and went back to reading.

The audience had ended.

"Yes, my lord." Felix bounced nervously out of the chair and scurried toward the door. "I'll start looking right away, my lord."

Lord Swartingham waited until Felix had almost reached the door before rumbling, "Hopple."

On the point of escape, Felix guiltily drew back his hand from the doorknob. "My lord?"

"You have until the morning after tomorrow."

Felix stared at his employer's still-downcast head and swallowed, feeling rather like that Hercules fellow must have on first seeing the Augean stables. "Yes, my lord."

EDWARD DE RAAF, the fifth Earl of Swartingham, finished reading the report from his North Yorkshire estate and tossed it onto the pile of papers, along with his spectacles. The light from the window was fading fast and soon would be gone. He rose from his chair and went to look out. The dog got up, stretched, and padded over to stand beside him, bumping at his hand. Edward absently stroked its ears.

This was the second secretary to decamp in the dark of night in so many months. One would think he was a dragon. Every single secretary had been more mouse than man. Show a little temper, a raised voice, and they scurried away. If even one of his secretaries had half the pluck of the woman he had nearly run down yesterday . . . His lips twitched. He hadn't missed her sarcastic reply to his demand of why she was in the road. No, that madam stood her ground when he blew his fire at her. A pity his secretaries couldn't do the same.

He glowered out the dark window. And then there was this other nagging . . . disturbance. His boyhood home was not as he remembered it.

True, he was a man now. When he had last seen Ravenhill Abbey, he'd been a stripling youth mourning the loss of his family. In the intervening two decades, he had wandered from his northern estates to his London town house, but somehow, despite the time, those two places had never felt like home. He had stayed away precisely because the Abbey would never be the same as when his family had lived here. He'd expected some change. But he'd not been prepared for this dreariness. Nor the awful sense of loneliness. The very emptiness of the rooms defeated him, mocking him with the laughter and light that he remembered.

The family that he remembered.

The only reason he persisted in opening up the mansion was because he hoped to bring his new bride here— his prospective new bride, pending the successful negotiation of the marital contract. He wasn't going to repeat the mistakes of his first, short marriage and attempt to settle elsewhere. Back then, he'd tried to make his young wife happy by remaining in her native Yorkshire. It hadn't worked. In the years since his wife's untimely death, he'd come to the conclusion that she wouldn't have been happy anywhere they'd chosen to make their home.

Edward pushed away from the window and strode toward the library doors. He would start as he meant to; go on and live at the Abbey; make it a home again. It was the seat of his earldom and where he meant to replant his family tree. And when the marriage bore fruit, when the halls once again rang with children's laughter, surely then Ravenhill Abbey would feel alive again.

Chapter Two

*Now, all three of the duke's daughters were equally
fair. The eldest had hair of deepest pitch that shone
with blue-black lights; the second had fiery locks
that framed a milky-white complexion; and the
youngest was golden, both of face and form, so that
she seemed bathed in sunlight. But of these three
maidens, only the youngest was blessed with her
father's kindness. Her name was Aurea. . . .*
—from *The Raven Prince*

Who would have guessed that there was such a paucity of
jobs for genteel ladies in Little Battleford? Anna had
known that it wouldn't be easy to find a position when she
left the cottage this morning, but she'd started with some
hope. All she required was a family with illiterate children
needing a governess or an elderly lady in want of a wool-
winder. Surely this was not too much to expect?

Evidently it was.

It was midafternoon now. Her feet ached from trudging
up and down muddy lanes, and she didn't have a position.
Old Mrs. Lester had no love of literature. Her son-in-law

was too parsimonious to hire a companion in any case. Anna called round on several other ladies, hinting that she might be open to a position, only to find they either could not afford a companion or simply did not want one.

Then she'd come to Felicity Clearwater's home.

Felicity was the third wife of Squire Clearwater, a man some thirty years older than his bride. The squire was the largest landowner in the county besides the Earl of Swartingham. As his wife, Felicity clearly considered herself the preeminent social figure in Little Battleford and rather above the humble Wren household. But Felicity had two girls of a suitable age for a governess, so Anna had called on her. She'd spent an excruciating half hour feeling her way like a cat walking on sharp pebbles. When Felicity had caught on to Anna's reason for visiting, she'd smoothed a pampered hand over her already immaculate coiffure. Then she'd sweetly enquired about Anna's musical knowledge.

The vicarage had never run to a harpsichord when Anna's family had occupied it. A fact Felicity knew very well, since she'd called there on several occasions as a girl.

Anna had taken a deep breath. "I'm afraid I don't have any musical ability, but I do have a bit of Latin and Greek."

Felicity had flicked open a fan and tittered behind it. "Oh, I do apologize," she'd said when she'd recovered. "But my girls will not be learning anything so masculine as Latin or Greek. It's rather unbecoming in a lady, don't you think?"

Anna had grit her teeth, but managed a smile. Until Felicity had suggested she try the kitchen to see if Cook needed a new scullery maid. Things had gone downhill from there.

Anna sighed now. She might very well end up a scullery maid or worse, but not at Felicity's house. Time to head home.

Rounding the corner at the ironmonger's, she just managed to avoid a collision with Mr. Felix Hopple hurrying in the other direction. She skidded to a halt inches shy of the Ravenhill steward's chest. A packet of needles, some yellow embroidery floss, and a small bag of tea for Mother Wren slid to the ground from her basket.

"Oh, do excuse me, Mrs. Wren," the little man gasped as he bent to retrieve the items. "I'm afraid I was not minding where my feet carried me."

"That's quite all right." Anna eyed the violet and crimson striped waistcoat he wore and blinked. *Good Lord.* "I hear the earl is finally in residence at Ravenhill. You must be quite busy."

The village gossips were all abuzz at the mysterious earl's reappearance in the neighborhood after so many years, and Anna was just as curious as everyone else. In fact, she was beginning to wonder about the identity of the ugly gentleman who had so nearly run her down the day before. . . .

Mr. Hopple heaved a sigh. "I'm afraid so." He pulled out a handkerchief and mopped his brow. "I am on the hunt for a new secretary for his lordship. It is not an easy search. The last man I interviewed kept blotting his paper, and I was not at all sure of his ability to spell."

"That would be a problem in a secretary," Anna murmured.

"Indeed."

"If you find no one today, do remember that there will be plenty of gentlemen at church on Sunday morning," Anna said. "Perhaps you will find someone there."

"I'm afraid that will do me no good. His lordship stated he must have a new secretary by tomorrow morning."

"So soon?" Anna stared. "That is very little time." A thought dawned.

The steward was trying without success to wipe the mud from the packet of needles.

"Mr. Hopple," she said slowly, "did the earl say he required a *male* secretary?"

"Well, no," Mr. Hopple replied absently, still involved with the packet. "The earl simply instructed me to hire another secretary, but what other—" He stopped suddenly.

Anna straightened her flat straw hat and smiled meaningfully. "As a matter of fact, I've been thinking lately about how much excess time I have. You may not be aware, but I've a very clear hand. And I do know how to spell."

"You are not suggesting . . . ?" Mr. Hopple looked stunned, rather like a gaffed halibut in a lavender wig.

"Yes, I do suggest." Anna nodded. "I think it will be just the thing. Shall I report to Ravenhill at nine or ten o'clock tomorrow?"

"Er, nine o'clock. The earl rises early. B-but really, Mrs. Wren—" Mr. Hopple stuttered.

"Yes, really, Mr. Hopple. There. It is all settled. I shall see you tomorrow at nine o'clock." Anna patted the poor man on the sleeve. He really did not look well. She turned to go but stopped when she remembered a very important point. "One more thing. What wage is the earl offering?"

"The wage?" Mr. Hopple blinked. "Well, er, the earl was paying his last secretary three pounds a month. Will that be all right?"

"Three pounds." Anna's lips moved as she silently repeated the words. It was suddenly a glorious day in Little Battleford. "That will do nicely."

"AND NO DOUBT MANY of the upper chambers will need to be aired and perhaps painted as well. Have you got that, Hopple?" Edward leapt down the last three steps in front of Ravenhill Abbey and strode toward the stables, the late-afternoon sun warm on his back. The dog, as usual, followed at his heels.

There was no reply.

"Hopple? Hopple!" He pivoted, his boots crunching on the gravel, and glanced behind him.

"A moment, my lord." The steward was just starting down the front steps. He seemed out of breath. "I'll be there . . . in . . . a . . . moment."

Edward waited, foot tapping, until Hopple caught up, then he continued around the back. Here the gravel gave way to worn cobblestone in the courtyard. "Have you got that about the upper chambers?"

"Er, the upper chambers, my lord?" the little man wheezed as he scanned the notes in his hand.

"Have the housekeeper air them," Edward repeated slowly. "Check to see if they need painting. Do try to keep up, man."

"Yes, my lord," Hopple muttered, scribbling.

"I trust you have found a secretary."

"Er, well . . ." The steward peered at his notes intently.

"I did tell you I needed one by tomorrow morn."

"Yes, indeed, my lord, and in fact I do have a-a person who I think may very well—"

Edward halted before the massive double doors to the stables. "Hopple, do you have a secretary for me or not?"

The steward looked alarmed. "Yes, my lord. I do think one could say that I have found a secretary."

"Then why not say so?" He frowned. "Is something wrong with the man?"

"N-no, my lord." Hopple smoothed his terrible purple waistcoat. "The secretary will, I think, be quite satisfactory as a, well, as a secretary." His eyes were fixed on the horse weather vane atop the stable roof.

Edward found himself inspecting the weather vane. It squeaked and revolved slowly. He tore his gaze from it and looked down. The dog sat beside him, head cocked, also staring at the weather vane.

Edward shook his head. "Good. I will be absent tomorrow morning when he arrives." They walked from the late-afternoon sunshine into the gloom of the stables. The dog trotted ahead, sniffing in corners. "So you will need to show him my manuscript and generally instruct him as to his duties." He turned. Was it his imagination or did Hopple look relieved?

"Very good, my lord," the steward said.

"I will be traveling up to London early tomorrow and shall be gone through the rest of the week. By the time I return, he should have transcribed the papers I have left."

"Indeed, my lord." The steward was definitely beaming.

Edward eyed him and snorted. "I shall be looking forward to meeting my new secretary when I return."

Hopple's smile dimmed.

RAVENHILL ABBEY WAS a rather daunting sort of place, Anna thought as she tramped up the drive to the manor the next morning. The walk from the village to the estate was almost three miles, and her calves were beginning to ache. Fortunately, the sun shone cheerily. Ancient oaks bordered the drive, a change from the open fields along the lane from Little Battleford. The trees were so old that two horsemen could ride abreast through the spaces between them.

She rounded a corner, gasped, and halted. Daffodils dotted the tender green grass beneath the trees. The branches above wore only a fuzz of new leaves, and the sunshine broke through with hardly any impediment. Each yellow daffodil shone translucent and perfect, creating a fragile fairyland.

What sort of man would stay away from this for almost two decades?

Anna remembered tales of the great smallpox epidemic that had decimated Little Battleford in the years before her parents moved into the vicarage. She knew the present earl's family had all died from the disease. Even so, wouldn't he have at least visited in the intervening years?

She shook her head and continued. Just past the daffodil field, the copse opened up and she could see Ravenhill clearly. It stood four stories high, built of gray stone in
the classic style. A single central entrance on the first floor
dominated the façade. From it, twin curving staircases descended to ground level. In a sea of open fields, the Abbey
was an island, alone and arrogant.

Anna started on the long approach to Ravenhill Abbey,
her confidence fading the closer she got. That front entrance was simply too imposing. She hesitated a moment
when she neared the Abbey, then veered around the corner. Just past the corner, she saw the servants' entrance.
This door, too, was tall and double, but at least she didn't
have to mount granite steps to reach it. Taking a deep
breath, she tugged on the big brass knob and walked directly into the huge kitchen.

A large woman with white-blond hair stood at a massive central table. She kneaded dough, her arms elbow-
deep in an earthenware bowl the size of a kettle. Strands
of hair came down from the bun at the top of her head and
stuck to the sweat on her red cheeks. The only other
people in the room were a scullery maid and a bootblack
boy. All three turned to stare at her.

The fair-haired woman—surely the cook?—held up
floury arms. "Aye?"

Anna raised her chin. "Good morning. I'm the earl's
new secretary, Mrs. Wren. Do you know where Mr. Hopple might be?"

Without taking her eyes from Anna, the cook yelled to
the bootblack boy, "You there, Danny. Go and fetch Mr.

Hopple and tell him Mrs. Wren is here in the kitchen. Be quick, now."

Danny dashed out of the kitchen, and the cook turned back to her dough.

Anna stood waiting.

The scullery maid by the massive fireplace stared, absently scratching her arm. Anna smiled at her. The girl quickly averted her eyes.

"Ain't never heard of a lady secretary before." The cook kept her eyes on her hands, swiftly working the dough. She expertly flipped the whole mass onto the table and rolled it into a ball, the muscles on her forearms flexing. "Have you met his lordship, then?"

"We've never been introduced," Anna said. "I discussed the position with Mr. Hopple, and he had no qualms about me becoming the earl's secretary." At least Mr. Hopple hadn't *voiced* any qualms, she added mentally.

The cook grunted without looking up. "That's just as well." She rapidly pinched off walnut-sized bits of dough and rolled them into balls. A pile formed. "Bertha, fetch me that tray."

The scullery maid brought over a cast-iron tray and lined up the balls on it in rows. "Gives me the chilly trembles, he does, when he shouts," she whispered.

The cook cast a jaundiced eye on the maid. "The sound of hoot owls gives you the chilly trembles. The earl's a fine gentleman. Pays us all a decent wage and gives us regular days off, he does."

Bertha bit her lower lip as she carefully positioned each ball. "He's got a terrible sharp tongue. Perhaps that's why Mr. Tootleham left so—" She seemed to realize the cook was glaring at her and abruptly shut her mouth.

Mr. Hopple's entrance broke the awkward silence. He wore an alarming violet waistcoat, embroidered all over with scarlet cherries.

"Good morning, good morning, Mrs. Wren." He darted a glance at the watching cook and scullery maid and lowered his voice. "Are you quite sure, er, about this?"

"Of course, Mr. Hopple." Anna smiled at the steward in what she hoped was a confident manner. "I am looking forward to making the acquaintance of the earl."

She heard the cook humph behind her.

"Ah." Mr. Hopple coughed. "As to that, the earl has journeyed to London on business. He often spends his time there, you know," he said in a confiding tone. "Meeting with other learned gentlemen. The earl is quite an authority on agricultural matters."

Disappointment shot through her. "Shall I wait for his return?" she asked.

"No, no. No need," Mr. Hopple said. "His lordship left some papers for you to transcribe in the library. I'll just show you there, shall I?"

Anna nodded and followed the steward out of the kitchen and up the back stairs into the main hallway. The floor was pink and black marble parquet, beautifully inlaid, although a bit hard to see in the dim light. They came to the main entrance, and she stared at the grand staircase. Good Lord, it was huge. The stairs led up to a landing the size of her kitchen and then parted into two staircases arching away into the dark upper floors. How on earth did one man rattle around in such a house, even if he did have an army of servants?

Anna became aware that Mr. Hopple was speaking to her.

"The last secretary and, of course, the one before him worked in their own study under the stairs," the little man said. "But the room there is rather bleak. Not at all fitting a lady. So I thought it best that you be set up in the library where the earl works. Unless," Mr. Hopple inquired breathlessly, "you would prefer to have a room of your own?"

The steward turned to the library and held the door for Anna. She walked inside and then stopped suddenly, forcing Mr. Hopple to step around her.

"No, no. This will do very nicely." She was amazed at how calm her voice sounded. So many books! They lined three sides of the room, marching around the fireplace and extending to the vaulted ceiling. There must be over a thousand books in this room. A rather rickety ladder on wheels stood in the corner, apparently for the sole purpose of putting the volumes within reach. Imagine owning all these books and being able to read them whenever one fancied.

Mr. Hopple led her to a corner of the cavernous room where a massive, mahogany desk stood. Opposite it, several feet away, was a smaller, rosewood desk.

"Here we are, Mrs. Wren," he said enthusiastically. "I've set out everything I think you might need: paper, quills, ink, wipers, blotting paper, and sand. This is the manuscript the earl would like copied." He indicated a four-inch stack of untidy paper. "There is a bellpull in the far corner, and I'm sure Cook would be happy to send up tea and any light refreshments you might like. Is there anything else you desire?"

"Oh, no. This is all fine." Anna clasped her hands before her and tried not to look overwhelmed.

"No? Well, do let me know if you need more paper, or anything else for that matter." Mr. Hopple smiled and shut the door behind him.

She sat at the elegant little desk and reverently ran a finger over the polished inlay. Such a pretty piece of furniture. She sighed and picked up the first page of the earl's manuscript. A bold hand, heavily slanted to the right, covered the page. Here and there, sentences were scratched out and alternative ones scrawled along the margins with many arrows pointing to where they should go.

Anna began copying. Her own handwriting flowed small and neat. She paused now and again as she tried to decipher a word. The earl's handwriting was truly atrocious. After a while, though, she began to get used to his looping Ys and dashed Rs.

At a little past noon, Anna laid aside her quill and rubbed at the ink on her fingertips. Then she rose and tentatively yanked at the bellpull in the corner. It was silent, but presumably a bell rang somewhere to summon someone to bring her a cup of tea. She glanced at the row of books near the pull. They were heavy, embossed tomes with Latin names. Curious, she drew one out. As she did so, a slim volume fell to the floor with a thud. Anna quickly bent to pick it up, glancing guiltily at the door. No one had yet responded to the bellpull.

She turned back to the book in her hands. It was bound in red morocco leather, buttery soft to the touch, and was without title. The sole embellishment was an embossed gold feather on the lower right corner of the cover. She frowned and replaced her first choice, then carefully opened the red leather book. Inside, on the flyleaf, was written in a childish hand, *Elizabeth Jane de Raaf, her book.*

"Yes, ma'am?"

Anna almost dropped the red book at the young maid's voice. She hastily replaced it on the shelf and smiled at the maid. "I wonder if I might have some tea?"

"Yes, ma'am." The maid bobbed and left without further comment.

Anna glanced again at Elizabeth's book but decided circumspection was the better part of valor and returned to her desk to await the tea.

At five o'clock, Mr. Hopple rushed back into the library. "How was your first day? Not too strenuous, I hope?" He picked up the stack of completed papers and glanced through the first several. "These look very well. The earl will be pleased to get them off to the printers." He sounded relieved.

Anna wondered if he had spent the day worrying about her abilities. She gathered her things and, with a last inspection of her desktop to make sure all was in order, bid Mr. Hopple good evening and set off home.

Mother Wren pounced the moment Anna arrived at the little cottage and bombarded her with anxious questions. Even Fanny looked at her as if working for the earl were terribly dashing.

"But I didn't even meet him," Anna protested to no avail.

The next several days passed swiftly, and the pile of transcribed pages grew steadily. Sunday was a welcome day of rest.

When Anna returned on Monday, the Abbey held an air of excitement. The earl had at last returned from London. Cook didn't even look up from the soup she stirred when Anna entered the kitchen, and Mr. Hopple wasn't there to greet her as had been his daily habit. Anna made her way to the library by herself, expecting to finally meet her employer.

Only to find the room empty.

Oh, well. Anna puffed out a breath in disappointment and set her luncheon basket down on the rosewood desk. She began her work, and time passed, marked only by the sound of her quill scratching across the page. After a while, she felt another presence and looked up. Anna gasped.

An enormous dog stood beside her desk only an arm's length away. The animal had entered without any sound.

Anna held herself very still while she tried to think. She wasn't afraid of dogs. As a child, she'd owned a sweet little terrier. But this canine was the largest she'd ever encountered. And unfortunately it was also familiar. She'd seen the same animal not a week ago, running beside the ugly man who had fallen off his horse on the high road. And if the animal was here now . . . *oh, dear.* Anna rose, but the dog took a step toward her and she thought better of escaping the library. Instead, she exhaled and slowly sat back down. She and the dog eyed each other.

She extended a hand, palm downward, for the dog to sniff. The dog followed her hand's movement with its gaze, but disdained the gesture.

"Well," Anna said softly, "if you will not move, sir, I can at least get on with my work."

She picked up her quill again, trying to ignore the huge animal beside her. After a bit, the dog sat down but still watched her. When the clock over the mantelpiece struck the noon hour, she put down her quill again and rubbed her hand. Cautiously, she stretched her arms overhead, making sure to move slowly.

"Perhaps you'd like some luncheon?" she muttered to the beast. Anna opened the small cloth-covered basket she brought every morning. She thought about ringing for some tea to go with her meal but wasn't certain the dog would let her move from the desk.

"And if someone doesn't come to check on me," she grumbled to the beast, "I shall be glued to this desk all afternoon because of you."

The basket held bread and butter, an apple, and a wedge of cheese, wrapped in a cloth. She offered a crust of the bread to the dog, but he didn't even sniff it.

"You are picky, aren't you?" She munched on the bread herself. "I suppose you're used to dining on pheasant and champagne."

The dog kept his own counsel.

Anna finished the bread and started on the apple under the beast's watchful eyes. Surely if it was dangerous, it would not be allowed to roam freely in the Abbey? She saved the cheese for last. She inhaled as she unwrapped it and savored the pungent aroma. Cheese was rather a luxury at the moment. She licked her lips.

The dog took that moment to stretch out his neck and sniff.

Anna paused with the lump of cheese halfway to her mouth. She looked first at it and then back to the dog. His eyes were liquid brown. He placed a heavy paw on her lap.

She sighed. "Some cheese, milord?" She broke off a piece and held it out.

The cheese disappeared in one gulp, leaving a trail of canine saliva in its former place on her palm. The dog's thick tail brushed the carpet. He looked at her expectantly.

Anna raised her eyebrows sternly. "You, sir, are a sham."

She fed the monster the rest of her cheese. Only then did he deign to let her fondle his ears. She was stroking his broad head and telling him what a handsome, proud fellow he was when she heard the sound of booted footsteps in the hallway. She looked up and saw the Earl of Swartingham standing in the doorway, his hot obsidian eyes upon her.

Chapter Three

A powerful prince, a man who feared neither God nor
mortal, ruled the lands to the east of the duke. This
prince was a cruel man and a covetous one as well.
He envied the duke the bounty of his lands and the
happiness of his people. One day, the prince gathered
a force of men and swept down upon the little
dukedom, pillaging the land and its people until his
army stood outside the walls of the duke's castle.
The old duke climbed to the top of his battlements
and beheld a sea of warriors that stretched from
the stones of his castle all the way to the horizon.
How could he defeat such a powerful army? He
wept for his people and for his daughters, who
surely would be ravished and slain. But as
he stood thus in his despair, he heard a croaking
voice. "Weep not, duke. All is not yet lost. . . ."
—from *The Raven Prince*

Edward halted in the act of entering his library. He
blinked. A woman sat at his secretary's desk.

He repressed the instinctive urge to back out a step and double-check the door. Instead he narrowed his eyes, inspecting the intruder. She was a small morsel dressed in brown, her hair hidden by a god-awful frilled cap. She held her back so straight, it didn't touch the chair. She looked like every other lady of good quality but depressed means, except that she was petting—*petting* for God's sake—his great brute of a dog. The animal's head lolled, tongue hanging out the side of his jaw like a besotted idiot, eyes half shut in ecstasy.

Edward scowled at him. "Who're you?" he asked her, more gruffly than he'd meant to.

The woman's mouth thinned primly, drawing his eyes to it. She had the most erotic mouth he'd ever seen on a woman. It was wide, the upper lip fuller than the lower, and one corner tilted. "I am Anna Wren, my lord. What is your dog's name?"

"I don't know." He stalked into the room, taking care not to move suddenly.

"But"—the woman knit her brow—"isn't it your dog?"

He glanced at the dog and was momentarily mesmerized. Her elegant fingers were stroking through the dog's fur.

"He follows me and sleeps by my bed." Edward shrugged. "But he has no name that I know of."

He stopped in front of the rosewood desk. She'd have to move past him in order to escape the room.

Anna Wren's brows lowered disapprovingly. "But he must have a name. How do you call him?"

"I don't, mostly."

The woman was plain. She had a long, thin nose, brown eyes, and brown hair—what he could see of it. Nothing about her was out of the ordinary. Except that mouth.

The tip of her tongue moistened that corner.

Edward felt his cock jump and harden; he hoped to hell she wouldn't notice and be shocked out of her maidenly mind. He was aroused by a frumpy woman he didn't even know.

The dog must've grown tired of the conversation. He slipped from beneath Anna Wren's hand and lay down with a sigh by the fireplace.

"You name him if you must." Edward shrugged again and rested the fingertips of his right hand on the desk.

The assessing stare she leveled at him stirred a memory. His eyes narrowed. "You're the woman who made my horse shy on the high road the other day."

"Yes." She gave him a look of suspicious sweetness. "I am so sorry you fell off your horse."

Impertinent. "I did not *fall* off. I was unseated."

"Indeed?"

He almost contested that one word, but she held out a sheaf of papers to him. "Would you care to see what I've transcribed today?"

"Hmm," he rumbled noncommittally.

He withdrew his spectacles from a pocket and settled them on his nose. It took a moment to concentrate on the page in his hand, but when he did, Edward recognized the handwriting of his new secretary. He'd read over the transcribed pages the night before, and while he'd approved of the neatness of the script, he'd wondered about the effeminacy of it.

He looked at little Anna Wren over his spectacles and snorted. Not *effeminate*. *Feminine*. Which explained Hopple's evasiveness.

He read a few sentences more before another thought struck him. Edward darted a sharp glance at the woman's hand and saw she wore no rings. Ha. All the men hereabouts were probably afraid to court her.

"You are unwed?"

She appeared startled. "I am a widow, my lord."

"Ah." Then she had been courted and wed, but not anymore. No male guarded her now.

Hard on the heels of that thought was a feeling of ridiculousness for having predatory thoughts about such a drab female. Except for that mouth . . . He shifted uncomfortably and brought his wandering thoughts back to the page he held. There were no blots or misspellings that he could see. Exactly what he would expect from a small, brown widow. He grimaced mentally.

Ha. A mistake. He glared at the widow over his spectacles. "This word should be *compost*, not *compose*. Can't you read my handwriting?"

Mrs. Wren took a deep breath as if fortifying her patience, which made her lavish bosom expand. "Actually, my lord, no, I can't always."

"Humph," he grunted, a little disappointed she hadn't argued. She'd probably have to take a lot of deep breaths if she were enraged.

He finished reading through the papers and threw them down on her desk, where they slid sideways. She frowned at the lopsided heap of papers and bent to retrieve one that had fluttered to the floor.

"They look well enough." He walked behind her. "I will be working here later this afternoon whilst you finish transcribing the manuscript thus far."

He reached around her to flick a piece of lint off the desk. For a moment, he could feel her body heat and smell the faint scent of roses wafting up from her warmth. He sensed her stiffen.

He straightened. "Tomorrow I'll need you to work with me on matters pertaining to the estate. I hope that is amenable to you?"

"Yes, of course, my lord."

He felt her twist around to see him, but he was already walking toward the door. "Fine. I have business to attend to before I begin my work here."

He paused by the door. "Oh, and Mrs. Wren?"

She raised her eyebrows. "Yes, my lord?"

"Do not leave the Abbey before I return." Edward strode into the hallway determined to hunt down and interrogate his steward.

IN THE LIBRARY, Anna narrowed her eyes at the earl's retreating back. What an overbearing man. He even looked arrogant from the rear, his broad shoulders straight, his head at an imperious tilt.

She considered his last words and turned a puzzled frown on the dog sprawled before the fire. "Why does he think I'd leave?"

The mastiff opened one eye but seemed to know that the question was rhetorical and closed it again. She sighed and shook her head, then drew a fresh sheet of paper from the pile. She was his secretary, after all; she'd just have to learn to put up with the high-handed earl. And, of course, keep her thoughts to herself at all times.

Three hours later, Anna had nearly finished transcribing the pages and had a crick in her shoulder for her efforts. The earl hadn't yet returned, despite his threat. She sighed and flexed her right hand, then stood. Perhaps a stroll about the room was in order. The dog looked up and rose to follow her. Idly, she trailed her fingers along a shelf of books. They were outsized tomes, geography volumes, judging by the titles on their spines. The books were certainly bigger than the red-bound one she'd looked at last week. Anna paused. She hadn't had the courage to inspect that little volume since she'd been interrupted by the maid, but now curiosity drove her to the shelf by the bellpull.

There it was, nestled beside its taller mates, just as she'd left it. The slim red book seemed to beckon her. Anna drew it out and opened it to the title page. The print was ornate and barely readable: *The Raven Prince.* There was no author given. She raised her eyebrows and flipped several pages until she came to an illustration of a giant black raven, far larger than the ordinary bird. It stood on a stone wall beside a man with a long white beard and a weary expression on his face. Anna frowned. The raven's head was tilted as if it knew something the old man didn't, and its beak was open as though it might—

"What do you have there?"

The earl's deep tones startled her so badly that Anna did drop the book this time. How had such a large man moved so silently? He crossed the carpet now, with no regard to the muddy tracks he left, and picked up the book at her feet. His expression went flat when he saw the cover. She couldn't tell what he was thinking.

Then he looked up. "I thought I'd order tea," he said prosaically. He tugged at the bellpull.

The big dog thrust his muzzle in his master's free hand. Lord Swartingham scrubbed the dog's head and turned to place the book in the drawer of his desk.

Anna cleared her throat. "I was just looking. I hope you don't mind—"

But the earl waved her to silence as a parlor maid appeared at the door. He spoke to the maid. "Bitsy, have Cook put together a tray with some bread and tea and whatever else she has about." He glanced at Anna, seemingly as an afterthought. "See if she has some cakes or biscuits, too, will you?"

He hadn't asked if Anna preferred sweets, so it was just as well that she did. The maid bobbed and hurried out of the room.

Anna pursed her lips. "I really didn't mean—"

"No matter," he interrupted. The earl was at his desk, pulling out ink and quills in a haphazard manner. "Look around if you choose. All these books should be put to some use. Although, I don't know that you'll find much of interest in them. Mostly boring histories, if I remember correctly, and probably moldy to boot."

He stopped to peruse a sheet lying on the desktop. She opened her mouth to try again but was distracted by the sight of him stroking the quill while he read. His hands were large and tanned, more so than a gentleman's hands should be. Black hairs grew on the back. The thought popped into her head that he probably had hair on his chest as well. She straightened and cleared her throat.

The earl looked up.

"Do you think 'Duke' is a good name?" she asked.

His face blanked for a second before it cleared. He glanced at the dog in consideration. "I don't think so. He would outrank me."

The arrival of three maids bearing heavily laden trays saved Anna from making a reply. They set up the tea service on a table near the window and then withdrew. The earl gestured her to the settee on one side while he took a chair on the other.

"Shall I pour?" she asked.

"Please." He nodded.

Anna served the tea. She thought she felt the earl watching her as she went through the ritual, but when she looked up, his gaze was on his cup. The quantity of the food was intimidating. There was bread and butter, three different jellies, cold sliced ham, pigeon pie, some cheese, two different puddings, small iced cakes, and dried fruit. She filled a plate for the earl with some of each, remembering how hungry a man could be after exercise; then she chose a few pieces of fruit and a cake for herself. Apparently the earl didn't need conversation during the meal. He methodically demolished the food on his plate.

Anna watched him while she nibbled at a lemon cake.

He lounged in the chair, one leg bent at the knee, the other extended half under the table. Her eyes followed the long length of his mud-splattered jackboots, up muscled thighs to trim hips, over a flat stomach to a chest that widened out to quite broad shoulders for such a lean man. Her gaze skittered to his face. His black eyes gleamed back at her.

She flushed and cleared her throat. "Your dog is so"— she glanced at the homely animal—"*unusual.* I don't believe I have ever seen one like it before. Where did you get it?"

The earl snorted. "The question should be, where did he get me?"

"I beg your pardon?"

The earl sighed and shifted in his chair. "He turned up one night about a year ago outside my estate in North Yorkshire. I found him along the road. He was emaciated, flea-bitten, and had a rope tangled about his neck and forelegs. I cut the rope off, and the damned animal followed me home." He scowled at the dog beside his chair.

It wagged its tail happily. The earl lobbed a piece of pie crust, which the dog snapped out of the air.

"Haven't been able to get rid of him since."

Anna pursed her lips to hide a smile. When she looked up, she thought the earl was staring at her mouth. Oh, dear. Did she have icing on her face? She hastily dabbed at her lips with a finger. "He must be quite loyal to you after you rescued him."

He grunted. "More like he's loyal to the kitchen scraps he gets here." The earl rose abruptly and rang for the tea things to be removed, the dog following his steps. Apparently tea was over.

The rest of the day passed companionably.

The earl wasn't a silent writer. He muttered to himself and ran his hand through his hair until strands of it became dislodged from his queue and fell around his cheeks in disarray. Sometimes he jumped up to pace the room before returning to his desk to furiously scribble. The dog seemed used to the earl's compositional style and snored by the fireplace, unperturbed.

When the hall clock chimed the five o'clock hour, Anna started to gather her basket together.

The earl frowned. "Are you leaving already?"

Anna paused. "The hour has struck five, my lord."

He looked surprised, then glanced out the darkening windows. "So it has."

He stood and waited while she finished and then escorted her to the door. Anna was very conscious of his presence beside her as she walked down the hall. Her head didn't quite come to his shoulder, reminding her again of how large a man he was.

The earl scowled when he saw the empty drive outside. "Where is your carriage?"

"I haven't one," she said rather tartly. "I walked from the village."

"Ah. Of course," he said. "Wait here. I'll have my carriage brought round."

Anna started to protest, but he ran down the steps and strode off toward the stables, leaving her with the dog for company. The animal groaned and sat down. She stroked his ears. They waited quietly, listening to the wind stirring the treetops. The dog suddenly pricked up his ears and got to his feet.

The carriage rumbled around the corner and pulled up before the front steps. The earl climbed out and held the door for Anna. Eagerly, the mastiff started down the front steps ahead of her.

Lord Swartingham frowned at the animal. "Not you."

The dog lowered its head and went to stand at his side. Anna placed her gloved hand in the earl's as he helped her into the carriage. For a moment, strong, masculine fingers tightened around hers; then she was released to sit on the red leather seat.

The earl leaned into the carriage. "You needn't bring a lunch tomorrow. You will be dining with me."

He signaled the driver before she could thank him and the carriage lurched forward. Anna craned her neck to look back. The earl still stood before the steps with the huge dog. For some reason, the sight filled her with a melancholy loneliness. Anna shook her head and faced forward again, chastising herself. The earl had no need of her pity.

EDWARD WATCHED THE carriage round the corner. He had an uneasy feeling that he shouldn't let the little widow out of his sight. Her presence beside him in the library that afternoon had been strangely soothing. He grimaced to himself. Anna Wren was not for him. She was of a different class than he, and, moreover, she was a respectable widow from the village. She wasn't a sophisticated society lady who might consider a liaison outside of wedlock.

"Come." He slapped his thigh.

The dog followed him back into the library. The room was cold and dreary again. Somehow it had felt warmer when Mrs. Wren had sat here. He strolled behind her rosewood desk and noticed a handkerchief on the floor. It was white with flowers embroidered in one corner. Violets, perhaps? Hard to tell since they were a bit lopsided. Edward lifted the cloth to his face and inhaled. It smelled of roses.

He fingered the handkerchief and walked to the darkened windows. His trip to London had gone well. Sir Richard Gerard had accepted the suit for his daughter. Gerard was only a baronet, but the family was old and sound. The mother had borne seven children, five of whom had lived to adulthood. Also, Gerard owned a small unentailed estate bordering his own in North Yorkshire. The man balked at adding this land to his eldest daughter's dowry, but Edward felt sure he would come around in time. After all, Gerard would be gaining an earl as a son-in-law. Quite a feather in his cap. As for the girl . . .

Edward's thoughts stopped, and for a horrible moment he couldn't think of her name. Then it came to him: Sylvia. Of course, Sylvia. He hadn't spent much time alone with her, but he'd made sure the match was agreeable to the girl. He'd asked her point-blank if the smallpox scars repelled her. She had said they did not. Edward balled his hand into a fist. Did she tell the truth? Others had lied about his scars and he had been fooled in the past. The girl could very well be telling him what he wished to hear and he would not find out her loathing until later. But what alternative did he have? To remain unmarried and childless the rest of his life for fear of a possible lie? That fate was untenable.

Edward stroked a finger across his cheek and felt soft linen against his skin. He still held the handkerchief. He stared at it a moment, rubbing the cloth with his thumb;

then he carefully folded the handkerchief and laid it on the desk.

He strode from the room, the dog shadowing him.

ANNA'S ARRIVAL HOME in a grand carriage caused an excitement in the Wren household. She could see Fanny's white face peering through the sitting room curtains as the coachman halted the horses outside the cottage. She waited for the footman to pull down the steps and then descended from the carriage self-consciously.

"Thank you." She smiled at the young footman. "And you, too, John Coachman. I'm sorry to put you all to such a bother."

"Twern't no bother, ma'am." The coachman touched his fingertips to the brim of his round hat. "Just glad we could see you safely home."

The footman leapt onto the back of the carriage, and with a nod to Anna, John Coachman clucked to the horses. The carriage had barely pulled away when Mother Wren and Fanny tumbled out of the cottage to bombard her with questions.

"The earl sent me home in his vehicle," Anna explained as she led the way back inside.

"My, what a kind man," her mother-in-law exclaimed.

Anna thought of the way the earl had ordered her to take the carriage. "Quite." She removed her shawl and bonnet.

"Did you meet the earl himself, then, mum?" Fanny asked.

Anna smiled at the girl and nodded.

"I've never seen an earl, mum. What was he like?"

"He's just a man like any other," Anna replied.

But she was uncertain of her own words. If the earl was like any other man, then why did she have a strange urge to goad him into arguments? None of the other men of her acquaintance made her want to challenge them.

"I heard he has terrible scars on his face from the smallpox."

"Fanny, dear," Mother Wren exclaimed, "our inner selves are more important than our outer husks."

They all contemplated this noble sentiment for a moment. Fanny puckered her brow as she worked it through.

Mother Wren cleared her throat. "I heard the pox scars ran across the upper half of his face."

Anna quashed a smile. "He does have pox scars on his face, but they aren't very noticeable, really. Besides, he has nice, thick black hair and handsome dark eyes, and his voice is very attractive, beautiful even, especially when he speaks softly. And he is quite tall, with very broad, muscular shoulders." She stopped abruptly.

Mother Wren looked at her strangely.

Anna twitched off her gloves. "Is supper ready?"

"Supper? Oh, yes, the supper should be ready." Mother Wren shooed Fanny toward the kitchen. "We have a pudding and a lovely roasted chicken Fanny got for quite a good price at Farmer Brown's. She has been practicing her bargaining skills, you know. We thought it would be a treat to celebrate your employment."

"How nice." Anna started up the stairs. "I'll freshen up."

Mother Wren laid a hand on her arm. "Are you sure you know what you are doing, my dear?" she asked in a low voice. "Sometimes ladies of a certain age get, well, *ideas* about gentlemen." She paused, then said in a rush, "He isn't of our class, you know. It would only lead to hurt."

Anna looked down at the fragile old hand on her arm; then she deliberately smiled and glanced up. "I am well aware that anything of a personal nature between Lord Swartingham and me would be improper. There's no need to worry."

The older woman searched her eyes a moment longer before patting Anna's arm. "Don't be too long, dear. We haven't burned the supper yet tonight."

Chapter Four

*The duke turned and saw a huge raven perched on the
wall of the castle. The bird hopped closer and cocked
its head. "I will help you defeat the prince if you give
me one of your daughters as my wife."
"How dare you, sirrah!" The old duke quivered in
indignation. "You insult me to imply I would even
think to wed one of my daughters to a dusty bird."
"Fine words, my friend," the raven cackled. "But
be not so quick. In a moment, you'll lose both
your daughters and your life."
The duke stared at the raven and saw that this was no
ordinary bird. It wore a golden chain around its neck,
and a ruby pendant in the shape of a small, perfect
crown hung on the chain. He looked back to the
threatening army at his gates and, seeing he had
little to lose, agreed to the unholy bargain. . . .*
—from *The Raven Prince*

"Have you considered the name 'Sweetie'?" Anna asked
as she spooned up some stewed apple.

She and the earl sat at one end of the immense dining

room table. From the fine layer of dust on the mahogany at the other end of the table, she guessed that this room must not be used much. Did the earl even take his supper here? Yet the dining room had been opened every day of the last week for their luncheon. In that week, she'd learned that the earl was not a conversationalist. After many days of grunts and monosyllabic replies, it'd become something of a game to provoke a response from her employer.

Lord Swartingham paused in the act of cutting a piece of steak and kidney pie. "Sweetie?"

His eyes were on her mouth, and Anna realized she'd licked her lips. "Yes. Don't you think 'Sweetie' a darling name?"

They both looked down at the dog beside the earl's chair. It was gnawing on a soup bone, sharp fangs glittering.

"I think 'Sweetie' may not be altogether suitable for his personality," Lord Swartingham said, placing the pie slice on his plate.

"Hmm. Perhaps you're right." Anna thoughtfully chewed. "Yet, you yourself haven't offered an alternative."

The earl sawed vigorously at a lump of meat. "That's because I'm content to let the animal remain nameless."

"Didn't you have any dogs as a boy?"

"I?" He stared at her as if she'd asked if he'd had two heads as a boy. "No."

"No pets at all?"

He scowled down at his pie. "Well, there was my mother's lapdog—"

"There, you see," Anna exclaimed in triumph.

"But the animal was a pug and an extremely irritable one at that."

"Even so—"

"Used to growl and snap at everyone but Mother," the earl mused, apparently to himself. "No one liked it. Once bit a footman. Father had to give the poor fellow a shilling."

"And did the pug have a name?"

"Fiddles." The earl nodded and took a bite of pie. "But Sammy called it Piddles. He also fed it Turkish delight just to see it get the candy stuck to the roof of its mouth."

Anna smiled. "Sammy was your brother?"

Lord Swartingham had raised a glass of wine to his lips, and he paused for a fraction of a second before sipping. "Yes." He placed the glass precisely beside his plate. "I'll need to check on various matters on the estate this afternoon."

Anna's smile died. Their play was apparently at an end.

He continued, "Tomorrow I'll need you to ride out with me. Hopple wants to show me some fields with a drainage problem, and I'd like you to take notes for us as we discuss possible solutions." He looked up. "You do have a riding habit, don't you?"

Anna tapped her fingers against her teacup. "As a matter of fact, I've never ridden."

"Never?" His eyebrows shot up.

"We don't have a horse."

"No, I suppose not." He frowned down at the pie on his

plate as if it were to blame for her lack of suitable attire. "Have you a gown you could use as a habit?"

Anna mentally ran through her meager wardrobe. "I could alter an old one."

"Excellent. Wear it tomorrow and I shall give you an elementary riding lesson. It shouldn't be too hard. We'll not be riding very far."

"Oh, but, my lord," Anna protested, "I don't want to put you to any trouble. I can ask one of the grooms to help me learn."

"No." He glared at her. "I will teach you to ride."

Overbearing man. She pursed her lips and refrained from a reply, sipping her tea instead.

The earl finished his pie in two more bites and pushed back his chair. "I'll see you before you leave this afternoon, Mrs. Wren." With a muttered "Come," he strode out of the room, the still-nameless dog following him.

Anna stared after the two. Was she peeved because the earl ordered her about, very much like the dog? Or touched that he insisted on teaching her to ride himself? She shrugged and finished the dregs of her tea.

Entering the library, she crossed to her desk and began writing. After a short while, she reached for a fresh sheet only to find there was none. Bother. Anna stood to ring for more paper and then remembered the stack in the earl's side drawer. She slipped behind his desk and pulled the drawer open. There on top of a pile of clean sheets lay the red leather book. Anna moved it aside and drew out a few sheets. A piece of paper drifted to the floor as she did so. She bent to pick it up and saw that it was a letter or a bill. A curious mark was engraved at the top. There appeared to be two men and a woman, but she could not make out what the diminutive figures were doing. She turned the letter this way and that in her hand, studying it.

The fire popped in the corner.

All at once, Anna understood and nearly dropped the paper. A nymph and two satyrs were engaged in an act that did not seem physically possible. She tilted her head to the side. Evidently, it *was* possible. The words *Aphrodite's Grotto* were engraved in ornate script beneath the rude illustration. The paper was a bill for two nights' stay at a house, and one could guess the type of house from the scandalous little picture at the top of the page. Who knew a bordello sent out monthly bills like a tailor?

Anna felt a sickening lurch in her stomach. Lord Swartingham must frequent this place if he had the bill in his desk. She sat down heavily and covered her mouth with a hand. Why should the discovery of his baser passions bother her so? The earl was a mature man who had lost his wife years ago. No person with any worldly knowledge at all would expect him to remain celibate the rest of his life. She smoothed the loathsome page on her lap. But the fact remained that the thought of him participating in such an activity with some beautiful woman brought a strange welling in her chest.

Anger. She felt anger. Society might not expect celibacy from the earl, but they certainly expected it of her. He, as a man, could go to houses of ill repute and romp all night with alluring, sophisticated creatures. While she, as a woman, was supposed to be chaste and not even think of dark eyes and hairy chests. It was simply not fair. Not fair at all.

She pondered the damning letter for a moment longer. Then she placed it carefully back in the desk drawer under the new paper. She made to close the drawer, but stopped, staring at the raven book. Anna's mouth thinned, and she impulsively snatched up the book. She slipped it in the center drawer of her own desk and returned to work. The rest of the afternoon dragged on. The earl never did return from the fields as promised.

Hours later, riding in the rattling carriage home, Anna tapped the back of one fingernail against the glass window and watched the fields turn into the muddy lanes of the village. The leather squabs smelled musty from the damp. She spotted a familiar street as they rounded a curve, and abruptly she stood and knocked on the carriage's roof. John Coachman called to the horses, and the carriage jerked to a stop. Anna descended and hastily thanked the coachman. She was in an area with houses that were both newer and a little more grand than her own cottage. The third house in from the lane was a redbrick with white trim. She knocked at the door.

In a moment, a maid peered out.

Anna smiled at the girl. "Hello, Meg. Is Mrs. Fairchild at home?"

"Good afternoon, Mrs. Wren." Black-haired Meg smiled cheerily. "The missus will be that glad to see you. You can wait in the sitting room while I tell her you're here."

Meg led the way into a little sitting room with bright yellow walls. A marmalade cat stretched on the rug, sunning itself in the dying light slanting through the windows. On the settee, a basket of sewing things lay, the threads trailing out untidily. Anna bent to greet the cat while she waited.

Footsteps pattered down the stairs, and Rebecca Fairchild appeared in the doorway. "For shame! It's been so long since you've visited, I'd begun to think you had abandoned me in my hour of need."

The other woman immediately contradicted her words by hurrying over and hugging Anna. Her belly made the embrace difficult, for it was round and heavy, thrusting before Rebecca like the full sails of a ship.

Anna returned her friend's hug fervently. "I'm sorry. You're right. I've been lax in coming to see you. How are you?"

"Fat. No, it's true," Rebecca talked over Anna's protest. "Even James, that dear man, has stopped offering to carry me up the stairs." She sat rather abruptly on the settee, narrowly missing the sewing basket. "Chivalry is quite dead. But you must tell me all about your employment at the Abbey."

"You've heard?" Anna took one of the chairs across from her friend.

"Have I heard? I've heard of practically nothing else." Rebecca lowered her voice dramatically. "The dark and mysterious Earl of Swartingham has employed the young Widow Wren for unknown purposes and daily closets himself with her for his own nefarious ends."

Anna winced. "I'm only transcribing papers for him."

Rebecca waved this mundane explanation away as Meg entered with a tea tray. "Don't tell me that. You realize that you're one of the few to actually meet the man? To hear the village gossips tell it, he hides himself away in his sinister mansion simply to deprive them of the opportunity to inspect him. Is he really as repulsive as the rumors say?"

"Oh, no!" Anna felt a spurt of anger. Surely they weren't saying Lord Swartingham was repulsive because of a few scars? "He's not handsome, of course, but he's not unattractive." Quite attractive to her anyway, a small voice whispered inside. Anna frowned down at her hands. When had she stopped noticing his scars and instead started focusing on the man underneath them?

"Pity." Rebecca appeared disappointed at the information that the earl wasn't a hideous ogre. "I want to hear of his dark secrets and his attempts to seduce you."

Meg quietly left.

Anna laughed. "He may have any number of dark secrets"—her voice hitched as she remembered the bill—"but he's very unlikely to try and seduce me."

"Of course he won't while you're wearing that awful cap." Rebecca gestured with the teapot at the offending article of clothing. "I don't know why you wear it. You're not that old."

"Widows are supposed to wear caps." Anna touched the muslin cap self-consciously. "Besides, I don't want him to seduce me."

"Why ever not?"

"Because—" Anna stopped.

She realized—horribly—that her mind had gone blank, and she couldn't think of a single reason why she didn't want the earl to seduce her. She popped a biscuit into her mouth and slowly chewed. Fortunately, Rebecca hadn't noticed her sudden silence and was now chattering on about hairstyles she thought would better suit her friend.

"Rebecca," Anna interrupted, "do you think all men have need of more than one woman?"

Rebecca, who had been in the act of pouring a second cup of tea, looked up at her in a far-too-sympathetic manner.

Anna felt herself flush. "I mean—"

"No, dear, I know what you mean." Rebecca slowly set the teapot down. "I can't speak for all men, but I'm fairly sure James has been faithful. And, really, if he was going to stray, I think he would do so now." She patted her tummy and reached for another biscuit.

Anna couldn't sit still any longer. She jumped up and started examining the bric-a-brac on the mantelpiece. "I'm sorry. I know James would never—"

"I'm glad you know." Rebecca snorted delicately. "You should've heard the advice Felicity Clearwater gave me on what to expect from a husband when one is with child. According to her, every husband is simply waiting—" Rebecca stopped suddenly.

Anna picked up a china shepherdess and touched the gilt on her bonnet. She couldn't see it very well. Her eyes were blurry.

"Now I'm the one who's sorry," Rebecca said.

Anna didn't look up. She'd always wondered if Rebecca had been aware. Now she knew. She closed her eyes.

"I think that any man who took his marriage vows so lightly," she heard Rebecca say, "has shamed himself unpardonably."

Anna set the shepherdess back on the mantel. "And the wife? Would she not be partly to blame if he went outside the marriage for satisfaction?"

"No, dear," Rebecca replied. "I don't think the wife is ever to blame."

Anna felt suddenly lighter. She tried a smile, though she feared it was a bit wobbly. "You are the best of friends, Rebecca."

"Well, of course." The other woman smiled like a self-satisfied and very pregnant cat. "And to prove it, I shall ring for Meg to bring us some cream cakes. Decadent, my dear!"

ANNA ARRIVED AT the Abbey the next morning dressed in an old blue worsted wool frock. She'd stayed up until well past midnight widening the skirt, but she hoped she could now sit a horse modestly. The earl was already pacing before the Abbey's entrance, apparently waiting for her. He wore buckskin breeches with brown jackboots that came to midthigh. These last were rather scuffed and dull, and Anna wondered, not for the first time, about his valet.

"Ah, Mrs. Wren." He eyed her skirt. "Yes, that will do nicely." Without waiting for a reply, he strode around the Abbey toward the stables.

Anna trotted to keep up.

His bay gelding was already saddled and busy baring its teeth at a stable boy. The boy held the horse's bridle at arm's length and looked wary. In contrast, a plump chestnut mare was standing placidly by the mounting block. The dog emerged from behind the stables and came bounding up to Anna. He skidded to a stop in front of her and tried belatedly to regain some of his dignity.

"I've found you out, you know," she whispered to him, and rubbed his ears in greeting.

"If you are through playing with that animal, Mrs. Wren." Lord Swartingham frowned at the dog.

Anna straightened. "I'm ready."

He indicated the mounting block, and Anna hesitantly approached it. She knew the theory of mounting a horse sidesaddle, but the reality was a bit more complicated. She could place one foot in the stirrup but had trouble pulling herself up to hook her other leg over the pommel.

"If you'll allow me?" The earl was behind her. She could feel his warm breath, smelling faintly of coffee, on her cheek as he bent over her.

She nodded, mute.

He placed his large hands around her waist and lifted her without any visible effort. Gently, he set her on the saddle and held the stirrup steady for her foot. Anna felt herself flush as she looked down at his bent head. He'd left his hat with the groom, and she could see a few strands of silver threading his queue. Was his hair soft or bristly? Her gloved hand lifted and, as if of its own accord, lightly touched his hair. She immediately snatched back her hand, but the earl seemed to have felt something. He looked up and stared into her eyes for what seemed a timeless moment. She watched as his eyelids lowered, and a faint flush seeped across his cheekbones.

Then he straightened and caught the horse's bridle. "This is a very placid mare," he said. "I think you'll have no trouble with her as long as there are no rats around."

She stared blankly down at him. "Rats?"

He nodded. "She has a fear of rats."

"I don't blame her," Anna murmured. She tentatively stroked the mare's mane, feeling the stiff hair beneath her fingers.

"Her name is Daisy," Lord Swartingham said. "Shall I lead you about the yard for a bit so you can get used to her?"

She nodded.

The earl clucked and the mare rocked forward. Anna clutched a handful of the mare's mane. Her whole body tensed at the unfamiliar sensation of moving so far off the ground. The mare shook her head.

Lord Swartingham glanced at her hands. "She can feel your fear. Isn't that right, my sweet girl?"

Anna, caught off guard by his last words, let go of the horse's mane.

"That's good. Let your body relax." His voice surrounded her, enfolding her in warmth. "She responds better to a gentle touch. She wants to be stroked and loved, don't you, my beauty?"

They walked around the stable yard, the earl's deep voice enchanting the horse. Something inside Anna seemed to heat and melt as she listened to him, as if she were enchanted, too. He gave simple instructions about how to hold the reins and sit. By the end of a half hour, she felt a good deal more confident in the saddle.

Lord Swartingham mounted his gelding and led off at a walk down the drive. The dog trotted beside them, sometimes disappearing into the high grass beside the drive only to reappear a few minutes later. When they reached the road, the earl let the bay have its head, galloping down the road a short distance and back again to work off some energy. The little mare watched the male antics without any sign that she wanted to break out of a walk. Anna lifted her face to the sun. She so missed its warmth after the long winter. She caught a flash of pale saffron beneath the hedges that lined the road.

"Look, primroses. I think those are the first this year, don't you?"

The earl glanced to where she pointed. "Those yellow flowers? I haven't seen them before."

"I've tried to grow them in my garden, but they don't like to be transplanted," she said. "I do have a few tulips, though. I've seen the lovely daffodils in the copse at the Abbey. Do you have tulips as well, my lord?"

He seemed a little startled by the question. "There may be tulips still in the gardens. I remember my mother gathering them, but I haven't seen the gardens in so long. . . ."

Anna waited, but he didn't elaborate. "Not everyone enjoys gardening, of course," she said to be polite.

"My mother loved to garden." He stared off down the lane. "She planted the daffodils you saw, and she renovated the great walled gardens behind the Abbey. When she died . . ." He grimaced. "When they all died, there were other, more important things to be seen to. And now the gardens have been neglected for so long, I should have them taken down."

"Oh, surely not!" Anna caught his lifted eyebrow and lowered her voice. "I mean to say, a good garden can always be restored."

He frowned. "To what point?"

Anna was nonplussed. "A garden always has a point."

He arched an eyebrow skeptically.

"My own mother had a lovely one when I was growing up at the vicarage," Anna said. "There were crocuses, daffodils, and tulips in the spring, followed by pinks, foxgloves, and phlox, with Johnny-jump-ups running throughout."

As she talked, Lord Swartingham watched her face intently.

"At my cottage now, I have the hollyhocks, of course, and many of the other flowers my mother grew. I wish I had more room to add some roses," she mused. "But roses are dear and take up quite a bit of space. I'm afraid I can't justify the expense when the vegetable garden comes first."

"Perhaps you could advise me on the Abbey's gardens later this spring," the earl said. He turned the bay's head and started down a smaller dirt track.

Anna concentrated on the business of turning the mare. When she looked up, she saw the flooded field. Mr. Hopple was already there, talking to a farmer in a woolen smock and straw hat. The man was having a hard time looking Mr. Hopple in the face. His eyes kept dragging lower to the amazing pink waistcoat Mr. Hopple wore. Something black was embroidered along the edges. As Anna drew nearer, she saw that the embroidery seemed to represent little black pigs.

"Good morning, Hopple, Mr. Grundle." The earl nodded to his steward and the farmer. His eyes flicked to the waistcoat. "That's a very interesting garment, Hopple. I don't know that I've seen the like before." The earl's tone was grave.

Mr. Hopple beamed and smoothed a hand down his waistcoat. "Why, thank you, my lord. I had it made at a small shop in London on my last trip."

The earl swung a long leg down from his horse. He gave the reins to Mr. Hopple and walked to Anna's horse. Gently grasping Anna's waist, he lifted her down. For the briefest moment, the tips of her breasts brushed the front of his coat and she felt his large fingers tighten. Then she was free, and he was turning to the steward and the farmer.

They spent the morning tramping through the field, examining the water problem. At one point, the earl stood knee-deep in muddy water and investigated a suspected source of the flood. Anna took notes in a small book he provided for her. She was glad she had chosen an old skirt to wear since it soon became thoroughly filthy about the hem.

"How do you intend to drain the field?" Anna asked as they rode back to the Abbey.

"We'll have to dig a trench across the north side." Lord Swartingham squinted thoughtfully. "That may be a problem because the land there runs into Clearwater's property, and for courtesy's sake, I'll have to send Hopple to ask permission. The farmer has already lost his pea crop, and if the field isn't made tillable soon, he'll miss his wheat—" He stopped and shot a wry look at her. "I'm sorry. You can't be interested in these matters."

"Indeed, I am, my lord." Anna straightened in her saddle and then hurriedly grabbed Daisy's mane when the horse sidestepped. "I've been most absorbed in your writings about land management. If I understand your theories correctly, the farmer should follow a crop of wheat with one of beans or peas and then with one of mangel-wurzels and so on. If that is the case, shouldn't this farmer plant mangel-wurzels instead of wheat?"

"In most instances, you would be right, but in this case . . ."

Anna listened to the earl's deep voice discussing vegetables and grains. Had agriculture always been this fascinating and she'd never realized it? Somehow she didn't think so.

AN HOUR LATER, Edward found himself bemusedly holding forth on various ways of draining a field during luncheon with Mrs. Wren. Of course the topic was an interesting one, but he'd never had occasion to talk to a woman about such masculine matters before. In fact, he had hardly any occasion to talk to women, at least since the death of his mother and sister. He'd flirted when young, naturally, and knew how to make light social chatter. But to exchange ideas with a woman as one did with a man was a new experience. And he liked talking with little Mrs. Wren. She listened to him with her head tilted to one side, the sun streaming in through the dining room window gently highlighting the curve of her cheek. Such utter attention was seductive.

Sometimes she smiled crookedly at what he was saying. He was fascinated by that lopsided smile. One edge of her rose-colored lips always tilted upward more than the other side. He became aware that he was staring at her mouth, hoping to see that smile again, fantasizing about what it would taste like. Edward turned his head aside and closed his eyes. His arousal was pressing against the front placket of his breeches, making them uncomfortably tight. He'd found he had this problem almost constantly of late when in the company of his new secretary.

Christ. He was a man above thirty, not a boy to moon over a woman's smile. The situation might be laughable if his cock didn't ache so much.

Edward abruptly realized that Mrs. Wren was asking him a question. "What?"

"I asked if you were all right, my lord," she said. She looked worried.

"Fine. I'm fine." He took a deep breath and wished irritably that she would call him by his given name. He longed to hear her say *Edward.* But no. It would be highly inappropriate for her to call him by his Christian name.

He gathered his scattered thoughts. "We should return to work." He stood and strode from the room, feeling as if he were fleeing fire-breathing monsters rather than one plain little widow.

WHEN THE CLOCK struck five, Anna tidied the small pile of transcripts she'd finished that afternoon and glanced at the earl. He was sitting scowling at the paper in front of him. She cleared her throat.

He looked up. "Is it time already?"

She nodded.

He rose and waited as she gathered her things. The dog followed them out the door, but then he bounded down the stairs to the drive. The animal sniffed intently at something on the ground and then rolled, happily rubbing his head and neck in whatever it was.

Lord Swartingham sighed. "I'll have one of the stable boys wash him before he enters the Abbey again."

"Mmm," Anna murmured thoughtfully. "What do you think of 'Adonis'?"

He gave her a look so full of incredulous horror that she was hard-pressed not to laugh. "No, I suppose not," she murmured.

The dog got up from his refreshment and shook himself, flipping one of his ears inside out. He trotted back to them and tried to look solemn with his ear still inside out.

"Self-control, lad." The earl righted the dog's ear.

At this Anna did chuckle. He looked at her sideways, and she thought his wide mouth twitched. The carriage trundled up then, and she entered with his assistance. The dog knew by now that he was not allowed to ride and merely watched wistfully.

Anna settled back and watched the familiar scenery roll by. As the carriage came upon the outskirts of town, she saw a wad of clothes in the roadside ditch. Curious, she leaned out the window to get a better look. The bundle moved, and a head with fine, pale-brown hair rose and turned toward the sound of the carriage.

"Stop! John Coachman, stop at once!" Anna pounded on the roof with her fist.

The carriage slowed to a halt, and she flung open the door.

"What is it, miss?"

She saw the startled face of Tom, the footman, as she ran past the back of the carriage with her skirts held in one hand. Anna reached the place where she had seen the clothes and stared down.

In the ditch lay a young woman.

Chapter Five

*The moment the duke agreed to his bargain, the raven
leapt into the air with a powerful rush of wings. At the
same time, a magical army streamed from the castle's
keep. First came ten thousand men, each armed with a
shield and sword. They were followed by ten thousand
archers carrying long, deadly bows and full quivers.
Finally, ten thousand mounted men galloped forth,
their horses gnashing their teeth and ready for battle.
The raven flew to the army's head and met the
prince's troops with a crash like thunder. Clouds
of dust covered both forces so that nothing could be
seen. Only the terrible cries of men at war were
heard. And when the dust finally cleared, not a trace
of the prince's army remained save for a few iron
horseshoes lying in the dirt. . . .*
—from *The Raven Prince*

The woman lay on her side in the ditch, both legs curled
as if seeking warmth. She clutched a dirty shawl about
pitifully thin shoulders. The dress beneath the shawl had
once been a bright pink but was now smeared with grime.

Her eyes were closed in a face that looked yellowish and unhealthy.

Anna held her skirt out of the way with one hand and used the other to steady herself against the bank as she clambered down to the stricken woman. She noticed a foul smell as she drew nearer.

"Are you hurt, ma'am?" She touched the pale face.

The woman moaned and her large eyes flew open, making Anna start. Behind her, the coachman and footman slid down the little slope with a rattle.

John Coachman made a disgusted noise in his throat. "Come away, Mrs. Wren. This here ain't for the likes of you."

Anna turned her eyes to the coachman in astonishment. He averted his face, watching the horses. She looked at Tom. He inspected the rocks at his feet.

"The lady is hurt or ill, John." She knit her brow. "We need to summon help for her."

"Aye, mum, we'll send back someone to take care of her," John said. "You should come to the carriage and go home now, Mrs. Wren."

"But I can't leave the lady here."

"She's no lady, if you understand my meaning." John spat to the side. "It ain't fit for you to bother yourself with her."

Anna looked down at the woman she'd drawn into her arms. She noticed now what she hadn't before: the unseemly show of skin at the woman's dress top and the tawdry nature of the material. She frowned in thought. Had she ever met a prostitute? She thought not. Such persons lived in a different world than poor country widows.

A world that her community explicitly forbade from ever intersecting with hers. She should do as John suggested and leave the poor woman. It was, after all, what everyone expected of her.

John Coachman was offering his hand to help her up. Anna stared at the appendage. Had her life always been this constrained, her boundaries so narrow that at times it was like walking a tightrope? Was she nothing more than her position in society?

No, she was not. Anna firmed her jaw. "Nevertheless, John, I do bother myself with this woman. Please carry her to the carriage with Tom's help. We must bring her to my cottage and send for Dr. Billings."

The two men didn't look happy with the situation, but under her determined gaze, they bore the slight woman between them to the carriage. Anna got in first and then turned around to help ease the woman onto the carriage seat. She braced the woman against herself with both arms to prevent her from falling off the seat on the way home. When the carriage stopped, she carefully laid the woman down and got out. John was still in the high driver's seat staring straight ahead with a furrowed brow.

Anna placed her hands on her hips. "John, come and help Tom get her into the cottage."

John muttered, but climbed down.

"What is it, Anna?" Mother Wren had come to the door.

"An unfortunate lady I found by the roadside." Anna watched the men maneuver the woman out of the carriage. "Bring her into the cottage, please."

Mother Wren backed out of the way as the men struggled to get the unconscious woman over the doorsill.

"Where shall we put her, ma'am?" Tom panted.

"I think in my room, up the stairs."

That earned Anna a disapproving look from John, but she ignored it. They carried the woman up the stairs.

"What is wrong with the lady?" Mother Wren asked.

"I don't know. I believe she may be ill," Anna said. "I thought it best to bring her here."

The men clomped back down the narrow stairs and outside.

"Don't forget to stop by Dr. Billings's," Anna called.

John Coachman waved a hand irritably over his shoulder to signify that he had heard. In a moment, the carriage had rattled away. By this time, Fanny was standing wide-eyed in the hallway.

"Could you put the kettle on for tea, Fanny?" Anna asked. She drew Mother Wren aside as soon as Fanny started for the kitchen. "John and Tom say this poor woman is not entirely respectable. I'll send her elsewhere if you say so." She looked anxiously at her mother-in-law.

Mother Wren raised her eyebrows. "Do you mean she's a whore?" At Anna's startled glance, she smiled and patted her hand. "It's very hard to get to my age without hearing the word at least once, dear."

"No, I suppose not," Anna replied. "Yes, John and Tom indicated that she is a whore."

Mother Wren sighed. "You know it would be best to send her away."

"Yes, undoubtedly." Anna lifted her chin.

"But"—Mother Wren threw up her hands—"if it is your wish to care for her here, I'll not stop you."

Anna blew out a breath in relief and ran upstairs to see to her patient.

A quarter of an hour later, there was a sharp knock on the door. Anna came down the stairs in time to see Mother Wren smooth her skirts and answer the door.

Dr. Billings, in a white bobbed wig, stood outside. "A good day to you, Mrs. Wren, Mrs. Wren."

"And to you, Dr. Billings," Mother Wren answered for them both.

Anna led the doctor to her room.

Dr. Billings had to duck to enter the bedroom. He was a tall, gaunt gentleman with a bit of a permanent stoop. The tip of his bony nose was always pink, even in summer. "Well, what have we here?"

"A woman I found in distress, Dr. Billings," Anna said. "Will you see if she is ill or injured?"

He cleared his throat. "If you'll leave me alone with this person, Mrs. Wren, I'll endeavor to examine her."

Clearly, John had told Dr. Billings the manner of woman they had found.

"I think I shall remain, if you do not mind, Dr. Billings," Anna said.

The doctor obviously did mind but could think of no reason to order Anna from the room. Despite his opinion of the patient, Dr. Billings was thorough but gentle in his examination. He looked down her throat and asked Anna to turn away so that he might scrutinize the sick woman's chest.

Then he straightened the covers over her and sighed. "I think we had better discuss this downstairs."

"Of course." Anna led the way from the room and down the stairs, stopping to ask Fanny to bring some tea to the sitting room. Then she indicated the only armchair for the doctor and sat across from him on the edge of the tiny settee, clasping her hands tightly in her lap. Was the woman dying?

"She's quite ill," Dr. Billings began.

Anna leaned forward. "Yes?"

The doctor avoided her eyes. "She has a fever, perhaps an infection of the lungs. She'll need some bed rest to recover."

He hesitated and then apparently saw the alarm in Anna's face. "Oh, it is nothing grave, I assure you, Mrs. Wren. She'll recover. She just needs time to heal."

"I am most relieved." Anna smiled. "I thought from your manner that the disease was fatal."

"Indeed not."

"Thank God."

Dr. Billings rubbed his finger along the side of his thin nose. "I'll send some men around immediately when I get home. She'll need to be taken to the poorhouse for care, of course."

Anna frowned. "But I thought you understood, Dr. Billings. We wish to nurse her here at the cottage."

A red stain seeped up the doctor's face. "Nonsense. It is entirely inappropriate for you and the elder Mrs. Wren to care for a woman of that sort."

She set her jaw. "I've discussed it with my mother-in-law, and we are both in agreement that we will care for the lady in our home."

Dr. Billings's face was now completely red. "It is quite out of the question."

"Doctor—"

But Dr. Billings interrupted her. "She's a prostitute!"

Anna forgot what she was about to say and closed her mouth. She stared at the doctor and saw the truth in his countenance: this was how the majority of the people in Little Battleford would react.

She took a deep breath. "We've decided to take care of the woman. Her profession doesn't change that fact."

"You must see reason, Mrs. Wren," the doctor grumbled. "It's impossible for you to care for that creature."

"Her condition is not contagious, is it?"

"No, no, probably not anymore," he admitted.

"Well, then, there is no reason we can't care for her." Anna smiled grimly.

Fanny chose that moment to bring in the tea. Anna poured for the doctor and herself, trying to remain as serene as possible. She wasn't used to having arguments with gentlemen, and she found it was most hard to remain resolute and not apologize. It was a rather unsettling feeling, knowing the doctor disagreed with her course, that in fact he disapproved of her. At the same time, she couldn't repress a clandestine thrill. How exhilarating to speak her mind frankly, uncaring of a man's opinion! Really, she ought to feel ashamed at the thought, but she couldn't bring herself to regret it. No, not at all.

They drank the tea in a charged silence, the good doctor having apparently decided he wasn't going to change her mind. After finishing his cup, Dr. Billings fished a small brown bottle out of his bag and gave it to Anna with instructions on how to administer the medication. Then the doctor crammed his hat on his head and wound a lavender muffler around his neck several times.

He halted by the front door as Anna was showing him out. "If you change your mind, Mrs. Wren, please call on me. I'll find an appropriate place for the young woman."

"Thank you," she murmured. She closed the door after the doctor and leaned against it, her shoulders slumping.

Mother Wren entered the hall and studied Anna. "What does she have, my dear?"

"A fever and infection of the lungs." Anna looked at her wearily. "Perhaps it would be better if you and Fanny stayed with friends until this is over."

Mother Wren raised her brows. "Who would look after her during the day while you are at Ravenhill?"

Anna stared, suddenly stricken. "I'd forgotten that."

Mother Wren shook her head. "Is it really necessary to stir up this amount of trouble, my dear?"

"I'm sorry." Anna looked down and noticed a grass stain on her skirts. It wouldn't come out—grass stains never did. "I don't mean to drag you into my mess."

"Then why not take the doctor's help? It's so much easier to simply do what people expect of you, Anna."

"It may be easier, but it isn't necessarily the right way, Mother. Surely you can see that?" She looked at her mother-in-law pleadingly, trying to find the words to explain. Her actions had made complete sense when she'd been staring at the woman's sickly face in the ditch. Now, with Mother Wren waiting so patiently, it was harder to articulate her logic. "I've always done what was expected, haven't I? Whether or not it was the right thing to do."

The older woman frowned. "But you've never done anything wrong—"

"But that's not the point, is it?" Anna bit her lip and found to her horror that she was close to tears. "If I've never stepped outside the role that's been assigned to me since birth, I've never tested myself. I've been too afraid of others' opinions, I think. I've been a coward. If that woman needs me, why not help her—for her . . . and for me?"

"All I know is that this way will lead to quite a lot of grief for you." Mother Wren shook her head again and sighed.

Anna led the way into the kitchen, and the two women prepared a thin beef tea. Anna carried it and the little brown bottle of medicine up the stairs to her room. Quietly, she cracked the door open and peeked in. The woman stirred feebly and tried to raise herself.

Anna put down her burden and crossed the room to her. "Don't try to move."

At the sound of Anna's voice, the woman's eyes flew open and she looked around wildly. "W-w-who are—?"

"My name is Anna Wren. You're in my home."

Anna hurried to bring the beef tea over to the woman. She put her arm around her patient, gently helping her to sit up. The woman sipped the warm broth and swallowed with difficulty. After she had drunk half the cup, her eyes began to close again. Anna lowered her back to the bed and gathered up the cup and spoon.

The woman caught her with a shaking hand as she turned away. "My sister," she whispered.

Anna knit her brow. "Do you wish me to notify your sister?"

The woman nodded.

"Wait," Anna said. "Let me get a bit of paper and pencil so I may write down her address." She hurried to her small dresser and tugged out the bottom drawer. Underneath a stack of old linens was a walnut writing case that had belonged to Peter. Anna took it out and settled on the bedside chair with the writing case on her lap. "Where shall I address a letter to your sister?"

The woman gasped out her sister's name and place of residence, which was in London, while Anna noted the address with a pencil on a scrap of paper. Then the woman lay back, exhausted, on the pillow.

Anna hesitantly touched her hand. "Can you tell me your name?"

"Pearl," she whispered without opening her eyes.

Anna carried the writing case from the room, shutting the door gently behind her. She ran down the stairs and went into the sitting room to compose a letter to Pearl's sister, a Miss Coral Smythe.

Peter's writing case was a flat rectangular box. The writer could place it on his or her lap and use it as a portable desk. On top was a hinged half lid that opened to reveal a smaller box for quills, a bottle of ink that fit next to it, and papers and other miscellaneous things used for correspondence. Anna hesitated. The writing case was a handsome thing, but she'd not touched it since Peter's death. While Peter lived, it had been his private possession. She felt almost a trespasser using it, especially as they had not been close toward the end of his life. She shook her head and opened the case.

Anna wrote carefully, but it still took several drafts to compose a letter. Finally, she had a missive she was satisfied with, and she put it aside to take to the Little Battleford Coach Inn tomorrow. She was putting the quill box back into the walnut writing case when she realized that something was jammed in the back. The quill box would not fit in. She opened the half lid all the way and shook out the shallow case. Then she felt with her hand at the back. There was something round and cool there. Anna gave a tug and the object came loose. When she withdrew her hand, a little gold locket nestled in her palm. The lid was prettily chased with curlicues, and on the back was a pin so a lady could wear it as a brooch. Anna pressed the thin wafer of gold at the seam. The locket popped apart.

It was empty.

Anna snapped the two halves back together. She rubbed her thumb thoughtfully over the engraving. The locket was not hers. In fact, she had never seen it before. She had a sudden urge to fling it across the room. How dare he? Even after his death, to torment her in this way? Hadn't she put up with enough when he lived? And now she found this little wretched thing lying in wait all these years later.

Anna raised her arm, the locket clenched in her fist. Tears blurred her vision.

Then she took a breath. Peter had been in his grave over six years. She was alive, and he had long ago turned to dust. She inhaled again and unfolded her fingers. The locket gleamed in her palm innocently.

Carefully, Anna placed it in her pocket.

THE NEXT DAY was Sunday.

The Little Battleford church was a small building of gray stone with a leaning steeple. Built sometime in the Middle Ages, it was terribly drafty and cold in the winter months. Anna had spent many a Sunday hoping the homily would end before the hot brick brought from home lost its heat and her toes froze completely.

There was a sudden hush when the Wren women entered the church. Several swiftly averted eyes confirmed Anna's suspicion that she was the topic of discussion, but Anna greeted her neighbors without any indication that she knew she was the center of attention. Rebecca waved from a front pew. She sat beside her husband, James, a big blond man with a rather stout middle. Mother Wren and Anna scrunched in beside them on the bench.

"You certainly have been leading an exciting life lately," Rebecca whispered.

"Really?" Anna busied herself with her gloves and bible.

"Mmm-hmm," Rebecca murmured. "I had no idea you were considering the world's oldest profession."

That got Anna's attention. "What?"

"They haven't actually accused you of it yet, but some are coming close." Rebecca smiled at the lady behind them who had leaned forward.

The woman drew back sharply and sniffed.

Her friend continued, "The town gossips haven't had this much fun since the miller's wife had her baby ten months after he died."

The vicar entered and the congregation quieted as the service began. Predictably, the homily was on the sins of Jezebel, although poor Vicar Jones did not look like he enjoyed delivering it. Anna had only to glance at the ramrod-straight back of Mrs. Jones sitting in the front pew to guess who had decided on the subject matter. At last the service came to a dreary close, and they stood to exit the church.

"Don't know why they left her palms and feet," James said as the congregation began rising.

Rebecca looked up at her husband with fond exasperation. "What are you blathering about, darling?"

"Jezebel," James muttered. "Dogs didn't eat her palms and the soles of her feet. Why? Hounds not usually that particular about their victuals, in my experience."

Rebecca rolled her eyes and patted her husband's arm. "Don't worry about it, darling. Perhaps they had different dogs back then."

James didn't look very satisfied with this explanation, but he responded to his wife's gentle nudge toward the door. Anna was touched to note that Mother Wren and Rebecca arranged themselves on either side of her with James guarding her rear.

As it turned out, however, she did not need such a loyal barricade. For while she received several censorious looks and one cut direct, not all the ladies of Little Battleford were disapproving. In fact, many of the younger ladies were so envious of Anna's new position as secretary to Lord Swartingham that it seemed to transcend her problematic championship of a prostitute in their eyes.

Anna was almost through the gauntlet of villagers outside the church and was beginning to relax when she heard an overly sweet voice at her shoulder. "Mrs. Wren, I do want you to know how very brave I think you are."

Felicity Clearwater carelessly held her small cape in one hand, the better to show off her fashionable frock. Orange and blue nosegays tumbled over a background of primrose yellow. The skirt parted in front to reveal a blue brocade underskirt, and the whole concoction draped over wide panniers.

For a moment, Anna thought wistfully of how nice it would be to wear a gown as fine as Felicity's; then Mother Wren bridled beside her. "Anna had not a thought for herself when she brought that poor woman home."

Felicity's eyes widened. "Oh, obviously. Why, to endure the displeasure of the entire village, not to mention the scolding from the pulpit she just received, Anna must not have had a thought at all."

"I don't think I shall take the lessons of Jezebel too seriously," Anna said lightly. "After all, they might apply to other women in this village, too."

For some reason, this rather weak rejoinder made the other woman stiffen. "I wouldn't know anything about that." Felicity's fingers ran blindly across her hair like spiders. "Unlike you, no one could fault me for the company I keep." Smiling tightly, Felicity swept off before Anna could think of a suitable riposte.

"Cat." Rebecca's own eyes narrowed rather like a feline.

Back at the cottage, Anna spent the rest of the day darning stockings, a talent that she'd by necessity become expert at. After her own supper, she crept up to Pearl's room and found the woman much better. Anna helped her sit up and eat some porridge thinned with milk. Pearl was quite a pretty woman, if worn looking.

Pearl fidgeted with a lock of her pale hair for several minutes before finally bursting out, "Why'd you take me in, then?"

Anna was startled. "You were lying by the side of the road. I couldn't leave you there."

"You know what kind of a girl I am, don't you?"

"Well—"

"I'm a trollop." Pearl said the last word with a defiant twist to her mouth.

"We thought you might be," Anna replied.

"Well, now you know."

"But I don't see that it makes any difference."

Pearl appeared stunned. Anna took the opportunity to spoon some more gruel into her open mouth.

"Here now. You aren't one of them religious types, are you?" Pearl's eyes narrowed in suspicion.

Anna paused with the spoon in midair. "What?"

Pearl agitatedly twisted the sheet covering her knees. "One of them religious ladies that grab girls like me to reform them. I heard that they feeds them nothing but bread and water and makes them do needlework till their fingers bleed and they repent."

Anna looked at the milky gruel in the bowl. "This isn't bread and water, is it?"

Pearl flushed. "No, ma'am, I suppose it isn't."

"We'll feed you more substantial fare when you are up to it, I assure you."

Pearl still looked uncertain, so Anna added, "You may go any time you like. I sent a letter to your sister. Perhaps she'll arrive soon."

"That's right." Pearl seemed relieved. "I remember giving you her direction."

Anna stood. "Try not to worry; just sleep well."

"Aye." Pearl's brow was still wrinkled.

Anna sighed. "Good night."

"'Night, ma'am."

Anna carried the bowl of gruel and the spoon back down the stairs and rinsed them out. It was quite dark by the time she retired to a small pallet made up in her mother-in-law's room.

She slept dreamlessly and didn't wake until Mother Wren gently shook her shoulder. "Anna. You had better get up, dear, if you're to get to Ravenhill on time."

Only then did it occur to Anna to wonder what the earl would think of her patient.

MONDAY MORNING, ANNA entered the Abbey library warily. She'd walked all the way from her cottage dreading the confrontation with Lord Swartingham, hoping against hope that he'd be more reasonable than the doctor had. However, the earl seemed just as usual—rumpled and grumpy with his hair and neckcloth askew. He greeted her by growling that he had found an error on one of the pages she had transcribed the day before. Anna breathed a grateful sigh of relief and settled down to work.

After luncheon, however, her luck ran out.

Lord Swartingham had made a short trip into town to consult with the vicar about helping to finance a renovation of the apse. His return was heralded by the front door crashing against the wall.

"MRS. WREN!"

Anna winced at the bellow and the subsequent slamming of the door. The dog by the fire lifted his head.

"Damnation! Where is the woman?"

Anna rolled her eyes. She was in the library where she always could be found. Where did he think she might be?

Heavy-booted feet stomped across the hall; then the earl's tall form darkened the doorway. "What's this I hear about an unsuitable refugee at your home, Mrs. Wren? The doctor was at great pains to tell me of your folly." He stalked over to the rosewood desk and braced his arms in front of her.

Anna lifted her chin and attempted to look down her nose at him, no small feat since he was employing his great height to tower over her. "I found an unfortunate person in need of help, my lord, and, naturally, brought her to my home so that I might nurse her back to health."

He scowled. "An unfortunate bawd, you mean. Are you insane?"

He was far more angry than she had anticipated. "Her name is Pearl."

"Oh, fine." He pushed away from her desk forcefully. "You are on intimate terms with the creature."

"I only wish to point out that she is a woman, not a creature."

"Semantics." The earl waved a dismissive hand. "Have you no care for your reputation?"

"My reputation is hardly the point."

"Hardly the point? *Hardly the point?*" He swung around violently and began pacing the carpet in front of her desk.

The dog laid back his ears and lowered his head, following his master's movements with his eyes.

"I wish you wouldn't parrot my words," Anna muttered. She could feel a flush creeping up her cheeks, and she wished she could control it. She didn't want to appear weak before him.

The earl, at the farther end of his track, seemed not to hear her reply. "Your reputation is the only point. You are supposed to be a respectable woman. A slip like this could paint you blacker than a crow."

Really! Anna straightened at her desk. "Are you questioning my reputation, Lord Swartingham?"

He stopped dead and turned an outraged face toward her. "Don't be a ninny. Of course I'm not questioning your reputation."

"Aren't you?"

"Ha! I—"

But Anna rode over him. "If I am a respectable woman, surely you can trust my good sense." She could feel her own anger rising, a great pressure inside her head threatening to escape. "As a respectable lady, I consider it my duty to help those less fortunate than I."

"Don't use sophistry with me." He pointed a finger at her from across the room. "Your position in the village will be ruined if you continue this course."

"I may come into some criticism"—she folded her arms—"but I hardly think I'll be ruined by an act of Christian charity."

The earl made an inelegant sound. "The Christians in the village will be the first to pillory you."

"I—"

"You are extremely vulnerable. A young, attractive widow—"

"Working for a single man," Anna pointed out sweetly. "Obviously, my virtue is in imminent peril."

"I didn't say that."

"No, but others have."

"That is exactly what I mean," he shouted, apparently under the impression that if he bellowed loud enough, it would make his point. "You cannot associate with this woman!"

This was simply too much. Anna's eyes narrowed. "I cannot associate with her?"

He crossed his arms on his chest. "Exactly—"

"I cannot associate with her?" she repeated over him, this time more loudly.

Lord Swartingham looked wary at her tone. As well he should.

"What of all the men who made her what she is by *associating* with her?" she asked. "No one worries about the reputation of the men who patronize whores."

"I can't believe you would speak of such things," he sputtered in outrage.

The pressure in Anna's head was gone, replaced by a rush of giddy freedom. "Well, I do speak of such things. And I know men do more than speak of them. Why, a man could visit a harlot regularly—every day of the week, even—and still be perfectly respectable. Whilst the poor girl who has engaged in the very same act as he is deemed soiled goods."

The earl seemed to have lost the power of speech. He produced a series of snorts.

Anna couldn't stop the river of words pouring from her mouth. "And I suspect it's not only the lower classes who patronize such women. I believe men and, indeed, *gentlemen* of quality frequent houses of ill repute." Anna's lips trembled uncontrollably. "Indeed, it seems hypocritical for a man to use a whore but not help one when she is in need." She stopped and blinked rapidly. She would not cry.

The snorts coalesced into a great roar. *"My God, woman!"*

"I think I shall go home now," Anna managed to say just before she ran from the room.

Oh, Lord, what had she done? She'd lost her temper with a man and argued with her employer. And in the process, no doubt, she had destroyed any chance of continuing her work as secretary to the earl.

Chapter Six

The people of the castle danced and shouted with joy.
Their enemy had been defeated, and they no longer
had anything to fear. But in the midst of their
celebration, the raven flew back and landed before
the duke. "I have done as I said and destroyed
the prince. Give me now my price."
But which daughter would be his wife? The eldest
cried that she would not waste her beauty on a nasty
bird. The second said now that the evil prince's
army was defeated, why fulfill the bargain? Only
the youngest, Aurea, agreed to uphold her father's
honor. That very night, in what was the strangest
ceremony any had witnessed, Aurea was wed to the
raven. And as soon as she was pronounced his wife,
the raven bade her climb on his back and he flew
away with his bride clinging atop him. . . .
—from *The Raven Prince*

Edward stared after Anna in baffled rage. What had just
happened? When had he lost control of the conversation?
He turned and snatched two china figurines and a

snuffbox from the mantelpiece and pelted them at the wall in rapid succession. Each exploded on impact, but it didn't help. What had gotten into the woman? He had merely pointed out—firmly, to be sure—how unsuitable it was for her to harbor such a person in her own home, and somehow it had blown up in his face.

What the hell had happened?

He strode into the hall where a startled-looking footman was staring out the front door.

"Don't just stand there, man." The footman jumped and spun at Edward's growl. "Run and tell John Coachman to take the carriage after Mrs. Wren. Silly woman'll probably walk all the way back to the village just to aggravate me."

"My lord." The footman bowed and scurried away.

Edward thrust both hands into his hair and pulled hard enough that he felt the hair come undone from his queue. *Women!* Beside him, the dog whined.

Hopple peered around the corner like a mouse popping out of its hole to see if the storm was past. He cleared his throat. "Females are quite unreasonable sometimes, are they not, my lord?"

"Oh, shut up, Hopple." Edward stomped out of the hall.

THE BIRDS HAD just begun their cheerful cacophony the next morning when the knocking started on the cottage's front door. At first Anna thought the noise part of a hazy dream, but then her eyes opened blearily and the dream dissipated.

The banging, unfortunately, did not.

Anna crawled out of her pallet and found her sky-blue wrapper. Bundling it about her, she stumbled down the cold stairs barefoot, yawning so widely her jaw creaked. The caller had by this time worked himself into a frenzy. Whoever it was had very little patience. In point of fact, the only person she knew who had such a temper was . . . "Lord Swartingham!"

He had one muscular arm braced against the lintel above her head, the other one raised in preparation for another blow to the door. Hastily he lowered his fisted hand. The dog by his side stood and wagged his tail.

"Mrs. Wren." He glowered at her. "Haven't you yet dressed?"

Anna looked down at her wrinkled wrapper and bare toes. "Evidently not, my lord."

The dog pushed past the earl's legs and shoved his muzzle into her hand.

"Why not?" he asked.

"Because it's too early to do so?" The dog leaned against Anna as she petted him.

Lord Swartingham scowled at the oblivious hound. "You mug," he said.

"I beg your pardon!"

The earl turned his scowl on her. "Not you, the dog."

"Who is it, Anna?" Mother Wren stood on the stairs, peering anxiously down. Fanny hovered in the hall.

"It's the Earl of Swartingham, Mother," Anna said as if it were usual for peers to come calling before breakfast. She turned back to him and said more formally, "May I present my mother-in-law, Mrs. Wren. Mother, this is his lordship, Edward de Raaf, the Earl of Swartingham."

Mother Wren, in a frothy pink wrapper, bobbed a perilous curtsy on the stairs. "How do you do?"

"A pleasure, I'm sure, ma'am," the man at the door muttered.

"Has he broken his fast yet?" Mother Wren asked Anna.

"I don't know." Anna swiveled to Lord Swartingham, whose scarred cheeks were reddening. "Have you broken your fast yet?"

"I . . ." He seemed uncharacteristically at a loss for words. He frowned harder.

"Ask him in, Anna, do," Mother Wren prompted.

"Won't you please join us for breakfast, my lord?" Anna inquired sweetly.

The earl nodded. Still frowning, he ducked his head to clear the lintel and stepped inside the cottage.

The elder Mrs. Wren swept down the staircase, fuchsia ribbons fluttering. "I am so glad to meet you, my lord. Fanny, hurry and put the kettle on."

Fanny squealed and dashed into the kitchen. Mother Wren ushered their guest into the tiny sitting room, and Anna noticed it seemed to shrink in size as he entered it. He sat down gingerly on the only armchair while the ladies took the settee. The dog happily made a circuit of the room, poking his nose into corners until the earl growled at him to sit down.

Mother Wren smiled brightly. "Anna must have been mistaken when she said you'd sacked her."

"What?" He gripped the arms of his chair.

"She was under the impression that you would no longer have need of a secretary."

"Mother," Anna whispered.

"That is what you said, dear."

The earl's eyes were intent on Anna. "She was mistaken. She is still my secretary."

"Oh, how nice!" Mother Wren positively beamed. "She was quite upset last night when she thought she was no longer employed."

"Mother—"

The older woman leaned forward confidentially as if Anna had disappeared from the room. "Why, her eyes were quite red when she came in from the carriage. I think she may have been weeping."

"*Mother!*"

Mrs. Wren turned an innocent gaze on her daughter-in-law. "Well, they were, dear."

"Were they, indeed?" the earl murmured. His own ebony eyes gleamed.

Fortunately, Fanny saved her from making a reply by entering with the breakfast tray. Anna noted with relief that the girl had thought to make coddled eggs and to toast some bread to go with their usual porridge. She'd even found a bit of ham. Anna sent an approving nod to the little maid, who grinned back cheekily.

After the earl had partaken of a truly amazing quantity of coddled eggs—what luck that Fanny had gone to market only yesterday—he rose and thanked Mother Wren for the breakfast. Mother Wren smiled flirtatiously at him, and Anna wondered how long it would be before the whole village heard that they had entertained the Earl of Swartingham in their wrappers.

"Can you dress for riding, Mrs. Wren?" the earl asked Anna. "I have my gelding and Daisy waiting outside."

"Of course, my lord." Anna excused herself and went to her room to change.

A few minutes later, she ran back down the stairs and found the earl waiting for her in the front garden. He was contemplating the wet earth to the side of her door where blue grape hyacinth and yellow daffodils were cheerfully blooming. He looked up when she came out of the house, and for an instant, there was an expression in his eyes that made her catch her breath. She glanced down to pull on her gloves and felt her cheeks heat.

"About time," he said. "We're later than I had planned."

Anna ignored his curtness and stood by the mare, waiting for his help to mount. The earl advanced and wrapped his big hands around her waist before throwing her up into the saddle. He stood below her for a moment, the wind teasing a lock of his dark hair, and searched her face. She stared back, all thought having fled from her mind. Then he turned to his own horse and mounted.

The day was bright. Anna didn't remember hearing rain during the night, but the evidence of it lay everywhere. Puddles stood in the lane, and the trees and fences they passed still dripped. The earl walked the horses out of the village and into the countryside.

"Where are we going?" she asked.

"Mr. Durbin's sheep have begun to lamb, and I wanted to see how the ewes are doing." He cleared his throat. "I suppose I should have told you about today's outing earlier."

Anna kept her eyes straight ahead and made a noncommittal sound.

He coughed. "I might've, had you not left so precipitously yesterday afternoon."

She arched a brow but did not reply.

There was a lengthy lull broken only by the dog's eager yelp as he flushed a rabbit from the hedge along the lane.

Then the earl tried again. "I've heard some people say my temper is rather . . ." He paused, apparently searching for a word.

Anna helped him. "Savage?"

He squinted at her.

"Ferocious?"

He frowned and opened his mouth.

She was quicker. "Barbaric?"

He cut her off before she could add to her list. "Yes, well, let us simply say that it intimidates some people." He hesitated. "I wouldn't want to intimidate you, Mrs. Wren."

"You don't."

He looked at her swiftly. He didn't say anymore, but his expression lightened. In another minute, he had kicked the bay into a gallop along the muddy lane, throwing up great clumps of earth. The dog gave chase with his tongue hanging from the side of his mouth.

Anna smiled for no reason and lifted her face to the soft morning breeze.

They continued down the lane until they came to a pasture bordered by a stream. The earl leaned down to unlatch the gate, and they rode in. As they neared the far corner, Anna saw that there were five men gathered close to the stream with a number of shepherd dogs milling about.

One of the men, an older fellow with grizzled hair, looked up at their approach. "Milord! Now, here's a right mess, then."

"Durbin." The earl nodded to the farmer and dismounted. He walked over to help Anna dismount. "What's the problem?" he asked over his shoulder.

"Ewes in th' stream." Durbin spat to the side. "Silly drabs. Must've followed each other down th' bank and now can't come up it. Three of them heavy with lamb, too."

"Ah." The earl approached the stream, and Anna followed. She could see now the five ewes caught in the swollen stream. The poor animals were tangled in the debris by an eddy. The bank was almost four feet deep at that particular point and was slippery with mud.

Lord Swartingham shook his head. "There's no help for it but to use brute force."

"Just what I was thinking meself." The farmer nodded approvingly at having his own idea confirmed.

Two men, along with the earl, lay flat on the stream's bank and reached down to pull on the sheep's wool. This, with the added incentive of the shepherd dogs harrying them from behind, convinced four of the ewes to scramble up the slimy bank. They tottered off, bleating their confusion at being so ill-used. The fifth ewe, however, was out of reach of the men on the bank. She was either too trapped or too stupid to climb from the stream on her own. Prostrate on her side, she bleated forlornly in the water.

"Gor. That one's good and stuck." Farmer Durbin sighed, and wiped his sweaty brow with the hem of his smock.

"Whyn't we send old Bess down to plague her, Da?" The farmer's eldest son fondled the ears of a black and white dog.

"Nay, lad. I don't want to lose Bess in the water. 'Tis over her head there. One of us'll have to go in after the daft beast."

"I'll do it, Durbin." The earl stepped away and took off his coat. He threw it to Anna, who barely caught it before it hit the ground. His waistcoat followed, and then he was pulling his fine lawn shirt over his head. He sat on the bank to wrestle off his jackboots.

Anna tried not to stare. She didn't often see a half-naked man. Actually, she couldn't remember ever seeing a man without a shirt in public. There were indented pox scars scattered across his torso, but she was more interested in other things. Her imagination had been correct. He did indeed have hair upon his chest. Quite a bit, in fact. Black swirls stretched across his breast and funneled down to his hard stomach. The hair narrowed to a thin ribbon that crossed his flat navel and then disappeared into his breeches.

The earl stood in his stockinged feet and half climbed, half slid down the steep bank and into the water. The muddy stream swirled around his hips as he waded to the side of the frightened ewe. He bent over the animal, working at the branches holding her. His wide shoulders gleamed with sweat and streaks of muck.

A shout rose from the watching men. The ewe was free, but in her haste to escape the stream, she had shouldered the earl, who went down in a geyser of muddy water. Anna gasped and started forward. Lord Swartingham's dog raced back and forth along the bank, barking excitedly. The earl emerged from the stream like a ragged Poseidon, water running in sheets off his torso. He was grinning even though his hair was plastered to his skull, the ribbon holding it having been lost in the stream.

The dog was still barking his disapproval of the whole proceeding. Meanwhile, the farmer and his relatives staggered about, gasping with laughter and slapping their knees. They were all but rolling on the ground in their hilarity. Anna sighed. Apparently an aristocrat getting a dunking was the most amusing thing the men had ever seen. Males were very perplexing at times.

"Oy! Milord! Do you always have trouble holding your wenches?" one of the men shouted.

"Nay, lad, she just didn't like the feel of his hand on her arse." The farmer made a graphic gesture that sent the men off again.

The earl laughed, but nodded toward Anna. Thus reminded of her presence, the men stopped their jests, although they continued to snigger. The earl lifted both hands to slick the water from his face.

Anna caught her breath at the sight. With his hands at the back of his head, squeezing the water from his hair, his muscles stood out in sharp relief. The sun glinted off his flexed arms and chest, and his black underarm hair curled damply. Rivulets of grimy water, mixed with blood from the ewe, ran down his chest and arms. His low-slung breeches clung to his hips and thighs, delineating the bulge of his manhood. He looked quite pagan.

Anna shivered.

The earl waded to shore and climbed the bank with a helping hand from the farmer's sons. Anna gave herself a shake and hurried over with his clothes.

He used the fine lawn shirt as a towel and then threw on his coat over his bare chest. "Well, Durbin, I hope you will call me the next time you are unable to handle a female."

"Aye, milord." The farmer slapped Lord Swartingham on the back. "My thanks for helping us out. Don't remember when I've seen a grander splash."

That set the men off again, and it was some little while before the earl and Anna could leave. By the time they were mounted, the earl's body was shaking with cold, but he showed no sign of hurry.

"You'll catch your death of cold, my lord," Anna said. "Please ride on to the Abbey ahead of me. You can go much faster without Daisy and me to slow you down."

"I'm quite all right, Mrs. Wren," he replied through teeth clenched to keep them from chattering. "Besides, I wouldn't want to be deprived of your dulcet company for even a moment."

Anna glared at him for she knew he was being sarcastic. "You don't have to prove how manly you are by catching the ague."

"So you consider me manly, Mrs. Wren?" He grinned like a little boy. "I was beginning to think that I battled a stinking sheep for nothing."

Anna tried, but it was impossible to keep her mouth from twitching. "I didn't know landowners helped their tenants so," she said. "Surely it is unusual?"

"Oh, certainly unusual," he replied. "I suppose the majority of my peers sit in London letting their arses widen while their stewards run their estates."

"Then why do you choose to wade into muddy streams after sheep?"

The earl shrugged his damp shoulders. "My father taught me that a good landowner knows his tenants and what they are doing. Then, too, I am more involved because of my agricultural studies." He shrugged again and smiled at her rather ironically. "And I'm fond of wrestling ewes and the like."

Anna returned the smile. "Did your father wrestle ewes as well?"

There was a silence, and she feared for a moment that she'd asked too personal a question.

"No, I don't remember him getting that dirty." Lord Swartingham watched the road ahead. "But he didn't mind wading into a flooded field in spring or overseeing the harvest in fall. And he always took me with him to mind the people and the land."

"He must've been a wonderful father," she murmured. *To have raised such a wonderful son.*

"Yes. If I'm only half as good a father to my own children, I'll be content." He looked curiously at her. "You had no children from your marriage?"

Anna glanced down at her hands. They were clenched in fists over the reins. "No. We were married for four years, but it was not God's will to grace us with children."

"I'm sorry." There seemed to be honest regret in the earl's eyes.

"As am I, my lord." *Every day.*

They were silent then until Ravenhill Abbey came into sight.

WHEN ANNA REACHED home that evening, Pearl was sitting up in bed and eating soup with Fanny's help. She was still thin, but her hair had been pulled back from her temples with a bit of ribbon, and she wore one of the little maid's old dresses. Anna took over the duty and sent Fanny down to finish making the supper.

"I forgot to thank you, ma'am," Pearl said shyly.

"It's quite all right." Anna smiled. "I only hope you feel better soon."

The other woman sighed. "Oh, I just need some rest, mostly."

"Are you from around here, or were you traveling through when you became ill?" Anna proffered a bit of beef.

Pearl chewed slowly and swallowed. "No, ma'am. I was trying to get back to London where I live. A gent brought me out here in a fine carriage promising to set me up proper like."

Anna raised her brows.

"I thought he was going to put me up in a little cottage." Pearl smoothed the sheet under her fingers. "I'm getting older, you know. I can't be working too much longer."

Anna remained silent.

"But it were just a con," Pearl said. "He only wanted me for a party with some friends."

Anna cast about for something to say. "I'm sorry it wasn't a permanent position."

"Yeah. And that weren't even the worst of it. He expected me to entertain him and his two friends." Pearl's mouth twisted down.

Two friends? "You mean you were to, um, entertain three gentlemen at once?" Anna asked faintly.

Pearl pursed her lips and nodded. "Yeah. All together or one after another." She must have seen Anna's shock. "Some of them fine gentlemen likes to do it together, sort of showing off to each other. But the girl gets hurt lots of times."

Good Lord. Anna stared at Pearl, appalled.

"But it don't really matter," Pearl continued. "I walked out."

Anna could only manage a nod.

"Then I started feeling bad on the coach back. I must've dozed off, 'cause next thing I knew, my purse was gone and I was having to try to walk since the coach wouldn't let mc back on without my money." Pearl shook her head. "I would've been dead for sure if you hadn't found me when you did."

Anna looked down at her palms. "May I ask you a question, Pearl?"

"Sure. Go ahead." The other woman folded her hands at her waist and nodded. "Ask me anything you want."

"Have you heard of an establishment called Aphrodite's Grotto?"

Pearl cocked her head back against the pillow and looked at Anna curiously. "I didn't think a lady like you knew about such places, ma'am."

Anna avoided Pearl's gaze. "I heard it mentioned by some gentlemen. I don't think they knew I'd overheard."

"I don't guess not," Pearl agreed. "Why, Aphrodite's Grotto is a real high-priced bawdy house. The girls who work there have it soft, that's for sure. 'Course, I've heard that some high-class ladies go there with their faces hidden by a mask to pretend to be what I am."

Anna's eyes widened. "You mean . . . ?"

"They take whatever gent that catches their fancy in the room below and spends the night with them." Pearl nodded matter-of-factly. "Or however long they want. Some even take a room and instruct the madam to send up a man of a certain description. Maybe a short, blond fellow or a tall, red-headed one."

"It sounds a bit like picking a horse." Anna wrinkled her nose.

Pearl gave the first smile Anna had seen. "That's clever, ma'am. Like picking a stud." She laughed. "I wouldn't mind being the one that does the choosing for once, instead of the gents always getting to do the deciding."

Anna smiled a little uncomfortably at this reminder of the realities of Pearl's profession. "But why would a gentleman submit to such an arrangement?"

"The gents like it because they know they're getting to spend the night with a real lady." The other woman shrugged. "If you can call her a lady."

Anna blinked and then shook herself. "I'm keeping you from your rest. I'd better go see about my own supper."

"All right, then." Pearl yawned. "Thank you again."

All through supper that evening, Anna was distracted. Pearl's comment that it would be nice to do the choosing for once kept running through her head. She poked rather absently at her meat pie. It was true, even on her level of society, that the men got to do most of the choosing. A young lady waited for a gentleman to come calling, while the gentleman was able to decide which young ladies to court. Once married, a respectable woman waited dutifully for her husband in the marriage bed. The man made the overtures of marital relations. Or not, as the case may be. At least it had been so in Anna's marriage. She'd certainly never let Peter know she might have needs of her own or that she might not be satisfied with what occurred in bed.

Later that night, as Anna got ready for sleep, she couldn't stop imagining Lord Swartingham in Aphrodite's Grotto as Pearl had described it. The earl being sighted and chosen by some daring woman of the aristocracy. The earl spending the night in a masked lady's arms. The thoughts made her chest hurt even as she fell asleep.

And then she was in Aphrodite's Grotto.

She wore a mask and searched for the earl. Men of every description, old, young, fair, and ugly, hundreds of men, filled a hall to overflowing. Frantically, she pushed through the mass, hunting for a singular pair of black, gleaming eyes, becoming more desperate the longer her search took. Finally, she saw him across the room, and she started running toward him. But as is the way with such nightmares, the faster she tried to run, the slower she went. Each step seemed to take an eternity. As she struggled, she saw another masked woman beckon to him. Without ever having seen her, he turned away and followed the other woman from the room.

Anna awoke in the dark, her heart pounding and her skin chilled. She lay absolutely still, remembering the dream and listening to her own roughened breathing.

It was some time before she realized she was weeping.

Chapter Seven

*The huge raven flew with his new wife on his back for
two days and two nights until on the third day, they
came to fields golden with ripened grain.
"Who owns these fields?" Aurea asked, looking
down from her perch.
"Your husband," the raven replied.
They came to an endless meadow filled with fat
cattle, their hides shining in the sun.
"Who owns these cattle?" Aurea asked.
"Your husband," the raven replied.
Then a vast emerald forest spread below, rolling
over hills as far as the eye could see.
"Who owns this forest?" Aurea asked.
"Your husband!" the raven cawed. . . .*
—from *The Raven Prince*

Anna walked to Ravenhill the next morning feeling tired
and low after a restless night. She paused for a moment to
admire the sea of bluebells blooming under the trees that
lined the drive. The azure dots sparkled in the sunlight,
like newly minted coins. Usually the sight of any flower

brought a lightness to her heart, but today they did not. She sighed and continued her journey until she rounded a curve and stopped short. Lord Swartingham, striding briskly in his habitual mud-spattered boots, was coming from the stables and hadn't caught sight of her yet.

He gave a terrific bellow. "DOG!"

For the first time that day, Anna smiled. Evidently the earl couldn't find the ever-present canine and was reduced to roaring its common name.

She strolled toward him. "I don't see why he should respond to that."

Lord Swartingham swung around at the sound of her voice. "I believe that I gave the job of naming the mongrel to you, Mrs. Wren."

Anna opened her eyes wide. "I did offer three different options, my lord."

"And all of them were out of the question, as you well know." He smiled evilly. "I think I've given you quite enough time to come up with a name. You shall produce one now."

She was amused by his obvious intention to put her on the spot. "Stripe?"

"Too juvenile."

"Tiberius?"

"Too imperial."

"Othello?"

"Too murderous." Lord Swartingham folded his arms across his chest. "Come, come, Mrs. Wren. A woman of your wit can do better than this."

"How about 'Jock,' then?"

"That won't do."

"Why not?" Anna retorted saucily. "I like the name Jock."

"Jock." The earl seemed to roll the name on his tongue.

"I wager the dog will come if I call him by that name."

"Ha." He stared down his nose in the superior manner of males the world over when dealing with silly females. "You are welcome to try."

"Very well, I shall." She tilted her chin. "And if he comes, you must show me around the Abbey's gardens."

Lord Swartingham raised his eyebrows. "And if he doesn't come?"

"I don't know." She hadn't thought that far ahead. "Name your prize."

He pursed his lips and contemplated the ground at his feet. "I believe it is traditional in wagers between a woman and a man for the gentleman to ask for a favor from the lady."

Anna drew in a breath and then had trouble releasing it.

The earl's black eyes glittered at her from beneath his brows. "Perhaps a kiss?"

Oh, dear. Possibly she had been precipitous. Anna let out her breath in a puff and straightened her shoulders. "Very well."

He waved a languid hand. "Proceed."

Anna cleared her throat. "Jock!"

Nothing.

"*Jock!*"

Lord Swartingham began to smirk.

Anna drew a deep breath and let loose a most unlady-like shriek. "JOCK!"

They both listened for the dog. Nothing.

The earl slowly pivoted to face her, the crunching of his boots in the gravel drive loud in the stillness. They stood only a few feet distant. He took a step, his beautiful, heavy-lidded eyes intent on her face.

Anna could feel the blood pounding in her chest. She licked her lips.

His gaze dropped to her mouth, and his nostrils flared. He took another step, and they were now only a foot apart. As if in a dream, she saw his hands rise and grip her arms, felt the pressure of his big fingers through her mantle and gown.

Anna began to tremble.

He bent his dark head toward hers, and his warm breath caressed her lips. She closed her eyes.

And heard the dog clatter into the yard.

Anna opened her eyes. Lord Swartingham was frozen. Slowly, he turned his head, still only inches from hers, to stare at the canine. The dog grinned back, tongue hanging from his mouth, panting.

"Shit," the earl breathed.

Quite, Anna thought.

He let go of her suddenly, stepped away, and turned his back. He ran both hands through his hair and shook his shoulders. She heard him take a deep breath, but his voice was still husky when he spoke. "It appears you have won the wager."

"Yes, my lord." She hoped she sounded sufficiently nonchalant, as if she was used to having gentlemen nearly kiss her in their driveways. As if she wasn't having trouble catching her breath. As if she didn't desperately wish the dog had stayed far, far away.

"I'll be pleased to show you the gardens," the earl muttered, "such as they are, after luncheon. Perhaps you can work in the library until then?"

"Won't you be coming to the library as well?" She tried to conceal her disappointment.

He still hadn't turned to face her. "I find that there are matters that need my attention around the estate."

"Of course," Anna murmured.

He finally looked at her. She noticed his eyes were still heavy lidded, and she rather fancied he glanced at her bosom. "I'll see you at luncheon."

She nodded, and the earl snapped his fingers at the dog. As he passed her, she thought she heard him mutter something to the beast. It sounded more like *idiot* than *Jock.*

JESUS GOD, WHAT was I thinking? Edward strode angrily around the Abbey.

He'd deliberately maneuvered Mrs. Wren into an untenable position. There was no way she could have denied his crude advances. As if a woman of her fine sensibilities would have welcomed a kiss from a pox-scarred man such as he. But he hadn't thought of his scars when he drew her into his arms. He hadn't thought of anything. He'd acted on pure instinct: the lust to touch that beautiful, erotic mouth. His cock had been full, achingly erect, in seconds at the mere thought. He'd nearly been unable to let go of Mrs. Wren when the dog had showed up, and then he'd been forced to turn his back to keep her from getting an eyeful. He still hadn't relaxed.

"And what were you doing, Jock?" Edward growled down at the happily oblivious mastiff. "Your timing needs work, lad, if you want to continue devouring the bounty of the Abbey's kitchen."

Jock grinned an adoring doggy grin up at him. One ear was flopped inside out, and Edward straightened it absently. "A minute earlier or a minute later—preferably later—would've been a better moment to come gamboling up."

He sighed. He couldn't let this rampant lust continue. He liked the woman, for God's sake. She was witty and unafraid of his temper. She asked questions about his agricultural studies. She rode about his fields through mud and muck without a word of complaint. She even seemed to enjoy their jaunts. And sometimes when she looked at him, her head tilted to the side and all her attention focused solely on him, there was something that seemed to turn in his chest.

He frowned and kicked a pebble on the path.

It was unfair and dishonorable to subject Mrs. Wren to his brutish advances. He shouldn't be combating thoughts of her soft breasts, wondering if she had pale pink nipples or if they were a deeper rose color. Contemplating whether her nipples would pucker up immediately when he drew his thumb across them or wait coyly for the feel of his tongue.

Hell.

He half laughed, half groaned. His cock was once again at stand and pulsing with blood at just the thought of her. His body hadn't been this out of control since he'd been a lad with a newly deepened voice.

He kicked another pebble and stopped on the path, hands on hips, to tip his head back to the sky.

It was no use. Edward rolled his head back against his shoulders, trying to ease the tension. He would have to make a trip to London soon to spend a night or even two at Aphrodite's Grotto. Perhaps after that he could be in his secretary's presence without lustful thoughts taking over his mind.

He ground the pebble he had been kicking into the mud as he pivoted and started back to the stables. He was approaching the idea of going to London as a chore. He no longer anticipated spending the night in a demimondaine's bed. Instead, he felt weary. Weary and yearning for a woman he could not have.

Later that afternoon, Anna was reading *The Raven Prince* when the banging started. She'd only gotten as far as the third page, which described a magical battle between an evil prince and an enormous raven. It was an odd little fairy tale, but it was engrossing, and it took her a minute to recognize the sound of the Abbey's front door knocker. She'd never heard it before. Most of the callers to the Abbey came by way of the servants' entrance.

She slipped the book back into her desk and picked up a quill as she listened to the sound of rapid footsteps, probably the footman, in the hall answering the door. A vague murmur of voices, one of them feminine, then a lady's heels tapped toward the library. The footman threw open the door, and Felicity Clearwater strolled in.

Anna stood. "Can I help you?"

"Oh, don't get up. I don't want to disturb your duties." Felicity flicked a hand in her direction as she inspected the rickety iron ladder in the corner. "I've just come to deliver an invitation for Lord Swartingham to my spring soiree." She stroked a gloved fingertip over an iron rail and wrinkled her nose at the rust-colored dust that came away.

"He isn't in at the moment," Anna said.

"No? Then I must entrust it with you." Felicity sauntered to the desk and produced a heavily embossed envelope from a pocket. "You will give this . . ." She was holding out the envelope, but her words trailed away as she looked at Anna.

"Yes?" Anna self-consciously brushed a hand over her hair. Did she have a smudge on her face? Something caught between her teeth? Felicity looked as if she'd solidified into marble. Surely dirt couldn't justify that much shock.

The embossed velum in Felicity's hand trembled and fell to the desk. She glanced away, and the moment was gone.

Anna blinked. Perhaps she'd imagined the look.

"Do make sure Lord Swartingham receives my invitation, won't you?" Felicity was saying. "I'm certain he won't want to miss the most important social event in the area." She aimed a brittle smile in Anna's direction and walked out the door.

Anna absently dropped her hand to her throat and felt cool metal under her palm. She wrinkled her brow as she remembered. This morning as she'd dressed, she had thought the fichu about her neck rather plain. She'd rummaged in the tiny box that held her meager stock of jewelry, but her only pin was too big. Then her fingers had touched the locket she'd found in Peter's case. This time she'd experienced only a twinge when she saw the locket. Perhaps it was losing the power to hurt her, and she'd thought, *Well, why not?* and defiantly pinned the locket at her neck.

Anna fingered the trinket at her throat. It was cold and hard under her hand, and she wished that she'd not given in to her morning impulse.

DAMN! DAMN! DAMN! Felicity stared sightlessly from her carriage as it bumped away from Ravenhill Abbey. She'd not endured eleven years of groping and poking by a man old enough to be her grandfather to have it all fall apart now.

One would think that Reginald Clearwater's quest for children had been satisfied with the four grown sons his first two wives had borne him, not to mention the six daughters. After all, Felicity's predecessor had died giving birth to his youngest male offspring. But no, Reginald was obsessed with his own potency and the task of getting children on his wife. There were times during his twice-weekly marital visits when she wondered if it were really worth all this trouble. The man had run through three wives and still didn't have any skill in the bedchamber.

Felicity snorted.

But despite its downside, she absolutely adored being the squire's wife. Clearwater Hall was the largest house in the county, excepting, of course, Ravenhill Abbey. She had a generous clothing allowance and her own carriage.

She looked forward to lovely—and very expensive—jewelry every birthday. And the local shopkeepers nearly genuflected when she called. All in all, it was a life well worth preserving.

Which brought her back to the problem of Anna Wren.

Felicity touched her hair, skimming over it, checking for strands out of place. How long had Anna known? Impossible that the locket had been an accident. Coincidences of that magnitude just did not happen, which meant the wretched woman was taunting her after all this time. The letter that Felicity'd written to Peter had been penned in the heat of lust and was quite, quite damning. She'd placed it in the locket he'd given her and handed it to him, never thinking he would keep the silly thing. And then he'd died, and she'd been on tenterhooks, waiting for Anna to come calling with the evidence. When the locket had not turned up in the first couple of years, she'd thought Peter had either sold it or buried it—along with the letter inside—before he'd died.

Men! What useless creatures they were—aside from the obvious.

Felicity drummed her fingers on the windowsill. The only reasons for Anna to show her the locket now were either revenge or blackmail. She grimaced and ran her tongue along her front teeth, feeling their edges. Dainty, smooth, and sharp. Very sharp. If little Anna Wren thought she could frighten Felicity Clearwater, she was about to find out just how very mistaken she was.

"I BELIEVE I OWE you a forfeit, Mrs. Wren," the earl announced as he stalked into the library later that afternoon.

The sun streaming in the windows highlighted silver threads in Lord Swartingham's hair. His boots were muddy again.

Anna laid down her quill and held out her hand to Jock, who had accompanied his master into the room. "I was beginning to think you'd forgotten this morning's debt, my lord."

He arched an arrogant brow. "Are you impugning my honor?"

"If I were, would you call me out?"

He made an inelegant sound. "No. You'd probably win if I did. I'm not a particularly good shot, and my sword work needs practice."

Anna raised her chin loftily. "Then perhaps you should be careful what you say to me."

One corner of Lord Swartingham's mouth curled up. "Are you coming to the garden, or do you wish to continue bandying words with me here?"

"I don't see why we cannot do both," she murmured, and gathered her wrap.

She took his arm, and they strolled out of the library. Jock trailed them, ears perked at the prospect of a ramble. The earl led her through the front door and around the corner of the Abbey past the stables. Here the cobblestones turned to mown grass. They passed a low hedge enclosing a kitchen garden to the side of the servants' entrance. Someone had already started leeks. Delicate green wisps lined a trench that would later be filled in as the plants grew. Beyond the kitchen garden was a sloped lawn at the bottom of which was a larger, walled garden. They picked their way down the slope on a gray slate walk. As they neared, Anna saw that ivy nearly obscured the old red bricks of the wall. A wooden door was hidden in the wall, overhung with brown vines.

Lord Swartingham took hold of the door's rusty iron handle and pulled. The door squeaked and opened an inch, then stopped. He muttered something and glanced at her.

She smiled encouragingly.

He wrapped both hands around the handle and braced his feet before yanking mightily. Nothing happened for a second, and then the door gave up with a groan. Jock shot through the opening into the garden. The earl stood aside and gestured her in with a wave of his hand.

She ducked her head to peer inside.

She saw a jungle. The garden appeared to be in the shape of a large rectangle. Or at least that had been its outline at one point. A brick path, barely discernible beneath debris, ran around the inside of the walls. It connected with a central walk in the shape of a cross that divided the garden into four smaller rectangles. The far wall held another door, almost hidden beneath the skeleton of a creeper. Perhaps a second garden or a series of gardens lay beyond.

"My grandmother laid out the original plans for these beds," the earl said from behind her. Somehow they'd gone through the doorway, although Anna didn't remember moving. "And my mother expanded and developed them."

"It must have been very beautiful once." She stepped over a break in the walkway where some of the bricks had heaved out of the ground. Was the tree in the corner a pear?

"Not much left of all her work, is there?" he replied. She could hear him kicking at something. "I suppose it would be best simply to have the walls torn down and the place leveled."

Anna jerked her head around to him. "Oh, no, my lord. You mustn't do that."

He frowned at her protest. "Why not?"

"There's too much here that can be saved."

The earl assessed the overgrown garden and ruined walk with clear skepticism. "I don't see even one thing worth saving."

She shot him an exasperated glance. "Why, look at the espaliered trees on the walls."

He swiveled to where she pointed.

Anna began picking her way to the wall. She stumbled over a rock hidden in the weeds and righted herself only to catch her toe again. Strong arms caught her from behind and lifted her easily. In two long strides, Lord Swartingham was by the wall.

He set her down. "Is this what you want to see?"

"Yes." Anna, breathless, peeked at him sideways.

He stared rather grimly at the espaliered tree.

"Thank you." She turned back to the pathetic tree against the wall and was immediately distracted. "I think it's an apple tree or perhaps a pear. You can see where they're planted all around the garden walls. And this one here is in bud."

The earl dutifully examined the branch indicated. He grunted.

"And really all they need is some good pruning," she chattered on. "You could make your own cider."

"I've never much liked cider."

She lowered her brows at him. "Or you could have Cook make apple jelly."

He arched an eyebrow.

She almost defended the merits of apple jelly, but then she spied a flower hiding in the weeds. "Do you think that's a violet or maybe a periwinkle?"

The flower was a couple of feet from the edge of a bed. Anna bent from the waist to get a closer look, placing one hand on the ground to steady herself.

"Or perhaps a forget-me-not, although usually they bloom in big groups." She carefully plucked the flower. "No, I'm silly. Look at the leaves."

Lord Swartingham was very still behind her.

"I think it may be a type of hyacinth." She straightened and turned to consult him.

"Oh?" The single word came out a baritone guttural.

She blinked at his voice. "Yes, and of course where there's one, there's always more."

"Of what?"

She narrowed her eyes suspiciously. "You haven't been listening to me, have you?"

He shook his head. "No."

He was watching her intently, in such a way that Anna's breath quickened. She could feel her face heat. In the quiet, the breeze playfully blew a thin lock of hair across her mouth. He reached out very slowly and brushed it away with the tips of his fingers. The calluses on his hand rasped against the sensitive skin of her lips, and she closed her eyes in yearning. He carefully tucked the lock back into her coiffure, his hand lingering at her temple.

She felt his breath caress her lips. *Oh, please.*

And then he dropped his hand.

Anna opened her eyes and met his obsidian gaze. She stretched out her own hand to protest—or perhaps touch his face, she wasn't sure, and it didn't matter anyway. He'd already whirled and paced a few steps away from her. She didn't think he had even noticed her own aborted gesture.

He turned his head so that she could see only his face in profile. "I beg your pardon."

"Why?" She tried to smile. "I—"

He made a chopping motion with the blade of his hand. "I will be traveling tomorrow to London. I fear I have some business there that can no longer wait."

Anna squeezed her hands into fists.

"You may continue admiring the garden if you wish. I need to return to my writing." He strode rapidly away, his boots grinding against the broken bricks.

Anna opened her clenched fists and felt the crushed flower slip from her fingers.

She glanced around the ruined garden. It had so many possibilities. Some weeding by the wall over there, some planting in the bed here. No garden was ever truly dead if a proper gardener knew how to nurture it. Why, it only needed a bit of care, a bit of love. . . .

A veil of tears obscured her eyes. She wiped at them irritably with a trembling hand. She'd forgotten her handkerchief inside. The tears overflowed her eyes and rolled to her chin. Bother. She'd have to use her sleeve to mop them. What sort of lady was caught without a handkerchief? A pitiful sort of one, obviously. The sort a gentleman couldn't bring himself to kiss. She scrubbed her face with the inside of her forearm, but the tears kept reappearing. As if she'd believe that nonsense about work in London! She was a mature woman. She knew where the earl meant to do his work. In that nasty brothel.

She caught her breath on a sob. He was going to London to bed another woman.

Chapter Eight

The raven flew with Aurea for another day and night,
and everything she saw in that time belonged to him.
Aurea tried to comprehend such wealth, such power,
but it was beyond understanding. Her own father had
only commanded a small portion of the people and
lands that this bird seemed to own. Finally, on the
fourth evening, she saw a great castle, made entirely
of white marble and gold. The setting sun reflecting
off it was so bright it made her eyes hurt.
"Who owns this castle?" Aurea whispered, and
a nameless dread filled her heart.
The raven turned his huge head and regarded her with
a glinting black eye. "Your husband!" he cackled. . . .
—from *The Raven Prince*

That evening, Anna trudged home alone. After she'd
pulled together her wits in the ruined garden, she'd returned to the library intending to work. She needn't have
bothered. Lord Swartingham hadn't appeared all the rest
of the afternoon, and as she was gathering her things at
the end of the day, a young footman had brought her a

small folded card. It was brief and to the point. His lordship would be leaving very early in the morning, and thus he would not see her before he left. He sent his regrets.

Since the earl wasn't around to protest, Anna walked home instead of taking the carriage, partly in rebellion, partly because she needed time alone to think and compose herself. It wouldn't do to return home with her face long and her eyes red. Not unless she wanted to be quizzed half the night by Mother Wren.

By the time Anna reached the outskirts of town, her feet were aching. She'd become used to the luxury of the carriage. She trudged on and turned into her lane, and there she stopped. A scarlet and black coach with gilt trim stood before her door. The coachman and the two footmen lounging against the vehicle wore matching black livery edged with scarlet piping and yards of gilt braid. Beside the vehicle, a gang of small boys hopped about, interrogating the footmen. Anna couldn't blame them—it looked like minor royalty had come to call on her. She sidled around the carriage and entered her cottage.

Inside, Mother Wren and Pearl were having tea in the sitting room with a third woman whom Anna had never seen before. The woman was quite young, barely in her twenties. Ice-white powdered hair swept up her forehead in a deceptively simple style, setting off strange, light green eyes. She wore a black gown. Black usually indicated mourning, but Anna had never seen a mourning gown quite like this one. A cascade of shining jet-black material flowed around the sitting woman, and the overskirt pulled back to reveal scarlet embroidery on the petticoat below. The vivid stitching repeated on the low, square neckline and triple tiers of lace falling from the half sleeves. She looked as out of place in Anna's little sitting room as a peacock in a hen yard.

Mother Wren looked up brightly at Anna's entrance. "Dear, this is Coral Smythe, Pearl's younger sister. We've just been having a dish of tea." She gestured with her cup, almost sloshing the tea into Pearl's lap in the process. "My daughter-in-law, Anna Wren."

"How do you do, Mrs. Wren?" Coral spoke in a deep, husky voice that sounded like it should be coming from a man instead of an exotic young woman.

"I'm pleased to meet you," Anna murmured as she accepted a cup of tea.

"We must be leaving soon if we're to make London before dawn," Pearl said.

"Are you recovered enough for the journey, sister?" Coral showed little emotion on her face, but she watched Pearl intently.

"Surely you will spend the night with us, Miss Smythe?" Mother Wren asked. "Then Pearl will have a fresh start in the morning."

Coral's lips curved in a meager smile. "I would not wish to inconvenience you, Mrs. Wren."

"Oh, it's not an inconvenience. It's nearly dark out, and I can't think it would be safe for two young ladies to travel right now." Mother Wren nodded toward the window, which was indeed almost black.

"Thank you." Coral inclined her head.

After they had finished the tea, Anna led Coral up to the room Pearl had been using so that the other woman could wash before supper. She brought some linens and fresh water for the basin and was turning to leave when Coral halted her.

"Mrs. Wren, I wish to thank you." Coral watched Anna with fathomless pale green eyes. Her expression did not mirror her words.

"It's nothing, Miss Smythe," Anna replied. "We could hardly have sent you off to the inn."

"Of course you could." Coral's lips twisted in a sardonic grimace. "But that is not what I speak of. I want to thank you for helping Pearl. She has told me how sick she was. Had you not brought her into your home and cared for her, she would have died."

Anna shrugged uncomfortably. "Another person would've been along in a minute and—"

"And they would have left her there," Coral interrupted. "Do not tell me anyone would do the same as you. Anyone did not."

Anna was at a loss for words. Much as she would like to protest Coral's cynical view of humanity, she knew the other woman was right.

"My sister walked the streets to put food in my mouth when we were younger," Coral continued. "We were orphaned when she was barely fifteen, and soon thereafter, she was let go from her position as an underhousemaid in a fashionable house. She could have simply let me go to the poorhouse. Without me, she might have found another respectable job, perhaps married and had a family." Coral's lips tightened. "Instead she entertained men."

Anna winced, trying to imagine such a dismal life. Such a total lack of options.

"I have tried to persuade Pearl to let me support her now." Coral turned her head away. "But you do not want to hear our history. Suffice it to say that she is the only living thing on this earth that I love."

Anna was silent.

"If there is ever anything I can do for you, Mrs. Wren"—Coral's queer eyes bored into her—"you have but to name it."

"Your thanks is enough," Anna finally said. "I was glad to help your sister."

"You do not take my offer seriously, I see. But keep it in mind. Anything within my power I will do for you. Anything at all."

Anna nodded and started out of the room. *Anything at all* . . . She paused on the threshold and turned impulsively, before she had time to reconsider. "Have you heard of an establishment called Aphrodite's Grotto?"

"Yes." Coral's expression became opaque. "Yes, and I know the proprietress, Aphrodite herself. I can get you a night or a week of nights at Aphrodite's Grotto if that is your wish."

She stepped toward Anna.

"I can get you a night with an accomplished male whore or a virginal schoolboy." Coral's eyes widened and seemed to flame. "Famous libertines or ragpickers off the street. One very special man or ten complete strangers. Dark men, red men, yellow men, men you've only dreamed of in the black of night, lonely in your bed, snug under your covers. Whatever you long for. Whatever you desire. Whatever you crave. You have only to ask me."

Anna stared at Coral like a mesmerized mouse before a particularly beautiful snake.

She started to stutter a denial, but Coral waved an indolent hand. "Sleep on it, Mrs. Wren. Sleep on it, and on the morrow give me your reply. Now, if you do not mind, I wish to be alone."

Anna found herself in the hallway outside her own door. She shook her head. Could the devil assume the guise of a woman?

Because temptation had surely been set before her.

She walked slowly down the stairs, Coral's seductive offer lodged in her brain. She tried to shake it off, but to her horror, she found that she simply couldn't. And the more she thought about Aphrodite's Grotto, the more acceptable it became.

During the night, Anna changed her mind about Coral's outrageous offer over and over again. She would wake from hazy, ominous dreams to lie debating, only to drift off again into a world where Lord Swartingham was eternally strolling away and she futilely running after. Toward morning, she gave up the pretense of sleep and lay on her back staring sightlessly at the still-dark ceiling. She clasped her hands beneath her chin like a little girl and prayed to God to let her resist this terrible proposition. A virtuous woman should have no trouble resisting, she was sure. A proper lady would never think of sneaking off to the dens of London to seduce a man who had made it abundantly clear that he was not interested in her.

When Anna opened her eyes again, it was daylight. She got up stiffly and washed her face and throat in the chilly water in the basin, then dressed and stole quietly out the door so as not to awaken her mother-in-law.

She went out to her flower garden. Unlike the earl's garden, hers was small and neat. The crocuses were mostly over now, but some late daffodils remained. She bent to deadhead a daffodil that had stopped blooming. The sight of the tulips in bud momentarily brought peace back to her soul. Then she remembered the earl would be traveling to London today. She squeezed her eyes tight to shut out the thought.

At that moment, she heard a footstep behind her. "Have you made your decision, Mrs. Wren?"

She swiveled and saw a lovely Mephistopheles with pale green eyes. Coral smiled at her.

Anna started to shake her head, but then heard herself say, "I'll accept your offer."

Coral's smile widened into a perfect, mirthless curve. "Good. You may accompany Pearl and me back to London in my carriage." She gave a low laugh. "This should prove interesting."

She reentered the cottage before Anna could think of a reply.

"WHOA, THERE," EDWARD murmured to the bay. He held its head and patiently waited as the horse stomped and mouthed the bit. The bay was often fractious in the morning, and he'd saddled the horse earlier than usual. The sky was only just beginning to brighten to the east.

"Whoa, you old bastard," he whispered. For the first time, it occurred to him that the horse he was talking to had no name. How long had he owned the bay? A half dozen years now, at least, and he'd never bothered to name him. Anna Wren would scold if she knew.

Edward winced as he finally mounted. That was exactly why he was making this trip: to drive thoughts of the widow from his mind. He'd chosen to work off some of the restlessness—both of body and of mind—by riding to London. His luggage and valet would follow behind in the carriage. But as if to mock that plan, the newly named Jock bounded up as soon as the bay clattered out of the stables. The dog raced out the door ahead of him; he had been missing the last half hour. Now his hindquarters were covered with malodorous mud.

Edward reined his horse around and sighed. He planned to visit his fiancée and her family this trip and finalize the engagement negotiations. An overlarge, smelly mongrel would not help his cause with the Gerard family.

"Stay, Jock."

The dog sat and regarded him with big, brown, only slightly bloodshot eyes. His tail swept the cobblestone behind him.

"I'm sorry, old man." Edward leaned down to ruffle the canine's ears. The nervous gelding sidled back a couple of steps, breaking the contact. "You'll have to stay here this time."

The dog cocked his head.

Edward felt a wash of unwelcome wistfulness. The dog didn't belong in his life and neither did the lady.

"Guard, Jock. Watch her for me, boy." He half smiled, half grimaced at his own whimsy. Jock was hardly a trained guard dog. And Anna Wren wasn't his to guard in any case.

Shaking the thoughts away, he wheeled the bay and cantered down the drive.

AFTER SOME CONSIDERATION, Anna told Mother Wren that she would be traveling to London with Pearl and Coral to buy material for new gowns.

"I'm so glad we can finally afford material, but are you sure?" Mother Wren responded. Her cheeks were a rose pink, and she continued in a lower voice, "They're very nice, of course, but they are, after all, courtesans."

Anna had difficulty meeting her eyes. "Coral is very grateful for the care we extended to Pearl. They're really quite close, you know."

"Yes, but—"

"And she has offered me the use of her carriage both to take me to London and to ride back again."

Mother Wren's brows knit uncertainly.

"It's a most generous offer," Anna said softly. "It'll save us the cost of a stagecoach ride, besides being more comfortable. I'll be able to buy additional fabric with the money we would've spent on the stage."

Mother Wren visibly wavered.

"Wouldn't you like a new gown?" she wheedled.

"Well, I do worry about your comfort, dear," Mother Wren finally said. "If you are happy with this arrangement, then so am I."

"Thank you." Anna kissed her on the cheek and ran up the stairs to finish packing.

The horses were already stomping outside when Anna came down again. She hurriedly said her good-byes and climbed in the carriage, where the Smythe sisters waited.

Anna waved out the window as they drove away, much to the amusement of Coral. She was about to draw her head back in when she caught sight of Felicity Clearwater standing down the street. Anna hesitated, her eyes meeting the other woman's. Then the carriage swept past, and she sat back in the seat. She bit her bottom lip. Felicity could not possibly know why she traveled to London, but seeing her still made Anna uneasy.

Across from her, Coral raised an eyebrow.

Anna grabbed the strap over her head as the carriage turned a corner, bouncing the women inside. She lifted her chin.

Coral smiled slightly and nodded.

They made a stop at Ravenhill Abbey so Anna could inform Mr. Hopple that she'd be absent from her work for a few days. The carriage waited at the end of the drive, out of sight, while she walked to the Abbey and back. It was not until she was almost returned to the carriage that she realized Jock was shadowing her.

She turned to face the dog. "Go back, Jock."

Jock sat down in the middle of the drive and regarded her calmly.

"Now, sir. Go home, Jock!" Anna pointed to the Abbey.

Jock turned his head to look in the direction of her finger, but didn't move.

"Fine, then," she huffed, feeling silly arguing with a dog. "I'll just ignore you."

Anna walked the rest of the way determinedly not paying attention to the enormous dog following her. But when she rounded the gates of the Abbey and saw the carriage, she knew she had a problem. The footman had caught sight of her and had opened the vehicle's door in anticipation of her entering it. There was a blur and a scrabble of claws on gravel as Jock dashed past her and leapt inside the carriage.

"Jock!" Anna was appalled.

From inside the carriage came a commotion that rocked it briefly from side to side; then it stood still. The footman stared in the door. She came alongside him and hesitantly peeked in as well.

Jock sat on one of the plush seats. Across from him, Pearl watched the dog, horrified. Coral, predictably, was unperturbed and smiling faintly.

Anna had forgotten how frightening Jock could be on first sight. "I'm so sorry. He's really quite harmless."

Pearl, rolling her eyes to the side to see her, looked unconvinced.

"Here, let me get him out," Anna said.

But this proved difficult. After one menacing growl from Jock, the footman made it clear that his job did not include handling dangerous animals. Anna scrambled into the carriage to try to cajole the dog out. When that did not work, she grabbed hold of the loose fur near his neck and attempted to drag him out. Jock simply set his feet and waited while she wrestled.

Coral started laughing. "It appears that your dog wants to come with us, Mrs. Wren. Leave him alone. I do not mind another passenger."

"Oh, I couldn't," Anna panted.

"Indeed you could. Do not let us argue. Come inside and protect Pearl and me from the beast."

Jock seemed content when Anna sat. Once it was established that he would not be ejected, he lay down and went to sleep. Pearl watched him tensely for a while. When he didn't move, her head began to nod. Anna rested against the fine plush carriage cushions and thought sleepily that they were even finer than Lord Swartingham's. In a little while, she, too, was asleep, weary from the lack of rest from the night before.

They stopped once in the afternoon for a late luncheon at an inn along the high road. Shouting ostlers ran out to hold the heads of the stomping horses while the women climbed down stiffly. The inn was surprisingly clean, and they enjoyed some nice boiled beef and cider. Anna made sure to bring a bit of the meat out to the carriage for Jock. Then she let him run around the yard and frighten the stable boys before they continued on their journey.

The sun had already set when the carriage drew up before a smart London row house. Anna was surprised at the luxury of the house, but then thought of Coral's carriage and realized she shouldn't be.

Coral must have noticed her gawking at the façade, because she smiled enigmatically. "All from the kindness of the marquis." She made a sweeping gesture, and her smile turned cynical. "My good friend."

Anna followed her up the front steps and into the shadowed entryway. Their footsteps echoed on gleaming white marble floors. The walls were paneled in white marble as well, leading up to a plastered ceiling with a glittering crystal chandelier. It was a very beautiful, but very empty entrance. She wondered if it reflected its current occupant or the absent owner.

Coral turned at that moment to Pearl, who was beginning to droop from the long ride. "I want you to stay here with me, sister."

"Your marquis won't like me staying here long. You know that." Pearl looked anxious.

Coral's lips twisted the slightest bit. "Let me worry about the marquis. He will understand my wishes. Besides, he is out of the country for the next two weeks." She smiled almost warmly. "Now let me show you to your rooms."

Anna's room was a pretty little chamber done in a dusky blue and white. Coral and Pearl bid her good night, and she made ready for bed. Jock sighed heavily and lay down before the fire in the grate. She brushed out her hair and talked to him. She very firmly didn't let herself think about the morrow. But as she lay down to sleep, all the thoughts she had tried to keep at bay rushed in. Was she about to commit a grave sin? Could she live with herself after tomorrow? Would she please the earl?

To her chagrin, it was this last thought that she worried over the most.

FELICITY LIT THE candelabra from her taper and set it carefully on the corner of the desk. Reginald had been particularly amorous tonight. A man of his age should have slowed down in his bed sport.

Felicity snorted to herself. The only thing that had slowed down was the time it took him to reach completion. She could've written a five-act play whilst he huffed and sweated over her. Instead, she'd pondered the reasons a provincial widow like Anna Wren might be journeying to London. The elder Mrs. Wren, when quizzed, had claimed the trip was to purchase materials for new dresses. A plausible excuse, true, but there were many other diversions an unattached lady might find in that city. So many, in fact, that Felicity thought it might be worthwhile to discover exactly what Anna did in London.

She pulled out a sheet of paper from her husband's desk and uncapped the inkwell. She inked her quill and then paused. Who among her acquaintances in London would be the best choice? Veronica was too curious. Timothy, while a racehorse between the sheets, had, unfortunately, the same mental capacity outside the bed. Then there was . . . Of course!

Felicity smiled in self-satisfaction as she traced the first letters in her missive. She wrote to a man who was not quite honest. Not quite a gentleman.

And not nice at all.

Chapter Nine

*The raven wheeled over the gleaming white castle,
and as he did so, scores of birds flew from the walls:
thrushes and titmice, sparrows and starlings, robins
and wrens. Every songbird Aurea could recognize and
many that she could not came to welcome them. The
raven landed and introduced them as his loyal
retainers and servants. But while the raven had the
power of human speech, these smaller birds did not.
That evening, the servant-birds led Aurea to a
magnificent dining room. There she saw a long table
splendidly prepared with delicacies she'd only
dreamed of. She expected the raven to dine with her,
but he did not appear, and she ate all alone.
Afterward, she was shown to a beautiful room and
found there a nightgown of gauzy silk that was
already laid out for her on the big bed. She dressed
in this and climbed into the bed, falling immediately
into a deep, dreamless sleep. . . .*
—from *The Raven Prince*

The damned wig itched like bloody hell.

Edward balanced a plate of meringues on his lap and wished he could poke a finger under his powdered wig. Or just take the cursed thing off. But wigs were de rigueur in polite society, and visiting his prospective bride and her family definitely qualified. He'd ridden all day yesterday to get to London and had arisen unfashionably early this morning, as was his wont. And then he'd had to cool his heels for several hours before it was deemed an appropriate time to go calling. Damn society and its asinine rules anyway.

Across from him, his future mother-in-law talked to the room at large. Or, rather, lectured. Lady Gerard was a handsome woman with a broad forehead and round, light blue eyes. She capably debated the current fashion in hats all by herself. Not a topic he himself would have chosen, and by the nodding of Sir Richard's head, not one of the older man's favorites either. It would seem, however, that once Lady Gerard started talking, only an act of God could stop her. Such as a bolt of lightning. Edward narrowed his eyes. Perhaps not even that.

Sylvia, his intended, sat gracefully across from him. Her eyes were as round and blue as Lady Gerard's. She had the true English coloring: a healthy peaches-and-cream complexion and thick golden hair. She reminded him not a little of his own mother.

Edward took a sip of tea and wished it was whiskey. On the little table beside Sylvia sat a vase of poppies. The flowers were bright scarlet, and they perfectly accented the yellow and orange room. They, along with the girl perched next to them in her indigo gown, made a picture worthy of a master. Had her mother posed her there? Lady Gerard's shrewd blue eyes flashed as she expounded on gauze.

Definitely posed.

Except poppies didn't bloom in March. These must have cost a pretty penny because it was impossible to tell unless one studied the blooms closely that they were made of silk and wax.

He set aside his plate. "Would you mind showing me your gardens, Miss Gerard?"

Lady Gerard, caught in a pause, gave permission with a satisfied smile.

Sylvia rose and proceeded him through the French doors into the compact town garden, her skirts swishing behind her. They strolled silently down the path, her fingers lightly resting on his sleeve. Edward tried to think of something to say, a light conversational topic, but his mind was strangely blank. One did not discuss crop rotation with a lady, nor how to drain a field or the newest techniques in composting. In fact, there was nothing at all that interested him that he could safely discuss with a young lady.

He glanced down at his feet and noticed a small yellow flower, not a daffodil or primrose. Edward stooped to finger it, wondering if Mrs. Wren had one like it in her garden.

"Do you know what this is?" he asked Miss Gerard.

Sylvia bent to examine the flower. "No, my lord." Her smooth brows knit. "Shall I ask the gardener for you?"

"No need." He straightened and dusted off his hands. "I just wondered."

They'd reached the end of the path where a little stone bench squatted against the garden wall.

Edward withdrew a large white handkerchief from his coat and laid it on the bench. He gestured with one hand. "Please."

The girl settled gracefully and folded her hands in her lap.

He clasped his hands behind his back and absently watched the little yellow flower. "Does this alliance suit you, Miss Gerard?"

"Perfectly, my lord." Sylvia didn't look at all perturbed by the bluntness of his question.

"Then will you do me the honor of becoming my wife?"

"Yes, my lord."

"Good." Edward bent to kiss the dutifully presented cheek.

His wig itched more than ever.

"THERE YOU ARE." Coral's voice broke the silence in the little library. "I am glad you found something of interest."

Anna nearly dropped the illustrated book in her hands. She whirled to find the other woman watching her with an amused look on her face.

"I'm sorry. I guess I'm still keeping country hours. When I came down to the breakfast room, they weren't ready yet. The maid said I could look in here." Anna held up the open book in her hands as evidence, and then hastily lowered it when she remembered the explicit engravings inside.

Coral glanced at the volume. "That one is very good, but you might find this one more helpful for what you plan tonight." She crossed to another shelf, took down a slim green volume, and pressed it into Anna's hands.

"Oh. Um . . . thank you." Anna knew she was turning seven shades of red. Rarely had she been so mortified in her life.

In her yellow-sprigged morning gown, Coral looked no older than sixteen. She might have been a young lady of good family about to go out calling on other girlish acquaintances. Only her eyes spoiled the illusion.

"Come. Let us break our fast together." Coral led the way into the breakfast room where Pearl already sat.

There was a full sideboard of hot dishes, but Anna found she didn't have much appetite. She settled in a chair across from Coral with a plate of toast.

After they ate, Pearl excused herself and Coral leaned back in her chair. Anna felt her shoulder blades tense.

"Now," her hostess said, "perhaps we should make some plans for this evening."

"What do you suggest?" Anna asked.

"I have several dresses you might want to look at. Any one of them can be altered to fit you. In addition, we should discuss sponges."

"I beg your pardon?" Anna blinked. How were bathing sponges going to help her?

"You may not be aware of them." Coral sipped her tea serenely. "Sponges that can be inserted into the female body to prevent a child."

Anna's mind froze on the thought. She'd never heard of such a thing. "I . . . that's probably not necessary. I was married for four years without conceiving."

"Then we will disregard them."

Anna fingered her teacup.

Coral continued, "Do you plan to attend the downstairs reception at Aphrodite's Grotto to pick out a likely male or"—she regarded Anna shrewdly—"or do you have a specific gentleman you would like to meet there?"

Anna hesitated and took a sip of tea. How far could she trust Coral? Until now, she had rather naïvely followed Coral's lead, had literally done everything the woman had suggested. But she hardly knew her, after all. Could she entrust her with what she really wanted—with, in fact, Lord Swartingham's name?

Coral seemed to understand her silence. "I am a whore," she said. "And in addition to that, I am not a nice woman. But despite these facts, my word is gold." She watched Anna intently, as if it were very important that she believe her. "Gold. I swear to you that I will not knowingly harm or betray you or anyone who you hold dear."

"Thank you."

Coral's mouth twisted. "It is I who should thank you. Not everyone would take the word of a prostitute seriously."

Anna ignored that. "Yes, as you have guessed, I'd like to meet a particular gentleman." She took a deep breath. "The Earl of Swartingham."

Coral's eyes widened infinitesimally. "Have you made an appointment to rendezvous with Lord Swartingham at Aphrodite's Grotto?"

"No. He has no knowledge of this," Anna said firmly. "Nor do I want him to."

The other woman gave a tiny, breathy laugh. "Forgive me, I am puzzled. You wish to spend the night with the earl—intimately—without him being aware of it. Do you plan to drug him?"

"Oh, no. You mistake me." Her face must be permanently stained a deep red by this point, but Anna struggled on. "I do wish to spend the night with the earl—intimately. I just don't want him to know it is me, as it were."

Coral smiled and tilted her head skeptically. "How?"

"I'm explaining this badly." Anna blew out a sigh and tried to order her thoughts. "You see, the earl has traveled to London on business. I have reason to believe that he'll visit Aphrodite's Grotto, probably tonight." She bit her lip. "Although, I'm not sure exactly when."

"That can be ascertained," Coral said. "But how do you propose that he not know you?"

"Pearl has said that many ladies and demimondaines wear a mask when they visit Aphrodite's Grotto. I thought I might wear one as well."

"Hmm."

"You don't think it will work?" Anna anxiously tapped at the side of her teacup.

"You are employed by the earl, are you not?"

"I'm his secretary."

"In that case, you must be aware there is a much higher chance of him finding you out," Coral warned.

"But if I wear a mask—"

"There is still your voice, your hair, your figure." Coral ticked off each point on the tips of her fingers. "Even your scent, if he has been near enough to you."

"You're right, of course." Anna felt close to tears.

"I am not saying it cannot be done," Coral reassured her coolly. "Just . . . You do understand the risks?"

Anna tried to think. It was difficult to concentrate this close to what she wanted. "Yes. Yes, I think so."

Coral regarded her a moment more. Then she clapped her hands once. "Good. I think we shall first work on the costume. We will need a mask that conceals most of your face. Let us consult my maid, Giselle. She is very good with a needle."

"But how do we know if Lord Swartingham will visit tonight?" Anna protested.

"I almost forgot." Coral rang for writing utensils and began composing a letter at the breakfast room table. She talked as she wrote. "I know the proprietor and part owner of Aphrodite's Grotto. She used to go by Mrs. Lavender, but now she is Aphrodite herself. A money-grubbing old witch, but she owes me a favor. A rather large one as it happens. She probably thinks I have forgotten the matter, so she will be all the more disconcerted to receive this letter." Coral lifted her lips in a feral smile. "I make it a habit to never let a debt go, so in a way, you are doing me a kindness."

She blew upon the ink to dry it, folded and sealed the letter, then rang for a footman. "The gentlemen who patronize Aphrodite's Grotto often make an appointment in advance so that they may be assured a room and a woman for the night," Coral explained. "Mrs. Lavender will inform us if that is the case with your earl."

"And if it is?" Anna asked anxiously.

"Then we will plan." Coral poured more tea for them both. "Perhaps you can take a room, and we will have Mrs. Lavender send Lord Swartingham to you." She narrowed her eyes thoughtfully. "Yes, I think that is the best idea. We will have the room lit by only a few candles so he will not be able to see you well."

"Wonderful." Anna grinned.

Coral looked briefly startled and then smiled back with the most sincere expression Anna had ever seen on her face.

The plan just might work.

APHRODITE'S GROTTO WAS a splendid sham, Anna reflected that night as she peered from the carriage window. A four-story building, all white marble columns and gold leaf, the place was apparently magnificent. It was only on second glance that one noticed the marble of the columns was painted on and that the "gold" was tarnished brass. The carriage pulled into the mews behind the building and stopped.

Coral, sitting in the shadows across from Anna, leaned forward. "Are you ready, Mrs. Wren?"

Anna took a deep breath and checked that her mask was firmly tied on. "Yes."

She stood on shaky legs and followed Coral down from the carriage. Outside, a lantern by the back door threw a feeble light into the mews. As they picked their way up the path, a tall woman with hennaed hair opened the door.

"Ah, Mrs. Lavender," Coral drawled.

"Aphrodite, if you please," the woman snapped.

Coral inclined her head ironically.

They stepped into the lit hall, and Anna saw that Aphrodite wore a violet gown fashioned to look like a classical toga. A gold mask dangled from one hand. The madam turned shrewd eyes on Anna. "And you are . . . ?"

"A friend," Coral replied before Anna could say a word.

Anna shot her a grateful glance. She was very glad that Coral had insisted she don the mask before leaving the town house. It wouldn't be wise to expose herself to the madam.

Aphrodite gave Coral a nasty look and led the way up the stairs and down the hall to pause before a door. She opened it and gestured inside. "You have the room until dawn. I will inform the earl that you wait for him when he arrives." With that, she swooshed away.

Coral's lips curved in a secret smile. "Good luck, Mrs. Wren." And then she, too, was gone.

Anna carefully closed the door behind her and took a moment to steady her breath as she looked around. The room was surprisingly tasteful. Well, considering it was in a brothel. She rubbed her arms, trying to make them warm. Velvet curtains draped the window, a banked fire glowed in a lovely white marble fireplace, and two uphol-stered chairs stood by the hearth. She flipped back the covers on the bed. The linens were clean—or at least they appeared so.

She removed her cloak and draped it over a chair. She wore a diaphanous gown underneath that she'd borrowed from Coral. Anna supposed it was meant to be a night-dress, but it was extremely impractical. The upper half consisted mostly of lace. Coral had assured her, neverthe-less, that this was the appropriate attire for a seduction. The satin mask on her face was butterfly shaped. It cov-ered her forehead and hairline and swept down over most of her cheeks. The eyeholes were oval and tilted at the corners, giving her eyes a vaguely foreign shape. Her hair flowed about her shoulders, the ends carefully curled. Lord Swartingham had never seen her with her hair down.

Everything was ready. Anna skittered to the mantel-piece and fiddled with a candle. What was she doing here? This was a silly plan that would never work. What had she been thinking? There was yet time to renege. She could leave this room and find the carriage—

The door opened.

Anna whirled and froze. A masculine shape loomed in the doorway, silhouetted by the hall light. For a fraction of a second, she felt fear and stepped back apprehensively. She couldn't even tell if it was Lord Swartingham. Then he entered, and she knew by the shape of his head, by his stride, by the movement of his arm as he took off his coat, that it was he.

The earl laid the coat on a chair and advanced toward her in his shirt, breeches, and waistcoat. Anna didn't know what to do or say. She nervously pulled her hair back from her face and tucked it behind her ear with the crook of her little finger. She couldn't see his expression in the dim candlelight any more than he could see hers.

He reached for her and took her in his arms. She relaxed at the movement and lifted her face, expecting his kiss. But he didn't kiss her lips. Instead, he bypassed her face altogether and laid his open mouth against the curve of her neck.

Anna trembled. To have waited so long for his touch and then suddenly to have his wet tongue tracing the tendon of her neck down to her shoulder was both shocking and wonderful. She gripped his upper arms. His lips ran back and forth on her collarbone, his hot breath raising goose bumps on her skin. Her nipples puckered against the rough lace on her gown.

He slowly pulled down one shoulder of the loose nightdress. The lace caught and dragged over her nipple almost painfully as her breast was exposed. His breathing grew deeper. He shifted his hand from her shoulder to slide a callused palm over her nipple. Anna caught her breath and exhaled raggedly. She'd not been touched by a man there in over six years, and then only by her husband. The heat of his palm almost burned against her cool breast. He rubbed his wide hand back and forth, taking his time to measure her with the span of his fingers. Then he caught the nipple in the crook of his forefinger and thumb and squeezed; at the same time, he bit gently down on her shoulder.

A jolt of exquisite pleasure lanced through Anna, traveling all the way to her woman's mound. Her belly tensed with excitement. She ran her fingers over his arms, pressing and rubbing, wishing desperately that she could feel his skin under the layers of clothes.

His hair was slightly damp from the mist outside, and she could smell him: sweat and brandy and his own unique male musk. She turned her face toward him, but he pulled his head away. She followed. She wanted to kiss him. But he suddenly pushed down the other shoulder of her gown, distracting her. Without her breasts to hold it up, the gown fell to her feet. She was nude before him. There was a moment when she blinked and began to feel vulnerable, but then he put his mouth to her nipple and licked.

She started. A low, hoarse sound came from her throat.

He licked her other nipple like a cat. Slow, languid strokes that rasped over her nerve endings. He made a sound almost like a purr, furthering the illusion that he was a big predator savoring the taste of her skin.

Her legs shook and she felt weak. She was surprised to find she couldn't stand. What was this feeling taking over her body? This had never happened before. Had it been so long that she could no longer remember what lovemaking was like? Her body—her emotions—felt foreign.

But he was supporting her now, even as her legs collapsed beneath her. His mouth never leaving her breast, he picked her up and laid her on the bed, and her thoughts scattered. He ran his hands down her bare sides, and taking hold of her thighs, he parted them widely. He settled his hips against her as if he had every right. His manhood lay on her feminine flesh, and he ground down in small circular motions so that her inner lips parted. She could feel him, big and thick and *there*.

The trembling spread throughout her body.

He made a sound somewhere between a growl and a purr. He seemed to relish his position and her helplessness. He continued to rock against her, and he sucked her nipple into his hot mouth. He pulled hard, and she arched up against him frantically, almost dislodging him. He did growl then as he turned to suck her other breast. At the same time, he moved his hips up fractionally to bear down on her. She arched again as a whimper escaped her lips. But this time he was ready and did not let her shift him. He ground more firmly on her sensitive flesh. He pressed her into the mattress and dominated her with his weight and strength.

She was caught, unable to move, as he relentlessly pleasured her. He didn't let up, cramming against her inexorably with his hard loins as he sucked and sucked and sucked at her wet nipples.

She shuddered, unable to control herself. Waves of pleasure flowed from her center toward the tips of her toes. Little ripples followed, and she gasped as pieces of herself seemed to fly apart. For an ecstatic moment, joy overwhelmed her anxiety. He rocked against her nonstop, but in soft, slow brushes now, as if he knew her flesh was too sensitive to handle a firmer contact. His hands flowed in long sweeps down her sides, and he feathered open-mouthed kisses against her aching breasts.

She didn't know how long she lingered in a half daze before she felt his fingers harden, and he reached between their bodies to unbutton his breeches. It was a tight squeeze, and every movement of his hand nudged the back of his knuckles into her wet woman's place. She squirmed wantonly against his hand. She wanted more from him, and she wanted it now. He rumbled a dark chuckle. Then he drew out his hard flesh and guided himself to her entrance. She could feel heat from the head as he nudged his manhood against her softness.

He was big—very big. Of course he was big. He was a big man all around. She just hadn't realized how big. Anna quivered in feminine anxiety, but he gave her no time to balk. He was pushing, pushing his large male presence into her, and she was giving way. Submitting.

She could feel the round, smooth crown of his erection pressing into the inner ring of muscles that guarded her keep. His chest vibrated with a groan. He braced himself up on stiff arms, flexed his buttocks, and drove his entire length home. She moaned at the wonder of it: to feel his masculine flesh inside her, warm and hard and *now*. Oh, goodness it was heaven. She lifted her legs and wrapped them high over his hips and was a little startled to feel the fabric of his breeches rubbing against the inner skin of her naked thighs.

Then he pulled his penis almost all the way out and shoved it back into her, and she forgot about his clothes.

He thrust into her again and again. Hard and steady. His chest and head arched up and away from her in the darkness while his hips kept in constant, mindless, pleasurable contact. She reached up to caress his face, but he gently knocked her hands aside and bent his head to nuzzle her ear. She could hear him breathing fast now as his rhythm began to break. She ran her fingers through the hair at the back of his head and tightened her thighs about him, trying to make this moment last. He groaned into her ear, and his buttocks suddenly flexed hard beneath her heels as he convulsed and poured himself into her.

She arched, wanting to receive all that he could give. If only it would never stop.

But it did, and he was done. He collapsed down, his breath and his body spent. She caught him and held him close, and then she shut her eyes to engrave this moment on her memory. She felt the rough brush of his breeches against her legs and each and every ripple of his muscles as he breathed. She listened to his unsteady breath in her ear. It was a wonderfully intimate sound, and tears pricked at her eyes.

For some reason, she felt bizarrely maudlin. The emotion startled her. This had been the most glorious experience of her life, but it had also been totally unexpected. She had thought it would be a simple physical release, but instead it had been a wonderful kind of transcendence. It made no sense to her, but she hadn't the clarity of mind to puzzle it out.

She pushed the thought aside to examine later. Right now her legs were spread wantonly wide, sprawled where they had fallen when he stopped moving. He was still in her body, pulsing now and then with the aftershocks. She closed her eyes and savored his heavy, hot weight on her. She felt the wet warmth of his seed and could smell his sweat and the pungent scent of sex. Odd how she liked the scent, and she smiled, feeling completely relaxed as she turned her head to brush her lips against his hair.

He shifted his weight and withdrew from her body. He went slowly, and she felt each of his movements as a spreading emptiness. The feeling kept growing as he rose off the bed and buttoned the front placket of his breeches. All too soon, he reached for his coat and walked to the door.

He opened it, but then paused, his head lit from behind by the light in the hall. "Meet me here again tomorrow night." The door closed quietly behind him.

And Anna realized it was the sole time he had spoken to her that night.

Chapter Ten

In the middle of the night, when all was black, Aurea
was awakened by passionate kisses. She was drowsy
and could not see, but the touch was gentle. She
turned and her arms wrapped around the form of a
man. He stroked and petted her so exquisitely that she
didn't even notice when he drew the nightgown from
her body. Then he made love to her in a silence broken
only by her cries of ecstasy. All night he stayed,
worshipping her body with his own, and as dawn
neared, she fell asleep again, replete with passion.
But in the morning when Aurea awoke, her lover of
the night before was gone. She sat up in her great,
lonely bed and searched for any sign of him. All she
could see was a single feather from the raven, and she
wondered if her lover had merely been a dream. . . .
—from *The Raven Prince*

Edward threw down his quill and pushed up his spectacles
to rub his eyes. Damn. The words just would not come.

Outside his London town house, in a not very fashionable
neighborhood, he could hear the sound of delivery carts

beginning to roll up and down the street. The front door banged, and a song drifted up to his window from the maid sweeping the steps. The room had lightened since he had risen from his bed, and he leaned over to blow out the candle guttering on his desk.

Sleep had eluded him the night before. He'd finally given up in the wee hours. It was strange. He'd just experienced the best sex in his lifetime and thus should have been completely exhausted. Instead, he'd spent the long night thinking about Anna Wren and the little whore he had taken to bed at Aphrodite's Grotto.

But was she a whore? That was the problem. The question had gone around and around in his head all the night long.

When he'd arrived at Aphrodite's Grotto the evening before, the madam had simply said that there was a woman already waiting for him. She hadn't indicated whether the woman was a working prostitute or a lady of the *ton,* out for an evening of illicit pleasure. He hadn't asked either. One didn't ask at Aphrodite's Grotto. That was why so many patronized the place: A man was guaranteed anonymity and a clean woman. He hadn't been curious until after he'd left.

On the one hand, she'd worn a mask like a lady eager to conceal her identity. However, sometimes the whores at Aphrodite's Grotto wore masks to give themselves an air of mystery. But then again, she'd been so tight when he'd entered her, as if she had been a very long while without a man. Perhaps that was his imagination, remembering only what he'd wanted to feel.

He groaned huskily under his breath. Thinking of her was making him hard as a rock. It was also making him feel guilty. Because that was the other thing that had kept him awake most of the night: guilt. Which was ridiculous. Everything had been fine, wonderful, even, until his mind turned to Mrs. Wren, *Anna,* again not even a quarter of an hour after he'd left Aphrodite's Grotto. The feeling the thought of her brought—a kind of melancholy, a sense of wrongness—had stayed with him all the way home. He felt as if he had betrayed her. Never mind that she had no claim on him. That she had never even shown that she reciprocated his longing. The notion that he had been unfaithful was still there, eroding his soul.

The little whore had been shaped like Anna.

Holding her, he imagined a little what it would be like to hold Anna Wren. How it would feel to caress her. And when he'd kissed her throat, he had become instantly aroused. Edward groaned into his hands. This was ridiculous. He must rid himself of these constant thoughts of his little secretary; they were unworthy of an English gentleman. This urge to corrupt an innocent must be overcome, and he would do it through sheer willpower if need be.

He jumped up from his desk, strode over to the bellpull hanging in the corner, and yanked it viciously. Then he began putting away his papers. He took off his reading glasses and stuffed them into a cubbyhole.

Five minutes later, his summons still hadn't been answered.

Edward exhaled and glared at the door. Another minute ticked by with no sign of a servant. He drummed his fingers on his desk impatiently. Goddamnit, he had a limit.

He marched to the door and bellowed into the hallway, "Davis!"

A shuffling sound, as if from a creature called forth from the stygian depths, came from the corridor. It drew nearer. Very slowly.

"It will be sundown before you get here if you don't *hurry up, Davis!*" Edward held his breath, listening.

The shuffling did not quicken.

He exhaled again and leaned on the door frame. "I'm going to dismiss you one of these days. I'm going to replace you with a trained bear. It couldn't possibly perform any worse than you. *Do you hear me, Davis?*"

Davis, his valet, materialized around the corner holding a tray with hot water. The tray trembled. The servant slowed his already-snaillike progress even more when he saw the earl.

Edward snorted. "That's right, don't exert yourself. I have all the time in the world to stand about the corridor in my nightshirt."

The other man appeared not to hear. His movements were down to a crawl now. Davis was an aged rascal with sparse hair the color of dirty snow. His back was bent in a habitual stoop. A large mole with sprouting hairs grew by the side of his mouth as if to make up for the lack of hair above the watery gray eyes.

"I know you can hear me," Edward shouted in his ear as he passed.

The valet started as if just noticing him. "Up early, are we, m'lord? So debauched we couldn't sleep, eh?"

"My sleep was dreamless."

"That so?" Davis gave a cackle that would have done credit to a buzzard. "'Tisn't good for a man your age, not sleeping well, if you don't mind me saying so."

"What are you mumbling about, you senile old coot?"

Davis set the tray down and shot a malicious glance at him. "Drains the manly vigor, it does, if you know what I mean, m'lord."

"No, I don't know what you mean, thank God." He poured the ewer of lukewarm water into a basin on his dresser and began to wet his jaw.

Davis leaned close and said in a hoarse whisper, "Tupping, m'lord." He winked, a hideous sight.

Edward eyed him irritably as he lathered.

"It's all fine for a young man," the valet continued, "but you're getting up there, m'lord. The elderly need to preserve their strength."

"You would certainly know."

Davis scowled and picked up the razor.

Edward immediately snatched it out of his hand. "I'm not such a fool as to allow you near my neck with a sharp blade." He began scraping the soap under his chin.

"'Course, some don't have to worry about saving their strength," the valet said. The blade approached the dent in Edward's chin. "Have a problem with their cock crowing, if you know what I mean."

Edward yelped as he nicked his chin. "OUT! Get out, you evil old pisspot."

Davis wheezed as he scurried to the door. Some, hearing the whistling sound, would have worried for the old man's health, but Edward wasn't fooled. It wasn't often his valet triumphed over him this early in the morning.

Davis was laughing.

THE TRYST HADN'T gone exactly as she'd expected, Anna reflected the next morning. They had made love, naturally.

And he hadn't seemed to have recognized her. That was a relief. But really, the more she thought about Lord Swartingham's lovemaking, the more uneasy she became. He'd been a good lover. A wonderful lover, actually. She had never known such physical pleasure before, so she hadn't been able to predict that. But the way he hadn't kissed her on the mouth . . .

Anna poured herself a cup of tea. Early again to breakfast, she had the room to herself.

He hadn't let her touch his face at all. It seemed impersonal somehow. Of course that was natural, wasn't it? He imagined she was a prostitute or a woman of loose morals, for goodness sake. Therefore, he'd treated her like one. Wasn't that what she had expected?

Anna beheaded a kipper and poked the tines of her fork into its side. She should have expected it, but she hadn't. The problem was that while she had been making love, he had been . . . well . . . having sex. With a nameless prostitute. It was very depressing.

She made a face at her decapitated kipper. And what in heaven's name was she supposed to do about tonight? She hadn't planned on staying in London more than two nights. She should be leaving for home today on the first coach. Instead, she sat in Coral's breakfast room mashing up an innocent kipper.

Anna was still frowning moodily when Coral strolled into the room wearing a sheer, pale-pink wrapper trimmed with swan's down feathers.

The other woman stopped and eyed her. "Did he not come to the room last night?"

"What?" It took a moment for Anna to register the question. "Oh. Yes. Yes, he came to the room." She blushed and hurriedly took a sip of tea.

Coral helped herself to some coddled eggs and toast from the sideboard and gracefully dropped into a chair across from Anna. "Was he too rough?"

"No."

"You did not enjoy it?" the other woman pressed. "He couldn't bring you to climax?"

Anna nearly choked on her tea in her embarrassment. "No! I mean, *yes*. It was quite enjoyable."

Coral unperturbedly poured herself a cup of tea. "Then why do I find you this morning morose when you should have stars in your eyes?"

"I don't know!" Anna found to her horror that she had raised her voice. What was the matter with her? Coral was right, she'd gotten her wish, spent a night with the earl, and still she was dissatisfied. What a contrary creature she was!

The other woman had arched her eyebrows at her tone.

Anna crumbled a bit of toast, unable to meet her eyes. "He wants me to go back tonight."

"Rea-lly." The other woman drew out the word. "That is interesting."

"I shouldn't go."

Coral sipped her tea.

"He might recognize me if we meet again." Anna pushed the kipper to one side of her plate. "It would be so unladylike to return a second night."

"Yes, I do see your problem," Coral murmured. "One night at a brothel is perfectly respectable, whilst two comes perilously close to being déclassé."

Anna glared.

Coral smiled whimsically at her. "Why don't we go shopping for those fabrics you told your mother-in-law you would be bringing back. It will give you time to think. You can make up your mind later this afternoon."

"What a very good idea. Thank you." Anna set her fork down. "I'd better go change."

She rose from the table and hurried out of the morning room, her spirits lifting. She only wished she could abandon her thoughts of tonight as easily as her breakfast. Despite what she'd told Coral, Anna was very much afraid that she'd already made up her mind.

She was going to return to Aphrodite's Grotto and Lord Swartingham again.

THAT NIGHT, THE earl entered the room where Anna waited without saying a word. The only sounds were the quiet shush of the door closing and the crackle of the fire. She watched him pace forward, his face in shadow. Slowly, he shrugged out of his coat, his big shoulders bunching. And then she glided to him before he could make the first move, before he could take control. She stood on tiptoe to kiss his mouth. But he deflected the movement, drawing her close to his body instead.

She was determined this time to make their dance more personal, to make him understand that she was real. To touch at least some of him. She took advantage of her position and quickly worked the buttons on his waistcoat open. It came undone and she attacked the shirt beneath.

He reached to catch her hands, but she already had the shirt partly undone. She greedily reached for her prize: his flat, masculine nipples. Her fingers stroked through his chest hair until she found them; then she swayed forward and licked his nipples as he'd done the night before to hers, feeling vaguely triumphant that she'd gained the upper hand so soon. His hands fell away from where they had risen to catch her wrists. He caressed her bottom instead.

His height was a hindrance to her—she couldn't reach all that she wanted. So she pushed him back into one of the armchairs by the fire. It was important to her that she win this battle tonight.

He sprawled there, his shirt half-open in the firelight. She knelt between his outspread legs and slid her hands into his shirt, all the way up to his shoulders; then her fingers smoothed down his arms, taking the fabric with them. She pulled the shirt off him and let it fall to the floor. That left her free to run her hands over his beautiful, muscled shoulders and arms. She moaned her delight in finally being able to feel the power and warmth of his body. She felt light-headed with anticipation.

He stirred and brought her hands to the front of his breeches. Her fingers trembled, but she brushed his hands aside when he tried to help her. She pushed the concealed buttons through their holes, feeling his erection growing all the while beneath her fingers; then she reached inside to draw him out.

He was gorgeous. Thick and large, with pulsing veins that stood out along his shaft. A swollen crest. The sight filled her with heat. She made a crooning sound in her throat and spread the placket of his breeches as far as it would go so she could look at his chest and stomach and penis. She adored the sight: the black wiry curls of his pubic hair, the thick column, standing now to his navel, and the heavy sac of his testes beneath. His naked skin gleamed, as if gilded by the firelight.

He growled and ran his fingers into the hair behind her head. He gently urged her mouth down to his penis. For a moment, she hesitated. She'd never . . . Did she dare? Then she remembered their battle. This was but one skirmish, but it was important she win them all. And besides, she was excited at simply the thought. It was this last that decided her.

Tentatively, she grasped his erection and brought it away from his belly to her lips. She looked up. His face was flushed with arousal. Her eyelids lowered, and she enveloped the crown of his penis in her mouth. His hips jerked when her tongue touched him, and she felt the triumph rise in her again. She could control a man this way. She could control *this* man. She glanced up again. He was watching her as she licked and suckled his manhood, his ebony eyes glittering in the firelight. His fingers flexed in her hair.

She let her eyelids fall as she brought her mouth down as far as she could over his length. Then she slowly pulled up, pursing her lips and sucking on the thick shaft as it withdrew from her mouth. She heard him moan, and his pelvis arched convulsively. She licked around the ridge below the head. It felt like chamois over iron and tasted of male musk, the salt of sweat, and victory. Surely after this—after tonight—things would somehow be different. She explored that area with her tongue for a while. Then she felt his hand cover hers. He guided her fingers in a slow stroke up and down.

He groaned.

She moved her hand faster as he urged her to take his penis into her mouth again with a nudge of his hips. This time when she drew back up to the head, she tasted a saline drop at the tip. She licked the slit at the top to see if there was more. He groaned again. Anna wriggled in excitement. She'd never done anything so sexually stimulating in her life. Her body was damp and slick, and her breasts seemed to throb with each groan she wrung from him.

His hips began to move rhythmically as she worked him. The sensuous, liquid sounds of her mouth on his body were explicit in the still room. Suddenly he bucked, gasping, and tried to withdraw from her mouth. She wanted to feel his finish, though, wanted to experience this intimacy together, wanted to be with him at his most vulnerable. She held on and sucked more strongly. Tangy warmth filled her mouth. She almost came herself with the knowledge that she'd brought him complete satisfaction.

He sighed and bent down to draw her into his lap. They sprawled there for a while, the fire in the grate snapping. She leaned her head on his shoulder and pulled her hair out of her eyes with a hooked little finger. After a time, he drew her gown from her breasts. Languidly, he played with her nipples, stroking and squeezing gently for many minutes.

Anna drifted, her eyes half closed.

Then he lifted her to pull the gown all the way off. He turned her around and settled her on his lap, naked and facing him. Her legs draped over the chair's arms. She was splayed before him. Vulnerable.

Was this what she wanted? She wasn't sure. But then his fingers feathered across her belly, down to where she was open to him, and she no longer cared. He played in her curls before skimming lower. She inhaled sharply, waiting—anticipating—where he would touch her next.

He stroked through her, parting her down there.

She bit her lip.

Then he brought his fingers up, wet with her juices and smeared them over her nipples. Vaguely she was aware that she should be shocked, but somehow in this place, with this man, she was beyond the mores of society. He worked her nipples, sliding and tugging as he made sure they were both thoroughly covered with her body's moisture.

She caught her breath at the animal sensation. It was so crude, what he was doing, and it excited her terribly.

He bent his head and sucked a nipple into his mouth. He had made sure to sensitize her flesh, and she moaned and arched uncontrollably at the contact. He returned to her mound and slid his long, strong middle finger into her hollow. His thumb flicked across her stiff bud, and at the same time, he moved his finger in her.

Mewling noises built in her throat. She felt moisture sliding between her thighs.

He chuckled and brought his thumb down firmly on her sensitive knot. He suckled at her other breast. The sharp sensations at two different points of her body mingled and compounded one another until she grabbed his shoulders and arched her hips involuntarily. He brought his other hand to her back and held her steady as his thumb began to rotate.

She came explosively, gasping and shaking. She tried to close her legs, but the chair held them open. She could only hump her hips mindlessly as he pleasured her. Finally, when she began to whimper, he lifted her bottom and pushed her down on his manhood.

His breathing was labored as he slowly penetrated her slick passage. He forced her down relentlessly until she'd taken all of his thick warmth and was stretched almost painfully open. Then he carefully lifted her legs, one at a time, over the chair arms and brought them to either side of him. He lifted her up onto her knees so that just the head of his erection remained, stretching her entrance. He kept her there, balanced on top of his penis while he sucked and licked at her swinging nipples.

She moaned. He was driving her out of her mind. Frantically she tried to sink down on his burning erection, but he laughed darkly and held her poised on the edge of pleasure. She tried swiveling her hips, swirling the crown in her passage.

He broke at that, pulling her down on him again and surging into her almost violently.

Oh, yes. She smiled savagely in satisfaction. She rode him, watching his face. He caressed her breasts and tilted his head against the chair. His eyes were closed, his lips drawn back from his teeth in a near snarl; the flickering firelight made a demon's mask of his features.

Then he lightly pulled on both her nipples at the same time, and her own head arched at the sensation. Her hair cascaded down her back, swinging and brushing both her legs and his. She began to come in long, drawn-out waves, her vision clouding. His hips bucked against hers. He grabbed the cheeks of her bottom to hold her down on him, his penis fully sheathed in her passage as he ground and ground and ground against her softness, his head rolling against the chair as he came.

She fell forward, panting in the aftermath, to lie against his naked shoulder as he cradled her in his arms.

His face was half turned away, and she lazily watched him as he recovered. The lines that habitually creased his forehead and bracketed his mouth were softened. His long, inky lashes lay on his cheeks, hiding his piercing eyes. She wanted to stroke his face, to feel it with her fingertips. But by this time, she knew that he would not allow it.

Had she won what she wanted? She felt tears sting the corners of her eyes. Somehow it wasn't right. The lovemaking had been even more wonderful tonight. But at the same time, as if in proportion to her physical ecstasy, she felt the gaping hole in her psyche more keenly. Something was missing.

He suddenly sighed and shifted. His flesh slid from hers. He lifted her in his arms and carried her to the bed, laying her down gently. She shivered and tugged the coverlet over her shoulders, watching him. She wanted to speak, but what could she say?

He buttoned his shirt, tucked it in his breeches, and then buttoned those as well. He ran his fingers through his hair and grabbed his coat and waistcoat, walking to the door in the loose-jointed way of a man recently satisfied. He paused by the door. "Tomorrow."

And then he was gone.

Anna lay there a minute, listening to his retreating footsteps, feeling melancholy. She was roused by bawdy laughter somewhere in the house. She got up and cleaned herself with the water and towels that sat conveniently by. Anna tossed the wet cloth down and then looked at it. The basin and linens were provided with the room to wash after a sexual encounter. It made her feel tawdry, like a whore, and wasn't she perilously close to that state? She was letting physical desire so rule her that she met a lover in a brothel.

She sighed and donned a nondescript dark dress that she had brought along, bundled in a bag with a hooded cape and boots. Once dressed, she folded the lace gown and stuffed it into the bag. Had she left anything? Glancing around the room, she saw nothing of her own. She opened the door a crack and looked up and down the hallway. All clear. She pulled up her hood, and with her face still covered by the butterfly mask, ventured forth.

Coral had instructed her yesterday to be careful in the hallways and to go in and out only by the back stairs. A carriage would be waiting outside when she was ready to leave.

Anna moved now to the back stairs that Coral had indicated and ran down the flight. She sighed with relief when she reached the door and saw the waiting carriage. Her mask had begun to rub on the bridge of her nose. She untied it. Just as she removed the mask, three young bucks reeled around the corner of the house. Anna hastened toward the carriage.

In a sudden move, one of the men slapped another on the back in a friendly gesture. But the second man was so drunk that he lost his balance and careened into Anna, knocking both of them to the ground. "A-a-awfully sorry, m'dear."

The dandy was giggling as he tried to push himself off of Anna, elbowing her in the stomach in the process. He got as far as bracing his body on his arms, but stayed there, swaying, as if too befuddled to move any farther. Anna shoved at him, trying to shift his weight. The back door to Aphrodite's Grotto opened. The light from the door fell across her face.

The buck grinned drunkenly. A gold canine glinted in his mouth. "Why, you're not too bad at all, love." He leaned down in what he obviously considered a seductive manner and breathed an ale-filled puff into her face. "What say you an' me—'?"

"Get off me, sir!" Anna hit the man's chest hard and managed to knock him off balance. He fell to the side, swearing foully as he did so. She scrambled quickly in the opposite direction, out of his reach.

"Come here, you tart. I'll—"

The dandy's friend saved her from hearing the rest of the undoubtedly obscene comment. The man hauled him up by the scruff of his shirt. "Come on, chum. No need to play with the downstairs help when we've got a couple of highfliers waiting inside."

Laughing, they dragged off their protesting friend.

Anna ran to the carriage, scrambled inside, and slammed the door behind her. She was shaking from the ugly incident. An incident that could have been much uglier.

She had never been mistaken for a woman of anything other than the highest morals. She felt degraded. Tainted. She took deep breaths and firmly reminded herself that she had nothing to be upset about. She hadn't been hurt by the fall, and the rude young man's friends had hustled him away before he had insulted her or even laid hands on her. True, he had seen her face. But it was highly unlikely that she would run into him in Little Battleford. Anna felt a little better. Surely there could be no repercussions.

TWO GOLD COINS flipped through the air, flashing in the light from the back door of Aphrodite's Grotto. They were caught by hands that were remarkably steady.

"That went well."

"Glad to hear it, old boy." One of the bucks smirked, looking almost as drunk as he was supposed to be. "Mind telling us what that was all about?"

"'Fraid I can't do that." The third man's lip lifted in a sneer, and his gold tooth gleamed. "It's a secret."

Chapter Eleven

Many months passed while Aurea lived in her raven-husband's castle. During the day, she amused herself by reading from the hundreds of illuminated books in the castle's library or by taking long walks in the garden. In the evening, she feasted on delicacies she had only dreamed of in her former life. She had beautiful gowns to wear and priceless jewels to decorate herself with. Sometimes the raven would visit her, appearing suddenly in her rooms or joining her at dinner without any notice. Aurea found that her strange spouse had a wide and intelligent mind, and he would engage her in fascinating conversations. But always the big black bird would disappear before she retired to her rooms in the evening. And every night, in the dark, a stranger came to her bridal bed and made exquisite love to her. . . .
—from *The Raven Prince*

"Hail, O defender of the turnip and master of the ewe," a deep sarcastic voice drawled the next morning. "Well met, my fellow Agrarian."

Edward squinted through the smoke in the cavernous coffeehouse. He could just make out the speaker, lounging at a table in the right rear corner. *Defender of the turnip, eh?* Winding his way through cluttered, age-blackened tables, Edward reached the man and slapped him hard on the back.

"Iddesleigh! It's not yet five in the afternoon. Why are you awake?"

Simon, Viscount Iddesleigh, didn't rock forward under the hearty back slap—he must have been bracing himself—but he did wince. A lean, elegant man, he wore a fashionable white-powdered wig and laced-edged shirt. To many he no doubt appeared a fop. But appearances in this case were deceiving.

"I've been known to see the light of day afore noon," Iddesleigh said, "although not often." He kicked a chair out from the table. "Sit, man, and partake of that hallowed brew called coffee. The gods, had they known of it, would've had no need of nectar on Olympus."

Edward waved at a boy serving drinks and took the proffered chair. He nodded at the silent third man sharing the table. "Harry. How're you?"

Harry Pye was a land steward on an estate somewhere in the north of England. He wasn't often in London. He must be here on business. In contrast to the flamboyant viscount, Harry almost blended into the woodwork. He was a man most would hardly notice in his ordinary brown coat and waistcoat. Edward knew for a fact that he carried a wicked dagger in his boot.

Harry nodded. "My lord. It's good to see you." He didn't smile, but there was an amused gleam in his green eyes.

"God's blood, Harry, how many times have I told you to call me Edward or de Raaf?" He signaled the boy again.

"Or Ed or Eddie," Iddesleigh cut in.

"*Not* Eddie." The boy banged a mug down, and Edward took a grateful sip.

"Aye, my lord," he heard Harry murmur, but Edward didn't bother replying.

He glanced around the room. The coffee at this house was very good. That was the main reason the Agrarian Society met here. It certainly wasn't because of the architecture. The room was crowded, with a too-low ceiling. The short door lintel was known to catch the taller members a nasty crack on the crown on entering. The tables had probably never been scrubbed, and the mugs didn't bear a close inspection. And the staff was a shifty lot who could be selectively hard of hearing when they didn't feel like serving, no matter the rank of the customer. But the coffee was fresh and strong, and any man was welcome to the house as long as he had an interest in agriculture. Edward recognized several titled men sitting at tables, but there were also small landowners up for a day in London and even working stewards such as Harry. The Agrarians were known for the strange equality of their club.

"And what does bring you to our lovely, if odoriferous, capital?" Iddesleigh asked.

"Negotiating a marital alliance," Edward replied.

Harry Pye's eyes sharpened over the rim of his mug. His hand was wrapped around the cup. There was a disconcerting space where his ring finger should have been but wasn't.

"Oh, braver man than I," Iddesleigh said. "You must have been celebrating the impending nuptials when I saw you last night at the fair Aphrodite's Grotto."

"You were there?" Edward felt oddly reticent. "I didn't see you."

"No." Iddesleigh smirked. "You looked quite, ah, *relaxed* when I saw you exit that establishment. I, myself, was engaged at the time with two eager nymphs, or I would have greeted you."

"Only two?" Harry asked, deadpan.

"We were joined later by a third." Iddesleigh's icy gray eyes sparkled almost innocently. "But I hesitated to admit the fact for fear it would cause you two to doubt your manhood by comparison."

Harry snorted.

Edward grinned and caught the boy's eye. He held up a finger for another mug. "Good God. Aren't you getting a trifle long in the tooth for such athletics?"

The viscount placed a lace-draped hand on his breast. "I assure you, on the honor of my dead and moldering forefathers, that all three wenches were wearing smiles when I left them."

"Probably because of the gold they were clutching," Edward said.

"You offend me deeply," the viscount said as he smothered a yawn. "Besides, you yourself must've engaged in debauchery of one sort or another at the goddess's domain. Admit it."

"True." Edward frowned at his mug. "But I won't be for very much longer."

The viscount looked up from inspecting the silver embroidery on his coat. "Never say you intend to be a chaste bridegroom?"

"I see no other option."

Iddesleigh's eyebrows arched. "Isn't that a rather literal—not to mention archaic—interpretation of the bridal vows?"

"Perhaps. But I think it will make for a successful marriage." Edward felt his jaw clench. "I want it to work this time. I need an heir."

"I wish you luck, then, my friend," Iddesleigh said quietly. "You must have chosen your lady carefully."

"I did indeed." Edward stared into his half-empty mug. "She is from an impeccable family; it goes back further than mine. She isn't repulsed by my scars; I know because I asked her myself—something I omitted to do with my first wife. She's intelligent and quiet. She's handsome, but not beautiful. And she comes from a large family. God willing, she should be able to give me strong sons."

"A Thoroughbred dam for a Thoroughbred sire." Iddesleigh's mouth quirked. "Soon your stables will overflow with hearty, squalling progeny. I'm sure you can hardly wait to begin getting offspring on your intended."

"Who is the lady?" Harry asked.

"Sir Richard Gerard's eldest, Miss Sylvia—"

Iddesleigh made a muffled exclamation. Harry glanced at him sharply.

"Gerard. Do you know her?" Edward finished slowly.

Iddesleigh studied the lace at his wrists. "My brother, Ethan's wife was a Gerard. As I remember, the mother was something of a tartar at the wedding."

"She still is." Edward shrugged. "But I doubt I'll have much contact with her after we're married."

Harry gravely raised his cup. "Congratulations on your betrothal, my lord."

"Yes, congratulations." The viscount lifted his cup as well. "And good luck, my friend."

A COLD NOSE against her cheek woke Anna. She peeked and saw brown canine eyes only inches from her own. They stared at her urgently. Pungent doggy breath panted in her face. She groaned and turned her head to glance at the window. Dawn was just brightening the sky from a drowsy peach color to the more alert bright blue of day.

She looked back at the watching canine eyes. "Good morning, Jock."

Jock took his forepaws from the mattress beside her head and backed up a step to sit down. He was very still, ears up, shoulder bunched, eyes alert to her every move. The very epitome of a dog waiting to go out.

"Oh, all right. I'm getting up." She padded over to the basin and made an abbreviated wash before dressing.

Dog and woman crept down the back stairs.

Coral lived in a fashionable street near Mayfair, which was lined with white stone houses only a few years old. Most of these were quiet now except for an occasional maid washing the front steps or polishing a doorknob. Normally, Anna might feel uncomfortable walking about in a strange place without an escort, but she had Jock to accompany her. He leaned closer as if to protect her whenever anyone else approached. They strolled in companionable silence. Jock was busy sniffing out the intriguing smells of the city, while she was lost in her own thoughts.

During the night, she'd thought over her situation, and when Anna awoke this morning, she'd already known what she must do. She couldn't meet him tonight. She was playing with fire, and she could no longer hide the fact from herself. In her need to be with Lord Swartingham, she'd flung aside all caution. She'd recklessly hared off to London and traipsed about a bordello as if it were a Little Battleford musicale. It was a miracle he hadn't discovered her. And the incident the night before with the drunken bucks was too close. She could've been raped or hurt or both. How hypocritical of her to scold men for doing the very thing she'd done for the past two nights. She winced at the thought of what Lord Swartingham would have said had he found her out. He was a very proud man with a terrible temper.

Anna shook her head and glanced up. They were only a few houses down from Coral's residence. Either her footsteps had led her back or Jock had a homing instinct.

She patted the dog's head. "Good boy. We had better go in and start packing for home."

Jock perked up his ears at the word *home.*

At that moment, a carriage pulled up in front of Coral's house. Anna hesitated, then retraced her steps around the corner and peeked back. Who could be calling at such an unfashionable hour? A footman jumped down from the carriage and placed a wooden step under the door before opening it. A male leg advanced, but withdrew inside the carriage again. She could see the footman moving the step an inch or two to the left; then a burly man with heavy shoulders descended. He stopped a moment to say something to the footman. From the way the servant bowed his head, it looked to be a set-down.

The burly man entered the house.

Was he Coral's marquis? Anna contemplated this turn of events while Jock waited patiently by her side. From what little she knew about the marquis, it would perhaps be prudent if she didn't meet him. She didn't want to cause trouble for Coral, and she was uneasy at the thought of letting someone of quality see her at Coral's residence. Although it was extremely unlikely she would cross paths again with a marquis, the incident the night before with the drunken bucks had made her wary. She decided to enter the house from the servants' entrance and thus perhaps escape notice.

"It's a good thing I'd planned to leave today anyway," she muttered to Jock as they crossed the kitchens.

There was a great flurry of activity in the kitchen. Maids scurried and the footmen helped bring in a mountain of luggage. Anna was hardly acknowledged as she climbed the dark back stair. Just as well. She and Jock moved soundlessly down the upper hall. Anna opened the door to her room and found Pearl anxiously waiting.

"Oh, thank God you're back, Mrs. Wren," the other woman said when she saw her.

"I took Jock for a walk," Anna said. "Was that Coral's marquis I saw coming in the front?"

"Yes," Pearl said. "Coral wasn't expecting him for another week or more. He'll be angry if he finds she has guests."

"I was just going to pack and leave, so I'll be out of his way."

"Thank you, ma'am. That'll make it ever so much easier for Coral, it will."

"But what will you do, Pearl?" Anna bent to drag out her soft bag from under the bed. "Coral said she wanted you here with her. Will the marquis let you stay?"

Pearl picked at a hanging thread on her cuff. "Coral thinks she can get him to let me stay, but I don't know. He's awful mean sometimes, even if he is a lord. And the house belongs to him, you know."

Anna nodded her understanding as she carefully folded her stockings.

"I'm glad Coral has such a nice place to live, with servants and carriages and things," Pearl said slowly. "But that marquis makes me nervous."

Anna paused with a handful of clothes in her arms. "You don't think he would hurt her, do you?"

Pearl stared back somberly. "I don't know."

EDWARD PROWLED THE bordello room like a caged tiger denied a meal. The woman was late. He checked the china clock over the hearth again. Half an hour late, damn her. How dare she make him wait for her? He reached the fireplace and stared into the blaze. He'd never obsessively gone back to the same woman. Not once, not twice, but three times now.

The sex had been so good each time. She was so responsive. She had held nothing back, acting like she was as much under his spell as he was under hers. He was not naïve. He knew women who were paid for sex often faked an excitement they did not feel. But a body's natural reaction could not be faked. She had been wet, literally soaked, in her desire for him.

He groaned. The thought of her wet pussy was having a predicable effect on his cock. Where the hell was she?

Edward swore and pushed himself away from the mantelpiece to resume his pacing. He'd even begun to daydream, in the manner of a starry-eyed stripling, about what her face looked like underneath the mask. More disturbing, he had imagined that she might look like Anna.

He stopped and placed the crown of his head against the wall, hands braced on either side. His chest expanded as he breathed deeply. He had come to London to rid himself of this awful fascination for his little secretary before he married. Instead, he'd found a new obsession. But had that stopped the original fixation? Oh, no. His longing for Anna had not only grown stronger, but was also mingled with lust for the mysterious little whore. He had two obsessions now instead of one, and they were tangled together in his overwrought brain.

He pounded his head against the wall. Perhaps he was going mad. That would explain everything.

Of course, none of this mattered to his cock. Mad or sane, it was still overeager to feel the woman's tight, slippery sheath. He stopped banging his head against the wall and looked at the clock again. She was thirty-three minutes late now.

By God's balls, he wasn't going to wait another minute more.

Edward snatched his coat up and slammed out of the room. Two gray-haired gentlemen were strolling down the hall. They took one look at his face and pressed to the side as he stormed past. He ran down the grand staircase two risers at a time and stalked into the parlor where the male customers went to mingle and meet disguised ladies and whores. He scanned the gaudy room. There were several women in bright colors, each surrounded by eager men, but only one woman wore a golden mask. She was taller than the other females and stood apart, alert to the currents in the room. Her full-face mask was smooth and serene, the eyebrows symmetrical incised arcs above the almond-shaped eyeholes. Aphrodite watched over her wares with a beady eagle eye.

Edward strode directly to her. "Where is she?" he demanded.

The madam, normally an unflappable woman, jerked at his sudden question by her side. "Lord Swartingham, isn't it?"

"Yes. Where is the woman I was to meet tonight?"

"She isn't in your room, my lord?"

"No." Edward grit his teeth. "No, she isn't in the room. Would I be down here asking after her if she were up in the room?"

"We have many other willing ladies, my lord." The madam's voice sounded ingratiating. "Perhaps I can send another to your room?"

Edward leaned forward. "I don't want another. I want the woman I had last night and the night before. Who is she?"

Aphrodite's eyes shifted behind the gold mask. "Now, my lord, you know we can't reveal the identity of our lovely doves here at the Grotto. Professional integrity, you know."

Edward snorted. "I don't give a bloody damn about the professional integrity of a whorehouse. Who. Is. She?"

Aphrodite backed a step, as if alarmed. Not surprisingly, since he now loomed above her. She made a signal with her hand to someone over his shoulder.

Edward narrowed his eyes. He knew he had only a few minutes. "I want her name—now—or I will enjoy starting a riot in your parlor."

"No need for threats. There are several other wenches here who would be eager to spend the night with you." Aphrodite's voice held a smirk. "Ones who don't mind a pockmark or two."

Edward went still. He knew well enough what his face looked like. It didn't distress him anymore—he was past the age of agonized vanity—but it did repel some women. The little whore hadn't seemed to mind his scars. Of course, last night they'd made love in the chair by the firelight. Perhaps it had been the first time she'd truly seen his face. Perhaps she had been so disgusted by the sight that she hadn't bothered to show up tonight.

Goddamn her.

Edward pivoted on his heel. He grabbed a faux Chinese vase, raised it above his head, and slammed it to the floor. It shattered explosively. Conversation in the room ceased as heads turned.

Too much thought was bad for a man. What he needed was action. If he couldn't work off his energy in bed, well, this was second best.

He was seized from behind and pulled around. A fist the size of a ham hurtled at his face. Edward leaned back. The blow went whistling past his nose. He brought his own right fist in low to the man's belly. The other man *oofed* out the air in his lungs—a lovely sound—and staggered.

Three men moved in to take the other's place. They were the big bruisers kept by the house to escort trouble-makers outside. One of them got in a roundhouse to the left side of his face. Edward saw stars, but it didn't stop him returning with a pretty uppercut.

Several of the patrons cheered.

And then after that, things became muddled. Many of the spectators appeared to be sporting men who thought the odds uneven. They joined the brawl with tipsy enthu-siasm. Girls frantically scrambled over settees, shrieking and upsetting furniture in their haste to get out of the way. Aphrodite stood in the middle of the room, shouting or-ders that no one could hear. She stopped abruptly when someone shoved her headfirst into a bowl of punch. Tables flew through the air. An enterprising demimondaine began taking bets in the hallway from the men and girls who had flooded the stairs to view the commotion. Four more bullies and at least as many men from the upstairs rooms joined the melee. Some of the guests had clearly been interrupted in their entertainment, as they wore only breeches or—in the case of one rather distinguished-looking old gent—a shirt and nothing else.

Edward was enjoying himself immensely.

Blood ran down his chin from a split lip, and he could feel one eye slowly swelling shut. A smallish villain clung to his back and hit him about the head and shoulders. In front of him, another, bigger man tried to kick his legs out from under him. Edward sidestepped the attempt and brought his own foot up to shove against the man's other leg while his weight was off balance. He went down like a colossus.

The imp on his back was becoming a nuisance. Grabbing the man by his hair, Edward swiftly rammed himself backward into a wall. He heard a *thunk* as the man's head met the solid surface. The man slid from Edward's shoulders and landed on the floor along with a good deal of the plaster from the wall.

Edward grinned and glared around through his good eye for more prey. One of the house thugs attempted to sidle out the door. He looked wildly over his shoulder when Edward's gaze settled on him, but there were none of his brethren to come to his aid.

"'Ave mercy, milord. I don't get paid enough to be beat bloody like you done with the rest of the lads." The thug held up his hands and backed away from Edward's advance. "Why, you even did Big Billy in, and I ain't never seen a man faster than him."

"Very well," Edward said. "Although, I can't see out of my right eye, which evens the odds. . . ." He looked hopefully at the cringing bully who smiled weakly and shook his head. "No? Well, then, I don't suppose you know of a place where a man can get properly drunk, do you?"

Thus, a little while later, Edward found himself at what had to be the seediest tavern in the East End of London. With him were the house thugs, including Big Billy, now nursing a swollen nose and two black eyes but no hard feelings. Big Billy had his arm around Edward's shoulders and was attempting to teach him the words to a ditty extolling the charms of a lass named Titty. The song seemed to have a lot of rather clever double entendres that Edward suspected were lost on him since he'd been standing drinks for everyone in the room for the last two hours.

"W-who was the whore you was looking for that started all this, milord?" Jackie, the thug asking, had not missed any of the rounds of drinks. He addressed the question to the air somewhere to Edward's right.

"Faithless woman," Edward muttered into his ale.

"All wenches are faithless tarts." This bit of masculine wisdom came from Big Billy.

The men present nodded somberly, although it caused one or two to lose their balance and sit down rather abruptly.

"No. S'not true," Edward said.

"What s'not true?"

"All women faithless," Edward said carefully. "I know a woman who's as p-pure as the driven snow."

"Who's that?" "Tell us, then, milord!" The men clamored to hear the name of this feminine paragon.

"Mrs. Anna Wren." He raised his glass precariously. "A toast! A toast to the most un-un-unblemished lady in England. Mrs. Anna Wren!"

The tavern erupted in boisterous cheers and toasts to the lady. And Edward wondered why all the lights went out suddenly.

HIS HEAD WAS coming apart. Edward opened his eyes, but then immediately thought better of that idea and squeezed them shut again. Carefully, he touched his temple and tried to think why the top of his head felt like it was about to explode.

He remembered Aphrodite's Grotto.

He remembered the woman not showing up.

He remembered a fight. Edward grimaced and gingerly probed with his tongue. His teeth were all intact. That was good news.

His mind strained.

He remembered meeting a jolly fellow. . . . Big Bob? Big Bert? No, Big Billy. He remembered—Oh, God. He remembered toasting Anna in the worst hellhole he had ever had the misfortune to drink watered-down ale in. His stomach rolled unpleasantly. Had he really bandied Anna's name about in such a place? Yes, he thought he had. And, if he recalled correctly, the whole roomful of disreputable rogues had bawdily toasted her.

He moaned.

Davis opened the door, letting it bang against the wall, and slowly shuffled into the room bearing a laden tray.

Edward moaned again. The sound of the door had nearly made his scalp separate from his skull. "Damn your eyes. Not now, Davis."

Davis continued on his snaillike course to the bed.

"I know you can hear me," he spoke slightly louder, but not too loud, for fear of setting his head off again.

"Been in our cups have we, m'lord?" Davis shouted.

"I didn't know you'd overindulged as well," Edward said from behind the hands covering his face.

Davis ignored this. "Lovely gents what brought you home last night. New friends of yours?"

Edward parted his fingers to shoot a glare at his valet.

Evidently it bounced harmlessly off the man. "Bit long in the tooth to be guzzling so much, m'lord. Might lead to gout at your age."

"I'm overwhelmed by your concern for my health." Edward looked at the tray Davis had now managed to set on the bedside table. It held a cup of tea, already cold, judging by the scum floating on top, and a bowl of milk-toast. "What the hell is this? Nursery pap? Bring me some brandy to settle this head."

Davis pretended deafness with an aplomb that would have done justice to the finest stage in London. He had had many years of practice, after all.

"Here's a lovely breakfast to put vigor back into you," the valet bawled in his ear. "Milk is very strengthening for a man at your age."

"Get out! Get out! Get out!" Edward roared, and then had to hold his head again.

Davis retreated to the door, but he couldn't resist a parting shot. "Need to watch your temper, m'lord. Might go all red in the face and buggy-eyed with apoplexy. Nasty way to go, that."

He scooted through the door with amazing dexterity for a man his age. Just before the bowl of milk-toast hit.

Edward groaned and closed his eyes, his head flopping back on the pillow. He ought to get up and start packing to go home. He'd obtained a fiancée and visited the Grotto, not once, but twice. He had, in fact, done all he'd meant to do when he'd decided to travel to London. And even if he felt far worse now than he had when he'd first come, there was no point in staying in the city. The little whore wouldn't return, he would never encounter her again, and he had responsibilities of his own to see to. And that was as it should be.

There was no room in his life for a mysterious masked woman and the transitory pleasure she brought.

Chapter Twelve

The days and nights passed as if in a dream, and
Aurea was content. Perhaps she was even happy. But
after several months, she began to have an urge to see
her father. The urge grew and grew until all her
waking moments were filled with a longing for her
father's face, and she became listless and sad.
One night at dinner, the raven turned the bright
ebony bead of his eye upon her and said, "What
causes this malaise I sense in you, my wife?"
"I long to see my father's face again, my lord,"
Aurea sighed. "I miss him."
"Impossible!" the raven squawked, and left
the table without another word.
But Aurea, although she never made complaint, so
missed her parent that she stopped eating and only
picked at the delicacies set before her. She began to
waste away until one day the raven could no longer
stand it. He flapped into her room angrily.
"Go, then, and visit your sire, wife," he cawed. "But
be very sure that you return within a fortnight, for
I would pine were you to stay longer."
—from *The Raven Prince*

"Oh, my goodness!" Anna exclaimed the next day. "What have you done to your face?"

She would notice the bruises. Edward halted and glowered at her. She hadn't seen him in five days, and the first words out of her mouth were an accusation. Briefly, he tried to imagine any of his previous, *male* secretaries daring to comment on his appearance. It was impossible. In fact, he couldn't think of anyone, save his current *female* secretary, who made such impertinent comments to him. Oddly, he found her impertinence endearing.

Not that he let it show. Edward raised a brow and tried to put his secretary in her place. "I have done nothing to my face, thank you, Mrs. Wren."

It had no noticeable effect.

"You can't call that black eye and the bruises on your jaw nothing." Anna looked disapproving. "Have you put any salve on it yet?"

She sat in her usual place at the small rosewood desk in his library. She looked serene and golden in the morning light from the window, as if she hadn't moved from the desk the entire time he had been in London. It was a strangely comforting thought. Edward noted that she had a small smudge of ink on her chin.

And something was different about her appearance.

"I haven't used any salve, Mrs. Wren, because there is no reason to." He tried to walk the remaining feet to his desk without limping.

Naturally, she noticed that, too. "And your leg! Why are you limping, my lord?"

"I am not limping."

She arched her eyebrows so high, they nearly disappeared into her hairline.

Edward was forced to glare in order to emphasize the lie. He tried to think of an explanation for his injuries that wouldn't make him look a total fool. He certainly couldn't tell his little secretary that he'd been in a brawl at a brothel.

What was it about her appearance?

"Did you have an accident?" she asked before he could think of a suitable excuse.

He seized on the suggestion. "Yes, an accident." Something about her hair . . . A new style, perhaps?

His respite was brief.

"Did you fall off your horse?"

"No!" Edward strove to lower his voice and had a sudden inspiration. He could *see* her hair. "No, I didn't fall off my horse. Where is your cap?"

As a distraction, it failed abysmally.

"I've decided not to wear it any longer," she said primly. "If you didn't fall off your horse, then what did happen to you?"

The woman would have been an outstanding success with the inquisition.

"I . . ." For the life of him, he could not think of a suitable story.

Anna looked worried. "Your carriage didn't overturn, did it?"

"No."

"Were you run down by a cart in London? I hear the streets are terribly crowded."

"No. I wasn't run down by a cart either." He tried to

smile charmingly. "I like you without your cap. Your tresses shine like a field of daisies."

Anna narrowed her eyes. Perhaps he hadn't any charm. "I wasn't aware that daisies were brown. Are you sure you didn't fall off your horse?"

Edward gritted his teeth and prayed for forbearance. "I did not fall off my horse. I have *never*—"

She raised one brow.

"*Hardly* ever been unseated from my horse."

A swift expression of enlightenment came over her features. "It's all right, you know," she said in an unbearably understanding voice. "Even the best horsemen fall off their mounts sometimes. It is nothing to be ashamed of."

Edward got up from his desk, limped across to hers, and placed both hands, palms down, upon it. He leaned over until his eyes were only inches from her hazel ones. "I am not ashamed," he said very slowly. "I did not fall off my horse. I was not thrown from my horse. I wish to end this discussion. Is that amenable to you, Mrs. Wren?"

Anna swallowed visibly, drawing his eyes to her throat. "Yes. Yes, that's quite amenable to me, Lord Swartingham."

"Good." His gaze rose to her lips, wet where she had licked them in her nervousness. "I thought of you while I was gone. Did you think of me? Did you miss me?"

"I—" she started to whisper.

Hopple breezed into the room. "Welcome back, my lord. I hope your sojourn in our lovely capital was pleasant?" The steward came to a halt when he noticed Edward's stance over Anna.

Edward slowly straightened, his eyes never leaving Anna. "My stay was pleasant enough, Hopple, although I found I missed the . . . loveliness of the country."

Anna looked flustered.

Edward smiled.

Mr. Hopple started. "Lord Swartingham! Whatever happened to—?"

Anna cut him off. "Mr. Hopple, have you time to show the earl the new ditch?"

"The ditch? But—" Hopple looked from Edward to Anna.

Anna twitched her eyebrows as if a fly had landed on her forehead. "The new ditch to drain Mr. Grundle's field. You did mention it the other day."

"The . . . Oh, yes, Farmer Grundle's ditch," Hopple said. "If you will come with me, my lord, I think you'll be interested in inspecting it."

Edward's eyes were back on Anna. "I'll meet with you in half an hour, Hopple. I've something I wish to discuss with my secretary first."

"Oh, yes. Yes. Er, very well, my lord." Hopple departed, looking befuddled.

"What was it you wished to discuss with me, my lord?" she asked.

Edward cleared his throat. "Actually, there's something I want to show you. If you'll come with me?"

Anna appeared mystified but stood and took his arm. He led her out to the hall, turning to the back door instead of the front. When they stepped into the kitchen, Cook nearly dropped her morning cup of tea. Three maids were clustered by the table where Cook sat, like acolytes around their priest. All four females came to their feet.

Edward waved them back down again. No doubt he'd interrupted a morning gossip. Without explanation, he continued through the kitchen and out the back door. They crossed the wide stable yard, his boot heels ringing on the cobblestones. The morning sun shone brightly, and the stables cast a long shadow behind them. Edward rounded a corner of the building and stopped in the shade. Anna glanced around, looking puzzled.

Edward had a sudden, awful feeling of uncertainty. It was an unusual gift. Maybe she wouldn't like it or—worse—be insulted.

"This is for you." He gestured abruptly at a muddy lump of burlap.

Anna looked from him to the burlap. "What—?"

Edward stooped and threw back a corner of the bundle. Underneath lay what looked like a bunch of dead, thorny sticks.

Anna squealed.

That noise had to be a good sign in a female, didn't it? Edward frowned uncertainly. Then she smiled up at him, and he felt warmth suffuse his chest.

"Roses!" she exclaimed.

She dropped to her knees to examine one of the dormant rosebushes. He'd carefully wrapped them in damp burlap to keep the roots from drying out before departing from London. Each bush had only a few thorny branches, but the roots were long and healthy.

"Careful, they're sharp," Edward murmured to her down-bent head.

Anna counted busily. "There's two dozen here. Do you mean to put them all in your garden?"

Edward scowled at her. "They're for you. For your cottage."

Anna opened her mouth and for a moment seemed at a loss for words. "But . . . even if I could accept them all, they must have been terribly expensive."

Was she refusing his gift? "Why can't you accept them?"

"Well, for one, I couldn't fit them all in my little garden."

"How many could you fit?"

"Oh, I suppose three or four," Anna said.

"Pick out the four you want, and I'll send the rest back." Edward felt relief. At least she wasn't rejecting the roses. "Or burn them," he added as an afterthought.

"Burn them!" Anna sounded horrified. "But you can't just burn them. Don't you want them for your own garden?"

He shook his head impatiently. "I don't know how to put them in."

"I do. I'll plant them for you in thanks for the others." Anna smiled up at him, looking a little shy. "Thank you for the roses, Lord Swartingham."

Edward cleared his throat. "You're welcome, Mrs. Wren." He had a strange urge to shuffle his feet like a little boy. "I suppose I ought to see Hopple."

She simply looked at him.

"Yes . . . Ah, yes." Good God, he was stuttering like an imbecile. "I'll just go find him, then." With a muttered farewell, he strode off in search of the steward.

Who knew giving presents to secretaries could be so stressful?

ANNA ABSENTLY WATCHED Lord Swartingham walk away, her hand fisting in the muddy burlap. She knew how this man felt against her in the dark. She knew how his body moved when he made love. She knew the deep husky sounds he produced in the back of his throat when he reached his climax. She knew the most intimate things one could know about a man, but she didn't know how to reconcile that knowledge to the sight of him in the daylight. To reconcile the man who made love so sublimely to the man who brought her rosebushes from London.

Anna shook her head. Perhaps it was too hard a question. Perhaps one could never understand the difference between the passion of a man at night and the civil face he showed during the day.

She hadn't realized what it would be like to see him again after spending two unbelievable nights in his arms. Now she knew. She felt sad, as if she'd lost something that had never truly been hers. She'd gone to London with the intention of making love to him, to enjoy the physical act as a man would: unemotionally. But as it turned out, she wasn't as stoic as a man. She was a woman, and where her body went, her emotions followed willy-nilly. The act had somehow bound her to him, whether he knew it or not.

And he could never know it now. What had transpired between them in that room at Aphrodite's Grotto must remain her secret alone.

She stared blindly down at the rose stems. Perhaps the roses were a sign that things could still be healed. Anna touched a prickly rose branch. They must mean something, surely? A gentleman didn't usually give such a lovely gift—such a perfect gift—to his secretary, did he?

A thorn pricked the ball of her thumb. Absentmindedly, she sucked on the wound. Maybe there was hope after all. As long as he never, ever discovered her deception.

LATER THAT MORNING, Edward stood calf-deep in muddy water, inspecting the new drainage ditch. A lark sang in the border of Mr. Grundle's field. Probably ecstatic it was dry. Nearby, two smock-clad laborers from Grundle's farm shoveled muck to keep the ditch free of debris.

Hopple also stood in muddy water, looking particularly aggrieved. This might be in part because he had slipped and fallen in the scummy water once already. His waistcoat, formerly an egg-yolk yellow with green piping, was filthy. The water from the ditch gushed into a nearby stream as the steward explained the engineering of the project.

Edward watched the laborers, nodded at Hopple's sermon, and thought about Anna's reaction to his gift. When Anna spoke, he had a hard time keeping his eyes off her exotic mouth. How such a mouth had come to be on such a plain little woman was a great mystery, one that apparently could enthrall him for hours. That mouth could lead the Archbishop of Canterbury to sin.

"Don't you think so, my lord?" Hopple asked.

"Oh, most definitely. Most definitely."

The steward looked at him strangely.

Edward sighed. "Just continue."

Jock bounded into view with a small, unfortunate rodent in his mouth. He leaped the ditch and landed with a splash of muddy water, completing the ruin of Hopple's waistcoat. Jock presented his find to Edward. It was immediately apparent that his treasure had left this life quite some time ago.

Hopple backed hastily away, waving a handkerchief before his face and muttering irritably, "Good gracious! I thought when that dog went missing for several days we were well rid of it."

Edward absently petted Jock, the odoriferous present still in the dog's mouth. A maggot fell with a plop into the water. Hopple swallowed and continued his explanation of the wonderful drain with his handkerchief over his nose and mouth.

Of course, after coming to know Anna, Edward had no longer found her so plain. In fact, he was at a loss to explain how he had so thoroughly discounted her the first time they met. How was it that he'd initially thought her rather ordinary? Except for her mouth, of course. He'd always been aware of her mouth.

Edward sighed and kicked at some debris under the water, sending up a splash of mud. She was a lady. That he had never been wrong about even if he had misjudged her attraction at first. As a gentleman, he shouldn't even be thinking about Anna in this way. That was what whores were for, after all. Ladies simply didn't contemplate kneeling in front of a man and slowly bending their beautiful, erotic mouths down to . . .

Edward shifted uncomfortably and scowled. Now that he was officially engaged to Miss Gerard, he must stop thinking about Anna's mouth. Or any other part of her for that matter. He needed to put Anna—*Mrs. Wren*—right out of his mind in order to have a successful second marriage.

His future family depended on it.

WHAT FUNNY THINGS roses were: prickly hard on the surface, yet so fragile inside, Anna mused that evening. Roses were one of the most difficult flowers to grow, needing much more coddling and worry than any other plant; yet, once established, they might grow for years, even if abandoned.

The garden behind her cottage was only about twenty feet by thirty, but there was still room for a small shed at the back. She'd used a candle in the gathering dusk to light her way as she had rummaged about in the shed and had found an old washbasin and a couple of tin buckets. Now she carefully laid the roses in the containers and covered them with the bitterly cold water from the little garden well.

Anna stood back and regarded her work critically. It had almost seemed like Lord Swartingham had avoided her after he'd given her the roses. He hadn't shown up for luncheon, and he'd only stopped by the library once that afternoon. But of course he had plenty of work built up over the five days that he had been gone, and he was a very busy man. She pulled the muddy burlap over the top of the washbasin and buckets. She'd set the containers in the shade of the cottage so they wouldn't burn in the sun tomorrow. It might be a day or two before she could plant them, but the water would keep them vital. She nodded and went in to wash up for supper.

The Wren household dined on roasted potatoes and a bit of gammon that night. The meal was almost over when Mother Wren dropped her fork and exclaimed, "Oh, I've forgotten to tell you, dear. While you were gone, Mrs. Clearwater invited us to her spring soiree the day after next."

Anna paused with her teacup halfway to her lips. "Really? We've never been invited before."

"She knows you're friends with Lord Swartingham." Mother Wren smiled complacently. "It would be a coup for her if he attended."

"I don't have any influence over whether the earl will attend or not. You know that, Mother."

"Do you really think so?" Mother Wren tilted her head. "Lord Swartingham hasn't made any effort to join our social diversions. He accepts no invitations to tea or dinner, and he hasn't bothered to attend church on Sundays."

"I suppose he does keep to himself," Anna admitted.

"Some are saying he is too proud to be seen at the country amusements here."

"That isn't true."

"Oh, I know he is quite nice." Mother Wren poured herself a second cup of tea. "Why, he had breakfast in this very cottage with us and very gracious he was, too. But he hasn't gone out of his way to endear himself with many others in the village. It doesn't do his reputation good."

Anna frowned down at her half-eaten potato. "I hadn't realized so many saw him in that light. The tenants on his land adore him."

Mother Wren nodded. "The tenants might. But he needs to be gracious to those higher up in society as well."

"I'll try to convince him to come to the soiree." Anna straightened her shoulders. "But it might be a job. As you say, he isn't very interested in social events."

Mother Wren smiled. "In the meantime, we need to discuss what we'll wear to the soiree."

"I hadn't even thought of that." Anna frowned. "All I have is my old green silk gown. There simply isn't enough time to have the material I brought from London made into dresses."

"It is a shame," Mother Wren agreed. "But your green gown is very becoming, my dear. The lovely color brings roses to your cheeks and sets off your hair so well. Although, I suppose the neckline is sadly out of date."

"Maybe we could use some of the trimmings Mrs. Wren bought in London," Fanny said shyly. She'd been hovering nearby throughout the conversation.

"What a good idea." Mother Wren beamed at her, making the girl flush. "We had better get started tonight."

"Yes, indeed, but there is something I want to find before we begin on the dresses."

Anna pushed back her chair and crossed to the old kitchen cupboard. She knelt and opened the bottom cabinet and peered in.

"Whatever are you looking for, Anna?" Mother Wren asked from behind her.

Anna backed out of the cabinet and sneezed before triumphantly holding up a dusty little jar. "My mother's salve for bruises and abrasions."

Mother Wren looked at the jar doubtfully. "Your mother was a wonderful amateur herbalist, my dear, and I've been grateful for her salve many times in the past, but it does have an unfortunate odor. Are you sure you need it?"

Anna got up, briskly shaking out the dust in her skirts. "Oh, it's not for me. It's for the earl. He had an accident with his horse."

"An accident with his horse?" Her mother-in-law blinked. "Did he fall off?"

"Oh, no. Lord Swartingham is much too good a horseman to fall off his horse," Anna said. "I'm not sure what exactly happened. I don't think he wants to discuss it. But he has the most terrible bruises on his face."

"On his face . . ." Mother Wren trailed off thoughtfully.

"Yes, one of his eyes looks quite bruised, and his jaw is black and blue."

"So you intend to put the salve on his face?" Mother Wren covered her own nose as if in sympathy.

Anna ignored her theatrics. "It will help him heal faster."

"I'm sure you know best," Mother Wren replied, but she didn't look particularly convinced.

THE NEXT MORNING, Anna ran her quarry to ground in the stable yard. Lord Swartingham stood firing instructions at Mr. Hopple, who was noting them as best he could in a little book. Jock lay nearby, but he got up to greet Anna when he saw her. The earl noticed, stopped, and turned his black eyes on Anna. He smiled.

Mr. Hopple glanced up at the cessation of directions. "Good morning, Mrs. Wren." He looked back to Lord Swartingham. "Shall I start on these, my lord?"

"Yes, yes," the earl replied impatiently.

The steward hurried away, looking relieved.

The earl sauntered over. "Is there something you need?" He kept walking until he stood too close to her.

She could see the fine threads of silver in his hair. "Yes," she said briskly. "I need you to hold still."

His beautiful ebony eyes widened. "What?"

"I have some salve for your face." She produced the little jar from her basket and held it up.

He eyed it dubiously.

"It's my late mother's own recipe. She swore by its healing properties."

Anna took the lid off, and the earl jerked his head back at the pungent smell that rolled up. Jock attempted to put his nose in the jar.

Lord Swartingham pulled the dog down by the scruff of his neck. "Good God. It smells like horse—" He caught her narrowed eye. "Hide," he finished lamely.

"Well, that's appropriate for the stable yard, don't you think?" she replied tartly.

The earl looked worried. "It doesn't actually have horse—"

"Oh, no." Anna was shocked. "It's composed of sheep fat and herbs and some other things. I'm not sure exactly what. I'd have to look up my mother's recipe to tell you.

But there is definitely no horse—uh, nothing objection-able in it. Now hold still."

He cocked an eyebrow at her tone but obediently stood motionless. She scooped out a greasy glob with her fin-ger, stretched on tiptoe, and began to smooth it over his cheekbone. He was very tall, and she had to crowd rather close in order to reach his face. Lord Swartingham was silent, breathing deeply as she spread the salve carefully up near his black eye. She could feel him watching her. She took another dollop and began to rub it gently on his discolored jaw. The salve was cool but became warm and slippery as his skin heated it. She felt the faint scrape of his beard under her fingers and had to fight the urge to linger. She completed the last pass and let her hand fall.

He looked down at her.

In moving closer to him in order to apply the salve, she'd crept between his spread legs. His heat surrounded her body. She started to step away. But his hands wrapped around her arms. His fingers flexed, and he seemed to gaze intently at her. Anna held her breath. Would he . . .?

He let her go.

"Thank you, Mrs. Wren." He opened his mouth as if to say something more and then shut it. "I have some work to attend to. I'll see you later this afternoon." He nodded curtly before turning away.

Jock looked at her, whined, and then followed his master.

Anna watched them stride away, then sighed and thoughtfully put the lid back on the salve jar.

Chapter Thirteen

So Aurea went home to visit her father. She traveled in a golden coach drawn by flying swans, and she carried with her many beautiful things to give to her family and friends. But when her older sisters saw the wonderful gifts that the younger girl had brought home, their hearts, instead of filling with gratitude and pleasure, wallowed in jealousy and spite. The sisters put their beautiful, cold heads together and began to quiz Aurea about her new home and her odd husband. And little by little, they heard all: the richness of the palace, the avian servants, the exotic meals, and finally—and most importantly—the silent, nocturnal lover. Hearing the last, they grinned behind their pale hands and set to planting the seeds of doubt in their little sister's mind. . . .

—from *The Raven Prince*

"Farther to the top." Felicity Clearwater wrinkled her brow and stared at the ceiling in her larger sitting room. The drawn curtains muted the afternoon sun outside. "No. No, more to the left."

A masculine voice muttered irritably.

"That's it," she said. "There. I think you've got it." In the corner, a crack snaked across the ceiling. She'd never noticed it before. It must be new. "Did you find her?"

Chilton Lillipin, "Chilly" to his intimates, one of whom was Felicity, spat out a hair. "My darling gosling, do try to relax. You're disturbing my artistry." He bent again.

Artistry? She suppressed a snort. She closed her eyes for a bit and tried to concentrate on her lover and what he was doing, but it was no use. She opened her eyes again. She really needed to have the plasterers in to repair that crack. And the last time they'd come, Reginald had been an absolute bear, stomping about and grumbling as if the workmen were only there to bother him. Felicity sighed.

"That's it, sweetheart," Chilly said from below. "Just lie back and let a master lover bring you to heaven."

She rolled her eyes. She'd almost forgotten the *master lover*. She sighed again. There was no help for it.

Felicity began to moan.

Fifteen minutes later, Chilly stood before the sitting room mirror, carefully adjusting his wig. He studied his reflection and slid the wig marginally to the right on his shaved head. He was a handsome man, but just a bit off, in Felicity's opinion. His eyes were pure blue, but they were set just a shade too close together. His features were regular, but his chin gave up and slid into his neck just a bit too soon. And his limbs were well muscled, but his legs were a fraction too short to be in proportion to the rest of his body. Chilly's offness continued into his personality. She'd heard rumors that, although skilled in swordplay,

Chilly proved his prowess by challenging less-accomplished men to duels and then killing them.

Felicity narrowed her eyes. She wouldn't trust Chilly at her back in a dark alley, but he did have his uses. "Did you find out where she went to in London?"

"Of course." Chilly smirked at himself in the glass. His gold canine winked back at him. "The little chit ended up at a bawdy house called Aphrodite's Grotto. Not once, but twice. Can you believe?"

"Aphrodite's Grotto?"

"It's a high-flying establishment." Chilly gave a last tug to his wig and abandoned the mirror to glance at her. "Ladies of the *ton* sometimes go there in disguise to meet their paramours."

"Really?" Felicity tried not to sound intrigued.

Chilly poured a tumblerful of the squire's best smuggled brandy. "Seems a little above a country widow."

Yes, it did. How had Anna Wren paid for such a place? The establishment Chilly described was expensive. Her lover would have to be rich. He must have a good knowledge of London and the less-reputable haunts of the *ton*. And the only gentleman who fit that description in Little Battleford, the only gentleman who had traveled to London during the same time period as Anna Wren, was the Earl of Swartingham. A triumphant shiver went down Felicity's spine.

"What's this all about, then?" Chilly peered over his glass at her. "Who cares if a brown mouse has a secret life?" He sounded a bit too curious for her taste.

"Never you mind." Felicity lounged back on the chaise and stretched luxuriantly, her breasts thrusting out.

Chilly's attention was immediately diverted. "I'll tell you someday."

"Don't I at least get a reward?" Chilly pretended to pout, an unattractive sight. He strolled closer and crowded against the edge of the chaise.

He had done well. And Felicity felt on good terms with the world. Why not humor the man? She stretched out a feline hand to the buttons on Chilly's breeches.

EDWARD PULLED THE mangled cravat from his neck that night. He had to get control of his body's impulses. He scowled and tossed the crumpled neckcloth on top of a chair. His room in the Abbey was a rather dismal place, the furniture big and clumsy, the colors drab and depressed. It was a wonder the de Raafs had been able to maintain the family line at all in such a setting.

Davis, as usual, wasn't around when he might be useful. Edward wedged the heel of his boot in the bootjack and began levering. He'd come very close to not letting go of Anna in the stable yard. To kissing her, in fact. It was exactly the sort of thing he'd been trying to prevent for the last few weeks.

The first boot fell to the floor, and he started work on the second. The trip to London was supposed to have solved this problem. And now with the marriage nearly finalized . . . Well, he had to start acting the part of a soon-to-be-married man. No pondering Anna's hair and why she had put off her cap. No contemplating how close she had stood when she'd applied the salve. And especially, he would not think of her mouth and how it would feel if he opened it wide beneath his own and . . .

Damn.

The second boot came off, and Davis, with exquisite timing, banged into the room. "Goramity! What is that smell? Pee-yeew!"

The valet held a stack of freshly laundered cravats in his hands, the apparent reason for his rare, voluntary visit to his employer's rooms.

Edward sighed. "A good evening to you, too, Davis."

"Christ all Jaysus! Fell in a pigsty, did you?"

Edward began pulling off his stockings. "Are you aware that some valets actually spend their time helping their masters to dress and undress rather than making rude comments about their person?"

Davis cackled. "Ha. Should've told me you were having problems buttoning your pantyloons, m'lord. I would've helped you."

Edward scowled. "Just put away the cravats and get out."

Davis tottered to the highboy, pulled out a top drawer, and dumped the cravats in. "What's that slimy stuff on your mug?" he asked.

"Mrs. Wren kindly gave me some salve for my bruises this afternoon," Edward said with dignity.

The valet tilted toward him and inhaled with a loud snuffling sound. "That's where the stank is coming from. It smells like horseshit."

"Davis!"

"Well, it do. Haven't smelled anything near that bad since you was a lad and fell on your arse into that pigsty back of Old Peward's farm. Remember that?"

"How could I forget with you around?" Edward muttered.

"Gor! Thought we'd never get the stank out of you that time. And I had to throw away them breeches."

"Pleasant as this recollection is—"

"'Course, you never would've fallen in if you hadn't been ogling Old Peward's daughter," Davis continued.

"I was not ogling anyone. I slipped."

"Naw." Davis scratched his scalp. "Your eyes were about falling out of your head they were, gawking at her big bubbies."

Edward grit his teeth. "I *slipped* and fell."

"Almost a sign from the Lord above, that," Davis said, waxing philosophical. "Gawp at a girl's bubbies and land in pig shit."

"Oh, for God's sake. I was sitting on the railing of the pigsty and I slipped."

"Prissy Peward sure did have big dugs, that lass did." Davis sounded a little wistful.

"You weren't even there."

"But that pigsty stank had nothing on the horseshit on your face now."

"*Dav*-vis."

The valet made his way back to the door waving a liver-spotted hand in front of his face as he went. "Must be balmy to let a woman smear horsesh—"

"*Davis!*"

"All over your face."

The valet reached the door and slanted around the corner, still mumbling. Since his progress was, as usual, slow, Edward could hear his nattering for a good five minutes more. Oddly, it became louder the farther Davis moved from the door.

Edward frowned at himself in his shaving mirror. The salve did smell terrible. He reached for a basin and poured some water into it from the pitcher on his dresser. He picked up a washcloth and then hesitated. The salve was already on his face, and it had pleased Anna to put it there. He rubbed his thumb across the edge of his jaw, remembering her soft hands.

He threw down the washcloth.

He could wash off the salve when he shaved in the morning. It wouldn't hurt to leave it on tonight. He turned from the dresser and took off the remainder of his clothes, folding and placing them on a chair as he did so. There was at least one advantage to having an unusual valet: He had learned to be neat with his apparel since Davis didn't deign to pick up after him. Standing naked, Edward yawned and stretched before climbing into the ancient four-poster bed. He leaned over and blew out the bedside candle and then lay there in the dark staring at the shadowy outlines of the bed curtains. He wondered fuzzily how old they were. Certainly older than the house itself. Had they originally been this awful shade of brownish yellow?

His eyes sleepily swept the room, and he saw near the door the shape of a woman.

He blinked and suddenly she stood by his bed.

She smiled. The same smile Eve wore when she'd held the fateful apple out to Adam. The woman was gloriously nude except for a butterfly mask on her face.

He thought, *It's the whore from Aphrodite's Grotto.*
And then, *I'm dreaming.*

But the thought drifted away. She slowly rubbed her
hands up her midriff, drawing his eyes with them. She
cupped her breasts and leaned forward so the tips were at
the level of his eyes. Then she began to pinch and tease
her own nipples.

His mouth went dry as he watched her nipples elongate
and turn cherry red. He lifted his head to kiss her breasts,
for his mouth fairly watered with the need to taste her, but
she moved away with a taunting smile. The woman lifted
her flowing, honey-brown hair away from her neck. Curling tentacles clung to her arms. She arched her slender
back, thrusting her breasts up and forward like juicy fruit
before him. He growled and felt his cock throb against his
stomach at her teasing.

The woman smiled a witchy smile. She knew exactly
what she was doing to him. She smoothed her hands back
down her torso, past her thrusting breasts, over her downy
belly, and paused. Her fingers just touched the glinting
curls of her bush. He willed her to move them farther, but
she teased him, lightly combing through her maiden hair.
Just when he could stand it no longer, she chuckled low
and spread her legs.

Edward didn't know if he still breathed. His eyes were
locked on her hands and her pussy. She parted her nether
lips for him. He could see the ruby skin glistening with
her fluid and smell her musk lifting from her flesh. She
dipped one slender finger into her cleft. Slowly, she
stroked up and found her clitoris. She petted herself, her
finger moving in slippery circles on the bud. Her hips

began to rotate, and she let her head fall back and moaned. The sound mingled with Edward's own groan of pure lust. He was rock hard, pulsing with need.

He watched as she tilted her pelvis toward him. She slid her middle finger into her pussy and moved it out and back again, slowly, languidly, the finger shining with her moisture. Her other hand moved faster on her clitoris, torturing the fragile nubbin. Suddenly she stiffened, her head still thrown back, and moaned, low and keening. Her finger worked furiously in and out of her body.

Edward groaned again. He could see the evidence of her orgasm sliding down her silky thighs. The sight nearly sent him over the edge. The woman sighed and relaxed, her hips swiveling sensuously one last time. She drew her fingers from herself and brought them, wet and shining, to his lips. She brushed her fingers over his mouth, and he tasted her desire. Dazedly, he looked up at her and realized that the mask had fallen away from her face.

Anna smiled down at him.

Then his orgasm took him, and he woke to the almost agonizing jerking of his cock as he gained his release.

ANNA'S EYES ADJUSTED to the cool dimness the next morning as she wandered down the packed-earth aisle of Ravenhill Abbey's stables. The building was venerable. It had served the Abbey through several reconstructions and expansions. Stones the size of a man's head formed the foundation and the lower walls. Six feet from the ground, the walls became sturdy oak that led up to the exposed rafters, vaulting twenty feet overhead. Below, stalls flanked a central aisle.

The Ravenhill stables had room for fifty horses easily, although fewer than ten were currently in residence. The relative paucity of horses saddened her. This must at one time have been a thriving, active place. Now the stables were quiet—like a grizzled, slumbering giant. It smelt of hay, leather, and decades, perhaps centuries, of horse manure. The odor was warm and welcoming.

Lord Swartingham was to meet her here this morning so they could ride out to inspect more fields. Anna's makeshift riding habit trailed in the dust behind her as she walked. Every now and then, an equine head poked curiously over a stall and nickered a greeting. She spotted the earl farther ahead, deep in conversation with the head groom. He towered over the older man. Both stood in a beam of dusty sunlight at the far end of the stables. As Anna neared, she could hear that they were discussing the problem of a gelding with a chronic limp. Lord Swartingham glanced up and caught sight of her. She paused by Daisy's stall. He smiled and turned back to the head groom.

Daisy was already saddled and bridled and tied loosely in the aisle. Anna waited, softly talking to the mare. She watched Lord Swartingham lean down to listen to the head groom, his full attention on the older man. The head groom was a wiry, aged specimen. His hands were knotted now with arthritis and healed bones, broken long ago. He carried himself proudly, his head stiffly erect. The old man, like many countrymen, talked slowly and liked to discuss a problem at length. Anna noticed that the earl patiently let him have his say, neither hurrying him nor cutting off his speech, until the head groom felt that the problem has been sufficiently mulled over. Then Lord Swartingham gently clapped the man on the back and watched him walk out of the stable. The earl turned and started for her.

Without any warning, Daisy—gentle, placid Daisy—reared. Iron-shod hooves cleaved the air only inches from Anna's face. She fell back against the stall door, cowering. A hoof thumped the wood next to her shoulder.

"Anna!" She heard the earl's shout over the startled neighing of the nearby horses and Daisy's own frantic whinnying.

A rat scurried underneath the stall door, flicking its naked tail as it disappeared. Lord Swartingham caught the horse's halter and pulled the mare forcibly away. Anna heard a grunt and the slam of a stall door.

Strong arms wrapped around her. "Dear God, Anna, are you hurt?"

She couldn't answer. Fear seemed to have clogged her throat. He ran his hands over her shoulders and arms, rapidly feeling and smoothing.

"Anna." His face lowered toward hers.

She couldn't help herself; her eyes closed.

He kissed her.

His lips were hot and dry. Soft and firm. They moved across hers lightly, before he angled his head and pressed strongly. Her nostrils flared, and she smelled horses and him. She thought irrelevantly that forever after she would associate the smell of horses with Lord Swartingham.

With *Edward.*

He skimmed her lips with his tongue, so softly that at first she thought she had imagined it. But he repeated the caress, a touch like suede leather, and she opened her mouth to him. She felt his warmth invading her mouth, filling it, stroking across her tongue. He tasted of the coffee he must have drunk at breakfast.

She clenched her fingers at the back of his neck, and he opened his own mouth wider and drew her closer to lean against him. One of his hands brushed across her cheek. She threaded her hands through the hair at his nape. His queue came undone, and she reveled in the silky feel of his hair between her fingers. He ran his tongue over her bottom lip and drew it between his teeth, gently sucking on it. She heard herself moan. She trembled, her legs hardly able to hold up her weight.

A clatter from the stable yard outside brought Anna abruptly back to her surroundings. Edward raised his head to listen. One of the stable hands was berating a boy for dropping equipment.

He turned his head back to Anna and smoothed his thumb over her cheek. "Anna, I . . ."

His train of thought seemed to slip away. He shook his head. Then, as if compelled, he brushed a gentle kiss over her mouth and lingered there a moment as the kiss deepened.

But something was wrong; Anna could feel it. He was slipping away. She was losing him. She pressed closer, trying to hold on. He ran his lips across her cheekbones and lightly, softly, over her closed eyelids. She felt his breath sift through her eyelashes.

His arms dropped, and she sensed him step away from her.

She opened her eyes to see him running his hands through his hair. "I'm sorry. That was—*God,* I'm so sorry."

"No, please don't apologize." She smiled, warmth spreading through her breast as she gathered her courage. Maybe this was the time. "I wanted the kiss just as much as you. As a matter of—"

"I'm engaged."

"What?" Anna recoiled as if he had struck her.

"I'm engaged to be married." Edward grimaced as if in self-disgust or possibly pain.

She stood frozen, struggling to comprehend the simple words. A numbness seeped throughout her body, driving out the warmth as if it had never been.

"That's why I went up to London. To finalize the marital settlements." Edward paced, his hands agitatedly running through his disheveled hair. "She's the daughter of a baronet, a very old family. I think they might have come over with the Conqueror, which is more than the de Raafs can say. Her lands—" He stopped suddenly as if she'd interrupted.

She hadn't.

He met her eyes for an agonizing moment and then looked away. It was as if a cord that had stretched between them had been severed.

"I'm sorry, Mrs. Wren." He cleared his throat. "I never should have behaved so badly with you. You have my word of honor that it won't happen again."

"I-I—" She struggled to force words through her swelling throat. "I ought to return to work, my lord." Her only coherent thought was that she must maintain her composure. Anna moved to go—to flee, really—but his voice stopped her.

"Sam . . ."

"What?" All she wanted was a hole to curl up in so she could never think again. Never feel again. But something in his face kept her from leaving.

Edward stared up at the loft as if searching for something, or someone. Anna followed his gaze. There was nothing there. The old loft was nearly empty. Where once mounds of hay must have lain, now only dust motes floated. The hay for the horses was stored below in empty stalls.

But still he stared at the loft. "This was my brother's favorite place," he said finally. "Samuel, my younger brother. He was nine years old, born six years after me. It was enough of a gap that I did not pay him much attention. He was a quiet boy. He used to hide in the loft, even though it gave Mother fits; she was afraid he'd fall and kill himself. It didn't stop him. He'd spend half the day up there, playing, I don't know, with tin soldiers or tops or something. It was easy to forget he was up there, and sometimes he'd throw hay down on my head just to aggravate me." His brows drew together. "Or, I suppose, he wanted his elder brother's attention. Not that I gave it to him. I was too busy at fifteen, learning to shoot and drink and be a man, to pay attention to a child."

He walked a few paces away, still studying the loft. Anna tried to swallow down the lump in her throat. Why now? Why reveal all this pain to her now, when it couldn't matter?

He continued, "It's funny, though. When I first came back, I kept expecting to see him here in the stables. I'd walk in and look up—for his face, I guess." Edward blinked and murmured, almost to himself, "Sometimes I still do."

Anna shoved her knuckle into her mouth and bit down. She didn't want to hear this. Didn't want to feel any sympathy for this man.

"This stable was full before," he said. "My father loved horses, used to breed them. There were lots of grooms and my father's cronies hanging around out here, talking horseflesh and hunting. My mother was in the Abbey, holding parties and planning my sister's coming-out. This place was so busy. So happy. It was the best place in the world."

Edward touched the worn door of an empty stall with his fingertips. "I never thought I would leave. I never wanted to."

Anna hugged herself and bit back a sob.

"But then the smallpox came." He seemed to stare into space, and the lines in his face stood out in sharp relief. "And they died, one by one. First Sammy, then Father and Mother. Elizabeth, my sister, was the last to go. They cut off her hair because of the fever, and she cried and cried inconsolably; she thought it her best feature. Two days later, they put her into the family vault. We were lucky, I guess, if you can call it luck. Other families had to wait for spring to bury their dead. It was winter and the ground was frozen."

He drew a breath. "But I don't remember that last, only what they told me later, because by then I had it, too."

He stroked a finger over his cheekbone where the smallpox scars clustered, and Anna wondered how often he had made the gesture in the years since.

"And, of course, I survived." He looked at her with the bitterest smile she'd ever seen, as if he tasted bile on his tongue. "I alone lived. Out of all of them, I survived."

He closed his eyes.

When he opened them again, his face was smoothed into a blank, firm mask. "I'm the last of my line, the last of the de Raafs," he said. "There are no distant cousins to inherit the title and the Abbey, no waiting obscure heirs. When I die—*if* I die without a son—it all reverts to the crown."

Anna forced herself to hold his gaze, though it left her trembling.

"I must have an heir. Do you understand?" He grit his teeth and said, as if he were pulling the words, bloody and torn, from his very heart, "I must marry a woman who can bear children."

Chapter Fourteen

*Who was her lover? Aurea's sisters inquired, their
brows creased with false concern. Why had she never
seen him in the light of day? And having never seen
him, how could she be sure he was human at all?
Perhaps a monster too horrible to be exposed to
daylight shared her bed. Perhaps this monster
would get her heavy with his child, and she would
bear something too awful to imagine. The longer
Aurea listened to her sisters, the more disquieted she
became until she knew not what to think or do.
It was then that the sisters suggested a plan. . . .*
—from *The Raven Prince*

For the rest of that day, Anna simply endured. She made
herself sit at the rosewood desk in the Abbey library. She
made herself dip her quill in the ink without spilling a
drop. She made herself copy out a page of Edward's manuscript. When she finished that first page, she made herself do it again. And again. And yet again.

That was the job of a secretary, after all.

Long ago, when Peter had first proposed to her, she'd thought about children. She'd wondered whether their children would have red or brown hair, and she'd day-dreamed possible names. When they'd married and moved into the tiny cottage, she'd worried if there would be enough room for a family.

She had never worried about not having children.

The second year of the marriage, Anna had begun to watch her monthly flow. The third year, she wept every month when she saw the rust-colored stain. By the fourth year of her marriage to Peter, she knew he had turned to someone else. Whether because she was inadequate as a lover or as a breeder or both, she never found out. And when Peter died . . .

When he died, she took her hopes for a child and wrapped them carefully in a box and buried that box deep, deep in her heart. So deep, she thought never to face that dream again. Except, with one sentence, Edward had ex-humed the box and ripped it open. And her hopes, her dreams, her *need* to bear a child were as fresh now as they had been when she was newly wed.

Oh, dear God, to be capable of giving Edward chil-dren! What she wouldn't do, what she wouldn't give up, to be able to hold a baby. A baby made from both of their bodies and souls. Anna felt a physical ache in her chest. An ache that expanded outward until she could hardly keep herself from curling up to hold it in.

But she must maintain her composure. She was in Edward's library—indeed, Edward sat not five feet away—and she couldn't show her pain. Fiercely, she concentrated on moving her quill across the paper. Never mind that the scratches she made with the quill were illegible, never mind that the page would have to be recopied later. She would get through this afternoon.

Several ghastly hours later, Anna slowly gathered her things, moving like a very old woman. As she did so, the invitation to Felicity Clearwater's dance fell from her shawl. She stared at it a moment. A lifetime ago she'd meant to remind Edward about the soiree. It seemed inconsequential now. But Mother Wren had said it was important that Edward participate in local social events. Anna straightened her shoulders. Just this one thing, then she could go home.

"Mrs. Clearwater's soiree is tomorrow night." Her voice creaked.

"I don't intend to accept Mrs. Clearwater's invitation."

Anna refused to look at him, but Edward's voice didn't sound much better than her own.

"You're the most important aristocrat in the area, my lord," she said. "It would be gracious to attend."

"No doubt."

"It is the best way to hear the latest village gossip."

He grunted.

"Mrs. Clearwater always serves her special punch. Everyone agrees it is the best in the county," she lied.

"I don't—"

"Please, *please* go." She still didn't look at him, but she could feel his gaze on her face, as palpable as a hand.

"As you wish."

"Good." Anna jammed her hat on her head and then remembered something. She opened her center desk drawer and took out *The Raven Prince.* She carried it over to Edward's desk, laying it softly on top. "This is yours."

She turned and left the room before he could reply.

THE HALL WAS stiflingly hot, the decorations from two years ago, and the music off-key. It was Felicity Clearwater's annual spring soiree. Every year, the citizens of Little Battleford who were lucky enough to receive an invitation put on their very best clothes and drank watery punch at the Clearwater home. Felicity Clearwater stood by the door to welcome her guests. She wore a new gown, an indigo-blue muslin this year with cascading flounce down the sleeves. The underskirt sported a pattern of flying crimson birds on a light blue field, and there were crimson bows in a V outlining her bodice. Squire Clearwater, a portly gentleman in orange-clocked stockings and the full-bottomed wig of his youth, fidgeted beside her, but it was clearly understood that the event belonged to Felicity.

Anna had made it through the receiving line with only a frosty greeting from Felicity and a rather abstracted one from the squire. Relieved to have gotten that ordeal out of the way, she hovered at the side of the room. She'd unwarily accepted a glass of punch from the vicar and now had no choice but to sip it.

Mother Wren stood beside Anna and cast anxious glances at her. Anna hadn't told her what had occurred in the stables between Edward and herself. Nor did she intend to. But her mother-in-law still sensed something was wrong. Evidently, Anna wasn't very good at pretending cheer.

She took another grim sip of the punch. She wore her best gown. She and Fanny had spent some time over it, trying to make the alterations as neat as possible. The dress was a light apple green, and they had freshened it with the addition of white lace at the neckline. The lace also hid the modification of the neckline from a curve to the more fashionable square. Fanny, in a fit of artistic invention, had devised a rosette for Anna's hair from some of the lace and a bit of green ribbon. Anna hardly felt festive, but it would have hurt Fanny's feelings not to wear the rosette.

"The punch isn't bad," Mother Wren whispered.

Anna hadn't noticed. She took another sip and was pleasantly surprised. "Yes. Better than rumored."

Mother Wren fidgeted for a moment before coming up with another conversational foray. "It's too bad Rebecca couldn't attend."

"I don't see why not."

"You know she can't be seen at social occasions, dear, so close to her confinement. In my day, we didn't dare set foot out of the house once we began to show."

Anna wrinkled her nose. "It's so silly. Everyone knows she's increasing. It isn't as if it's a secret."

"It's the propriety that matters, not what everyone knows. Besides, Rebecca is so far along, I don't think she would like to stand for hours. There are never enough seats at these dances." Mother Wren looked around the room. "Do you think your earl will come?"

"He's not *my* earl, as you well know," Anna said somewhat bitterly.

Mother Wren glanced at her sharply.

Anna tried to modulate her tone. "I told him that I thought it a good idea for him to attend the soiree."

"I hope he comes before the dancing commences. I do like to see a fine, manly figure on the dance floor."

"He mayn't come at all, and then you'll have to be content with Mr. Merriweather's form on the dance floor." Anna gestured with her cup to that gentleman, standing across the room.

Both women looked at Mr. Merriweather, a skeletal gentleman with knock-knees, who was talking to a substantial matron in a peach-colored frock. As they watched, Mr. Merriweather leaned closer to make a point and absentmindedly tilted his punch cup. A thin stream of liquid trickled down the décolletage of the lady's dress.

Mother Wren shook her head sadly.

"Do you know," Anna said thoughtfully, "I'm not sure Mr. Merriweather has ever made it through a reel without losing his place."

Mother Wren sighed. Then she glanced over Anna's shoulder at the door and visibly brightened. "I don't think I'll have to make do with Mr. Merriweather after all. There's *your* earl at the door."

Anna turned to view the entrance to the dance room and raised her cup to her lips. For a moment, she forgot it there as she caught sight of Edward. He wore black knee breeches with a sapphire coat and waistcoat. His black hair, brushed in an uncharacteristically neat queue, gleamed like a bird's wing in the candlelight. He stood nearly a head taller than any other man in the room. Felicity was plainly delighted with her luck at being the first to entice the elusive earl into a social setting. She had a firm hand on his elbow and was introducing Edward to anyone within speaking distance.

Anna smiled wryly. Edward's shoulders were bunched, and his expression was grim. Even across the room, she could tell that he was holding on to his temper by a thread. He looked to be in danger of making the faux pas of walking away from his hostess. He glanced up at that moment and caught her eye.

She sucked in her breath at the contact. Impossible to read his expression.

He turned back to Felicity and said something, then began to make his way through the crowd toward Anna. She felt liquid coolness on her wrist and glanced down. Her hand was trembling so hard she was sloshing the remains of the punch on her arm. Anna clasped her other hand around the cup to steady it. For an instant, she came close to bolting, but Mother Wren was right beside her. And she'd have to face him again sometime.

Felicity must have signaled the musicians. The violins let out a shriek.

"Ah, Mrs. Wren. A pleasure to meet you again." Edward bowed over Mother Wren's hand. He didn't smile.

Her mother-in-law didn't seem to care. "Oh, my lord, I'm so glad you could attend. Anna has been dying to dance." Mother Wren lifted her eyebrows meaningfully.

Anna wished she had bolted when she'd had the chance.

The broad hint hung there in the air between them for an uncomfortably long time before Edward spoke. "If you would do me the pleasure?"

He didn't even look at her. For goodness sake, he had been the one to kiss her!

Anna pursed her lips. "I didn't know you danced, my lord."

Edward's gaze snapped around to her. "Of course I can dance. I am an earl after all."

"As if I'd forget that," she muttered.

Edward narrowed his obsidian eyes.

Ha! She certainly had his attention now.

He held out a gloved hand, and she demurely placed her own in it. Even with two layers of fabric between their palms, she could feel his body heat. For a moment, she remembered what it was like to run her fingertips down his nude back. Hot. Sweaty. Achingly good. She swallowed.

With only a nod to Mother Wren, he towed her out onto the dance floor where he proved he could indeed dance, albeit rather heavily.

"You do know the steps," Anna said as they met to promenade down the center of the dancers.

She saw him scowl out of the corner of her eye. "I wasn't born under a rock. I know how to behave in polite society."

The music ended before Anna could form an appropriate reply. She curtsied and started to tug her hand from Edward's grasp.

He pulled her hand firmly to him and tucked it in the crook of his elbow. "Don't you dare think of deserting me, Mrs. Wren. It's your fault I'm at this bloody soiree to begin with."

Must he keep touching her? She looked around for a distraction. "Perhaps you would care for some punch?"

He looked at her suspiciously. "Would I?"

"Well, maybe not," she admitted. "But it's the only thing to drink at the present, and the refreshment table is in the opposite direction from Mrs. Clearwater."

"Then let us try the punch by all means."

He walked toward the punch table, and she found that people stepped aside naturally for him. In no time at all, Anna was sipping her second glass of weak punch.

Edward had pivoted slightly to the side to answer a question from the vicar when she heard a sly voice at her elbow. "I'm surprised to see you here, Mrs. Wren. I'd heard you had taken up a new *profession*."

EDWARD TURNED SLOWLY to face the speaker, a florid man in an ill-fitting wig. He didn't look familiar. Beside him, Anna had stiffened, her face frozen.

"Have you learned any new *skills* from your recent guests?" The man's entire attention was fixed on Anna.

She opened her mouth, but for once Edward beat her to it. "I don't believe I heard you correctly."

The swine seemed to notice him for the first time. His eyes widened. Good.

The silence in their immediate vicinity began to spread outward through the room as the guests became aware that something interesting was happening.

The fellow was braver than he looked. "I said—"

"Be very, very careful what you say next." Edward could feel the muscles in his shoulders flexing.

The other man finally appeared to comprehend the danger he was in. His eyes widened, and he visibly swallowed.

Edward nodded once. "Good. Perhaps you'd care to apologize to Mrs. Wren for what you did *not* say."

"I—" The man had to stop and clear his throat. "I am most sorry if anything I said offended you, Mrs. Wren."

Anna nodded stiffly, but the man was correctly looking toward Edward to see if he had redeemed himself.

He had not.

The man swallowed again. A bead of sweat slid greasily along the edge of his wig. "I don't know what came over me. I am most abjectly sorry to have caused you any pain whatsoever, Mrs. Wren." He pulled at his neckcloth and leaned forward to add, "I really am an ass, you know."

"Yes, you are," Edward said gently.

The man's complexion turned a sickly hue.

"Well!" Anna said. "I think it is about time for the next dance. Isn't that the music beginning?"

She spoke loudly in the general direction of the musicians, and they immediately took her up on the suggestion. She snatched Edward's hand and began marching toward the dance floor. She had quite a strong grip for such a little thing. Edward shot one last, narrow-eyed glare at the swine, and then docilely permitted himself to be led away.

"Who is he?"

Anna looked up at him as they formed the set. "He didn't really hurt me, you know."

The dance began and he was forced to wait until the figures drew them together again. "Who is he, Anna?"

She looked exasperated. "John Wiltonson. He was a friend of my husband's."

Edward waited.

"He made a proposition to me after Peter's death."

"He wanted to marry you?" His brows drew together.

"An indecent proposition." Anna's eyes were averted. "He was—is—already married."

He stopped dead, causing the couple next in line to bump into them. "He assaulted you?"

"No." She pulled on his arm, but he remained steadfast. She hissed in his ear, "He wanted me to become his mistress. I refused." The dancers behind them were beginning to pile up. "My lord!"

Edward allowed himself to be pulled into the dance again, although they were no longer in time to the music. "I never want to hear someone speak so of you again."

"A fine sentiment, I'm sure," she replied tartly. "But you can hardly spend the rest of your life following me about intimidating the impertinent."

Unable to think of a reply, he simply glared. She was right. The thought tore at him. Anna was only his secretary, plain and simple. He couldn't be with her all the time. He couldn't stop any insults. He couldn't even protect her from insulting advances. Such guardianship was the prerogative of a husband only.

Anna interrupted his thoughts. "I shouldn't have danced with you again so soon. It isn't proper."

"I don't give a damn what's proper," Edward said. "Besides, you knew it was the only method to get me away from that baboon."

She smiled up at him, and something inside his chest wrenched. How was he to keep her safe?

Edward was still pondering that question two hours later. He leaned against a wall and watched Anna lead a panting gentleman in a country reel. She clearly needed a husband, but he couldn't imagine her with a man. Or rather, he couldn't imagine her with *another* man. He scowled.

Someone coughed deferentially at his elbow. A tall young man with a bob wig stood next to him. His Geneva collar identified him as Vicar Jones.

The vicar coughed again and smiled nearsightedly at him through his pince-nez. "Lord Swartingham. So good of you to attend our little local entertainment."

Edward wondered how he managed to sound like a man twice his age. The vicar couldn't be over thirty. "Vicar. I'm enjoying Mrs. Clearwater's soiree." To his surprise, he realized that he spoke the truth.

"Good, good. Mrs. Clearwater's social events are always so well planned. And her refreshments are just delicious." The vicar demonstrated by gulping enthusiastically at his punch.

Edward eyed his own punch and made a mental note to check on the vicar's stipend. Obviously the man was not used to decent food.

"I say, Mrs. Wren is certainly cutting a dashing figure on the dance floor." The vicar squinted as he watched Anna. "She looks different tonight."

Edward followed his gaze. "She isn't wearing a cap."

"Is that it?" Vicar Jones sounded vague. "You have sharper eyes than I, my lord. I wondered if she'd bought a new dress on her trip."

Edward was raising his own cup of punch to his lips when the vicar's words sunk in. He frowned and lowered the cup. "What trip?"

"Hmm?" Vicar Jones still watched the dancers, his mind obviously not on the conversation.

Edward was about to repeat the question a little more forcefully this time when Mrs. Clearwater interrupted them. "Ah, Lord Swartingham. I see you know the vicar."

Both men started as if they'd been goosed simultaneously in the arse. Edward turned a strained smile on his hostess. He noticed out of the corner of his eye that the vicar was peering around as if for escape. "Yes, I've met Vicar Jones, Mrs. Clearwater."

"Lord Swartingham has most graciously helped with the new church roof." Vicar Jones made eye contact with another guest. "I say, is that Mr. Merriweather? I must have a word with him. If you'll excuse me?" The vicar bowed and hurried away.

Edward eyed the vicar's retreating form with envy. The man must have attended the Clearwater soirees before.

"How lovely to have a moment alone with you, my lord," Mrs. Clearwater said. "I did want to discuss your trip to London."

"Oh?" Maybe if he caught the elder Mrs. Wren's eye. It wasn't done to just abandon a lady.

"Yes, indeed." Mrs. Clearwater leaned closer. "I have heard that you were seen at some most unusual places."

"Really?"

"In the company of a lady we both know."

Edward's attention swung back to Felicity Clearwater. What the devil was the woman talking about?

"Fe-*lee*-ci-ty!" A male voice, rather the worse for drink, yodeled nearby.

Mrs. Clearwater winced.

Squire Clearwater was making his way unsteadily toward them. "Felicity, m'dear, mustn't monopolize the earl. He's not interested in talk of fashions and fr-fr-fripperies." The squire dug a pointy elbow into Edward's ribs. "Eh, my lord? Hunting's the thing. A man's sport! What? What?"

Mrs. Clearwater made a sound that, in a male, might have been considered a snort.

"Actually, I don't hunt much," Edward said.

"Hounds baying, horses galloping, the smell of blood . . ." The squire was in his own world.

Across the room, Edward saw Anna put on a wrapper. Damn it. Was she leaving without bidding him good-bye?

"Excuse me."

He bowed to the squire and his wife and pushed through the mass of people. But at this hour, the soiree had become quite crowded. By the time Edward reached the door, Anna and Mrs. Wren were already outside.

"Anna!" Edward shoved past the footmen in the hall and pushed open the door. "Anna!"

She was only a few steps away. At his shout, both she and Mrs. Wren turned.

"You shouldn't walk home alone, Anna." Edward glowered, then realized his slip. "Nor you, Mrs. Wren."

Anna looked confused, but the older woman beamed. "Have you come to escort us home, Lord Swartingham?"

"Yes."

His carriage was waiting nearby. They could ride, but then the evening would be over in a matter of minutes. Besides, it was a beautiful night. He signaled the carriage to follow behind them as they walked. He offered Anna one arm and Mrs. Wren the other. Although the ladies had left the party early, the hour was late and it was dark. A full moon shone, gloriously large in the black sky, casting long shadows before them.

As they neared a crossroads, Edward heard the sudden clatter of running feet ahead of them, loud in the quiet air. Immediately he set the ladies behind him. A slight form flew around the corner. It veered toward them.

"Meg! Whatever is the matter?" Anna cried.

"Oh, ma'am!" The girl bent double, clutching her side as she tried to catch her breath. "It's Mrs. Fairchild, ma'am. She's fallen down the stairs, and I can't help her up. I think the baby's coming, too!"

Chapter Fifteen

So Aurea flew back in her magnificent golden
carriage, her sisters' plan churning in her head.
The raven greeted his returned wife almost
indifferently. Aurea ate a splendid dinner with him,
bade the raven good night, and went to her room
to wait for her sensuous visitor.
Suddenly he was there beside her, more urgent,
more demanding than he had ever been before. His
attentions left Aurea sleepy and satiated, but she stuck
stubbornly to her plan and kept herself awake even as
she heard her lover's breath settle into the evenness of
sleep. Quietly, she sat up and felt for the candle she
had earlier left on the table beside the bed. . . .
—from *The Raven Prince*

"Oh, my Lord!" Anna tried to remember when exactly
Rebecca had thought the baby would come. Surely not for
another month?

"Dr. Billings is at the soiree," Edward said with calm
authority. "Take my carriage, girl, and fetch him quickly."
He turned and shouted instructions to John Coachman as
he waved the carriage forward.

"I'll go with Meg," Mother Wren said.

Edward nodded and helped her and the maid into the carriage. "Is there a midwife to find as well?" He directed the question at Anna.

"Rebecca was going to have Mrs. Stucker—"

"The midwife is attending Mrs. Lyle," her mother-in-law interrupted. "She lives four or five miles out of town. Several ladies were talking about it at the party."

"Fetch Dr. Billings to Mrs. Fairchild first, and then I'll send my carriage for Mrs. Stucker," Edward ordered.

Mother Wren and Meg nodded from inside the carriage.

Edward slammed the door shut and stepped back. "Go, John!"

The coachman shouted to the horses, and the carriage rattled away.

Edward caught Anna's hand. "Which way is Mrs. Fairchild's house?"

"It's just ahead." Anna snatched up her skirts and ran toward the house with Edward.

The front door to Rebecca's house stood ajar. All was dark except for a curtain of light that fell from the entrance onto the walkway. Edward pushed open the door and Anna followed. She looked around. They stood in the front hall with the stairs to the upper floor immediately before them. The lower part could be seen in the light from the hall, but the higher steps were in darkness. There was no sign of Rebecca.

"Could she have moved herself?" Anna gasped.

They heard a low moan from the upper stairs. Anna ran up before Edward could move. She heard him curse behind her.

Rebecca lay on a landing midway up the staircase. Anna thanked the fates that she had stopped here, instead of falling down the longer, second flight of stairs. Her friend was on her side, the great mound of her belly more prominent in that position. Her face shone white and greasy with perspiration.

Anna bit her lip. "Rebecca, can you hear me?"

"Anna." Rebecca held out her hand, and she caught it. "Thank God you are here." She gasped and her hand tightened painfully.

"What is it?" Anna asked.

"The baby." Rebecca expelled her breath. "It's coming."

"Can you rise?"

"I'm so clumsy. My ankle is hurt." There were tears in Rebecca's eyes and traces of others on her face. "The baby is too soon."

Anna's own eyes were suddenly flooded with tears. She bit the inside of her cheek as she tried to control them. Tears would not help her friend.

"Let me carry you up to your room, Mrs. Fairchild." Edward's deep voice interrupted her thoughts.

Anna glanced up. Edward stood behind her, his face grave. She stepped to the side, letting Rebecca's hand go. Edward eased his palms under the laboring woman, then squatted and positioned her in his arms before rising in one fluid movement. He was obviously careful not to jostle Rebecca's ankle, but she whimpered and squeezed her hands in the front of his coat. Edward's lips tightened. He nodded to Anna, and she went ahead of him up the stairs and down the upper hall. A single candle flickered on a bedside table in Rebecca's room. Anna hurried to take it and to light several others. Edward turned sideways to enter, and then laid her friend gently on the bed. For the first time, Anna noticed that he was very pale.

She pushed a damp lock of hair off Rebecca's forehead. "Where is James?"

Anna had to wait for the answer as another pain hit her friend. Rebecca moaned low, and her back arched off the bed. When it was over, she was panting. "He went to Drewsbury for the day on business. He said he would return tomorrow after midday." Rebecca bit her lip. "He will be so cross with me."

Edward muttered something sharp behind them and paced to the dark bedroom windows.

"Nonsense," Anna scolded softly. "None of this is your fault."

"If only I hadn't fallen down the stairs," Rebecca sobbed.

Anna was trying to comfort her when the front door slammed below. The doctor had obviously arrived. Edward excused himself to direct the man up.

Dr. Billings tried to wear an impassive face, but it was evident that he was quite worried. He bandaged Rebecca's ankle, which had swollen already and turned purple. Anna mostly sat by Rebecca's head, holding her hand and talking to her in an attempt to calm her. It wasn't easy. According to the calculations of the midwife and Rebecca, the baby was a month early. As the night progressed Rebecca's agony grew worse, and she became despondent. She was convinced she'd lose the baby. Nothing Anna said seemed to help, but she stayed by the other woman, holding her hand and stroking her hair.

A little over three hours after the doctor had arrived, Mrs. Stucker, the midwife, blew into the room. A short, rotund woman with red cheeks and black hair, now liberally sprinkled with gray, she was a welcome sight.

"Ho! This is a night for babies, it is," the midwife said. "You'll all be glad to know Mrs. Lyle has another boy baby, her fifth, would you believe it? I don't know why she even bothers to call me. I just sit in the corner and knit until it's time to catch the wee one." Mrs. Stucker took off her wrapper and a great many scarves and threw them over a chair. "Do you have some water and a bit of soap, Meg? I do like to wash me hands before I help a lady."

Dr. Billings was looking disapproving, but he made no protest at the midwife seeing his patient.

"And how are you, Mrs. Fairchild? Holding on well, despite that ankle? My, that must have been painful." The midwife laid her hand on Rebecca's tummy and looked at her face shrewdly. "The babe's eager, isn't it? Coming early just to aggravate his mother. But you're not to worry about it. Babies sometimes have minds of their own about when they want to come out."

"Will he be all right?" Rebecca licked dry lips.

"Well now, you know I can't promise anything, luv. But you're a good, strong lady, if you don't mind me saying so. I'll do my very best to help you and that baby."

Things looked brighter after that. Mrs. Stucker got Rebecca to sit up in the bed because "babies slide better downhill than up." Rebecca seemed to regain hope. She was even able to chat between pains.

Just as Anna felt as if she were going to drop from fatigue right there in the chair, Rebecca began to moan deeply. At first Anna was terribly alarmed, thinking something must be wrong. But Mrs. Stucker wasn't perturbed and stated cheerfully that the babe would soon be there. And indeed, in another half hour, during which Anna came wide awake, Rebecca's baby was born. It was a little girl, wrinkled and small but able to bawl quite loudly. The sound brought a smile to her mother's exhausted face. The baby had dark hair that stood on end like a baby chick's fluff. Her blue eyes blinked slowly, and she turned her head to Rebecca's breast when she was snuggled against it.

"Now, then, isn't that about the prettiest baby you've ever seen?" Mrs. Stucker asked. "I know you're tuckered out, Mrs. Fairchild, but perhaps you'll take a little tea or broth."

"I'll go see what I can find," Anna said, yawning.

She slowly stumbled down the stairs. When she got to the landing, she noticed a light gleaming in the downstairs sitting room. Puzzled, Anna pushed the door open and stood there a moment, staring.

Edward sprawled on Rebecca's damask settee, his long legs hanging off the end. He'd removed his neckcloth and unbuttoned his waistcoat. One arm draped over his eyes. His other arm stretched to the floor where his hand almost enveloped a half-empty glass of what looked like James's brandy. Anna stepped inside the room, and he immediately raised his arm from his eyes, belying the impression that he had been asleep.

"How is she?" His voice was raspy, his countenance ghastly. The fading bruises stood out starkly in his pale face, and the stubble on his jaw made him look dissolute.

Anna felt ashamed. She'd forgotten about Edward, had assumed he'd gone home long ago. All this time he'd been waiting downstairs to see how Rebecca fared.

"Rebecca is fine," she said brightly. "She has a baby girl."

His expression didn't change. "Alive?"

"Yes." Anna faltered. "Yes, of course. Both Rebecca and the baby are alive and well."

"Thank God." His face hadn't lost the strained look.

She began to feel uneasy. Surely he was overly concerned? He'd just met Rebecca tonight, hadn't he? "What is the matter?"

He sighed and his arm returned to cover his eyes. There was a long moment of silence—so long she thought he wasn't going to answer the question. Finally, he spoke, "My wife and babe died in childbirth."

Anna slowly sat down on a stool near the settee. She hadn't really thought about his wife before. She knew he'd been married and that his wife had died young, but not how she'd died. Had he loved her? Did he love her still?

"I'm sorry."

He lifted his hand from the brandy glass, made an impatient movement, and then let it settle on the glass again as if too weary to find another resting place for it. "I didn't tell you to elicit your pity. She died a long time ago. Ten years now."

"How old was she?"

"She'd turned twenty a fortnight before." His mouth twisted. "I was four and twenty."

Anna waited.

When he next spoke, the words were so low she had to lean forward to hear them. "She was young and healthy. It never occurred to me that bearing the child might kill her, but she miscarried in her seventh month. The baby was too small to live. They told me it would have been a boy. Then she started bleeding."

He took his arm away from his face, and Anna could see that he was staring sightlessly at some inner vision.

"They couldn't stop it. Doctors and midwives, they couldn't stop it. The maids kept running in with more and more linens," he whispered to the horror in his memory. "She just bled and bled until her very life bled away. There was so much blood in the bed, the mattress was soaked through. We had to burn it afterward."

The tears she'd withheld for Rebecca's sake ran down Anna's cheeks. To have lost someone you loved so horribly, so tragically, how awful it must have been. And he must have wanted that baby very badly. She already knew that having a family was important to him.

Anna pressed a hand to her mouth, and the movement seemed to bring Edward out of his reverie. He swore softly when he saw the tears on her face. He sat up on the settee and reached for her. Without any sign of strain, he lifted her off the stool and onto his lap and settled her there so she sat across him, her back held by his arm. He brought her head to his chest.

One big hand gently stroked her hair. "I'm sorry. I shouldn't have told you about that. It's not for a lady's ears, especially after you've been up all night worrying about your friend."

Anna allowed herself to lean against him, his mascu-

line warmth and the petting hand wonderfully comforting. "You must have loved her very much."

The hand paused, and then resumed. "I thought I did.
As it turned out, I didn't know her that well."

She tilted her head back to see his face. "How long
were you married?"

"A little over a year."

"But—"

He pushed her head back to his chest. "We hadn't known
each other long when we became engaged, and I suppose
I never really talked to her. Her father was very eager for
the match, told me that it was agreeable to the girl and I
simply assumed . . ." His voice roughened. "I found out
after we were married that my face repulsed her."

Anna tried to speak, but he hushed her again.

"I think she was afraid of me, too," he said wryly. "You
may not have noticed, but I've something of a temper."
She felt his hand touch the top of her head softly. "By the
time she was pregnant with my child, I knew that something was wrong, and in her last hours she cursed him."

"Cursed who?"

"Her father. For forcing her to marry such an ugly man."

Anna shivered. What a silly little girl his wife must
have been.

"Apparently her father had lied to me." Edward's voice
turned as icy as winter. "He desperately desired the match
and, not wanting to offend me, forbade my fiancée to tell
me that my scars revolted her."

"I'm sorry, I—"

"Shh," he murmured. "It happened a long time ago,
and I have learned since to live with my face and to discern

those who would try to hide an aversion to it. Even if they lie, I usually know it."

But he didn't know her lies. Anna felt cold at the thought. She'd deceived him, and he'd never forgive her if he found out.

He must've mistaken her tremble for continued sadness at his tale. He whispered something into her hair and held her closer until the warmth from his body had chased her chill away. They sat quietly then for a little while, taking comfort from each other. It was beginning to grow light outside. There was a halo around the closed sitting room curtains. Anna took the opportunity to rub her nose against his rumpled shirt. He smelled like the brandy he'd drunk—very masculine.

Edward leaned back to look down at her. "What are you doing?"

"Sniffing you."

"I probably smell fetid right now."

"No." Anna shook her head. "You smell . . . nice."

He studied her upturned face for a minute. "Please forgive me. I don't want you to hope. If there were any way—"

"I know." She got to her feet. "I even understand." She walked briskly to the door. "I came down to get something for Rebecca. She must be wondering what happened to me."

"Anna . . ."

But she pretended she didn't hear and left the sitting room. Rejection from Edward was one thing. Pity she didn't have to take.

The front door banged open at that moment to admit a disheveled James Fairchild. He was like a vision from Bedlam: his blond hair stood on end, and his neckcloth was missing.

He looked wildly at Anna. "Rebecca?"

At that moment, as if in answer from on high, there came the wavering wail of a newborn baby. James Fairchild's expression changed from frantic to dumbstruck. Without waiting for Anna's answer, he bounded up the stairs, taking the risers three at a time. Anna noticed as he passed out of sight that he was wearing only one stocking on his feet.

She half smiled to herself as she turned to the kitchen.

"I BELIEVE IT'S almost time to plant, my lord," Hopple said chummily.

"No doubt." Edward squinted at the bright afternoon sun.

After a night of very little sleep, he wasn't in the mood for chitchat. He and the steward were walking a field, checking to see if it would need a drainage ditch like Mr. Grundle's. It appeared the local ditch diggers had an assured living for the foreseeable future. Jock bounded along the hedges lining the fields, poking his muzzle down rabbit holes. Edward had sent a note to Anna this morning to tell her that she need not come to the Abbey today. She could use the day to rest. And he needed a respite from her presence. He had come close to kissing her again last night, despite his word of honor. He should let her go; after he was married, he could hardly retain a female secretary anyway. But then she would have no source of income, and he'd a feeling that the Wren household needed the money.

"Perhaps if we put the drainage ditch there?" Hopple pointed to a spot where Jock was currently digging and sending up a spume of mud.

Edward grunted.

"Or perhaps—" Hopple turned and nearly tripped on a clump of debris. He looked down disgustedly at his muddy boot. "It was wise of you not to include Mrs. Wren on this outing."

"She's at home," Edward said. "I told her to spend the day sleeping. You heard about Mrs. Fairchild's confinement last night?"

"The lady had a difficult time as I understand. What a miracle that both mother and child are well."

Edward snorted. "A miracle, indeed. Damned foolish for a man to leave his wife all alone, save a little maid, that close to her confinement."

"I heard the father was quite appalled this morning," Hopple offered.

"Not that it did his wife any good last night," Edward said dryly. "Be that as it may, Mrs. Wren was up all night with her friend. I thought it only reasonable that she take the day off. After all, she's worked every day excepting Sundays since she began as my secretary."

"Yes, indeed," Hopple said. "Except for the four days when you first left for London, of course."

Jock flushed a rabbit and gave chase.

Edward stopped and turned to the steward. "What?"

"Mrs. Wren didn't come to work whilst you were in

London." Hopple swallowed. "Except for the day before you came back, that is. She worked that day."

"I see," Edward said. But he didn't see.

"It was only for four days, my lord." Hopple hastened to smooth things over. "And she was all caught up on the paperwork, so she told me. It wasn't as if she let her work lie."

Edward stared thoughtfully at the mud beneath his feet. He remembered the vicar's mention of a "trip" the night before. "Where did she go?"

"Go, my lord?" Hopple looked to be stalling. "I, er, don't know if she went anywhere at all. She didn't say."

"The vicar said she had made a trip. He intimated that she'd gone to do some shopping."

"Maybe he was mistaken," Hopple said. "Why, if a lady couldn't find what she wanted in the shops in Little Battleford, she'd have to go to London to discover better. Surely Mrs. Wren didn't go that far."

Edward grunted. He went back to staring at the ground at his feet. Only now he knit his brows. Where had Anna gone? And why?

ANNA BRACED HER feet and hauled on the old garden door with all her might. Edward had given her the day to herself, but she couldn't stay that long asleep. Instead, after spending the morning resting, she thought she'd use the free time this afternoon to plant the roses. The door remained stubbornly shut for a moment, then it gave suddenly and flew open, almost throwing her on her rear. She dusted her hands and picked up her basket of gardening tools before slipping into the neglected garden. Edward had brought her here just over a week ago. In that little time, there'd been a great change within the old walls. Green shoots were poking up in the beds and between the cracks in the walkway. Some were obviously weeds, but others had a more refined air. Anna even recognized a few: the reddish tips of tulips, the unfurling rosettes of columbine leaves, and the dew-spangled palms of lady's mantle.

Each was a treasure she discovered with delight. The garden wasn't dead. It only lay dormant.

She set down her basket and went back out the garden door to bring in the remaining rosebushes Edward had given her. She'd already planted three in her own little garden. The rosebushes lay outside, still wet from the buckets of water. Each had begun to sprout tiny green buds. She looked down at them. They had brought her such hope when Edward had given them to her. Even though that hope was dead, it didn't seem fair to let the roses languish. She would plant them today, and if Edward never visited the garden again, well, she'd know they were here.

Anna dragged the first batch into the garden and let them flop down in the muddy path. She straightened and glanced around in search of a likely spot to plant them. The garden had a pattern once upon a time, but now it was almost impossible to discern what it had been. She shrugged and decided to divide the plants evenly between the four main flower beds. She picked up her shovel and began hacking through the tangled growth in the first bed.

Anna was in the garden when Edward found her that afternoon. He was irritable. He'd been searching for her some fifteen minutes, ever since Hopple had informed him that she was at the Abbey. Really, he shouldn't have sought her out at all; he'd made just that resolution this morning. But something inside him seemed constitutionally incapable of keeping away from his secretary when he knew her to be nearby. So he was frowning at his own lack of fortitude when he spotted her. Even then he paused by the garden door to admire the picture she made. She had dropped to her knees in the dirt to plant a rose. Her head was uncovered, and her hair was coming down from the knot at the nape of her neck. In the bright afternoon sunlight, the brown locks gleamed gold and auburn.

Edward felt a tightening in his chest. He rather thought it might be fear. He scowled and paced down the path. Fear was not an emotion that a strong man such as himself should feel when confronting a meek little widow, he was sure.

Anna caught sight of him. "My lord." She brushed the hair from her brow, leaving a smear of dirt behind. "I thought I would plant your roses before they died."

"So I see."

She gave him an odd look but evidently decided to make nothing of his strange mood. "I'll plant some in each bed since the garden is laid out in such symmetrical lines. Later, if you wish, we could surround them with lavender. Mrs. Fairchild has some lovely lavender plants by her back walk, and I know she would be pleased to let me take some cuttings for your gardens."

"Hmm."

Anna stopped her monologue to brush away her hair again, further smearing the dirt on her forehead. "Bother. I forgot to bring the watering can."

She frowned and started to climb to her feet, but he forestalled her. "Stay there. I can fetch the water for you."

Edward ignored her aborted protest and strode back up the path. He reached the garden door, but something made him hesitate. Forever after, he would ponder what impulse made him pause. He turned and looked back at her, still kneeling by the rosebush. She was packing the earth around it. While he watched, Anna raised her hand and with her little finger hooked back a lock of hair behind her ear.

He froze.

All sound stopped for a terrible, timeless minute, as his world shuddered and toppled around him. Three voices whispered, murmured, babbled in his ear and then coalesced into coherent language:

Hopple by the ditch: *I thought when that dog went missing for several days, we were well rid of it.*

Vicar Jones at Mrs. Clearwater's soiree: *I wondered if she'd bought a new dress on her trip.*

And Hopple again just today: *Mrs. Wren didn't come to work whilst you were in London.*

A scarlet haze obscured his vision.

When it cleared, he was almost upon Anna and knew that he had started for her even before the voices had become understandable. She was still bent beside the rosebush, unaware of the approaching storm until he stood over her and she glanced up.

He must have worn the knowledge of her deceit on his face because Anna's smile died before it had fully formed.

Chapter Sixteen

Cautiously, Aurea lit the candle and turned to hold it
high over her lover's form. Her breath caught, her
eyes widened, and she gave a start. A very small start,
but enough of one to send a drop of hot wax spilling
over the lip of the candle and onto the shoulder of
the man who lay beside her. For it was a man—not
monster or beast—but a man with smooth, white skin;
long, strong limbs; and black, black hair. He opened
his eyes, and Aurea saw that they, too, were black.
A piercing, intelligent black that, somehow, was
familiar. On his chest glinted a pendant.
It was in the shape of a small, perfect crown
inlaid with glowing rubies. . . .
—from *The Raven Prince*

Anna was debating whether or not she'd set the rosebush at the right depth in the hole when a shadow fell across her. She glanced up. Edward stood over her. Her first thought was that he had returned too soon to have brought the watering can.

And then she saw his expression.

His lips were drawn back in a rictus of rage, and his eyes burned like black holes in his face. In that moment, she felt an awful premonition that he'd somehow found out. In the seconds before he spoke, she tried to rally, to reassure herself that there was no possible way he could have discovered her secret.

His words killed all hope.

"You." She didn't recognize his voice, it was so low and terrible. "You were there at the whorehouse."

She'd never been good at lying. "What?"

He squeezed his eyes shut as if at a bright light. "You were there. You waited for me like a female spider, and I fell neatly into your web."

Dear Lord, this was even worse than she had imagined. He thought she'd done it for some kind of sick revenge or joke. "I didn't—"

His eyes snapped open, and she threw up a hand to ward off the hell she saw in them. "You didn't what? Didn't travel to London, didn't go to Aphrodite's Grotto?"

Her eyes widened, and she started to rise, but he was already on her. He grasped her by the shoulders and lifted her easily, effortlessly, as if she weighed no more than thistledown. He was so strong! Why had she never before realized how much stronger the male was in relation to the female? She felt like a butterfly seized by a great black bird. He swung her body against the nearby brick wall and pinned her there. He lowered his face to hers until their noses nearly touched, and he could surely see his own reflection in her wide, frightened eyes.

"You waited there, wearing nothing but a bit of lace." His words washed over her face in a hot, intimate breath.

"And when I came, you flaunted yourself, offered yourself, and I fucked you until I couldn't see straight."

Anna felt each puff of his exhalation against her own lips. She flinched at the obscenity. She wanted to deny it, to say that it did not describe the sublime sweetness they'd discovered together in London, but the words caught in her throat.

"I was actually worried that contact with the prostitute you sheltered would ruin your good name. What a fool you made me. How could you hold back your laughter when I begged your pardon for kissing you?" His hands flexed on her shoulders. "All this time I've been restraining myself because I thought you were a respectable lady. All this time when you only wanted *this*."

He swooped in then and devoured her mouth with his own, ravishing her softness, making no allowances for her smaller size, for her femininity. His lips crushed hers against her teeth. She moaned, whether in pain or desire, she could not tell. He thrust his tongue into the cavern of her mouth without preamble or warning, as if he had every right.

"You should have told me that this was what you wanted." He raised his head to gasp. "I would've obliged you."

She seemed incapable of coherent thought, let alone speech.

"You had only to say the word and I could have taken you on my desk in the library, in the carriage with John Coachman up front, or even here in the garden."

She tried to form words through the fog of her confusion. "No, I—"

"God knows I've been hard for days—*weeks*—around you," he ground out. "I could've tumbled you at any time. Or can't you admit that you want to bed a man whose face looks like mine?"

She tried to shake her head, but it fell helplessly as he bent her back over his arm. His other hand dropped to her hips and jerked them into his own. The unyielding hardness of his erection pressed against her soft belly.

"*This* is what you crave. What you traveled all the way to London for," he whispered against her mouth.

She moaned in denial even as her hips arched into his.

He stilled her movement with an iron grip and tore his mouth away from hers. But almost as if he couldn't leave the lure of her skin, he returned. His mouth trailed across her face to catch an earlobe between his teeth.

"Why?" His question sighed into her ear. "Why, why, why? Why did you lie to me?"

She tried again to shake her head.

He punished her with a sharp nip. "Was it a jest? Did you find it amusing to lay with me one night and then play the virtuous widow the next? Or was it a perverse need? Some women find the thought of bedding a pox-scarred man stimulating."

She jerked her head violently then, despite the pain when his teeth scraped across her ear. She couldn't—*could not*—let him think that. "Please, you must know—"

He turned his head. She tried to face him, and he did the most terrifying thing yet.

He let her go.

"Edward! *Edward!* For God's sake, please listen to

me!" Strange that this was the first time she had called him by his Christian name.

He strode down the garden path. She ran after him, her eyes blinded by tears, and tripped over a loose brick.

He stopped at the sound of her fall, his back still to her. "Such tears, Anna. Can you produce them at will like the crocodile?" And then, so softly she might have imagined it, "Were there other men?"

He walked away.

She watched as he disappeared through the gate. Her chest felt tight. She thought vaguely that perhaps she'd hurt herself in the fall. But then she heard a guttural, rasping sound, and a cold little part of her brain took note of what a strange noise her crying made.

How swift, how harsh was the punishment dealt for stepping outside her staid widow's life. All the lessons and warnings, spoken and unspoken, that she'd been taught growing up had, in fact, come true. Although, she supposed her punishment wasn't that envisioned by the moralizers of Little Battleford. No, her fate was far worse than exposure and censure. Her punishment was Edward's hatred. That and the knowledge that she had never gone to London merely for the sex. All along it had been to be with him, Edward. It was the man she'd craved, not the physical act. It seemed she had been lying to herself just as much as she'd lied to him. How ironic to have finally tumbled to that realization now when all was ashes around her.

Anna didn't know how long she lay there, her old brown dress growing damp from the overturned dirt. When her sobs finally died away, the afternoon sky had become overcast. She pushed herself up with both arms to a kneeling position and from there lurched to her feet. She wavered, but caught herself, one hand holding the garden wall for support. She closed her eyes and breathed in deeply. Then she picked up the shovel.

Soon she would have to go home and tell Mother Wren that she no longer had a job. She would face a lonely bed tonight and a thousand nights after for the rest of her life.

But for now, she'd simply plant roses.

FELICITY PLACED A cloth dampened with violet water on her forehead. She'd retired to the little morning room, a place that usually brought her quite a bit of satisfaction, especially when she thought about how much it had cost to refurbish. The price of the canary-colored damask settee alone would have fed and clothed the Wren household for five years. But at the moment, her head was simply killing her.

Matters were *not* going well.

Reginald was moping about, moaning that his prize mare had miscarried. Chilly had gone back to London in a sulk because she wouldn't tell him about Anna and the earl. And that same earl had been annoyingly obtuse at the soiree. Granted, most men in her experience were slow to one degree or another, but she wouldn't have guessed Lord Swartingham was so thickheaded. The man had seemed not to know what she hinted at. How was she going to convince him to keep Anna quiet if he was too dim to realize he was being blackmailed?

Felicity winced.

Not blackmail. That sounded too gauche. Incentive. That was better. Lord Swartingham had an *incentive* to stop Anna from blathering Felicity's past peccadilloes all over the village.

The door banged open at that moment, and the younger of her two daughters, Cynthia, skipped in. She was followed by her sister, Christine, at a more sedate pace.

"M'man," Christine said. "Nanny says we must get your permission to go to the sweet shop in town. May we?"

"Pepp-er-mint sticks!" Cynthia skipped around the settee Felicity lay on. "Le-mon drops! Turk-ish delight!" Oddly, her youngest resembled Reginald in many ways.

"Please stop that, Cynthia," Felicity said. "M'man has a headache."

"I'm so sorry, M'man," Christine replied, not sounding sorry at all. "We'll leave as soon as we get your permission." She smiled coyly.

"M'man's per-mission! M'man's per-mission!" Cynthia chanted.

"Yes!" Felicity said. "Yes, you have my permission."

"Huzzah! Huzzah!" Cynthia ran from the room, her red hair streaming behind her.

The sight made her frown. Cynthia's red hair was the bane of Felicity's life.

"Thank you, M'man." Christine closed the door primly.

Felicity groaned and rang for more toilet water. If only she hadn't written that incriminating note in a fit of sentimentality. And what had Peter been thinking to save that locket? Men truly were idiots.

She pressed her fingertips over the cloth on her forehead. Perhaps Lord Swartingham really hadn't known what she was talking about. He'd seemed confused when she had said they both knew the identity of the lady he'd met at Aphrodite's Grotto. And if, in fact, he did not know her . . .

Felicity sat up, the cloth falling unheeded to the floor. If he did not know the woman's identity, then she'd been trying to blackmail the wrong person.

ANNA KNELT IN her little garden in back of the cottage the next morning. She hadn't the heart to tell Mother Wren she'd lost her employment. It had been late when she'd arrived home the night before, and this morning she hadn't wanted to talk about it. Not yet, anyway, when the subject would only bring up questions she couldn't answer. Eventually, she'd have to work up the courage to apologize to Edward. But that could wait, too, while she licked her wounds. Which was why she worked in the garden today. The mundane tasks of caring for vegetables and the smell of the freshly dug earth provided a kind of solace to her soul.

She was digging up horseradish roots to replant when she heard a shout from the front of the cottage. She frowned and lay down the shovel. Surely nothing was wrong with Rebecca's baby? She lifted her skirts to trot around the cottage. The sound of a carriage and horses receded. A clearly feminine voice shouted again as she rounded the corner.

Pearl stood on the front step, holding another woman against her. At her approach, they both turned and Anna gasped. The other woman had two black eyes, and her nose looked as if it might be broken. It took Anna a couple of seconds to recognize her.

It was Coral.

"Oh, Lord!" Anna gasped.

The front door opened.

Anna rushed to take Coral's other arm. "Fanny, hold the door for us, please."

Fanny, wide-eyed, obeyed as they awkwardly maneuvered Coral in.

"Told Pearl," Coral whispered, "not to come here." Her lips were so swollen, the words were indistinct.

"Thank goodness she didn't listen to you," Anna said.

She judged the narrow stairs to the upper floor. They'd never make it up the steps with Coral leaning so heavily on them. "Let's bring her into the sitting room."

Pearl nodded.

They gently lowered Coral to the settee. Anna sent Fanny up the stairs for a blanket. Coral's eyes had closed, and Anna wondered if she'd fainted. The other woman was breathing sonorously through her mouth, her nose too misshapen and swollen to let in air.

Anna pulled Pearl to the side. "What happened to her?"

The other woman darted an anxious glance at Coral. "It was that marquis. He came home last night fallingdown drunk; only, he wasn't so drunk he couldn't do *that* to her."

"But why?"

"He didn't have a reason as I could see." Pearl's lips trembled. At Anna's shocked stare, she grimaced. "Oh, he mumbled something 'bout her seeing other men, but that was a crock. Coral thinks of bed sport as business. She wouldn't be doing it with someone else while she had a protector. He just enjoyed putting his fists into her face."

Pearl wiped away an angry tear. "If I hadn't gotten her out when he went to piss, he probably would've killed her."

Anna put an arm around her shoulder. "We must thank the Lord that you were able to save her."

"I didn't know where else to bring her, ma'am," Pearl said. "I'm sorry to bother you after how kind you were before. If we can stay a night or two, just until Coral can get back on her feet."

"You're welcome to stay however long it takes for Coral to become well again. But I fear it'll be more than a night or two." Anna looked worriedly over at her battered guest. "I must send Fanny for Dr. Billings right away."

"Oh, no." Pearl's voice rose in panic. "Don't do that!"

"But she needs to be seen to."

"It'd be better if no one knows we're here 'sides Fanny and the other Mrs. Wren," Pearl said. "He might try looking for her."

Anna slowly nodded. Coral was obviously still in danger. "But what about her wounds?"

"I can take care of them. There aren't any broken bones. I already checked, and I can straighten her nose again."

"You can fix a broken nose?" Anna looked at Pearl strangely.

The other woman tightened her lips. "I've done it before. It comes in handy in my trade."

Anna closed her eyes. "I'm sorry. I didn't mean to doubt you. What do you need?"

Under Pearl's direction, Anna quickly gathered water, rags, and bandages, as well as the jar of her mother's salve.

Pearl worked over her sister's face with her help. The little woman was matter-of-fact, even when Coral moaned and tried to knock away her hands. Anna held down the injured woman's arms so that Pearl could finish bandaging. She sighed with relief when Pearl indicated they were done. They made sure that Coral was as comfortable as possible before retiring to the kitchen for a much-needed cup of tea.

Pearl sighed as she lifted the hot tea to her lips. "Thank you. Thank you so much, ma'am. You're so good."

Anna half laughed, a funny little croak. "It's I who should thank you, if only you knew. I need to do something good right now."

EDWARD THREW DOWN his quill and paced to the library windows. He hadn't written a coherent sentence all day. The room was too quiet, too big for his peace of mind anymore. All he could think of was Anna and what she'd done to him. Why? Why choose him? Was it his title? His wealth?

God! His *scars?*

What possible reason could a respectable woman have to don a disguise and act the part of a whore? If she'd wanted a lover, couldn't she have found one in Little Battleford? Or was it that she liked playing the whore?

Edward rubbed his forehead against the cold glass of the window. He remembered everything he had done to Anna in those two nights. Every exquisite place his hand had touched, every inch of skin his mouth had tongued. He remembered doing things he would never have dreamed of performing with a lady, let alone one he knew and liked. She'd seen a side of himself that he'd made pains to hide away from the world, a private, secret side. She'd seen him at his most bestial. What had she felt when he had pressed her head toward his cock? Excitement? Fear?

Revulsion?

And there were more thoughts he could not stop. Had she met other men at Aphrodite's Grotto? Had she shared her beautiful, lush body with men she didn't even know? Had she let them kiss her wanton mouth, let them paw her breasts, let them rut on her willing, spread body? Edward pounded the window frame with his fist until the skin cracked and blood splattered. Impossible to wipe the obscene images from his mind of Anna—*his* Anna—with another man. His vision blurred. Christ. He was crying like a lad.

Jock nudged his leg and whimpered.

She'd brought him to this. He was completely undone. And yet it made no difference because he was a gentleman and she, despite her actions, was a lady. He would have to marry her, and in doing so give up all his dreams, all his hopes, of having a family. She couldn't have children. His line would die with his last breath. There would be no girls that looked like his mother, no boys that reminded him of Sammy. No one to open his heart to. No one to watch grow. Edward straightened. If that was what life held for him, so be it, but he would make damn sure Anna knew her price.

He wiped his face and jerked the bellpull savagely.

Chapter Seventeen

The man in her bed stared at Aurea and then spoke
softly. Sorrowfully. "So, my wife, you could not let
well enough alone. I will quench your curiosity, then.
I am Prince Niger, the lord of these lands and this
palace. I have been cursed to assume the form of that
foul raven by day and all my minions to become birds
as well. My tormentor made one caveat to the spell: If
I could find a lady to agree of her own will to marry
me in my raven form, then I could live as a man from
midnight to dawn's first glow. You were that lady. But
now our time together is at an end. I will spend the
remainder of my days in that hated feathered form,
and all that follow me are also so doomed. . . ."
—from *The Raven Prince*

The next morning, Felix Hopple shifted from one foot to
the other, sighed, and knocked at the cottage door again.
He twitched his freshly powdered wig straight and ran a
hand over his neckcloth. He'd never been on an errand
quite like this one before. In fact, he wasn't sure his job
really entailed it. Of course, it was impossible to say that

to Lord Swartingham. Especially when he stared at him with smoldering, black, devilish eyes.

He sighed again. His employer's temper had been even worse than usual this past week. Very few knickknacks remained intact in the library, and even the dog had taken to hiding when the earl stalked through the Abbey.

A pretty woman opened the door.

Felix blinked and stepped back a pace. Was he at the right house?

"Yes?" The woman smoothed her skirt and smiled tentatively at him.

"Er, I-I was looking for Mrs. Wren," Felix stuttered. "The *younger* Mrs. Wren. Have I the right address?"

"Oh, yes, this is the right address," she said. "I mean, this is the Wren cottage. I'm just staying here."

"Ah, I see, Miss . . . ?"

"Smythe. Pearl Smythe." The woman blushed for some reason. "Won't you come in?"

"Thank you, Miss Smythe." Felix stepped into the tiny entryway and stood awkwardly.

Miss Smythe was staring, seemingly entranced by his middle. "Coo!" she blurted. "That's the loveliest waistcoat ever."

"Why, er, why thank you, Miss Smythe." He fingered the buttons on his leaf-green waistcoat.

"Are those bumblebees?" Miss Smythe bent down to peer closer at the purple embroidery, giving him a quite inappropriate view down the front of her dress.

No true gentleman would take advantage of a lady's accidental exposure. Felix looked at the ceiling, at the top of her head, and finally down her dress. He blinked rapidly.

"Isn't that clever?" she said, straightening again. "I don't think I've ever seen anything so pretty on a gentleman before."

"What?" he wheezed. "Er, yes. Quite. Thank you again, Miss Smythe. One rarely encounters a person of such fine sentiment about fashion."

Miss Smythe appeared a little confused, but she smiled at him.

He couldn't help but notice how lovely she was. All over.

"You said you came for Mrs. Wren. Why don't you wait in there"—she waved toward a small sitting room—"and I'll go fetch Mrs. Wren from the garden."

Felix stepped into the small room. He heard the pretty woman's retreating footsteps and the close of the back door. He paced to the mantel and looked at a little china clock. He frowned and took out his pocket watch. The mantel clock was fast.

The back door opened again, and Mrs. Wren came in. "Mr. Hopple, how can I help you?"

She was intent on rubbing the garden loam from her hands and didn't meet his eyes.

"I've come on an, er, errand from the earl."

"Indeed?" Mrs. Wren still did not look up.

"Yes." He was at a loss as to how to continue. "Won't you have a seat?"

Mrs. Wren glanced at him in puzzlement and took her seat.

Felix cleared his throat. "There comes a time in every man's life when the winds of adventure blow out, and he feels a need for rest and comfort. A need to toss aside the careless ways of youth—or at least early adulthood in this case—and settle down to domestic tranquility." He paused to see if his words had registered.

"Yes, Mr. Hopple?" She appeared more confused than before.

He mentally girded his loins and labored on. "Yes, Mrs. Wren. Every man, even an earl"—here he paused significantly to emphasize the title—"even an *earl* needs a place of repose and calm. A sanctuary tended by the gentle hand of the feminine sex. A hand guided and led by the stronger masculine hand of a, er, guardian so that both may weather the storms and travails that life brings us."

Mrs. Wren stared at him in a dazed way.

Felix began to feel desperate. "Every man, every *earl,* needs a place of hymeneal comfort."

Her brow puckered. "Hymeneal?"

"Yes." He mopped his brow. "Hymeneal. Of or pertaining to marriage."

She blinked. "Mr. Hopple, why did the earl send you?"

Felix blew out his breath in a gust. "Oh, hang it all, Mrs. Wren! He wants to marry you."

She went completely white. "What?"

Felix groaned. He knew he would make a hash of this. Really, Lord Swartingham was asking too much of him. He was only a land steward, for pity's sake, not cupid with his golden bow and arrows! There was no other choice now but to muddle on.

"Edward de Raaf, the Earl of Swartingham, asks for your hand in marriage. He would like a short engagement and is considering—"

"No."

"The first of June. Wh-what did you say?"

"I said no." Mrs. Wren spoke in a staccato. "Tell him that I am sorry. Very sorry. But there is no possible way that I can marry him."

"But-but-but . . ." Felix took a deep breath to quell his stutter. "But he is an earl. I know his temper is quite foul, really, and he does spend a good deal of time in mud. Which"—he shuddered—"he actually seems to like. But his title and his considerable—one might even say *obscene*—wealth make up for that, don't you think?"

Felix ran out of breath and had to stop.

"No, I don't." She moved toward the door. "Just tell him no."

"But, Mrs. Wren! How will I face him?"

She closed the door gently behind her, and his despairing cry echoed in the empty room. Felix slumped into a chair and wished for an entire bottle of Madeira. Lord Swartingham was not going to like this.

ANNA PLUNGED A trowel into the soft earth and viciously dug up a dandelion. What could Edward have been thinking when he sent Mr. Hopple to propose to her this morning? Obviously he hadn't been overcome by love. She snorted and attacked another dandelion.

The back door to the cottage scraped open. She turned and frowned. Coral was dragging a kitchen stool into the garden.

"What are you doing outside?" Anna demanded. "Pearl and I had to half carry you up the stairs to my room this morning."

Coral sat on the stool. "Country air is supposed to heal, is it not?"

The swelling on her face had gone down somewhat, but the bruising was still evident. Pearl had packed her nostrils with lint in an attempt to heal the break. Now they flared grotesquely. Coral's left eyelid drooped lower than the right, and Anna wondered if it would rise again with time or if the disfigurement was permanent. A small, crescent-shaped scar was scabbed over under the drooping eye.

"I expect I should thank you." Coral tilted her head back against the cottage wall and closed her eyes, as if enjoying the sunlight on her damaged face.

"It is the usual thing to do," Anna said.

"Not for me. I do not like being in other people's debt."

"Then don't think of it as a debt," Anna grunted as she uprooted a weed. "Consider it a gift."

"A gift," Coral mused. "In my experience, gifts usually have to be paid for in one way or another. But perhaps with you that truly is not so. Thank you."

She sighed and shifted position. Although she had sustained no broken bones, there'd been bruises all over her body. She must still be in a great deal of pain.

"I value the regard of women more than men," Coral continued. "It is so much rarer, especially in my profession. It was a woman who did this to me."

"What?" Anna was horrified. "I thought the marquis . . . ?"

The other woman made a dismissive sound. "He was but her instrument. Mrs. Lavender told him I was entertaining other men."

"But why?"

"She wanted my position as the marquis' mistress. And we have some history between us." Coral waved a hand. "But that does not matter. I will deal with her when I am well. Why are you not working at the Abbey today? That is where you usually spend your days, is it not?"

Anna frowned. "I've decided not to go there anymore."

"You have had a falling out with your man?" Coral asked.

"How—?"

"That is who you saw in London, is it not? Edward de Raaf, the Earl of Swartingham?"

"Yes, that's who I met," she sighed. "But he's not my man."

"It has been my observation that women of your ilk— principled women—do not bed a man unless their heart is involved." Coral's mouth quirked sardonically. "They place a great deal of sentimentality on the act."

Anna took an unnecessarily long time to find the next root with the tip of her trowel. "Perhaps you are right. Perhaps I did place a great deal of sentimentality on the-the *act*. But that is neither here nor there now." She bore down on the trowel handle, and the dandelion popped out of the soil. "We argued."

Coral regarded her with narrowed eyes for a moment and then shrugged and closed her eyelids again. "He found out it was you—"

Anna looked up, startled. "How did you—?"

"And now I suppose you will meekly accept his disapproval," Coral continued without pause. "You will hide your shame behind a façade of respectable widowhood. Perhaps you could knit stockings for the poor of the village. Your good works will surely comfort you when he marries in a few years and beds another woman."

"He's asked me to marry him."

Coral opened her eyes. "Now that is interesting." She looked at the growing pile of wilted dandelions. "But you refused him."

Whack!

Anna started hacking at the dandelion pile. "He thinks me a wanton."

Whack!

"I'm barren and he needs children."

Whack!

"And he doesn't want me."

Whack! Whack! Whack!

Anna stopped and stared at the heap of broken, oozing weeds.

"Doesn't he?" Coral murmured. "And what about you? Do you, ah, *want* him?"

Anna felt heat flooding her cheeks. "I've been without a man for many years now. I can be alone again."

A smile flickered across Coral's face. "Have you ever noticed that once you have had a taste of certain sweets—raspberry trifle is my own despair—it is quite impossible not to think, not to want, not to *crave* until you have taken another bite?"

"Lord Swartingham is not a raspberry trifle."

"No, more of a dark chocolate mousse, I should think," Coral murmured.

"And," Anna continued as if she hadn't heard the interruption, "I don't need another bite, uh, *night* of him."

A vision of that second night rose up before her eyes: Edward bare-chested, his trousers undone, lounging in that chair before the fire like a Turkish pasha. His skin, his *penis,* had gleamed in the firelight.

Anna swallowed. Her mouth was watering. "I can live without Lord Swartingham," she declared very firmly.

Coral raised an eyebrow.

"I can! Besides, you weren't there." Anna suddenly felt as wilted as the dandelions. "He was horribly angry. He said terrible things to me."

"Ah," Coral said. "He is uncertain of you."

"I don't see why that should make you happy," Anna said. "And, anyway, it's much more than that. He'll never forgive me."

Coral smiled like a cat watching a sparrow hop near. "Maybe. Maybe not."

"WHAT DO YOU mean, you won't marry me?" Edward paced from the curio shelf at one end of the small sitting room to the settee at the other end, pivoted, and came back again. Not such a great feat since he could cross the entire room in three strides. "I'm an earl, goddamnit!"

Anna grimaced. She should never have let him into the cottage. Of course, she hadn't had much choice at the time, since he'd threatened to break down the door if she didn't open it.

He had looked quite capable of doing it, too.

"I won't marry you," she repeated.

"Why not? You were eager enough to fuck me."

Anna winced. "I do wish you would stop using that word."

Edward swung around and assumed a hideously sarcastic expression. "Would you prefer *swive? Tup? Dance the buttock jig?*"

She compressed her lips. Thank goodness Mother Wren

and Fanny had gone shopping this morning. Edward was making no effort to lower his voice.

"You don't want to marry me." Anna spoke slowly and enunciated each word as if talking to a hard-of-hearing village idiot.

"Whether I want to marry you or not isn't the issue, as you well know," Edward said. "The fact is, I must marry you."

"Why?" She blew out a breath. "There is no possibility of a child. As you have made abundantly clear, you know I am barren."

"I have compromised you."

"I'm the one who went to Aphrodite's Grotto in disguise. It seems to me that *I* compromised *you*." Anna thought it commendable that she did not wave her arms in the air in exasperation.

"That's ridiculous!" Edward's bellow could probably be heard back at the Abbey.

Why did men think that saying something louder made it true? "No more ridiculous than an earl who is already engaged proposing marriage to his secretary!" Her own voice was raised now.

"I'm not proposing. I'm telling you we must marry."

"No." Anna crossed her arms.

Edward stalked across the room toward her, each step deliberate and meant to be intimidating. He didn't stop until his chest was inches from her face. She craned her neck to meet his gaze; she refused to back away from him.

He leaned down until his breath brushed across her forehead intimately. "You will marry me."

He smelled of coffee. Anna dropped her eyes to his

mouth. Even in anger, it was disgustingly sensual. She re-treated a step and turned her back. "I am not going to marry you."

Anna could hear him breathing heavily behind her. She peeked over her shoulder.

Edward was looking thoughtfully at her bottom.

His eyes snapped up. "You will marry me." He held up a hand when she started to speak. "But I'll quit the discussion of when for now. In the meantime, I still need a secretary. I want you at the Abbey this afternoon."

"I hardly think"—Anna had to stop to steady her voice—"I hardly think in light of our past relationship that I should continue as your secretary."

Edward's eyes narrowed. "Correct me if I am wrong, Mrs. Wren, but weren't you the one who initiated that relationship? Therefore—"

"I said I was sorry!"

He ignored her outburst. "*Therefore,* I fail to see why I should be the one to suffer the loss of a secretary merely because of your discomfort, if that is the problem."

"Yes, that's the problem!" Discomfort didn't begin to describe the agony it would be to try and carry on as before. Anna took a fortifying breath. "I can't return."

"Well, then," Edward said softly, "I fear I'll be unable to pay you your wages to date."

"That's . . ." Anna lost her power of speech in sheer horror.

The Wren household had been counting on the money that would be paid at the end of the month. So much so that they'd already accrued several small debts at the local shops. It would be bad enough, not having a job. If she couldn't have the wages she'd already earned as Edward's secretary, the results would be disastrous.

"Yes?" Edward inquired.

"That's unfair!" Anna burst out.

"Now, dear heart, whatever gave you the idea that I played fair?" He smiled silkily.

"You can't do that!"

"Yes, I can. I keep telling you that I'm an earl, but it hasn't seemed to have sunk in yet." Edward propped a fist beneath his chin. "Of course, if you come back to work, your wages will be paid in full."

Anna closed her mouth and breathed rather forcefully through her nostrils for a bit.

"Fine. I'll come back. But I want to be paid at the end of the week," she said. "*Every* week."

He laughed. "You are so untrusting."

He lunged forward and, catching her hand, kissed the back of it. Then he turned her hand over and quickly pressed his tongue into her palm. For a second, she felt the soft, wet warmth and her intimate muscles clenched. He let go and was out the door before she could protest.

At least, she was fairly certain she would have protested.

OBSTINATE, OBSTINATE WOMAN. Edward swung himself into the bay's saddle. Any other female in Little Battleford would've sold their grandmother to marry him. Hell, most of the women in England would sell their entire family, the family retainers, *and* the family pets to become his bride.

Edward snorted.

He wasn't egotistical. It had nothing to do with him

personally. It was the title he bore that had such a high market value. Well, that and the money that came with the title. But not for Anna Wren, impoverished widow of no social standing. Oh, no. For her and her only, he was good enough to bed, but not wed. What did she think he was? A cock for hire?

Edward tightened the reins as the bay shied at a blowing leaf. Well, that same sensuality that had led her to meet him in a brothel was going to be her downfall. He'd caught her staring at his mouth in midargument, and it had dawned on him: Why not use her sexuality for his own purposes? What matter *why* she had decided to seduce him—whether because of his scars or no—the more important point was that she had. She liked his mouth, did she? She would see it all day, every day, as his secretary. And he would be sure to remind her what other things she was missing until she consented to be his bride.

Edward grinned. In fact, it would be his pleasure to show her just what rewards awaited her when they wed. With her lustful nature, Anna wouldn't be able to hold out long. And then she would be his wife. The thought of Anna as his wife was strangely comforting, and a fellow could get used to such feminine lust in a wife. Oh, yes, indeed.

Smiling grimly, Edward kicked the gelding into a gallop.

Chapter Eighteen

*Aurea stared, horrified, at her husband. Then the
first rays of dawn streamed through the high palace
window and fell upon the prince, and his form began
to shrink and convulse. The broad, smooth shoulders
shriveled and diminished; his wide, elegant mouth
protruded and hardened; and the fingers of his strong
hands metamorphosed into wispy, tarnished feathers.
And as the raven appeared, the walls of the palace
shook and trembled until it dissolved and disappeared.
There was a great whirring and flapping of wings as
the raven and all his followers took to the skies.
Aurea found herself alone. She was without clothing,
food, or even water in a dry plain that stretched in all
directions as far as the eye could see. . . .*
—from *The Raven Prince*

Anna was just about at the end of her patience. She caught
herself tapping a toe and carefully stilled her foot. She
stood in the stable courtyard while Edward argued with a
groom about Daisy's saddle. Apparently there was something wrong with it. What, exactly, she did not know,
since no one deigned to tell her, a woman, the problem.

She sighed. For nearly a week she'd bitten her tongue and dutifully done Edward's bidding as his secretary. Never mind that some of his orders were clearly calculated to make her lose her self-possession. Never mind that at least once a day Edward made some remark about the perfidy of women. Never mind that every time she'd happened to glance up, her eyes had collided with Edward's staring back at her. She'd been ladylike, she'd been meek, and it was almost killing her.

Anna closed her eyes now. Patience. Patience was a virtue she must master.

"Are you falling asleep?" Edward spoke right beside her, making Anna jump and glare, a reaction he missed, as he'd already turned away. "George says the girth is too worn. We'll have to take the phaeton instead."

"I don't think—" Anna started.

But he strode to where a team was being hitched to the vehicle.

Anna gaped and then trotted after him. "My lord."

He ignored her.

"*Edward,*" she hissed

"Darling?" He stopped so suddenly, she nearly skidded into him.

"Don't. Call. Me. That." She'd said it so many times in the last week, the words had become a chant. "There isn't room on that thing for a groom or maid."

He glanced at the phaeton casually. Jock had already jumped into the high seat and was sitting alertly, ready for a ride. "Why would I want to take a groom or maid to look at fields?"

Anna pursed her lips. "You know very well."

He raised his eyebrows.

"As a chaperone." She smiled sweetly for the benefit of the stablemen.

He leaned close. "Sweetheart, I'm flattered, but even I can't seduce you whilst driving a phaeton."

Anna blushed. She knew that. "I—"

Edward seized her hand before she could say more, pulled her to the carriage, and tossed her on the seat. He went to help the grooms hitching the horses.

"Overbearing man," she muttered to Jock.

The mastiff thumped his tail and laid his massive head on her shoulder, smearing it with canine drool. After another few minutes, Edward vaulted to the seat, making the carriage shake, and caught the reins. The horses stepped out, and the phaeton started forward with a jerk. Anna grabbed the back of her seat. Jock leaned into the wind, ears and jowls flapping. The phaeton rounded a corner fast, and she jostled against Edward. For a moment, her breast pressed against the hard slab of his arm. She righted herself and took a firmer hold of the side.

The carriage veered, and Anna bumped against him again. She glared, but it had no effect. Every time she let go of the seat back, the vehicle lurched and she was forced to grab it.

"Are you doing that on purpose?"

There was no answer.

"If you are shaking me about to put me in my place," she huffed, "I do think it is rather infantile of you."

An ebony eye glanced at her through sooty lashes.

"If you want to punish me," she said, "I can understand, but surely wrecking the phaeton would inconvenience you as well."

He slowed fractionally.

Anna placed her hands in her lap.

"Why would I want to punish you?" he asked.

"You know." Really, he was the most exasperating creature when he wanted to be.

They bowled along the lane for a bit in silence. The sky began to lighten and then blush a shy crimson. Anna could see his features more clearly. They did not look confiding.

She sighed. "I *am* sorry, you know."

"Sorry you were found out?" Edward's voice was suspiciously silky.

She bit the inside of her cheek. "I'm sorry I deceived you."

"I find that hard to believe."

"Are you implying that I'm lying?" Anna grit her teeth to hold fast to her temper, trying to remember her vow about patience.

"Why, yes, my sweet, I believe I am." His teeth sounded as if they were being ground. "You seem to have an innate facility for lying."

She took a deep breath. "I understand why you would think that, but please believe that I never meant to hurt you."

Edward snorted. "Fine. Good. You were in one of the most notorious brothels in London dressed as a high-priced whore, and I happened to walk in on you. Yes, I can see that you've been misunderstood."

Anna counted to ten. Then she counted to fifty. "I was waiting for you. *Only* you."

That appeared to take the wind out of his sails for a bit. The sun had risen fully now. They rattled around a curve and frightened two hares in the middle of the road.

"Why?" he barked.

She'd lost the thread of the conversation. "What?"

"Why did you choose me after, what, six years of celibacy?"

"Nearer seven."

"But you've been widowed six."

Anna nodded without explanation.

She could feel Edward looking curiously at her. "Whatever the time period, why me? My scars—"

"It had nothing to do with your bloody scars!" she burst out. "The scars don't matter, can't you see that?"

"Then why?"

And it was her turn to be mute. The sun was very bright now, picking out every detail, leaving nothing hidden.

She tried to explain. "I believed . . . No. I *knew* we had an attraction. Then you left and I realized you were taking what you felt for me and giving it to another woman. A woman you didn't even know. And I wanted—needed—" Anna threw up her hands in frustration. "I wanted to be the one you-you *swived* with."

Edward choked. She couldn't tell if he was appalled, sickened, or simply laughing at her.

Her temper suddenly came to a boil. "You were the one who left for London. You were the one who decided to-to *tup* another woman. You were the one who turned away from me. From us. Who is the greater sinner? I will no longer—urp!"

She gulped her words as Edward pulled the horses up so abruptly that they half reared. Jock was nearly catapulted from the seat. Anna opened her lips in alarm, but before she could protest, her mouth was covered by his. He thrust his tongue into her mouth without preamble. She tasted coffee as he stroked along her tongue, opening her lips farther for his access. Blunt fingers massaged the nape of her neck. She was surrounded by the musky scent of a man in his prime. Slowly, reluctantly, his mouth left hers. His tongue tenderly licked along her bottom lip as if in regret.

Anna blinked in the bright sunlight as he lifted his head. Edward studied her dazed features and must have been satisfied by what he saw there. He grinned, flashing white teeth. He caught up the reins and set the horses cantering down the lane, manes flying. Anna grabbed the seat back once again and tried to figure out what had just happened. It was rather hard to think with the taste of him still in her mouth.

"I'm going to marry you," Edward shouted.

For the life of her, she didn't know what to say. So she said nothing.

Jock barked once and let his tongue hang out of his mouth, flying in the wind.

CORAL TILTED HER face to the sky and felt the rays of the sun slide like liquid heat down her cheeks. She sat at the back door to the Wrens' cottage, just as she had every day since she was well enough to rise from her sickbed. Around her, small green things were poking their fingers through the black earth, and nearby, a funny little bird was making quite a lot of noise. Strange how one never noticed the sun in London. The raucous cries of thousands of voices, the sooty smoke, the sewage-laden streets distracted and obscured until one no longer looked up. No longer felt the gentle touch of the sun.

"Oh, Mr. Hopple!"

Coral opened her eyes at the sound of her sister's voice but otherwise remained still. Pearl had paused just inside the gate to the back garden. She was accompanied by a bantam man wearing the gaudiest waistcoat Coral had ever seen. He seemed shy, judging by the way he repeatedly tugged at the waistcoat. That was not surprising. Many men were anxious in the company of a woman they were attracted to. At least, the nicer ones were. But Pearl was playing with her hair, twirling and tangling it in her fingers, indicating that she was ill at ease as well. And that was surprising. One of the first things a whore learned was how to maintain a confident, indeed bold, mask when in the company of the stronger sex. It was the key to their living.

Pearl took leave of her escort with a pretty titter. She opened the gate and entered the small yard. She was almost to the back door when she noticed her sister.

"Goodness me, ducks, I didn't see you sitting there." Pearl fanned her flushed face. "You gave me a proper start, you did."

"So I see," Coral said. "You are not looking for a new prospect are you? You don't have to work anymore. Besides, we will be leaving for London soon, now that I am better."

"He's not a prospect," Pearl said. "At least not the kind

you mean. He's offered me a job as a downstairs maid at the Abbey."

"Downstairs maid?"

"Yes." Pearl was blushing. "I'm trained as one, you know. I'd make a good maid again, I would."

Coral frowned. "But you need not work at all. I told you I would look after you, and I will."

Her sister pulled back her thin shoulders and thrust her chin forward. "I'm going to stay here with Mr. Felix Hopple."

Coral stared for a short moment. Pearl's stance never wavered.

"Why?" she finally asked, her voice even.

"He's asked leave to court me, and I've told him he may."

"And when he learns what you are?"

"I think he already knows." Pearl saw her question and quickly shook her head. "No, I haven't told him, but my last stay here wasn't a secret. And if he doesn't know, I'll tell him. I think he'll have me anyway."

"Even if he accepts your former life," Coral said gently, "the other villagers may not."

"Oh, I know it will be rough. I'm not a young girl with pixie dust in her eyes anymore. But he's a proper gentleman." Pearl knelt beside Coral's chair. "He treats me so kindly, and he looks at me like I might be a lady."

"And so you will stay here?"

"You could stay, too." Pearl spoke low and reached to grasp Coral's hand. "We could both start a new life here, have families like normal folk. We could have a wee cottage like this one, and you could live with me. Wouldn't that be lovely?"

Coral looked down at her hand intertwined with her older sister's. Pearl's fingers were biscuit-colored with small, light scars around the knuckles, mementos of her years of service. Her own hand was white, smooth, and unnaturally soft. She withdrew it from Pearl's clasp.

"I'm afraid I cannot stay here." Coral tried to smile but found she couldn't. "I belong in London. I'm just not comfortable any other place."

"But—"

"Hush, dear. My lot in life was drawn a long time ago." Coral stood and shook out her skirts. "Besides, all this fresh air and sunshine can't be good for my complexion. Come inside and help me pack."

"If that's what you want," Pearl said slowly.

"It is." Coral held out her hand to pull her sister to her feet. "You have told me how Mr. Hopple feels, but you never said how you feel about him."

"He makes me feel safe and warm." Pearl blushed. "And he kisses so nicely."

"A lemon curd tart," Coral murmured. "And you always were so very fond of lemon curd."

"What?"

"Never mind, dear." Coral brushed her lips across her sister's cheek. "I'm glad you have found the man for you."

"AND FURTHERMORE, THIS crackpot theory only deepens the suspicion that your senility of the brain is now in an advanced stage. My commiserations."

Anna frantically scribbled the words as Edward paced before her rosewood desk. She'd never taken dictation before and found to her dismay that it was harder than she would have thought. The fact that Edward composed his scathing letters at a breakneck pace certainly did not help.

Out of the corner of her eye, she noticed that *The Raven Prince* was back on her desk. Ever since that ride in the phaeton two days ago, she and Edward seemed to be playing a game with the book. One morning she'd found the book lying in the center of her desk. She'd returned it to him silently, but after luncheon it'd been back on her desk again. She'd put it on Edward's desk, again, and the process had been repeated. Several times. So far, she hadn't worked up the courage to ask what, exactly, the book meant to him and why he seemed to be giving it to her.

Now Edward wandered over in the midst of his dictation. "Perhaps your sad mental deterioration has a family root." He braced a fist on her desk. "I remember your uncle, the Duke of Arlington, was similarly stubborn on the issue of swine breeding. Indeed, some say his final apoplectic fit was the result of a too-heated discussion about farrowing pens. Do you find it hot in here?"

Anna had gotten as far as writing *hot* when she realized that the last question was directed at her. She glanced up in time to see him discard his coat.

"No, the room seems most temperate." Her tentative smile froze as Edward drew off his neckcloth.

"I'm overly warm," he said. He unbuttoned his waistcoat.

"What are you doing?" Anna squeaked.

"Dictating a letter?" He arched his eyebrows in a parody of innocence.

"You're disrobing!"

"No, I would be disrobing if I removed my shirt," Edward said, doing just that.

"Edward!"

"My dear?"

"Put your shirt back on this instant," Anna hissed.

"Why? Do you find my torso offensive?" Edward leaned nonchalantly against her desk.

"Yes." Anna winced at his expression. "No! Put your shirt back on."

"You're sure you're not repulsed by my scars?" He leaned closer, his fingers trailing across the marks on his upper chest.

Her eyes helplessly followed his hypnotic hand before she snapped her gaze away. A scathing reply teetered on the edge of her tongue. She was stopped by Edward's studied ease. The question was clearly important to the impossible man.

She sighed. "I don't find you repulsive at all, as well you know."

"Then touch me."

"Edward—"

"Do it," he whispered. "I need to know." He caught her hand and pulled her to stand in front of him.

Anna looked into his face, struggling between propriety and the desire to reassure him. The true problem was, of course, that she wanted to touch him. Too much.

He waited.

She raised her hand. Hesitated. Then touched. Her

palm rested, trembling, on the juncture of Edward's throat and chest, just where she could feel the implacable beat of his heart. His eyes seemed to darken impossibly to a deeper shade of black as he stared at her. Her own breast labored to fill with air as her hand glided down over firm muscle. She could feel the indentations of the pox scars, and she paused to circle one gently with her middle finger. His eyelids fell, as if weighted. She moved to another scar and traced it as well. She watched her own hand and thought about the long-ago pain these scars represented. The pain to a young boy's body and the pain to his soul. The room was quiet save for the whisper of their mutual strained breaths. She'd never explored a man's chest in such minute detail. It felt too good. Sensual. More intimate in some ways than the act of sex itself.

Her gaze flicked to his face. His lips were parted, wet where he'd run his tongue over them. Obviously he was as affected as she. The knowledge that her mere touch had that kind of power over him sparked her own arousal. Her hand encountered the black, curling hair on his chest. It was damp with perspiration. She slowly furrowed her fingers into the tangle, watching as the wisps curled around her fingertips as if to hold her. She could smell his masculine essence rising with the heat from his body.

She swayed forward, drawn by a force beyond her will. His chest hair tickled her lips. She buried her nose in his warmth. His chest moved jerkily now. She opened her mouth and exhaled. Her tongue crept forward to taste the salt on his skin. One of them, maybe both, moaned. Her hands clutched at his sides, and she could dimly feel his arms urging her closer. Her tongue continued to explore:

tickling hair, tangy sweat, the corrugation of a male nipple.

The salt of her own tears.

She found that her eyes were leaking slowly, tears dripping down her face and mingling with the moisture on Edward's body. It made no sense, but she couldn't stop the tears. Any more than she could stop her body from yearning for this man or her heart from—*loving him.*

The realization brought her up short, cleared some of the haze from her mind. She inhaled shakily, and then pushed away from Edward's embrace.

His arms tightened. "Anna—"

"Please. Let me go." Her voice sounded scratchy to her own ears.

"Damn it." But his arms opened, releasing her.

She backed swiftly away.

He scowled. "If you think I'll forget this . . ."

"No need to warn me." She laughed too shrilly, teetering on the edge of completely losing her composure. "I already know you don't forget—or forgive—anything."

"God*damn*it, you know damn—"

A knock sounded at the library door. Edward cut himself off and straightened, running his hand impatiently through his hair and dislodging his queue. "What?"

Mr. Hopple peered around the door. He blinked when he saw the earl's state of undress but stuttered into speech nevertheless. "B-begging your pardon, my lord, but John Coachman says one of the rear carriage wheels is still being repaired by the blacksmith."

Edward scowled at the steward and snatched up his shirt.

Anna took the opportunity to surreptitiously swipe at her wet cheeks.

"He assures me it will take only a day more," Mr. Hopple continued. "Two at the most."

"I haven't that amount of time, man." Edward had finished re-dressing and now swung around and began rummaging in his desk, knocking papers to the floor as he did so. "We'll take the phaeton, and the servants can follow behind when the carriage is repaired."

Anna looked up suspiciously. This was the first she'd heard of a trip. Surely, he wouldn't dare?

Mr. Hopple frowned. "*We,* my lord? I wasn't aware—"

"My secretary will accompany me to London, of course. I'll be in need of her services, if I am to finish the manuscript."

The steward's eyes widened in horror, but Edward missed the reaction. He was staring at Anna challengingly.

She drew in a quick breath, mute.

"B-but, my lord!" Mr. Hopple stuttered, apparently scandalized.

"I'll need to finish the manuscript." Edward addressed his reasons to her, his eyes burning with a black fire. "My secretary will take notes at the Agrarian's meeting. I'll have to deal with various business matters pertaining to my other estates. Yes, I do believe it is essential that my secretary travel with me," he finished in a lower, more intimate tone.

Mr. Hopple lurched into speech. "But she's a-a—well! A female. An unmarried female, pardon my candor, Mrs. Wren. It isn't at all proper for her to be traveling—"

"Quite. Quite," Edward interrupted. "We'll have a chaperone. Be sure and bring one with you tomorrow, Mrs. Wren. We leave just before daybreak. I shall expect you in the courtyard." And he stomped out of the room.

Mr. Hopple trailed after, muttering ineffectual objections.

Anna truly didn't know whether to laugh or cry. She felt a rough, wet tongue on her palm and looked down to see Jock panting by her side.

"Whatever am I to do?"

But the dog only sighed and rolled onto his back so that his paws waved in the air absurdly, which hardly answered her question.

Chapter Nineteen

Aurea wept for all that she had lost, alone there in the endless desert. But after a while, she realized that her only hope was to find her vanished husband and redeem both herself and him. So she set out to search for the Raven Prince. The first year, she hunted for him in the lands to the east. There, strange animals and stranger people lived, but no one had heard of the Raven Prince. The second year, she traveled the lands to the north. There, freezing winds ruled the people from dawn to dusk, but no one had heard of the Raven Prince. The third year, she explored the western lands. There, opulent palaces rose to the sky, but no one had heard of the Raven Prince. The fourth year, she sailed to the farthest south. There, the sun burned too close to the earth, but no one had heard of the Raven Prince. . . .

—from *The Raven Prince*

"I'm very sorry, dear." Mother Wren wrung her hands that evening as she watched Anna pack. "But you know how open carriages make my tummy do loops. Just the thought, in fact, is almost enough t-to . . ."

Anna looked up swiftly. Her mother-in-law had turned a delicate shade of green.

She pushed the older woman into a chair. "Sit down and breathe. Would you like some water?" Anna tried to open the only window in the room, but it was stuck.

Mother Wren pressed a handkerchief to her mouth and closed her eyes. "I'll be all right in a moment."

Anna poured some water from a pitcher on the dresser and pressed the glass into her hand. The older woman sipped it, and the color began to return to her cheeks.

"It's just too bad Coral left so suddenly." Mother Wren had repeated the sentiment with variations all day.

Anna flattened her mouth.

Fanny had roused them that morning after finding a note in the kitchen. In the note, Coral had simply thanked them for their care. Anna had run upstairs to look in the room where Coral had been sleeping, but it was empty and the bed already made. There she discovered another note pinned to the pillow. Coral asked that Pearl be allowed to stay a while longer, and she'd included gold coins that clinked to the floor when Anna unfolded the note.

Anna had tried to give the money to Pearl, but the other woman had shaken her head and backed away. "No, ma'am. That there money is for you and Mrs. Wren. You've been the best friends me and Coral have ever had."

"But you'll need it."

"You and Mrs. Wren need it, too. Besides, I have a position I'll be starting soon." She had blushed. "Up at the Abbey."

Anna shook her head. "I hope Coral is all right. Her

bruises had barely begun to fade. Pearl doesn't even know where she could have gone besides back to London."

Mother Wren pressed a hand to her forehead. "Had she only waited, she could've accompanied you to London."

"Maybe Pearl wouldn't mind delaying her work at the Abbey and going with me first." Anna pulled out a drawer in her dresser and hunted for a pair of stockings without any holes.

"I rather think Pearl will want to stay here." Her mother-in-law set the glass down carefully on the floor beside her chair. "She seems to have met a gentleman at the Abbey."

"Really?" Anna half turned, her hands full of stockings. "Who do you think it is? One of the footmen?"

"I don't know. The day before last, she asked me about the household and who worked there. And then she muttered something about bees."

"Does the Abbey have a beekeeper?" Anna wrinkled her brow in thought before shaking her head and folding a pair of stockings and placing them in her bag.

"Not that I know of." Mother Wren shrugged. "In any case, I'm glad Lord Swartingham has decided to take you to London. He's such a nice man. And he's interested in you, dear. Perhaps he'll be asking you an important question there."

Anna winced. "He's already asked me to marry him."

Mother Wren jumped up and let out a squeal worthy of a girl a quarter of her age.

"And I told him no," Anna finished.

"No?" Her mother-in-law looked aghast.

"No." She carefully folded a chemise and placed it in her bag.

"Damn Peter!" The other woman stamped her foot.

"Mother!"

"I'm sorry, dear, but you know as well as I do that you wouldn't have turned that lovely man down if it hadn't been for my son."

"I don't—"

"Now, there's no use making excuses for him." Mother Wren actually looked stern. "The good Lord knows I loved Peter. He was my only son, and he was such a darling little boy. But what he did to you in your marriage was just plain unforgivable. My dear husband, had he been alive at the time, would've taken a horsewhip to Peter."

Anna felt tears prick her eyes. "I didn't realize you knew."

"I didn't." Mother Wren sat down again with a thump. "Not until that last illness. He was feverish and started talking one night when I was up with him. You'd gone to bed already."

Anna looked down at her hands to hide the fact that tears were blurring her vision. "He was so upset when he found out I couldn't have babies. I'm sorry for that."

"I'm sorry, too. Sorry that you couldn't have children together."

Anna wiped her face with her palm and heard her mother-in-law's skirts rustle as she came near.

Plump, warm arms wrapped around her. "But he had you. Do you know how happy I was when Peter married you?"

"Oh, Mother . . ."

"You were—*are*—the daughter I never had," Mother Wren murmured. "You've taken care of me all these years. In many ways, I've grown closer to you than I ever was to Peter."

For some reason, this made Anna weep harder.

Mother Wren held her, rocking slightly from side to side. Anna cried great, heaving sobs that tore from her chest and made her head hurt. It was so painful to have this part of her life exposed when she'd kept it hidden away from the light so long. Peter's infidelity had been her own secret shame to bear and suffer alone. Yet, all this time, Mother Wren had known, and what was more, she did not blame her. Her words felt like an absolution.

Finally, Anna's sobs slowed and quieted, her eyes still closed. She felt so weary, her limbs heavy and listless.

The older woman helped her to lie down and smoothed the coverlet over her. "Just rest."

Mother Wren's cool, soft hand gently brushed the hair from her forehead, and she heard her murmur, "Please be happy, dear."

Anna lay dreamily and listened to the click of the other woman's heels as she went downstairs. Even with her headache, she felt at peace.

"GONE TO LONDON?" Felicity's voice rose until it nearly cracked.

Two ladies walking by the Wren cottage glanced over at her. She turned her back to them.

The elder Mrs. Wren was looking at her oddly. "Yes, just this morning with the earl. Lord Swartingham said he couldn't do without her at his club meeting. I can't think now what they are called, the Aegeans or some such. It's amazing what these society gentlemen find to amuse themselves with, isn't it?"

Felicity fixed a smile on her face as the old woman babbled on, though she wanted to scream with impatience. "Yes, but when will Anna return?"

"Oh, I shouldn't think for another day or so." Mrs. Wren's brow knit in thought. "Perhaps even a week? Surely by the fortnight."

Felicity felt her smile congeal into a grimace. Good God, was the woman senile? "Quite. Well, I have to go. Errands, you know."

She could tell by Mrs. Wren's faltering smile that her parting was less than genteel, but Felicity didn't have the time right now. She climbed into her carriage, banged on the ceiling, then groaned as the carriage pulled away. Why had Chilly been so indiscreet? And which of her servants had gossiped? When she got her hands on the traitor, she would make sure they wouldn't work again in this county. Only this morning the squire had become irate at the breakfast table. He'd demanded to know who had been sneaking from her rooms the week before. It had quite put her off her coddled eggs.

If only Chilly had climbed through the window instead of using the servant's entrance. But no, he'd insisted that the stone on the window ledge would tear his stockings. Silly, vain man. And as if Reginald's suspicions about Chilly weren't enough, he'd commented only yesterday on Cynthia's red hair. It seemed red hair hadn't appeared in the Clearwater family in living memory. If ever.

Well, of course not, you stupid man, Felicity had wanted to scream. *Her red hair doesn't come from your family.* Instead, she'd made some vague references to her grandmother's auburn locks and hastily turned the conversation to hounds, a subject that always enthralled her spouse.

Felicity ran her fingers over her own perfect coiffure. Why was the squire finally looking at his daughters now after all this time? If that letter turned up on top of his suspicions about Chilly, her standing would take a considerable fall. She shuddered. Banishment to a shoddy little farmhouse was possible. Even *divorce,* that most awful of fates, might happen to her. Inconceivable. Not to Felicity Clearwater.

She had to find Anna and get that letter.

ANNA ROLLED OVER and punched the heavy down pillow for what seemed like the hundredth time. Impossible to sleep while waiting to be swooped down on by a circling earl.

She hadn't been surprised early this morning when Fanny, her chaperone by default, had been relegated to a following carriage. That had left Anna to drive alone with Edward in the phaeton to London. She'd been sure to position Jock between them on the phaeton's seat and had been almost disappointed when Edward hadn't seemed to notice. They'd driven all day and arrived at Edward's London town house after dark. Apparently they'd woken the staff. The butler, Dreary, had opened the door in nightshirt and cap. Still, the yawning maids had lit fires and found a cold meal for them.

Then Edward had wished her a polite good night and bid the housekeeper show her to a room. Since the servant's carriage with Fanny hadn't yet appeared, Anna had the bedroom to herself. In her room was a small connecting door, and she had grave suspicions about it. The bedroom was far too grand to be simply a guest room. He couldn't have put her in the countess's suite, could he? He wouldn't dare.

She sighed. Actually, he would.

The clock on the mantel had already chimed the one o'clock hour. Surely if Edward was coming to her, he would have done so before now? Not that it would do him any good to try her doors. She'd locked both.

Steady, masculine footsteps thumped up the stairs.

She stilled like a hare overshadowed by a bird of prey. She looked at the hall door. The footsteps drew near, the tread slowing as it reached her door. They stopped.

All of her being focused on the doorknob.

There was a pause, and then the footsteps resumed. A door farther down the hall opened and shut. Anna flopped back on her pillows. Naturally, she was relieved at this turn of events. Very, very relieved. Wouldn't any proper lady be relieved to find that she *wasn't* going to be ravished by a demon earl?

She was debating how a proper lady would present herself at a demon earl's bedroom for ravishment when the lock on the connecting door snicked open. Edward sauntered in, holding a key and two glasses.

"I thought you might like to share my brandy?" He gestured with the glasses.

"I, um . . ." Anna paused to clear her throat. "I don't care for brandy."

He held the glasses up for a moment longer before lowering them. "No? Well—"

"But you are welcome to drink it here." Anna's words collided with Edward's.

He stared at her silently.

"With me, I mean." She could feel her cheeks heating.

Edward turned his back, and for a ghastly moment, Anna thought he would leave after all. But he put the glasses down on a table, faced her again, and began removing his cravat. "Actually, I didn't come for a nightcap."

Her breath caught.

He tossed the cravat on a chair and pulled his shirt off over his head. Her eyes immediately fixed on his bare chest.

He looked at her. "No comment? I think this may be a first."

He sat on the bed to pull off first his boots and then his stockings. The bed sagged with his weight. He stood and dropped his hands to the buttons on his buckskins.

She stopped breathing.

Edward smiled wickedly and slowly flicked open the buttons. He hooked his thumbs in the waistband and shucked both pants and drawers with one movement. Then he straightened, and his smile faded. "If you're going to say no, do it now." He sounded just a bit uncertain.

Anna took her time looking him over. From hooded ebony eyes to broad muscular shoulders and lean belly to thickening manhood and weighty balls to corded thighs and hairy calves and finally to large, bony feet. The light had been dim at Aphrodite's Grotto, and she wanted to save this picture of him should she never see it again. He was beautiful standing there, offering himself to her in the candle's glow. She found her throat was too thick to speak, so she simply held out her arms.

Edward closed his eyes for a second. Had he really thought she would send him away? Then he walked soundlessly to the bed. He halted beside her. Bowing his head with unexpected elegance, he raised one hand to pull the ribbon from his queue. Black silk flowed around his scarred shoulders. He climbed in the bed and crouched over her, his hair tickling the sides of her face. He lowered his head to brush soft kisses over her cheeks, her nose, and her eyes. She tried to lift her lips to his, but he evaded her. Until she grew impatient.

She needed his mouth so much. "Kiss me." She drove her fingers into his mane and drew his face down to hers.

He opened his lips over hers, taking her breath into himself, and it felt like a benediction. This was so right. She knew that now. This passion between them was the most perfect thing in the world.

She squirmed, trying to get closer to him, but his hands and knees on either side of her body weighed down the sheet covering her. She was trapped. He ravished her mouth at his pleasure. He took his time, roughly, then softly, and then roughly once more until she felt her want melt within her.

Suddenly he reared back on his knees. There was a fine sheen of sweat on his chest, and seed dewed the tip of his penis. She moaned low in her throat at the sight. He was so magnificent, so beautiful, and at this instant in time, he was all hers.

He flicked his gaze at her face, then downward as he pulled the sheet from her breasts. She wore only her shift. He drew the thin garment tight across her bosom and examined the result. She could feel her nipples stiffening against the fabric. Tight and yearning. Waiting for his touch. He leaned down, placed his wet mouth over a nipple, and sucked at it through the shift. The sensation was so sharp she bucked. He moved to the other nipple and suckled that one as well until the tips of her breasts were draped in wet, transparent fabric. He drew back and blew on first one, and then the other nipple, making her gasp and struggle.

"Stop playing. For pity's sake, touch me." She didn't recognize her own voice, it was so husky.

"As you wish."

He grasped the neckline of the shift and with one motion, tore open the flimsy material. Her bare breasts tumbled into the chilly night air. For a second, Anna was shy. She wore no concealing mask tonight. This was her real self making love to Edward. She had no pretense to hide behind; he could see her face, her emotions. Then he swooped once again and captured her nipple in his mouth. The heated sucking after the coolness of the wet fabric almost sent her over the edge. At the same time, he burrowed long fingers in her maiden hair.

She stilled, breathlessly waiting, as he delicately sought and then found what he searched for. He began an insidious circling with his thumb. Oh, God, it felt so good. He knew exactly how to touch her. She mewled, her hips instinctively following his hand. He thrust his finger deep inside her, and she shuddered in the sudden storm of her climax.

His breath whispered over her closed eyelids. "Look at me."

She turned her head to the sound of his growl, her eyes still closed in bliss.

"Anna, look at me."

She opened her eyes.

Edward loomed over her, his face flushed, his nostrils flared. "I am putting myself in you now."

She could feel his erection nudging at her wet opening. The head began squeezing in, and her eyelids dropped in reaction.

"Anna, sweet Anna, look at me," Edward crooned.

He was halfway in now, and she struggled to keep her eyes focused. He bent his head and licked the tip of her nose.

Her eyes widened.

And he drove all the way home.

She moaned and arched against him. *So right. So perfect.* He filled her as if they were both made for this. As if they were made for each other. She curved her thighs around his hips, cradling him with her pelvis, and looked into his face. His eyes were closed, his face stark with want. A strand of inky hair had plastered itself against his jaw.

He opened his eyes then and speared her with their black intensity. "I am in you, and you are holding me. There is no going back from this moment."

She cried out at his words, and the breath within her chest seemed to tremble. His hips rocked. She wrapped her arms around him and held on as the slide of his penis shoving in and out of her drove all thought from her mind. He quickened his pace and groaned. His eyes were locked with hers; as if he was trying to communicate something unutterable. She touched the side of his face with one hand.

His big body seemed to break apart. He jerked against her hard. She began coming in waves, a joy so exquisite flooded her that she couldn't contain it. She moaned her rapture. He threw back his head at the same time and bared his teeth in a shout of pleasure. Warmth flooded her womb, her heart, and her very soul.

His heavy body lay on hers, and she felt his heartbeat. Anna sighed. Then he lethargically rolled off her. She curled into a ball on her side, her limbs pleasantly achy. The last thing she felt before surrendering to oblivion was Edward's hands on her stomach, pulling her back against his warmth.

Chapter Twenty

In the fifth year of her search, late on a rainy night,
Aurea stumbled through a grim, dark wood. She wore
thin rags that only just covered her body; her feet
were bare and blistered, and she was lost and weary.
A single crust of bread was the only food she had. In
the gloom, she spied a flickering light. A tiny shack
stood all alone in a clearing. At her knock, a toothless
crone, bent nearly double by age, appeared at the
door and beckoned her inside.
"Ah, dearie," the old woman croaked. "'Tis a cold,
wet night to be alone. Come share my fire, do. But I
fear I've no victuals to offer you; my table is bare. Oh,
but what I wouldn't give for something to eat!"
Hearing this, Aurea took pity on the crone. She
reached into her pocket and offered the old woman
her last bit of bread. . . .
—from *The Raven Prince*

A high, womanish scream jolted Edward from sleep the
next morning. He lurched up, shocked, and stared toward
the source of the awful noise. Davis, his gray locks strag-

gling about his grizzled face, stared back in abject horror. Beside Edward, a feminine voice made a sleepy protest. Christ! He quickly threw the sheets over Anna.

"In the name of all that's holy, Davis, what's got into you now?" Edward bellowed even as he felt his face heating.

"It's not enough that you're always at them whorehouses; now you've brought home a-a . . ." The valet's mouth worked.

"Woman," Edward finished the sentence. "But not the kind you're thinking of. This is my fiancée."

The bedsheets began to heave. He placed a hand on the upper edge, trapping the occupant within.

"Fiancée! I may be old, but I'm not stoopid. That's not Miss Gerard."

The bedcovers muttered ominously.

"Fetch the maid to start the fire," Edward ordered in desperation.

"But—"

"Go now."

Too late.

Anna had worked her way to the top of the bedclothes, and her head now emerged. Her hair was delightfully tousled, her mouth sinfully swollen. Edward felt a part of his own anatomy swell. She and Davis regarded each other. Their eyes narrowed simultaneously.

Edward groaned and dropped his head into his hands.

"You're Lord Swartingham's valet?" Never had a naked woman caught in a compromising position sounded so prim.

"'Course I am. And you're—"

Edward shot a glare at Davis that held the promise of dismemberment, mayhem, and the apocalypse.

Davis stopped and continued more cautiously. "M'lord's uh, lady."

"Quite." She cleared her throat and withdrew one arm from the covers to push back her hair.

Edward scowled and tucked the sheets more firmly around her shoulders. He needn't have bothered. Davis was carefully studying the ceiling.

"Perhaps," Anna said, "you could bring up his lordship's tea and send the maid to tend the fire?"

Davis jumped at this novel idea. "Right away, mum."

He was actually backing out the doorway when Edward's voice stopped him. "In another hour."

The valet looked scandalized but didn't say a word, a first in Edward's experience. The door shut behind Davis. Edward leaped from the bed, strode to the door, and turned the key in the lock. He flung it across the room where it clanged against the wall. He was back in the bed before Anna had time to sit up.

"Your valet is rather unusual," she said.

"Yes." Catching the sheet, he pulled it entirely off the bed, provoking a squeal from her. She lay all warm and sleepy and naked for his delectation. He growled in approval, and his early morning erection hardened even more. What a wonderful way to wake up.

She licked her lips, a move his cock thoroughly approved of. "I-I've noticed your boots are seldom shined."

"Davis is terminally incompetent." He placed his hands on either side of her hips and began to nip his way up her legs.

"Oh!" For a moment he thought he'd succeeded in distracting her, but she rallied. "Why do you keep him, then?"

"Davis was my father's valet before me." He paid scant attention to the conversation. He could smell his own scent on Anna's body, and it satisfied him in a primal way.

"So you keep him for sentimental—Edward!"

She gasped as he buried his nose in her maiden hair and inhaled. His scent was strongest here, in her gilded curls so soft and pretty in the morning light.

"I suppose so." He spoke into her hair, making Anna squirm. "And I'm fond of the evil old reprobate. Sometimes. He's known me since childhood and treats me without an iota of respect. It's refreshing. Or at least different."

He drew a finger through her cunny. The lips parted shyly, revealing a deep-pink interior. He angled his face to see better.

"Edward!"

"Would you like to know how I hired Hopple?" He propped himself on his elbows between her legs. Holding her spread with one hand, he teased her bud with the forefinger of his other hand.

"Ohhh!"

"And you've hardly met Dreary, but he has an interesting past."

"Ed-*ward!*"

God, he loved the sound of his name on Anna's lips. He debated licking her but decided he couldn't hold out that long this early in the morning. He moved on to her breasts where he suckled at first one and then the other.

"Then there's the entire staff at the Abbey. Would you like to hear about them?" He breathed the question in her ear.

Thick eyelashes almost hid her hazel eyes. "Make love to me."

Something inside him, maybe his heart, stopped for a second. "Anna."

Her lips were soft and yielding. He was not gentle, but she didn't protest. She opened her mouth sweetly and gave and gave and gave until he couldn't stand it anymore.

He pulled back and carefully turned her to her belly. He filled his hands with her plump arse and pulled her up toward him until she was on elbows and knees. He paused to study her vulnerable sex from this angle. His chest heaved at the sight. This was his woman, and only he would ever be privileged to see her this way.

He took hold of his cock and guided it to her wet entrance. It felt so good, he thrust in more roughly than he'd intended. Paused to gasp. Then thrust again. And again. Until her slick walls gave and he'd made a home for himself in her heat. Her muscles squeezed around him.

He grit his teeth to keep from spilling too soon.

Reaching, he stroked his palm down her spine. From her neck to her arse to the place where he entered her. He circled her there, feeling her stretched tissues and his own hard flesh impaling her.

She moaned and nudged him.

He withdrew to the head of his cock. And thrust. So hard her body slithered up the bed. He withdrew and thrust again. His hips swung faster and faster, and he flung back his head and ground his teeth.

He could hear Anna's heated cries, and he reached around her hips to find that tender nub and pinch it. The walls of her vagina began contracting in waves, and he could hold out no longer. He came in jets of almost painful pleasure, pumping into her, marking her as his. She was collapsing beneath him, and he followed her down to the bed, grinding his hips into her. Shuddering in the aftershocks.

He lay a moment, panting, and then rolled off Anna before he could crush her. He rested on his back, one arm over his eyes, and tried to catch his breath.

As the sweat dried on his body, he began to think about the position he'd put her in. She was now undoubtedly compromised. He'd nearly hurt Davis merely because of the look he'd given Anna. God only knew what he would do when someone made a comment to her, as inevitably would happen.

"You need to marry me." He winced. That had been rather blunt.

Anna apparently thought so, too. Her body jerked next to his. "What?"

He scowled. Now wasn't the time to appear weak. "I've compromised you. We must marry."

"No one knows but Davis."

"And the entire household. Do you think they haven't noticed by now that I didn't sleep in my own bed?"

"Even so. Nobody knows in Little Battleford, and that's what matters." She rose from the bed and pulled a chemise from her bag.

Edward grimaced. She couldn't be that naïve. "How long do you think before the news gets back to Little Battleford? I wager it'll return before we do."

Anna threw on the chemise and bent to rummage for something else in her bag, her bottom temptingly displayed through the thin linen. Was she trying to distract him? "You're already engaged," she said, her voice firm.

"Not for long. I've an appointment with Gerard tomorrow."

"What?" That got her attention. "Edward, don't do anything that you'll regret. I'll not marry you."

"For Christ's sake, why not?" He sat up impatiently.

She perched on the bed and rolled on a stocking. He noticed it was darned near the knee, and the sight made him even more angry. She shouldn't have to wear rags. Why wouldn't she marry him so he could take proper care of her?

"Why not?" he repeated as quietly as he could.

She swallowed and began on the other stocking, carefully smoothing it over her toes. "Because I don't want you to marry out of a sense of misplaced duty."

"Correct me if I'm wrong," he said. "Wasn't I the man making love to you last night and this morning?"

"And I was the woman making love to you," Anna said. "I share just as much responsibility for the act as you."

Edward watched her, searching for the words, the argument that would convince her.

She began tying a garter. "Peter was unhappy when I didn't become pregnant."

He waited.

She sighed, not looking at him. "Eventually, he went to another woman."

Damned, stupid bastard. Edward flung back the bedcovers and paced to the window. "Were you in love with him?" The question was bitter on his tongue, but he was compelled to ask it.

"In the beginning, when we were first married." She still smoothed the tattered silk over her calves. "Not at the end."

"I see." He paid for another man's sins.

"No, I don't think you can." She picked up the remaining garter and stared at it in her hands. "When a man betrays a woman in such a way, it breaks something in her that I'm not sure can ever be repaired."

Edward stared out the window, trying to form a reply. His future happiness depended on what he said next.

"I already know you are barren." He finally turned to face her. "I'm content with you as you are. I can promise you that I'll never take a mistress, but only time will provide real proof of my faithfulness. In the end, you must trust me."

Anna stretched the garter between her fingers. "I don't know if I can."

Edward turned back to the window so she couldn't see his expression. For the first time, he realized that he might not be able to convince Anna to marry him. The thought brought him close to something very like panic.

"OH, FOR GOD'S SAKE!"

"Hush. He'll hear you," Anna hissed in Edward's ear.

They were attending Sir Lazarus Lillipin's afternoon lecture on the rotation of crops using swedes and mangel-wurzels. So far, Edward disagreed with almost every word the poor man said. And he wasn't keeping his opinion of the man or his theories to himself.

Edward glared at the speaker. "No, he won't. The man's deafer than a post."

"Then others certainly will."

Edward looked at her indignantly. "I should hope they do." He turned back to the talk.

Anna sighed. He was behaving no worse than the rest of the assemblage and better than quite a few. The audience could only be called *eclectic*. They ranged from aristocrats in silks and lace to men in muddy jackboots, smoking clay pipes. All were crowded into a rather grimy coffeehouse that Edward had assured her was perfectly respectable.

She was doubtful.

Even now, a shouting match was breaking out in the back corner between a country squire and a dandy. She hoped it would not come to fisticuffs—or swords, for that matter. Every aristocrat in the room wore a sword as a badge of his rank. Even Edward, who eschewed the affectation in the country, had belted on a sword this morning.

He'd instructed her, before setting out, to take notes of the important points of the lecture so he could compare them to his own research later. She'd made some half-hearted scribbles, but she was uncertain how useful they'd be. Most of the lecture was incomprehensible to her, and she was a bit hazy about what exactly a mangel-wurzel was.

She'd begun to suspect that the main reason for her presence was so Edward could keep her in his sight. Since this morning he'd stubbornly maintained his argument that they must be married. He seemed to be under the impression that if he simply repeated it often enough, she would eventually wear down. And he might be right—if she could just let go of her fear of trusting him.

She closed her eyes and thought what it would be like to be Edward's wife. They would ride about his estates in the mornings, then argue politics and people over supper. He'd drag her to arcane lectures like the present one. And they would share the same bed. Every night.

She sighed. Heaven.

Edward let out an explosive snort. "No, no, no! Even a lunatic knows you cannot follow rye with turnips!"

Anna opened her eyes. "If you dislike the man so very much, why attend his presentation?"

"Dislike Lillipin?" He looked genuinely surprised. "He's a fine fellow. Simply backward in his thinking is all."

A wave of applause—and catcalls—signified the end of the lecture. Edward seized her hand in a possessive grip and started shouldering toward the door.

A voice hailed them from the left. "De Raaf! Drawn back to London by the lure of mangel-wurzels?"

Edward stopped, forcing Anna to halt as well. She peered over his shoulder at an exceedingly elegant gentleman in red heels.

"Iddesleigh, I hadn't hoped to see you here." Edward shifted so she couldn't see the man's face.

Anna tried leaning to the right but was blocked by a massive shoulder.

"And how could I miss Lillipin's impassioned rhetoric on the subject of swedes?" A hand draped in lace waved gracefully in the air. "I've even left my prize roses in bud to attend. By the by, how are the roses you procured from me when last you were in the capital? I never knew you were interested in ornamentals."

"Edward purchased my roses from you?" Anna pushed around him in her eagerness.

Icy gray eyes narrowed. "Well, well, what have we here?"

Edward cleared his throat. "Iddesleigh, may I present Mrs. Anna Wren, my secretary. Mrs. Wren, this is Viscount Iddesleigh."

She dropped into a curtsy as the viscount bowed and produced a lorgnette. The gray eyes that examined her through the lenses were much sharper than the style of speech and mode of dress had led her to imagine.

"Your *secretary?*" the viscount drawled. "*Fas*-cin-ating. And, as I remember, you hauled me out of bed at six in the morning to select those roses." He slowly smiled at Edward.

Edward scowled.

Anna backtracked. "Lord Swartingham was very generous in letting me have a few of the roses he'd purchased for the Abbey garden," she fibbed. "They're doing quite well, I assure you, my lord. In fact, all of the roses have branched out, and a few are developing buds."

The viscount's icy eyes returned to hers, and a corner of his mouth twitched. "And the wren defends the raven." He swept another, even more flamboyant bow, and mur-

mured to Edward, "I congratulate you, my friend," before
sauntering away into the crowd.

Edward's hand tightened briefly on her shoulder, then
he grabbed her elbow once more and tugged her toward
the door. A dam of bodies blocked the entrance. Several
philosophical discussions were being carried on all at
once, some by the same people.

A young man paused to watch the arguments with a
look of contempt on his face. He wore a ridiculously
small tricorn perched atop a yellow-powdered wig with
an extravagantly curled tail. Anna had never seen a macaroni, but she'd studied the cartoons depicting them in the
newspapers. The young man glanced at Anna as they
neared the entrance. His eyes widened and then shifted
to Edward. He leaned over and was muttering to another
man when they made the sidewalk. The carriage was waiting around the block on a less-crowded street. As they
turned the corner, Anna glanced back.

The macaroni stared after her.

A shiver ran down her spine before she turned away.

CHILLY WATCHED THE COUNTRY widow round the corner
on the arm of one of the richest men in England. *The Earl
of Swartingham.* No wonder Felicity had held back the
name of the widow's lover. The potential for profit was
enormous. And he had a perpetual need of blunt. Quite a
bit of it, in fact. The accoutrements of a fashionable London gentleman didn't come cheaply.

His eyes narrowed as he estimated how much he could
demand for the first payment. Felicity had the right idea
there. In her latest letter, she'd implored him to contact

Anna Wren on her behalf. As Lord Swartingham's mistress, Mrs. Wren must have loads of jewelry and other valuable gifts that she could turn to money. Obviously, Felicity planned to blackmail Mrs. Wren without letting him in on the scheme.

He sneered. Now that he knew the setup, he could cut Felicity out altogether. She'd never been properly appreciative of his bed skills anyway.

"Chilton. Come to hear my lecture?" His elder brother, Sir Lazarus Lillipin, looked nervous.

As well he should, since Chilly had originally tracked down his brother to ask for another loan. Of course, now that he knew about Anna Wren, he wouldn't need his brother's money. On the other hand, that tailor had been quite uppity in his last communication. A little extra blunt never hurt.

"Hello, Lazarus." He linked arms with his elder brother and began making his pitch.

"EDWARD?"

"Hmm?" Edward furiously scribbled at his desk. He'd discarded his coat and waistcoat long ago, and his shirt cuffs were ink stained.

The candles were guttering. Anna suspected that Dreary had snuck off to bed after sending in their supper on a tray. The fact that the butler hadn't bothered to lay the dining room table for the meal spoke volumes about his experience with his master after an Agrarian Club lecture. Edward had been writing rebuttals to Sir Lazarus's ever since they'd returned.

She sighed.

Standing, she strolled over to where Edward worked and began playing with the gauze scarf tucked into the neckline of her dress. "It's quite late."

"Really?" He didn't look up.

"Yes."

She propped a hip on the desk and leaned over his elbow. "I'm so fatigued."

The scarf came loose over one breast. Edward's hand stilled. His head swiveled to watch her fingers at her bosom, only inches from his face.

Her ring finger wandered to her cleavage and dipped between her breasts. "Don't you think it's time for bed?"

In. Out. In. Out . . .

Edward surged to his feet, nearly knocking her over. He caught her and tossed her high in his arms.

Anna clutched him about the neck as she tilted. "Edward!"

"Darling?" He strode out the study door.

"The servants."

"If you think, after that little display"—he took the stairs two at a time—"that I'd waste time worrying about the servants, you don't know me."

They gained the upper hall. Edward bypassed her room and stopped at his own.

"The door," he prompted.

She turned the doorknob, and Edward pushed it open with his shoulder. Inside his bedroom, she glimpsed two heavy tables covered in books and papers. More books were stacked haphazardly on chairs and the floor.

He crossed to set her by his huge bed. Without a word, he turned her and began to unhook her dress. She caught her breath, suddenly shy. This was the first time she'd initiated their play when he knew it was her. He didn't seem repelled by her boldness, however. Far from it. She was very aware of the blunt fingertips brushing her spine through the layers of clothes. The dress sagged about her shoulders, and Edward pulled it down as she stepped out of it. He slowly untied her petticoats one by one and unlaced her stays. She faced him in only her chemise and stockings. His eyes were heavy lidded and intense, his gaze serious as he rubbed one thumb over the shoulder strap of her chemise.

"Beautiful," he whispered.

He bent and brushed a kiss over her shoulder as the strap fell. She shivered, whether at his touch or the look in his eyes, she didn't know. She could no longer pretend that this was only a physical act between them, and he must sense her emotion. She felt exposed.

His lips slid along her sensitive skin and he nipped. He moved to the other shoulder and that strap fell as well. Gently, he inched the front of the chemise down, exposing her breasts. Her nipples were already tight. He spread his hands over both mounds, his palms warm and possessive. He seemed to examine the contrast between his dark hands framing her white skin. High on his cheekbones color flamed. Anna imagined her pale pink nipples peeking between his callused fingers, and her head fell back as if weighted.

He lifted her breasts and squeezed.

She pushed herself into his hands. She could feel his gaze on her face, and then he stripped the chemise from her and lifted her to the bed. She watched as he swiftly removed his clothes and he lowered himself beside her. His hand smoothed across her naked belly. She raised her arms to draw him to her, but he gently caught her wrists and placed them by her head. Then he slid down her body until his head was level with her belly. His hands were on her inner thighs, and he pressed her legs apart.

"There's something I've always wanted to do with a woman." His voice was black velvet.

What did he mean? Shocked, she resisted. Surely he didn't want to look *there?* It had been different this morning when she'd been half asleep. Now she was fully awake.

"It's not something a man can do with a whore," he said.

Oh, Lord, could she do this? Expose herself so intimately? She craned her neck to look at his face.

His gaze was implacable. He wanted this. "Let me. Please."

Blushing, she lay back, surrendering to him and his needs. She let her knees fall open, feeling almost as if she were offering a gift of love to him. He looked down as her legs widened, then widened more until he was kneeling between her outstretched thighs, her most private places exposed. She squeezed her eyes shut, unable to watch him examine her.

He didn't do anything more, and finally she couldn't bear the waiting any longer. She opened her eyes. He was staring at her body, at her woman's place, and his nostrils flared, and his mouth curled in a look so possessive it was almost frightening.

Anna felt her opening contract in reaction. Liquid seeped from within her. "I need you," she whispered.

Then he truly shocked her. He swooped down and swiped right across her wetness with his tongue.

"Oh!"

He looked up at her face and slowly licked his lips. "I want to taste and tongue and suck you until you've forgotten your name." He smiled carnally. "Until I've forgotten mine as well."

She arched and gasped at just his words, but his hands were on her hips now, holding her down. His tongue searched through the folds of her femininity, each rasp going straight to her center. He found her clitoris and licked.

And she lost her mind. A long, low moan broke from her lips, and she twisted the pillow on either side of her head with her fists. Her hips bucked. But he wasn't going to be kept from his objective. He relentlessly tongued the nub until she saw stars and shamelessly shoved her pelvis into his face.

Then he drew her clitoris between his lips and sucked gently.

"Edward!" His name keened from her as a wave of warmth flooded her body, rolling all the way to her toes.

He was up and over her, his penis invading her, before she had time to open her eyes. She shuddered and clasped him as he pounded against oversensitive flesh. And she felt the wave rising again, carrying her endlessly on its crest. Her thighs quivered helplessly open, and she ground her pelvis up against his hardness. He responded by hooking his arms beneath her knees and pushing her legs toward her shoulders. She was as open as possible, exposed and held down as he loved her. As she took all he had to give.

"God!" It burst from his lips, more a guttural than a word. His great body was shaking helplessly, and he stiffened against her.

Her vision fractured into tiny rainbows as he drove his hard flesh into her softness again and again and again. She gasped. She never wanted this moment to end, they were linked right now, in body and in soul.

Until he slumped over her, his chest heaving in enormous gasps. She ran her hands over his buttocks, her eyes still closed, trying to make the intimacy last. Oh, how she wanted this man! She wanted to hold him like this tomorrow and fifty years hence. She wanted to be by his side every morning when he woke, she wanted his to be the last voice she heard before she fell asleep at night.

Edward shifted then and rolled to his back. She felt the cool air brush her damp skin. One lean arm bundled her close to his side.

"I have something for you," he said.

She felt a weight on her chest and picked it up. It was *The Raven Prince*. She blinked back tears and stroked the red morocco cover, feeling the indentations of the embossed feather beneath her fingers. "But, Edward, this was your sister's, wasn't it?"

He nodded. "And now it is yours."

"But—"

"Hush. I want you to have it."

He kissed her so tenderly she felt her heart fill and overflow with emotion. How could she continue to deny her love for this man? "I-I think—" she began.

"Shh, sweet. We'll talk in the morning," he murmured huskily.

Anna sighed and snuggled against him, inhaling his sharp, male scent. She hadn't felt this blissfully happy in years. Maybe never.

The morning would come soon enough.

Chapter Twenty-One

Aurea and the old woman shared the crust of bread
before the little fire. As Aurea swallowed the last bite,
the door flew open and a tall, bony fellow came in.
The wind blew the door shut behind him.
"How fair you, Mother?" he greeted the crone.
The door opened once more. This time a man with
hair standing on end like the fluff of a dandelion
entered. "A good evening to you, Mother," he said.
Next, two more men stomped in, the wind whistling behind
them. One was tall and tanned, the other plump and
ruddy cheeked. "Hello, Mother," they cried together.
All four men sat by the fire, and as they did, the
flames blew and flickered, and the dust swirled
and spun on the floor around their feet.
"And have you guessed who I am?" The old
woman grinned toothlessly at Aurea. "These are
the Four Winds, and I am their mother. . . ."
—from The Raven Prince

Anna was dreaming of a black-eyed baby the next morning
when a masculine voice chuckled in her ear and woke her.

"I've never seen anyone sleep so deeply." Lips brushed from her earlobe to her jaw.

She smiled and snuggled closer, only to find that there wasn't a warm body next to hers. Confused, she opened her eyes. Edward was standing by the bed already dressed.

"Wha—?"

"I'm going to see Gerard. Hush." He placed a finger against her lips when she would have spoken. "I'll be back as soon as I can. We'll make plans when I return." He leaned down to give her a kiss that made her thoughts scatter. "Don't leave my bed."

And he was gone before she could reply. She sighed and rolled over.

The next time she woke, a maid was drawing the curtains.

The girl looked up as she stretched. "Oh, you're awake, mum. I've brought some tea and fresh buns."

Anna thanked the maid and sat to take the tray. She noticed a folded note sitting next to the teapot. "What's this?"

The maid looked over. "I don't know, mum, I'm sure. A boy delivered it to the door and said it was for the lady in the house." She curtsied and left.

Anna poured herself a cup of tea and picked up the note. It was rather grubby. On the reverse side, it had been sealed with wax, but without any mark. She used the butter knife to open it, then raised the teacup to her lips as she read the first line.

The cup clattered to the saucer.

It was a blackmail note.

Anna stared at the nasty thing. The author had seen her at Aphrodite's Grotto and knew she'd met Edward there.

In sordid terms, he threatened to tell the Gerard family. She could prevent this disaster by coming to the salon at Aphrodite's Grotto tonight at nine o'clock. She was instructed to bring one hundred pounds hidden in a muff.

Anna set aside the missive and contemplated her cooling tea and dying dreams. Just moments before, happiness had seemed so close. She'd almost grasped it in her hand, almost held its fluttering wings. Then it had darted and flown, and she was left with empty air in her palm.

A tear fell from her cheek onto the breakfast tray.

Even if she had one hundred pounds—which she didn't—what would keep the blackmailer from demanding the same sum again? And again? He might even raise the price of his silence. If she were to become the Countess of Swartingham, she would be a prime mark. And it hardly mattered that Edward was at this very moment breaking off his engagement to Miss Gerard. She would be disgraced if the rest of society were to find out about her visits to Aphrodite's Grotto.

Worse, Edward would insist on marrying her anyway, despite a scandal. She would bring shame and disaster to Edward and his name. The name that meant so very much to him. It was impossible for her to destroy him like this. There was only one thing to do. She must leave London and Edward. Now, before he returned.

She knew no other way to protect him.

"YOU WOULD REJECT my daughter for a-a . . . !" Sir Richard's face darkened to a dangerous shade of puce. He looked in imminent danger of an apoplectic fit.

"A widow from Little Battleford," Edward finished the other man's sentence before he could find a less-suitable description for Anna. "Yes, sir."

The two men faced off in Sir Richard's study.

The room reeked of stale tobacco smoke. The walls, already a muddy brown color, were made dimmer by the soot streaks that started halfway up and disappeared into the gloom near the ceiling. A single oil painting hung slightly askew over the mantel. It was a hunting scene, with white and tan hounds closing in on a hare. Moments from being torn limb from limb, the hare's flat black eyes were serene. On the desk, two cut-glass tumblers stood half full with what was undoubtedly a fine brandy.

Neither glass had been touched.

"You have played with Sylvia's good name, my lord. I'll have your head for this," Sir Richard bawled.

Edward sighed. This discussion had turned even uglier than he'd anticipated. And his wig, as always, itched. Surely the old fellow wasn't going to call him out? Iddesleigh would never let him hear the end of it were he forced to duel a stout, gout-ridden baronet.

"Miss Gerard's reputation will not suffer from this at all," Edward said as soothingly as possible. "We'll put it out that she dismissed me."

"I'll take you to court, sir, for breach of promise!"

Edward narrowed his eyes. "And lose. I've infinitely more funds and contacts than you. I will not marry your daughter." Edward let his voice soften. "Besides, court would only serve to make Miss Gerard's name the talk of London. Neither of us wants that."

"But she has lost this entire season to find a suitable husband." The pendulous flesh under Sir Richard's chin trembled.

Ah. Now the real reason for the man's temper. He was less worried about his daughter's name than the prospect of funding another season for her. For a moment, Edward felt pity for the girl with such a parent. Then he seized the opening.

"Naturally," he murmured, "I'll want to recompense you for your disappointment."

Sir Richard's little eyes creased greedily at the corners. Edward sent up a prayer of thanks to whatever gods watched over him. He'd come altogether too close to having this man as his father-in-law.

Twenty minutes later, Edward emerged into the sunlight on the Gerard's front stoop. The old man had been a keen bargainer. Like a pudgy bulldog with one end of a bone he refused to relinquish, he'd growled and tugged and shook his head furiously, but in the end they'd come to an agreement. Edward was considerably lighter in the pocket as a result, but he was free of the Gerard family. All that remained was to return to Anna and make wedding plans.

He grinned. If his luck held out, she'd still be in his bed.

Whistling, he ran down the steps to his carriage. He only paused to pull off the awful wig and toss it to the ground before entering the vehicle. He glanced out the window as the carriage pulled away. A ragpicker was trying the wig on for size. The white-powdered wig with its stiff side curls and tail contrasted strangely with the man's filthy clothes and unshaven face. The ragpicker bent, grasped the handles of his wheelbarrow, and jauntily trundled off.

By the time the carriage pulled up before his town house, Edward was humming a bawdy tune. With the Gerard engagement out of the way, he saw no reason why he shouldn't be a married man in a month. A fortnight, if he could get a special license.

He shoved his tricorn and cape at a footman and took the stairs two at a time. He still had to win an assent from Anna, but after last night, he felt sure that she'd capitulate soon.

He rounded the stairs and strode down the hall. "Anna!" He pushed open the door to his room. "Anna, I—"

He stopped short. She wasn't in the bed. "Damnation."

He strode through the connecting door into the sitting room. It, too, was empty. He heaved a sigh of exasperation. Walking back into his bedroom, he stuck his head out the door and bellowed for Dreary. Then he paced across the room. Where was the woman? The bed was made, the curtains drawn. A fire had burned out on the grate. She must've left the room some time ago. He noticed Elizabeth's red book sitting on the dresser. There was a scrap of paper on top of it.

He started for the book as Dreary entered the room.

"My lord?"

"Where's Mrs. Wren?" Edward picked up the folded paper. His name was written on the front in Anna's hand.

"Mrs. Wren? The footmen informed me that she left the house at about ten o'clock."

"Yes, but where did she go, man?" He opened the note and began to read it.

"That's just it, my lord. She didn't say where . . ." The butler's voice buzzed in the background as Edward comprehended the words written in the note.

So sorry . . . must go away . . . Yours always, Anna

"My lord?"

Gone.

"My lord?"

She'd left him.

"Are you all right, my lord?"

"She's gone," Edward whispered.

Dreary buzzed around some more, and then he must have left, because after a while, Edward found that he was alone. He sat in front of a dead fire in his bedroom, alone. But then that was what, until very recently, he'd been most used to.

Being alone.

THE COACH RATTLED and bumped over a pothole in the road.

"Ouch," Fanny exclaimed. She rubbed her elbow, which had hit the door. "Lord Swartingham's carriage sure was better sprung."

Anna murmured an assent, but she really didn't care. She supposed she should be making plans. Deciding where to go once they reached Little Battleford. Thinking about how to raise some money. But it was terribly hard to think, let alone plan right now. It was much easier to stare out the window of the coach and let it take her where it would. Across from them, the only other occupant of the coach, a spare little man with a gray wig tilted over one brow, snored. He'd been asleep when they began their trip in London and hadn't woken since, despite the jostling of the coach and the frequent stops. From the smell that emanated from him, a pungent blend of gin, vomit, and unwashed body, he wouldn't waken if trumpets announced the second coming. Not that she cared very much either way.

"Do you think we'll be in Little Battleford by night?" Fanny asked.

"I don't know."

The maid sighed and plucked at her apron.

Anna felt a brief moment of guilt. She hadn't told Fanny why they were leaving London when she'd woken her this morning. Indeed, she'd hardly spoken to the girl at all since departing Edward's town house.

Fanny cleared her throat. "Will the earl be following us, do you think?"

"No."

Silence.

Anna glanced at the maid. Her brow was puckered.

"I thought you might be marrying the earl soon?" The girl phrased the statement as a question.

"No."

Fanny's mouth trembled.

Anna said more softly, "It's hardly likely, is it? An earl and me?"

"It is if he loves you," the little maid said earnestly. "And Lord Swartingham does. Love you, I mean. Everyone says so."

"Oh, Fanny." She turned her eyes to the window as they blurred.

"Well, it is possible," the girl insisted. "And you love

the earl, so I don't see why we're going back to Little Battleford."

"It's more complicated than that. I-I would be a liability to him."

"A what?" Fanny's mouth scrunched up.

"A liability. A millstone about his neck. I can't marry him."

"I don't know why—" Fanny broke off as the carriage clattered into an inn yard.

Anna seized gratefully on the interruption. "Let's get out here and stretch our legs."

Moving past the still-sleeping third passenger, they jumped down from the coach. In the yard, ostlers ran back and forth, tending the team of horses, unloading packages from on top of the coach, and bringing more out to replace them. The driver leaned down from his perch, shouting gossip to the innkeeper. To add to the noise and confusion, a private carriage was also stopped at the inn. Several men were bent over the right near horse, examining its hoof. The animal appeared to have either thrown a shoe or come up lame.

Anna took Fanny's elbow and moved them both beneath the inn's eaves so as not to be in the way of running men and boys. Fanny stood on one foot and then the other and finally blurted, "Excuse me, mum. I have to use the necessary."

Anna nodded and the little maid scurried off. She idly watched the men tending to the lame horse.

"When exactly will the carriage be ready?" a strident voice exclaimed. "I've been waiting an hour already in this filthy inn."

Anna stiffened at the familiar tones. Oh, God, not Felicity Clearwater. Not now. She shrank back against the inn wall, but fate wasn't pulling its punches today. Felicity walked out of the inn and immediately saw her.

"Anna Wren." The other woman's mouth pinched until unbecoming lines radiated from her lips. "Finally."

Felicity marched up and seized her arm in a commanding grip. "I can't believe I've had to travel almost all the way to London just to talk to you. And I had to cool my heels at this wretched inn. Now listen carefully." Felicity shook her arm for emphasis. "I don't want to repeat myself. I know all about your little entanglement at Aphrodite's Grotto."

Anna felt her eyes widen. "I—"

"No." Felicity cut her off. "Don't try to deny it. I've a witness. And I know you met the Earl of Swartingham there. Aiming a bit high, weren't you? I never would've guessed it of a timid little mouse like you."

For a moment, the other woman almost looked curious, but she recovered and continued before Anna could get her mouth to work.

"That's neither here nor there. This is the important part." She shook Anna's arm again, this time more roughly. "I want my locket and the letter in it back, and if you ever breathe a word about Peter and me, I'll make sure every single soul in Little Battleford hears about your indiscretion. You and your mother-in-law will be driven out of town. I'll see to it personally."

Anna's eyes widened. How dare . . . ?

"I hope"—she gave a final nasty shake—"I've made myself clear." Felicity nodded as if she'd finished with

some small, domestic business. Dismissing an impertinent maid, perhaps. Unpleasant, but necessary. Now on to
more important matters. She turned to walk off.

Anna stared.

Felicity truly thought she was a *timid little mouse*, one
who would crumple in a heap of fear at threats by her late
husband's lover. And wasn't she? She was running from
the man she loved. The man who cared for her and wanted
to marry her. Running because of a filthy blackmail note.
Anna felt ashamed. No wonder Felicity thought she could
tread all over her!

Anna whipped out a hand and caught the other woman
by the shoulder. Felicity almost went over in the inn yard
muck.

"What—?"

"Oh, you have made yourself clear," Anna purred as
she backed the taller woman into the wall. "But you've
made one slight miscalculation: that I'd give two farthings
for your threats. You see, if I don't care what you say
about me, well then you have nothing to hold over me,
now, do you, Mrs. Clearwater?"

"But, you—"

Anna nodded as if Felicity had said something pro-
found. "That's right. But I, on the other hand, have something quite substantial about you. The fact that you tupped
my husband."

"I-I—"

"And if memory serves me right"—Anna touched a
finger to her cheek in mock amazement—"why it was just
about the time your younger daughter was conceived. The
one with red hair like Peter's."

Felicity slumped against the wall and looked at her as if she'd grown a third eye right in the middle of her forehead.

"Now what do you think the squire would say about that?" Anna asked sweetly.

The other woman tried a recovery. "Now see here—"

Anna stabbed a finger in her face. "No. You see here. If you ever try to threaten me or anyone I love again, I'll tell all the inhabitants of Little Battleford that you were bedding my husband. I'll have leaflets printed up and delivered to every house, cottage, and hovel in Essex. In fact, I'll tell the whole country. You may very well have to leave England."

"You wouldn't," Felicity breathed.

"No?" Anna smiled, not at all nicely. "Try me."

"That's—"

"Blackmail. Yes. And you should know."

Felicity's face blanched.

"Oh, and one more thing. I need a ride to London. Immediately. I'm taking your carriage." Anna wheeled and started for the carriage, grabbing Fanny, who was gawking beside the inn door, as she went past.

"But how am I to return to Little Battleford?" Felicity wailed behind her.

Anna didn't bother to look back. "You are welcome to my seat on the coach."

HE SAT IN A CRACKED leather armchair in the town house library because he could not bear the memories in his bedroom.

There was one bookcase to lend the room its name. Dusty religious volumes filled the shelves, lined in rows like tombstones in a graveyard, untouched for generations. The only window was draped in blue velvet, pulled to one side by a tarnished gilt rope. He could see the phantom roofline of the next building over. Earlier, the festering red sun had silhouetted the multiple chimneys on the roof as it set. Now it was near dark outside.

The room was cold because the fire had died.

A maid had come some time back—he wasn't sure when—to rebuild the fire, but he'd ordered her out. No one had bothered him since. Now and then, he heard murmured voices outside in the hall, but he ignored them.

He didn't read.

He didn't write.

He didn't drink.

He simply sat, holding the book on his lap, and thought and stared at nothing as the night entombed him. Jock nudged his hand once or twice, but he ignored that contact as well, until the dog gave up and lay down by his side.

Was it the pox scars? Or his temper? Hadn't she enjoyed his lovemaking? Was he too enthralled with his work? Or did she simply not love him?

That only. So small and yet everything.

If his title, his wealth, his—*God!*—his *love* had not mattered to her, he had nothing. What had driven her away? It was a question he couldn't answer. A question he couldn't let go. It engulfed him, consumed him, became the only thing that counted at all. Because without her, there was nothing. His life stretched before him in gray, ghostly tones.

Alone.

He was without anyone to touch his soul as Anna had, without the completeness she had provided. He hadn't even noticed until she was gone: there was a great, gaping hole in his being without her.

Could a man live with such a void inside of him?

SOMETIME LATER, EDWARD vaguely noticed a flurry of raised voices in the hall drawing nearer. The library door opened, revealing Iddesleigh.

"Oh, this is a pretty sight." The viscount closed the door behind him. He set the single candle he carried on a table and threw his cape and hat on a chair. "A strong, intelligent man brought low by a woman."

"Simon. Go away." Edward didn't move, didn't even turn his head at the intrusion.

"I would, old boy, if I hadn't a conscience." Iddesleigh's voice echoed eerily about the room. "But I find I have. A conscience, that is. Damned inconvenient." The viscount knelt at the cold fireplace and began assembling a pile of tinder.

Edward frowned a little. "Who sent for you?"

"Your strange elderly man." Iddesleigh reached for the coal scuttle. "Davis, I think? He was concerned for Mrs. Wren. He seems to have taken a liking to her, rather like a pullet imprinting on a swan. He may have been worried about you as well, but it was hard to tell. I can't think why you keep the creature on."

Edward didn't answer.

Iddesleigh delicately stacked lumps of coal around his tinder. It was odd to see the fastidious viscount working at such a dirty job. Edward hadn't suspected he knew how to lay a fire.

Iddesleigh spoke over his shoulder, "So, what's the plan? To sit here until you freeze? A bit passive, what?"

"Simon, for the love of God, leave me be."

"No, Edward. For the love of God—and you—I'll stay." Iddesleigh struck flint and steel, but the tinder wouldn't catch.

"She's gone. What would you have me do?"

"Apologize. Buy her an emerald necklace. Or, no, in this lady's case, buy her more roses." A spark caught and began to lick at the coals. "Anything, man, but sit here."

For the first time, Edward stirred, an uncomfortable shifting of muscles still too long. "She doesn't want me."

"Now that," Iddesleigh said as he stood and took out a handkerchief, "is an out and out lie. I saw her with you, remember, at Lillipin's lecture. The lady is in love with you, although God only knows why." He wiped his hands on the handkerchief, turning it black, then contemplated the ruined square of silk for a moment before throwing it into the flames.

Edward turned his head away. "Then why did she leave me?" he muttered.

Iddesleigh shrugged. "What man knows a woman's mind? Certainly not I. You might've said something to offend, almost surely did, in fact. Or she might've taken a sudden dislike to London. Or"—he dipped his hand into his coat pocket and held out a piece of paper between two fingers—"she might've been blackmailed."

"What?" Edward jolted upright and grabbed the slip of paper. "What are you talking . . ." His voice trailed away as he read the damned note. Someone had threatened Anna. *His* Anna.

He looked up. "Where the hell did you get this?"

Iddesleigh showed his palms. "Davis again. He gave it to me in the hall. Apparently it was on the grate in your room."

"The goddamn son of a whore. Who is this man?" Edward brandished the paper before viciously screwing it into a ball and throwing it into the fire.

"I have no idea," Iddesleigh said. "But he must frequent Aphrodite's Grotto to know so much."

"Jesus!" Edward jumped from the chair and shoved his arms into his coat. "When I finish with him, he won't be able to visit a drab. I'll cut off his stones. And then I'm going after Anna. How dare she not tell me someone was threatening her?" He stilled at a sudden thought, then swung around to Iddesleigh. "Why didn't you give the note to me at once?"

The viscount shrugged again, unperturbed by his scowl. "The blackmailer won't be at the Grotto until nine." He took out a penknife and began cleaning underneath his thumbnail. "It's only half past seven now. Didn't see much point in rushing things. Perhaps we can have a bite to eat first?"

"If you weren't so useful once in a while," Edward growled, "I would have strangled you by now."

"Oh, undoubtedly." Iddesleigh put away the knife and reached for his cape. "But it would be nice to at least bring along some bread and cheese in the carriage."

Edward scowled. "You're not coming with me."

"I'm afraid I am." The viscount adjusted his tricorn to the proper angle in the mirror by the door. "And so is Harry. He's waiting in the hall."

"Why?"

"Because, my dear friend, this is one of those times when I can be useful." Iddesleigh smiled ferally. "You'll be needing seconds, won't you?"

Chapter Twenty-Two

*The old woman smiled at Aurea's startled expression.
"My sons roam the four corners of the earth.
There isn't a man or beast or bird that they
don't know. What is it you search for?"
Then Aurea told of her strange marriage to the Raven
Prince and his avian followers and her search for her
lost husband. The first three Winds shook their heads
regretfully; they had not heard of the Raven Prince.
But the West Wind, the tall bony son, hesitated.
"Sometime back, a wee shrike told me a strange
story. She said there was a castle in the clouds
where birds spoke with human voices. If you like,
I'll take you there." So Aurea climbed on the back
of the West Wind and wrapped her arms tightly
around his throat so that she might not fall off,
for the West Wind flies more swiftly than any bird. . . .
—from* The Raven Prince

Harry tugged at his black silk demimask. "Tell me again why we're going masked, my lord."

Edward drummed his fingers against the carriage door, wishing they could gallop through the London streets. "There was a small misunderstanding the last time I was at the Grotto."

"A misunderstanding." Harry's voice was soft, noncommittal.

"It would be better were I not recognized."

"Really?" Iddesleigh stopped fiddling with his own mask. He sounded fascinated. "I wasn't aware Aphrodite barred anyone from her doors. What, exactly, did you do?"

"It doesn't matter." Edward waved an impatient hand. "All you need to know is that we must be discreet when we enter."

"And Harry and I are also masked because . . . ?"

"Because if this man follows me closely enough to know about my engagement to Miss Gerard, he'll also know we three are comrades."

Harry grunted in apparent assent.

"Ah. In that case, perhaps we ought to mask the dog as well." The viscount looked pointedly at Jock, sitting upright on the bench next to Harry. The dog gazed alertly out the window.

"Try to be serious," Edward growled.

"I was," Iddesleigh muttered.

Edward ignored the other man to watch out the window himself. They were in an area near the East End that was not quite disreputable, yet not entirely respectable. He caught the movement of a skirt in a doorway as they passed. A trull displaying her wares. Less-benign shapes skulked in the shadows as well. Part of the Grotto's allure was that it straddled the narrow line between the illicit and the truly dangerous. The fact that on any given night a small portion of the Grotto's patrons were robbed or worse didn't seem to diminish its attraction; to a certain sort, no doubt, it increased the appeal.

The glow of lights up ahead gave notice that they were nearing the Grotto. In another moment, the faux Greek façade came into view. White marble and an abundance of gilt lent Aphrodite's Grotto a magnificently vulgar air.

"How do you plan to find the blackmailer?" Harry asked sotto voce as they descended from the carriage.

Edward shrugged. "At nine we'll know how big the field is." He strolled to the entrance with all the arrogance of his nine generations of aristocracy behind him.

Two burly fellows in togas guarded the doors. The drapes on the man nearest were a bit too short, revealing astonishingly hairy calves.

The guard squinted suspiciously at Edward. "'Ere now. Ain't you the Earl of—"

"I'm so glad you recognized me." Edward put one hand on the man's shoulder and extended the other in a seemingly friendly shake.

The extended palm held a guinea. The guard's fist closed smoothly over the gold piece and disappeared into the folds of his toga.

The man smiled greasily. "That's all fine and good, my lord. But after last time, perhaps you wouldn't mind . . . ?" The man rubbed his fingers together suggestively.

Edward scowled. What cheek! He leaned into the other man's face until he could smell the rot of his teeth. "Perhaps I would mind."

Jock growled.

The guard backed up, hands thrust out in a calming motion. "That's good! That's good, my lord! Step right in."

Edward nodded curtly and climbed the steps.

Beside him, Iddesleigh murmured, "You really must tell me about this misunderstanding sometime."

Harry chuckled.

Edward ignored them. They were in, and he'd more important matters to consider.

"BUT WHERE DID HE GO?" Anna stood in the entrance hall to Edward's town house, interrogating Dreary. She still wore her musty traveling clothes.

"I'm sure I don't know, ma'am." The butler seemed genuinely at a loss.

She stared at him in frustration. She'd spent all day traveling, had composed and recomposed her apology to Edward, had even daydreamed about making up afterward, and now the silly man wasn't even here. It was a bit anticlimactic, to say the least.

"Doesn't anyone know where Lord Swartingham is?" She was beginning to whine.

Fanny shifted from one foot to the other beside her. "Maybe he went looking for you, mum."

Anna switched her gaze to Fanny. In doing so, a movement at the back of the hall caught her eye. Edward's valet was tiptoeing away. Sneakily.

"Mr. Davis." She snatched at her skirts and trotted after the man more briskly than was ladylike. "Mr. Davis, wait a moment."

Drat! The old man was faster than he looked. He darted around the corner and up a back staircase, feigning deafness.

Anna panted after him. "Stop!"

The valet turned at the top of the stairs. They were in a narrow hallway, evidently the servants' quarters. Davis made for a door at the end of the corridor, but Anna was faster on level ground. She put on an extra burst of speed and reached the door before the little man. She slammed her back to the closed door, her arms outstretched on either side, barring him from his sanctuary.

"Mr. Davis."

"Oh, was you wanting me, mum?" He opened rheumy eyes wide.

"Quite." She inhaled deeply, trying to catch her breath. "Where is the earl?"

"The earl?" Davis looked around as if expecting Edward to pop out of the shadows.

"Edward de Raaf, Lord Swartingham, the Earl of Swartingham?" Anna leaned closer. "Your master?"

"Don't have to be snotty." Davis actually looked wounded.

"Mr. Davis!"

"M'lord might've had an idea," the valet said carefully, "that he was needed somewheres else."

Anna tapped her foot. "Tell me right now where he is."

Davis cast his eyes up and then to the side, but there was no help in the dim hallway. He heaved a sigh. "He might've found a letter." The manservant didn't meet her eyes. "He might've gone to a nasty house. Had an awful strange name, Aphroditty or Aphro—"

But Anna was already running down the servant's stair, skidding on the turns as she rounded them. *Oh, my God. Oh, my God.*

If Edward had found the blackmail note . . .

If he'd gone to confront the blackmailer . . .

The blackmailer obviously had no sense of honor and was probably dangerous. What would he do when cornered? Surely Edward wouldn't take on such a man by himself? She whimpered. Oh, yes, he would. If anything happened to him, it would be her fault.

Anna ran flat out through the hall, shoved past Dreary, still dithering, and banged open the door.

"Mum!" Fanny started after her.

Anna did a little spin. "Fanny, stay here. If the earl returns, tell him I'll be back soon." She turned again and cupped her hands to bellow at the carriage pulling away from the town house. *"Stop!"*

The coachman yanked hard on the reins, causing the front horses to half rear. He looked around. "What is it now, mum? Don't you want to rest a bit now you're in London? Mrs. Clearwater—"

"I need you to drive me to Aphrodite's Grotto."

"But, Mrs. Clearwater—"

"Now."

The coachman sighed wearily. "Which way is it, then?"

Anna gave succinct directions, then scrambled into the carriage she'd so recently exited. She gripped the leather straps and prayed, *Oh, dear God, let me be in time.* She couldn't live with herself if Edward were hurt.

The carriage ride was hellishly interminable, but finally she alighted and ran up the long marble steps. Inside,

Aphrodite's Grotto echoed with the chatter and laughter of London's denizens of the night. Every young buck, every aging roué, every lady mincing on the fine edge of respectability seemed to be gathered at Aphrodite's. It was a quarter to nine, and the throng was boisterous, uninhibited, and more than slightly drunk.

Anna drew her cloak tightly about her. The rooms were hot and smelled of burning wax, unwashed bodies, and alcoholic spirits. Nevertheless, she kept the wrap on, a thin barrier between herself and the crowd. Once she glanced up and noticed leering cupids on the ceiling. They were pulling back a painted veil to reveal a voluptuously pink Aphrodite surrounded by a . . . well, an orgy.

Aphrodite seemed to wink down at her with knowing eyes.

Anna hastily averted her gaze and continued her search. Her plan was simple: find the blackmailer and lure him away from the Grotto before Edward got to him. The problem was that she didn't know who the blackmailer was. In fact, she didn't even know if it was a man. Nervously, she kept an eye out for Edward as well. Perhaps if she could find him before the blackmailer appeared, she could convince him to just leave. Although she had a hard time imagining Edward backing away from a fight, even one he might lose.

She entered the main salon. Here couples lounged on settees, and young bucks prowled for their evening's entertainment. She saw at once that it would be prudent to keep moving, so she perambulated about the room. The classical theme was continued here, with various scenes of Zeus seducing young ladies. The one of Europa and the Bull was particularly graphic.

"I told you to bring a muff." A peevish voice at Anna's elbow interrupted her thoughts.

Finally.

"I'm not paying your ridiculous price." The blackmailer didn't look that frightening. He was younger than she'd expected, with a familiar, receding chin. Anna frowned. "You're the macaroni from the lecture."

The man looked irritated. "Where's my money?"

"I've already told you, I'm not paying. The earl is here, and it's in your best interest to leave now, before he finds you."

"But, the money—"

Anna stamped her foot in exasperation. "Look, you pea-brained nit, I haven't got any money with me, and you really must—"

A large furry form leapt from behind Anna. There was a shout and a horrible, low growling. The blackmailer sprawled on the floor, his body nearly obliterated by Jock. The mastiff's bared fangs were only inches from the man's eyes, and a ridge of fur bristled down the dog's back as he continued his menacing rumbling.

Belatedly, a woman screamed.

"Hold, Jock," Edward said as he advanced. "Chilton Lillipin. I should've guessed. You must have been at your elder brother's lecture yesterday."

"Damnation, Swartingham, get this beast off me! What do you care about a sl—"

Jock barked, nearly taking off the man's nose.

Edward placed a hand on the back of the dog's neck. "I do, most certainly, care about this *lady*."

Lillipin's eyes narrowed craftily. "Then you'll no doubt want satisfaction."

"Naturally."

"I'll have my seconds contact—"

"Now." Although Edward spoke softly, his voice carried over the other man's.

"Edward, no!" This was exactly what Anna had wanted to avoid.

Edward ignored her. "I have my seconds here."

Viscount Iddesleigh and a shorter man with watchful green eyes stepped forward. Their faces were intent on this masculine game.

The viscount smiled. "Pick your seconds."

Lillipin glanced around the room from his prone position. A young man, his shirt untucked, pulled his staggering companion to the front of the crowd. "We'll second you."

Oh, God! "Edward, stop this, please." Anna spoke low.

He pulled Jock off Lillipin and toward her. "Guard."

The dog obediently stood braced in front of Anna.

"But—"

Edward looked at her sternly, cutting off her words. He shed his coat. Lillipin jumped to his feet, removed his coat and waistcoat, and drew his sword. Edward unsheathed his own weapon. The two men stood in a suddenly cleared space.

This was happening too fast. It was like a nightmare she couldn't stop. The room had grown silent, faces turned avidly at the prospect of bloodshed.

The men saluted, bringing their swords up before their faces; then each bent slightly at the knee, their blades in front of them. Slimmer and shorter than Edward, the younger man's stance was consciously elegant with his left hand curved in a graceful arc behind his head. Lillipin wore a linen shirt trimmed in fountains of Belgian lace that flowed as he moved. Edward stood solidly, his unarmed hand held out behind him for balance, not grace. His black waistcoat had only a thin line of black braid along the edge, and his white shirt was unadorned.

Lillipin sneered. "En garde!" The younger man lunged. His rapier moved in a glinting flurry.

Edward blocked the attack. His sword slid and scraped against his opponent's. He stepped back two paces as Lillipin advanced, weapon flashing. Anna bit her lip. Surely he was on the defensive? Lillipin seemed to think so as well. His lips curved in an oily grin.

"Chilly Lilly killed two men last year," a voice crowed from the crowd behind her. Anna drew in her breath sharply. She'd heard of the bucks in London who amused themselves by challenging and killing less-skilled swordsmen. Edward spent most of his time in the country. Could he even defend himself?

The men moved in a tight circle, sweat gleaming on their faces. Lillipin lunged forward, and his sword chattered against Edward's. Edward's right sleeve shredded. Anna moaned, but no telltale red stained the sleeve. Lillipin's blade darted out again, a snake striking, and bit into Edward's shoulder. Edward grunted. This time crimson drops fell to the floor. Anna started forward, only to be halted by Jock's jaws clamped gently around her arm.

"Blood," Iddesleigh called out, echoed closely by Lillipin's seconds.

Neither duelist wavered. The swords sang and attacked. Edward's sleeve steadily bloomed a bright red. With each movement of his arm, blood sprayed over the floor, bright droplets that were immediately smeared into streaks by the combatants' feet. Weren't they supposed to stop at the first blood drawn?

Unless they fought to the death.

Anna stuffed her fist into her mouth to stifle a scream. She couldn't distract Edward now. She stood absolutely still, her eyes brimming with tears.

Suddenly, Edward lunged and lunged again. His lead foot stomped against the floor with the ferocity of his attack. Lillipin fell back and brought his sword up to defend his face. Edward's arm made a controlled circular movement; his blade flashed up and over his opponent's weapon. Lillipin squealed in pain. The sword flew from his hand, sliding with a clatter across the room. Edward stood with the tip of his weapon pressed into the soft skin at the base of Lillipin's throat.

The younger man breathed hard, his bleeding right hand cradled in his left.

"You may have won by luck, Swartingham," Lillipin panted, "but you cannot stop me from talking once I leave this—"

Edward flung down his sword and slammed his fist into the other man's face. Lillipin staggered back, arms flailed wide, and fell to the floor with a thump. He lay still.

"Actually, I can stop you," Edward muttered, and shook his right hand.

There was a long-suffering sigh from directly behind Anna. "I knew you'd resort to fisticuffs eventually." Viscount Iddesleigh stepped around her.

Edward looked affronted. "I did duel him first."

"Yes, and your form was atrocious as always."

The man with the green eyes rounded Anna's other side and silently bent to pick up Edward's sword.

"I won," Edward said pointedly.

The viscount sneered. "Sadly so."

"Would you have preferred he best me?" Edward demanded.

"No, but in a perfect world, classic form would win every time."

"This isn't a perfect world, thank God."

Anna couldn't stand it any longer. *"Idiot!"* She hit Edward's chest, but then remembered and frantically tore at his bloody sleeve.

"Darling, what—?" Edward sounded nonplussed.

"It's not enough that you had to fight that awful man," she panted, her vision half obscured by tears. "You let him hurt you. You're bleeding all over the floor." Anna got the sleeve open and felt dizzy when she saw the terrible gash marring his beautiful shoulder. "And now you're probably going to die." She sobbed as she pressed her handkerchief, pitifully inadequate, against his wound.

"Anna, sweetheart, hush." Edward tried to put his arms around her, but she batted them aside.

"And for what? What was worth dueling that horrible man over?"

"You." Edward spoke softly, and her breath caught midsob. "You are worth anything and everything to me. Even bleeding to death in a brothel."

Anna choked, unable to speak.

He brushed his hand tenderly along her cheek. "I need you. I told you that, but you didn't seem to believe me." He took a breath and his eyes glittered. "Don't ever leave me again, Anna. I won't survive the next time. I want you to marry me, but if you can't do that . . ." He swallowed.

Her eyes filled with tears anew.

"Just don't leave me," he whispered.

"Oh, Edward." She sighed as he framed her face with bloody hands and kissed her tenderly.

He husked across her lips, "I love you."

Distantly, she heard a whoop and several catcalls. The viscount cleared his throat nearly in her ear.

Edward lifted his head but kept his eyes on Anna's face. "Can't you see I'm busy, Iddesleigh?"

"Oh, indeed. The whole Grotto can see you're busy, de Raaf," the viscount said dryly.

Edward looked up and seemed to notice their audience for the first time. He scowled. "Right. I need to take Anna home and get this"—he gestured to his shoulder—"seen to." He glanced at the unconscious Lillipin, who was now drooling. "Can you take care of that?"

"I suppose I'll have to." The viscount pursed his lips in distaste. "There must be a ship sailing somewhere exotic tonight. You don't mind, do you, Harry?"

The green-eyed man grinned. "Sailoring will do this lout a world of good." He grabbed Lillipin's feet. Viscount Iddesleigh took the other end, none too gently, and together they lifted Chilly Lilly.

"Congratulations." Harry nodded at Anna.

"Yes, felicitations, de Raaf," the viscount drawled as he walked past. "I do hope I'll merit an invite to the impending nuptials?"

Edward growled.

Chuckling, the viscount sauntered out, holding half of an unconscious man. Edward immediately clamped a hand around Anna's arm and began pushing her through the mass of people. For the first time, she noticed that Aphrodite herself watched from the edge of the crowd. Anna's mouth dropped open. The madam now stood a head shorter than previously and had catlike green eyes behind her golden mask. Her hair was powdered with gold dust.

"I knew he would forgive you," Aphrodite purred as Anna threaded her way past; then she raised her voice. "Drinks on the house for everyone in celebration of love!"

The crowd roared behind them as Anna and Edward ran down the front steps into the waiting carriage. Edward thumped on the roof and collapsed on the cushions. He hadn't let go of her for a second, and now he pulled her into his lap and covered her mouth with his own, taking advantage of her parted lips to thrust his tongue in. It was several minutes before she could draw a breath.

He drew back only to deliver a series of little nips along her bottom lip. "Will you marry me?" he breathed so close to her that the air from his body whispered across her face.

More tears blurred Anna's eyes. "I love you so much, Edward," she said brokenly. "What if we never have a family?"

He cupped her face in his hands. "You are my family. If we never have children, I will be disappointed, but if I never have you, I will be devastated. I love you. I need you. Please trust me enough to be my wife."

"Yes." Edward was already nibbling a row of kisses down her neck, so it was hard for her to get the word out, but she said it again anyway, because saying it was important.

"*Yes.*"

Epilogue

*The West Wind flew with Aurea to a castle in the
clouds surrounded by wheeling birds. As she
stepped from his back, a giant raven alighted
beside her and transformed into Prince Niger.
"You have found me, Aurea, my love!" he said.
As the Raven Prince spoke, the birds drifted down
from the sky and turned one by one into men and
women again. A great shout of exultation arose from
the Raven Prince's followers. At the same time, the
clouds dissolved from around the castle to reveal
that it sat at the summit of a great mountain.
Aurea was dazed. "But how is this possible?"
The prince smiled, and his ebony eyes glinted.
"Your love, Aurea. Your love has broken the curse...."*
—from *The Raven Prince*

THREE YEARS LATER . . .

"And Aurea and the Raven Prince lived happily ever
after." Anna closed the red morocco leather book softly.
"Is he asleep?"

Edward shifted the silk screen so it would shade the toddler from the afternoon sun. "Mmm. For some time now, I think."

They both looked at the deceptively cherubic face. Their son lay on ruby-red silk cushions, piled in the center of the walled garden at the Abbey. His short limbs sprawled, as if sleep had overcome him in midmotion. Rosebud lips pursed over the two fingers in his mouth, and a gentle wind stirred his raven curls. Jock lay beside his favorite human, unconcerned by the chubby hand that clutched his ear. Around them, the garden bloomed in full glory: Flowers spilled onto the pathways in multicolored exuberance, and climbing roses nearly covered the walls. The air was filled with the scent of roses and the hum of bees.

Edward reached over and plucked the book from her hand. He set it down next to the remains of their luncheon; then he took a pink rose from the vase in the center of the picnic cloth and shifted closer to his wife.

"What are you doing?" Anna hissed, although she had a very good idea.

"Me?" Edward tried to look innocent as he trailed the rose over the tops of her exposed breasts. He didn't succeed nearly as well as his son.

"Edward!"

One petal fell down her cleavage. He knit his brows in mock alarm. "Oh, dear."

His long fingers delved between her breasts, searching for the petal but only pushing it farther down. He wasn't doing a very good job finding it, his fingertips kept brushing over Anna's nipples.

She batted at his hand halfheartedly. "Stop that. It tickles." She squeaked as he pinched a nipple between two fingers.

Edward frowned sternly. "Shh. You'll wake Samuel." Her bodice gave way. "You must be very, very quiet."

"But Mother Wren—"

"Is seeing how Fanny fares at her new post in the next county." His breath tickled her exposed breasts. "She shan't be home until supper."

He took a nipple into his mouth.

Anna's breath caught. "I think I'm breeding again."

Edward lifted his head, his black eyes glittering. "Would you mind another child so soon?"

"I'd adore one," she said, and then sighed happily.

Edward was taking the news of her second pregnancy much better than he had the first. From the moment Anna had told him of her first pregnancy, he'd been terribly grim. She'd done her best to comfort him at the time, but she had been resigned to the fact that he wouldn't truly recover until she was safely delivered of their child. And indeed, Edward had sat white-faced beside her bed the entire labor. Mrs. Stucker had taken one look at the expectant father's face and sent for brandy, which Edward had refused to touch. Five hours later, Samuel Ethan de Raaf, Viscount Herrod, was born. He was possibly the most beautiful baby in the history of the world, in his mother's opinion. Edward had drunk nearly a third of the bottle of brandy before climbing into the big bed with his wife and newborn son and wrapping his arms around both.

Now he flipped Anna's skirts up and settled between her bared thighs. "It'll be a daughter this time."

He was trailing kisses up her neck. Both of his hands covered her breasts, and his thumbs flicked her nipples.

Anna gasped. "Another boy would be nice, too, but if it is a girl, I know what I'll name her."

"What?" He was nibbling her ear, and Anna could feel his erection pressing against her.

He probably wasn't listening, but she answered him anyway. "Elizabeth Rose."

About the Author

Elizabeth Hoyt lives in central Illinois with three untrained dogs, two angelic, but bickering children, and one long-suffering husband. There is some debate on whether a golden hamster resides with her family as well. The freethinking rodent decided to live *sans* cage sometime during the summer of '05. It has not been reliably spotted since, although Elizabeth's youngest child holds out hope of its return. The hermit crabs are best not mentioned at all.

Winters are long, cold, and monotonous in central Illinois. Elizabeth would be most appreciative of any mail you'd care to send her. You may e-mail her at: elizabeth@ elizabethhoyt.com or mail her at: PO Box 17134, Urbana, Illinois 61803. Please visit her Web site at www. elizabethhoyt.com for giveaways, book excerpts, and author updates.

More Historical Romance from

Elizabeth Hoyt!

Please turn this page
for a preview of

The Leopard Prince

AVAILABLE IN FALL 2007.

Chapter One

Yorkshire, England
September, 1760

After the carriage wreck and a bit before the horses ran away, Lady Georgina Maitland noticed that her land steward was a man. Well, that is to say, naturally she knew Harry Pye was a man. She wasn't under the delusion that he was a lion or an elephant or a whale, or indeed any other member of the animal kingdom—if one could call a whale an animal and not just a very big fish. What she meant was that his *male*ness had suddenly become very evident.

George knit her brow as she stood on the desolate high road to East Riding in Yorkshire. Around them, the gorse-covered hills rolled away into the gray horizon. Dark was rapidly falling, brought on early by the rainstorm. They could've been standing at the ends of the earth.

"Do you consider a whale to be an animal or a very big fish, Mr. Pye?" she shouted into the wind.

Harry Pye's shoulders bunched. They were covered only by a wet lawn shirt that clung to him in an aesthetically pleasing way. He'd previously discarded his coat and waistcoat to help John Coachman unhitch the horses from the overturned carriage.

"An animal, my lady." Mr. Pye's voice was, as always, even and deep with a sort of gravelly tone toward the bottom.

George had never heard him raise his voice or show passion in any other way. Not when she'd insisted on accompanying him to her Yorkshire estate; not when the rain had started, slowing their travel to a crawl; not when the carriage had overturned twenty minutes ago.

How very irritating. "Do you think you will be able to right the carriage?" She pulled her soaked cloak up over her chin as she contemplated the remains of her vehicle. The door hung from one hinge, banging in the wind, two wheels were smashed, and the back axle had settled at an odd angle. It was a thoroughly idiotic question.

Mr. Pye didn't indicate by action or word that he was aware of the silliness of her query. "No, my lady."

George sighed.

Really, it was something of a miracle that they and the coachman hadn't been hurt or killed. The rain had made the roads slippery with mud, and as they had rounded the last curve, the carriage had started to slide. From inside, she and Mr. Pye had heard the coachman shouting as he tried to steady the vehicle. Harry Pye had leapt from his seat to hers, rather like a large cat. He'd braced himself against her before she could even utter a word. His warmth had surrounded her, and her nose, buried intimately in his shirt, had inhaled the scent of clean linen and male skin. By that time, the carriage had tilted, and it was obvious they were falling into the ditch.

Slowly, awfully, the contraption had tipped over with a grinding crash. The horses had whinnied from the front, and the carriage had moaned as if protesting its fate. She'd clutched Mr. Pye's coat as her world upended, and Mr. Pye grunted in pain. Then they were still again. The vehicle had rested on its side, and Mr. Pye rested on her like a great warm blanket. Except Harry Pye was much firmer than any blanket she'd ever felt before.

He'd apologized most correctly, disentangled himself from her, and climbed up the seat to wrest open the door above them. He'd crawled through and then pulled her bodily out. George rubbed the wrist he'd gripped. He was disconcertingly strong—one would never know it to look at him. At one point, almost her entire weight had hung from his arm, and she wasn't a petite woman.

The coachman gave a shout, which was snatched away by the wind, but it was enough to bring her back to the present. The mare he'd been unhitching was free.

"Ride her to the next town, Mr. Coachman, if you will," Harry Pye directed. "See if there is another carriage to send back. I'll remain here with her ladyship."

The coachman mounted the horse and waved before disappearing into the downpour.

"How far is the next town?" George asked.

"Ten or fifteen miles." He pulled a strap loose on one of the horses.

She studied him as he worked. Aside from being wet, Harry Pye didn't look any different than he had when they'd started out this morning from an inn in Lincoln. He was still a man of average height. Rather lean. His hair was brown, neither chestnut nor auburn, merely brown.

He tied it back in a simple queue, not bothering to dress it with pomades or powder. And he wore brown—breeches, waistcoat, and coat—as if to camouflage himself. Only his eyes, a dark emerald green that sometimes flickered with what might be emotion, gave him any color.

"It's just that I'm rather cold," George muttered.

Mr. Pye looked up swiftly. His gaze darted to her hands, trembling at her throat, and then shifted to the hills behind her.

"I'm sorry, my lady. I should have noticed your chill earlier." He turned back to the frightened gelding he was trying to liberate. His hands must be as numb as her own, but he labored steadily. "There's a shepherd's cottage not far from here. We can ride this horse and that one." He nodded at the horse next to the gelding. "The other is lame."

"Really? How can you tell?" She hadn't noticed the animal was hurt. All three of the remaining carriage horses shivered and rolled their eyes at the whistling of the wind. The horse he had indicated didn't look any more ragged than the rest.

"She's favoring her right foreleg." Mr. Pye grunted, and suddenly all three horses were free of the carriage, although they were still hitched together. "Whoa, there, sweetheart." He caught the lead horse and stroked it, his tanned right hand moving tenderly over the animal's neck. The last two joints on his ring finger were missing.

She turned her head away to look at the hills. Servants—and, really, a land steward was just a superior sort of servant—should have no gender. Of course, one knew they were people with their own lives and all that, but it made things so very much easier if one saw them as sexless. Like a chair. One wanted a chair to sit in when one was tired. No one ever thought about chairs much other-wise and that was how it should be. How uncomfortable to go about wondering if the chair had noticed that one's nose was running, wishing to know what it was thinking, or seeing that the chair had rather beautiful eyes. Not that chairs had eyes, beautiful or otherwise, but men did.

And Harry Pye did.

George faced him again. "What will we do with the third horse?"

"We'll have to leave her here."

"In the rain?"

"Yes."

"That can't be good for her."

"No, my lady." Harry Pye's shoulders bunched again, a reaction that George found oddly fascinating. She wished she could make him do it more often.

"Perhaps we should take her with us?"

"Impossible, my lady."

"Are you sure?"

The shoulders tensed and Mr. Pye slowly turned his head. In the flash of lightning that lit up the road in that in-stant, she saw his green eyes gleam, and a thrill ran up her spine. Then the following thunder crashed like the herald-ing of the apocalypse.

George flinched.

Harry Pye straightened.

And the horses bolted.

"OH, DEAR," SAID Lady Georgina, rain dripping from her narrow nose. "We seem to be in something of a fix."

Something of a fix, indeed. More like well and truly buggered. Harry squinted up the road where the horses had disappeared, running as if the Devil himself were chasing them. There was no sign of the daft beasts. At the rate they'd been galloping, they wouldn't stop for half a mile or more. No use going after them in this downpour. He switched his gaze to his employer of less than six months. Lady Georgina's aristocratic lips were blue, and the fur trimming the hood of her cloak had turned into a sopping mess. She looked more like an urchin in tattered finery than the daughter of an earl.

What was she doing here?

If not for Lady Georgina, he would've ridden a horse from London to her estates in Yorkshire. He would've arrived a day ago at Woldsly Manor. Right now he would be enjoying a hot meal in front of the fire in his own cottage. Not freezing his baubles off, standing in the middle of the high road in the rain with the light fading fast. But on his last trip to London to report to Lady Georgina on her holdings, she had decided to travel with him back to Woldsly Manor. Which had meant taking the carriage, now lying in a heap of broken wood in the ditch.

Harry swallowed a sigh. "Can you walk, my lady?"

Lady Georgina widened eyes that were as blue as a thrush's egg. "Oh yes. I've been doing it since I was eleven months old."

"Good." Harry shrugged on his waistcoat and coat, not bothering to button either; they were soaked through like the rest of him. He scrambled down the bank to retrieve the rugs from inside the carriage. Thankfully, they were still dry. He rolled them together and snagged the still-lit carriage lantern. Then he gripped Lady Georgina's elbow, just in case she was wrong and fell on her aristocratic little arse, and started trudging up the gorse-covered hill.

At first he'd thought her urge to travel to Yorkshire a childish fancy. The lark of a woman who never worried where the meat on her table or the jewels at her throat came from. To his mind, those who didn't labor to make their living often had flighty ideas. But the more time he spent in her company, the more he began to doubt that she was such a woman. She said gormless things, true, but he'd seen almost at once that she did it for her own amusement. She was smarter than most society ladies. He had a feeling that Lady Georgina had a good reason for traveling with him to Yorkshire.

"Is it much farther?" The lady was panting, and her normally pale face sported two spots of red.

Harry scanned the sodden hills, looking for a landmark in the gloom. Was that twisted oak growing against an outcropping familiar? "Not far."

At least he hoped not. It had been years since he'd last ridden these hills, and he might've mistaken where the cottage lay. Or it might have tumbled down since he last saw it.

"I trust you are skilled at starting fires, Mr. P-pye." Her voice shook, and his name chattered on her lips.

She needed to get warm. If they didn't find the cottage soon, he'd have to make a shelter from the carriage robes. "Oh, yes. I've been doing it since I was four, my lady."

That earned him a cheeky grin. Their eyes met, and he wished . . . A sudden bolt of lightning interrupted his half-formed thought, and in the flash, he saw a stone wall.

"There it is." *Thank God.*

The tiny cottage still stood at least. Four stone walls with a thatched roof black with age and the rain. He put his shoulder to the slick door, and after one or two shoves, it gave. Harry stumbled in and held the lantern high to illuminate the interior. Small shapes scurried into the shadows. He checked a shudder.

"Gah! It does smell." Lady Georgina walked in and waved her hand in front of her pink nose as if to shoo the stink of mildew.

He banged the door closed behind her. "I'm sorry, my lady."

"Why don't you just tell me to shut my mouth and be glad I'm out of the rain?" She smiled and pulled back her hood.

"I think not." Harry walked to the fireplace and found some half-burned logs. They were covered with cobwebs.

"Oh, come, Mr. Pye. You know you wish t-t-to." Her teeth still chattered.

Four rickety wooden chairs stood around a lopsided table. Harry placed the lantern on the table and picked up a chair. He swung it hard against the stone fireplace. It shattered, the back coming off and the seat splintering.

Behind him, Lady Georgina squeaked.

"No, I don't, my lady," he said.

"Truly?"

"Yes." He knelt and began placing small splinters of the chair against the charred logs.

"Very well. I suppose I must be nice, then." Harry heard her draw up a chair. "That looks very efficient, what you're doing there."

He touched the lantern flame to the slivers of wood. They lit and he added larger pieces of the chair, careful not to smother the flame.

"Mmm. It feels good." Her voice was throaty behind him.

For a moment, Harry froze, thinking of what her words and tone might imply in a different context. Then he banished the thoughts and turned.

Lady Georgina held out her hands to the blaze. Her ginger hair was drying into fine curls around her forehead, and her white skin glowed in the firelight. She was still shivering.

Harry cleared his throat. "I believe you should remove your wet gown and wrap the rugs about yourself." He strode over to the door where he'd dumped the carriage robes.

From behind him, he heard a breathless laugh. "I don't believe I have ever heard such an improper suggestion made so properly."

"I didn't mean to be improper, my lady." He handed her the robes. "I'm sorry if I offended." Briefly his eyes met hers, so blue and laughing; then he turned his back.

Behind him there was a rustling. He tried to discipline his thoughts. He would not imagine her pale, naked shoulders above—

"You aren't improper, as well you know, Mr. Pye. Indeed, I'm beginning to think it would be impossible for you to be so."

If she only knew. He cleared his throat but made no comment. He forced himself to gaze around the little cottage. There was no kitchen dresser, only the table and chairs. A pity. His belly was empty.

The rustling by the fire ceased. "You may turn around now."

He braced himself before looking, but Lady Georgina was covered in furs. He was glad to see her lips were pinker.

She freed a naked arm from the bundle to point at a robe at the other side of the fireplace. "I've left one for you. I'm too comfortable to move, but I'll close my eyes and promise not to peek if you wish to disrobe as well."

Harry dragged his gaze away from the arm and met her clever blue eyes. "Thank you."

The arm disappeared. Lady Georgina smiled, and her eyelids fell.

For a moment, Harry simply watched her. The reddish arcs of her eyelashes fluttered against her pale skin, and a smile hovered on her crooked mouth. Her nose was thin and overlong, the angles of her face a bit too sharp. When she stood, she almost equaled his own height. She wasn't a beautiful woman, but he found himself having to control his gaze when he was around her. Something about the twitching of her lips when she was about to taunt him. Or the way her eyebrows winged up her forehead when she smiled. His eyes were drawn to her face like iron filings near a lodestone.

He shucked his upper garments and drew the last robe around himself. "You may open your eyes now, my lady."

Her eyes popped open. "Good. And now we both look like Russians swathed for the Siberian winter. A pity we don't have a sleigh with bells as well." She smoothed the fur on her lap.

He nodded. The fire crackled in the silence as he tried to think of how else he could look after her. There was no food in the cottage, nothing to do but wait for dawn. How did the upper crust behave when they were in their palatial sitting rooms all alone?

Lady Georgina was plucking at her robe, but she suddenly clasped her hands together as if to still them. "Do you know any stories, Mr. Pye?"

"Stories, my lady?"

"Mmm. Stories. Fairy tales, actually. I collect them."

"Indeed." Harry was at a loss. The way the aristocracy thought was truly amazing sometimes. "How, may I ask, do you go about collecting them?"

"By inquiring." Was she having fun with him? "You'd be amazed at the stories that people remember from their youth. Of course, old nursemaids and the like are the best sources. I believe I've asked every one of my acquaintances to introduce me to their old nurse. Is yours still alive?"

"I didn't have a nursemaid, my lady."

"Oh." Her cheeks reddened. "But someone—your mother?—must've told you fairy tales growing up."

He shifted to put another piece of the broken chair on the fire. "The only fairy tale I can remember is *Jack and the Beanstalk.*"

Lady Georgina gave him a pitying look. "Can't you do better than that?"

"I'm afraid not." The other tales he knew weren't exactly fit for a lady's ears.

"Well, I heard a rather interesting one recently. From my cook's aunt when she came to visit Cook in London. Would you like me to tell it to you?"

No. The last thing he needed was to become any more intimate with his employer than the situation had already forced him to be. "Yes, my lady."

"Once upon a time, there was a great king, and he had an enchanted leopard to serve him." She wiggled her rump on the chair. "I know what you're thinking, but that's not how it goes."

Harry blinked. "My lady?"

"No. The king dies right away, so he's not the hero." She looked expectantly at him.

"Ah." He couldn't think of anything else to say.

It seemed to do.

Lady Georgina nodded. "The leopard wore a sort of gold chain around its neck. It was enslaved, you see, but I don't know how that came about. Cook's aunt didn't say. Anyway, when the king was dying, he made the leopard promise to serve the *next* king, his son." She frowned. "Which doesn't seem very fair, somehow, does it? I mean, usually they free the faithful servant at that point." She shifted again on the wooden chair.

Harry cleared his throat. "Perhaps you would be more comfortable on the floor. Your cloak is drier. I could make a pallet."

She smiled blindingly at him. "What a good idea."

He spread out the cloak and rolled his own clothes into a pillow shape.

Lady Georgina shuffled over in her robes and plopped down on the crude bed. "That's better. You might as well come lie down as well. We'll be here until morning, most likely."

Christ. "I don't think it advisable."

She looked down her narrow nose at him. "Mr. Pye, those chairs are hard. Please come lie on the rugs at least. I promise not to bite."

He felt his jaw clench, but he really had no choice. It was a veiled order. "Thank you, my lady."

Harry gingerly sat beside her—he was damned if he would lie down next to this woman, order or no—and made sure to leave a space between their bodies. He wrapped his arms around his bent knees and tried not to notice her scent.

"You are stubborn, aren't you?" she muttered.

He looked at her.

She yawned. "Where was I? Oh, yes. So the first thing the young king does is to see a painting of a beautiful princess and fall in love with her. A courtier or a messenger or some such shows it to him, but that doesn't matter."

She yawned again, squeaking this time, and for some reason his prick responded to the sound. Or perhaps it was her scent, which reached his nose whether he wished it to or not. It reminded him of spices and exotic flowers.

"The princess has skin as white as snow, lips as red as rubies, hair as black as, oh, pitch or the like, et cetera, et cetera." Lady Georgina paused and stared into the fire.

He wondered if she was done and his torment over.

Then she sighed. "Have you ever noticed that these fairy-tale princes fall in love with beautiful princesses without knowing a thing about them? Ruby lips are all very well, but what if she laughs oddly or clicks her teeth when she eats?" She shrugged. "Of course, men in our times are just as apt to fall in love with glossy black curls, so I suppose I shouldn't quibble." Her eyes widened suddenly, and she turned her head to look at him. "No offense meant."

"None taken," Harry said gravely.

"Hmm." She seemed doubtful. "Anyway, he falls in love with this picture, and someone tells him that the princess's father is auctioning her off to the man who can bring him the Golden Horse, which is presently in the possession of a terrible ogre. So"—Lady Georgina turned to face the fire and cradled her cheek in her hand—"he sends for the Leopard Prince and tells him to go out quick and fetch him the Golden Horse, and what do you think?"

"I don't know, my lady."

"The leopard turned into a man." She closed her eyes and murmured, "Imagine that. He was a man all along. . . ."

Harry waited, but this time there was no more story. After a while, he heard a soft snore.

He drew the robes up over her neck and tucked them around her face. His fingers brushed against her cheek, and he paused, studying the contrast in the tones. His hand was dark against her skin, his fingers rough where she was soft and smooth. Slowly, he stroked his thumb across the corner of her mouth. So warm. He almost recognized her scent, as if he'd inhaled it in another life or long ago. It made him ache.

If she were a different woman, if this were a different place, if he were a different man. . . . Harry cut short the whisper in his mind and drew back his hand. He stretched out next to Lady Georgina, careful not to touch her. He stared at the ceiling and drove out all thought, all feeling. Then he closed his eyes, even though he knew it would be a long while before he slept.

ABOVE: Construction of the
Will Rogers Stadium, 1938.
Photo taken from the roof of
the Broadmoor Riding Academy.

Courtesy World Arena Pictorial Collection

January 1, 1938, with a gala ice show and was well received by all. The space was extremely functional, for the ice could be covered and used as an indoor arena for many different types of events. The ice arena gave the hotel's patrons and city residents yet another sports facility and the rink and its skaters soon achieved national prominence as a training and competition facility. Amateur, professional and collegiate ice hockey teams also competed in the new rink. The Broadmoor even had its own team, the Broadmoor Broncs which competed against local teams and those from other states.

Just months after the Ice Palace opened, the stadium was completed beside it. The stadium boasted a large central oval field, a quarter mile track around the perimeter and covered seating for ten thousand spectators in a horseshoe around the track. To maximize the utility of the construction, apartments for hotel guests who wished to have their own kitchens were built into the area under the graduated seating on the east side (These apartments had a beautiful view of the lake and were much sought after by summer guests.) The opening event was the first Will Rogers Rodeo held on August 19, 1938. The stadium was immediately subject to heavy use. Horse shows, exhibition events and even a professional football game between the Pittsburgh Pirates and the Los Angeles Bulldogs,[7] all took place during its first season. Penrose's vision of a multi-faceted sports facility had become a reality, and the Pikes Peak Region was much the richer for it. As a sign of Colorado Springs residents' appreciation, the Penroses were given a silver punch bowl with the inscription "In appreciation of our foremost citizens, MR. AND MRS. SPENCER PENROSE for their untiring and generous devotion to the community. From the business and professional men of Colorado Springs."

Thus, as Penrose's illness worsened, he felt confident that his great project was in excellent condition and prepared to march into the future,

---

7. This Armistice Day event included a star player from Colorado, Byron "Whizzer" White, who played for the Pirates and then went on to a successful career in law. Justice White resigned from the Supreme Court the year of this book's publication, 1993.

without him if necessary. He and Mrs. Penrose spent more time in Hawaii and with physicians across the country. Numerous doctors saw to it that Penrose obtained the best possible care, but it was clear that Spencer's lease on life was soon to draw to a close. Penrose was not a maudlin man and faced his destiny with his usual aplomb. In order to ensure that he would have an appropriate final resting place, he began making plans for his tomb.

Speck wished to be interred on the mountain that had been his beacon and which overlooked his favorite accomplishment. Given his grand view of life, however, he could have no simple tomb and the plans for a building grew larger and larger until it became the Will Rogers Shrine of the Sun on the slopes of Cheyenne Mountain. The building would function not only as his tomb, but also as a spot for tourists to stop on their way up to the Cheyenne Lodge. Penrose was, to the very end, a businessman.

The shrine, designed by Charles Thomas, was built at a cost of $250,000 out of one single slab of granite, cement and steel. Above it rises a tower equipped with a powerful amplification system. The tower stands over a hundred feet in height and rests on a concrete mat fifty-six feet square and three feet thick. It is built of light pink native granite. The entire amount of stone, some five thousand cubic yards, came from one gigantic boulder a short distance above the shrine. The tower's chimes can sound muted and bell-like, or ring out melodies loudly enough to be heard throughout the hotel's grounds and golf courses. The interior was decorated with murals painted by Broadmoor Art Academy artist Randall Davey. Penrose was fond of Davey because in addition to being an artist he was also an excellent polo player who played on the Broadmoor Polo team. Davey painted a history of Colorado Springs from its inception through the construction of the Broadmoor Hotel in a series of murals around the interior of the shrine. Many of the people that have been discussed in this history can be seen depicted there.

Penrose's original idea was to name this modest structure after himself, but in light of its commercial function he was convinced to name it after a personage that many, including himself, knew and loved. Will Rogers, a popular cowboy actor and singer (in addition to being a talented polo

player), had been killed in a plane crash shortly before the construction of the shrine. Speck decided to name it after Rogers, who had been his guest at the hotel and for whom he had great respect. Will Rogers is not and never was buried there himself.

The shrine was completed in the summer of 1938 and was dedicated with a theatrical ceremony that included the leading of a horse without a saddle up the highway to the shrine, music from the tower speakers which echoed over the plains and the unveiling of a bust of Will Rogers by Jo Davidson. Some of the members of the Sioux tribe who were an integral part of the yearly rodeo and had been coming to the Broadmoor since the first Roundup performed a "Ghost dance" for Will Rogers' spirit. Among the dancers was Chief Blue Horse who had become an artist under Penrose's sponsorship and did a series of murals, which were hung on the walls of the Ice Palace.

Thus, as the end approached, Speck could look around, see what he had accomplished, and know that he had fulfilled his ambitions. The fruits of his labor surrounded him and filled his heart with joy, but also with anxiety; for after he was gone who would tend to his empire? Most of the projects that he had developed in the last two decades were not extremely stable economically, although they contained the seeds of their own and the region's future success. In the late thirties they still depended on his own personal ingenuity and fortune for their maintenance. Penrose, determined not to lose control of what he had worked so hard to build, had a plan.

ABOVE: Penrose's modest resting place on the slopes of Cheyenne Mountain grew in both size and purpose until it became the Will Rogers Shrine of the Sun, which Penrose hoped would be a stopping place for tourists on their way up to the Cheyenne Lodge. Circa 1946.

Broadmoor Historical Collection

A New Perspective

S PENCER PENROSE HAD NOT neglected to see to the fate of his ever-increasing fortune. Just as he had fitted out the Broadmoor Hotel for its embarkation into a new decade, so had he tended to his personal affairs. Pragmatic as always, he had begun taking steps in 1937 to ensure that his fortune and the many initiatives that he had launched in his lifetime would not be scattered to the winds, but rather maintained as part of a complete whole and properly tended. Penrose realized that upon the death of such a wealthy person as himself, the government could help itself to at least a third of his estate. The election of President Roosevelt in 1933 further strengthened his resolve: He, a staunch Republican, would rather give his money away than hand it over to a Democrat whose New Deal policies were anathema to Penrose's way of thinking. Given that Julie was independently wealthy, and they had no issue, Penrose decided that giving it away was not such a bad idea after all.

Speck's friends and business partners from Utah, the Guggenheims, had set up the Guggenheim Foundation to administer funds for charitable causes in 1922. Penrose determined that a foundation of his own was the perfect solution to his problem. In December of 1937, El Pomar Foundation was incorporated. Among its assets were the Broadmoor Hotel Incorporated and El Pomar Investment Company, the holding company which managed most of Penrose's investments and business interests. The Foundation was (and is) governed by a board of five members who make all of the decisions regarding the properties owned by the Foundation and the distribution of funds to those in need. The first members of the board were: Spencer Penrose, President; Henry McAllister, Penrose's lawyer from Denver; William Howbert, a Colorado Springs businessman; Charles L. Tutt, Jr.; and Merton W. Bogart, Penrose's personal secretary.

The Foundation's purpose as stated in its Articles of Organization is *"To receive and maintain a fund or funds and to apply the principal and*

The resort is transformed into an internationally known meeting place for athletes, world-class competitions, conferences and travelers.

LEFT: Oil painting of Spencer Penrose by Julian Story dated 1915, it hangs in El Pomar Office Building.

Courtesy El Pomar Foundation
Bill Bowers photo

income thereof and any other property or funds of the corporation to such charitable uses and purposes (including public, educational, scientific and benevolent uses and purposes) exclusively, as will, in the absolute and uncontrolled discretion of the Trustees of the corporation, most effectively assist, encourage and promote the general well-being of the inhabitants of the State of Colorado . . ." Although the Foundation's primary purpose is a charitable one, its implicit purpose was to provide the financial support and guidance necessary to maintain Penrose's empire. In the years since 1937, El Pomar Foundation has made more than 160 million dollars in grants, all within the state of Colorado, Penrose's adopted home. The foundation's assets have continued to increase in value; in 1993 they totalled 300 million dollars.

This done, Penrose, like a tired Atlas, could hand the responsibility for this world of his own creation onto another's back and prepare himself for the end. He spent his last year, 1939, in Hawaii with Julie, with various physicians in Chicago and elsewhere, and, ultimately in his bedroom at El Pomar. The south wall of this room contains a large picture window which frames Cheyenne Mountain and the Broadmoor Hotel. Speck spent his last days gazing at the vista that had so inspired him when he first arrived in Colorado Springs, and the many things that he had done to change it. He died in his El Pomar bedroom at 12:50 am on December 7, 1939, at the age of seventy-four.

Julie was shattered by the loss of the man who had been the center of her life for thirty-three years, but she took up the reins where he had dropped them and business continued as usual at the Broadmoor Hotel. Upon the death of Spencer Penrose, Julie assumed the presidency of El Pomar Foundation and El Pomar Investment Company, the parent company of the Broadmoor Hotel. During 1940 she also acted as President of the Broadmoor Hotel, but before the end of the year she hired Charles L. Tutt Jr. to hold this position. He was also made Vice President of El Pomar Investment Company and of El Pomar Foundation.

Charles Tutt had worked for Penrose in his offices in the Mining Exchange building in downtown Colorado Springs since shortly after his

Mrs. Spencer Penrose gratefully acknowledges your kind expression of sympathy

ABOVE: When Spencer died, Julie sent mourning cards such as this one to friends and associates.

Courtesy Fountion Valley School
Bill Bowers photo

RIGHT: Although Spencer Penrose had a reputation as a taciturn and difficult person, he was not without sentiment. When he visited his beloved zoo, he enjoyed riding on this elaborate carousel with children who neither knew nor cared of his exalted position in society.

Myron Wood photo,
Broadmoor Historical Collection

Aerial view of the Broadmoor area after Penrose's death. The hotel's success brought many other residents to the area. The large oval in the foreground is the Cheyenne Mountain Country Club polo field.

father's death in 1909. While working for Penrose he also maintained some of the business interests left to him by his father. In 1918, he joined Julie Penrose on the first board of the Broadmoor Art Academy, and the two established a friendship that would continue for decades. Tutt was one of the few members of the Broadmoor Hotel and Land Company board of directors who had been actively involved in the running of the hotel. During the twenties he served as President of the Broadmoor Golf Club and assisted Penrose in many other aspects of the hotel's management. When Penrose moved his offices from the Mining Exchange Building out to the Broadmoor Hotel, Tutt moved with him. In the 1930s, Tutt became Managing Director of the hotel and assumed positions on the boards of several of Penrose's companies. In the late thirties, however, he resigned from the Penrose enterprises, returned to his downtown office and continued the operations of his own affairs until Julie offered him the Presidency of the hotel after Spencer Penrose's death.

In the midst of her grief, Julie Penrose set about the task of settling Spencer's estate. The size of the estate and the number of beneficiaries necessitated an enormous amount of paperwork and appearances in probate court. At the time of his death, the value of Penrose's estate was just sixteen million dollars due to the fact that he had already given the bulk of his fortune to El Pomar Foundation before his death. The beneficiaries included staff, relatives and several clubs and organizations he had belonged to. She took her new role as administrator quite seriously and was active in the boards on which she served. She maintained offices on the second floor of Northmoor (where the sales and conference offices are today) with her secretary Roland Giggey and his secretary Lillian McDermott. She continued to travel, though not as often as before, and mourned Spencer until the day of her death. She wore black in some proportion for the remaining fifteen years of her life and tears sprang to her eyes whenever his name was mentioned. Although she chose not to be involved in the administration of the hotel, she continued to monitor all of the design and artistic aspects of the building and ensured that its character and charm remained intact.

BELOW: Zoo Director Robert Menary taking one of his charges for a walk in the snow.

Courtesy of John and Catherine Calder

Charley Tutt took up where Penrose had left off, and continued the building and development of the Broadmoor properties as Penrose would have wished. He took particular care of the zoo, which had been near to Penrose's heart, and a great source of pleasure for himself as well. In 1938, Penrose had incorporated the Cheyenne Mountain Zoo as a separate non-profit organization whose purpose was to provide recreational, educational and scientific facilities in the field of zoology, but the hotel and the Foundation remained involved in the zoo's administration. Under Robert Menary's direction, the zoo continued to expand, with emphasis on exotic and little-known animals. Animals were garnered from all over the world, and despite the altitude and climate, which were unfamiliar for some, seemed to thrive on the mountain air.

Business steadily improved at the hotel: There was, after all, no way to go but up! Levels of occupancy in 1941 were better than they had been in ten years. The number of conventions slowly increased, as did the number of out-of-town visitors. It became more and more difficult, however, for Americans to stay out of the war that was raging in Europe, and on December 7, 1941 when the Japanese bombed Pearl Harbor, America was, once again, at war.

The war, however, had begun in 1939 for Julie Penrose with the commencement of hostilities in Europe. Remembering their internment during World War I, the Count and Countess de Ways Ruart left Europe as soon as it was clear that war was imminent. They stayed at El Pomar for the duration. Gladys' presence helped Julie make it through the terrible time following Spencer's death. They worried constantly, however, about the fate of Pauline who was still in German-occupied Belgium with her husband the Baron de Selys Longchamps and six young children. Julie spent hours praying in the Pauline Chapel in the hopes that God would not force yet another tragedy into a life that had suffered so many of them. Her prayers went unanswered, however, for although all of the De Selys Longchamps survived the war, Pauline died during an operation to remove a tumor from her brain in 1953.

Shortly thereafter, Gladys fell ill with Multiple Sclerosis and was confined to a wheelchair for the rest of her life.

Although travel was restricted for most Americans during the war, the Broadmoor Hotel did not lack for residents nor for patrons at its many bars and restaurants. In summer of 1942 a small army camp south of Colorado Springs named Camp Carson was transformed into an infantry training base and became the destination for over 35,000 troops and their families. This influx of people doubled the population of Colorado Springs in less than a year, and although the soldiers did not flood the Broadmoor Hotel, military officials frequented the Tavern and the Hawaiian Village with great regularity.

Broadmoor sporting events continued: Golf, tennis and polo tournaments were held, but the names of the participants all had military titles before them. As the war went on, the Broadmoor made all of its sporting venues

ABOVE: Charles L. Tutt Jr. as a young man.

Courtesy R. Thayer Tutt Jr.

available to soldiers at no or minimal charge, especially those who had returned from the front and were recovering from injuries. The most famous of these was Major General Uzal G. Ent, former commander of the Second Air Force who was paralyzed from the waist down when the plane he was flying was hit in 1944. He spent the summer of 1946 at the Broadmoor Hotel where he broadcast radio programs for disabled veterans describing his recovery and encouraging them to "build hope out of despair."

Guests at the hotel also included officer overflow from Camp Carson and Peterson Air Force Base who took rooms in the hotel at reduced rates and found little to complain about. The Broadmoor's hospitality, and par-

ticularly its excellent liquor supply, endeared the hotel and the Pikes Peak region to numerous military officers. Many came back to visit or to settle in Colorado Springs when they retired.

The hotel was seriously understaffed, for many employees had left to join the war effort, but those that remained kept the standards of service as high as possible. The staff was supplemented by Julie Penrose's decision to hire Japanese Americans who had been interned in camps in southern Colorado. Julie was affronted by the government's behavior towards its own citizens and sought to remedy the insult by a personal gesture of her own. She had a great deal of respect and admiration for Japanese culture as a result of her many trips to China and Japan and her fondness for Oriental art. Executive Chef, Louis Stratta, and other managers were sent to the camps with instructions to hire those that had some aptitude for the hotel-restaurant business. Many employees who were hired at that time stayed on at the Broadmoor long after the end of the hostilities and contributed greatly to the Broadmoor's success.

The Broadmoor Hotel was not without important civilian guests during this period. The Baron Von Seidlitz, a German nobleman who had left Germany with the rise of Fascism, and the Baroness, an American (née Frieda Frausch an heiress from New Orleans whose family was in the sugar processing business) were asked by the United States government to leave the East Coast. They had a suite at the Broadmoor Hotel for the duration of the war and gave some of the most lavish parties that the hotel had ever hosted.

Thus, the Broadmoor survived yet another difficult time in America's history and emerged unscathed and ready to greet what would hopefully be a long period of prosperity. After the war, the hotel once again required a great deal of renovation and restoration. The need for new furniture, paint and a general putting in order sent staff and workmen scrambling all over the hotel. The prospect of increased occupancy dictated the construction of two more wings, Northeastmoor and Southeastmoor, which were built on either side of the hotel's circular drive. To make outdoor swimming a possibility all year round, a heated outdoor pool was constructed out onto the lake which supplanted the guest beach. The pool is surrounded by a high glass wall which blocks the wind and allows swimmers to bask under the Colorado sun even in the midst of winter.

In the 1950s the lobby was expanded to the north and escalators were installed to partially resolve one of the few problems inherent in the design

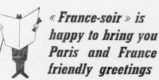

France-soir

LE SEUL QUOTIDIEN FRANÇAIS VENDANT PLUS D'UN MILLION

« France-soir » is happy to bring you Paris and France friendly greetings

N° 5.012 - Gui. 98-80. Cen.20-90
100, rue Réaumur — PARIS (2ᵉ)
Boîte Postale 142-02

Vendredi 2 Septembre 1960
344ᵉ jour de l'année

NF 0,25
(25 fr.)

ALGERIE : NF 0.30 - MAROC : 33 fr. mar. TUNI-
SIE : 27 m. - BELG.-LUX. : 3 fr. 50 SUISSE :
0 h. 25 - ESPAGNE : Pesetas 3.50 - ITALIE : 50 lires

ÉDITION SPÉCIALE SOUVENIR

Directement de Paris (Seine) à Colorado Springs (Colorado)

LE PAQUEBOT « FRANCE » ACCOSTE
DEVANT L'HOTEL BROADMOOR

Les premières photos de ce merveilleux exploit

17 HEURES : Le « France » débouche dans le lac

(De notre envoyé spécial)
COLORADO SPRINGS, 2 septembre. — Miraculeusement piloté par Mlle Carol Truax et M. Leslie Dorsey, le paquebot « France » est arrivé à l'hôtel Broadmoor. Le magnifique navire s'est amarré dans la piscine du Palace.

Les opérations d'accostage se sont déroulées sans incidents. Elles étaient terminées à 18 heures (heure locale).

Passeport s'il vous plait...

SEULS participent à ce voyage féerique, dont le bénéfice reviendra à la « Maison de l'Espoir », une école pour les enfants caractériels, les titulaires du passeport ci-contre.

Ils ont été sélectionnés par les dirigeantes de l'Association des Jeunes de Colorado Springs. Vous les voyez au travail, à l'ombre de la Tour Eiffel.

De gauche à droite, voici Mrs. Philip W. Bissel, rapporteur de la Commission des ressources ; Mrs. John E. M. C. Williams, vice-présidente et Mrs. Edwards B. Liddle, présidente de l'Association des Jeunes.

---

of the hotel: the lack of elevators. The main building has only one guest elevator which serves all of the residential floors as well as the mezzanine. The installation of the escalators made it possible for large numbers of people to ascend and descend rapidly, especially during social functions. The Tavern, which had become a favorite spot for Colorado Springs' residents and hotel guests alike, also needed to be expanded. The architects Lord and Burnham created a transitional area out of what were originally the children's and servants' dining rooms and then added on a glassed-in greenhouse complete with trees growing up through the floor and a fountain at the north end.

ABOVE: When the Chambre Syndicale de la Haute Couture Parisienne held its 1960 fashion show at the Broadmoor Hotel, the French newspaper *France-soir* printed a special edition from Colorado Springs.

Broadmoor Historical Collection
Bill Bowers photo

The lobby and transitional area of the Tavern, called the Mayan Room, were painted by a local artisan/craftsman by the name of Theobald Christen Willumsen, a Danish immigrant who had worked on the interior decorations of many of Europe's great manor houses. In the lobby he created ceiling panels which continued the themes on the ceiling of the original lobby and added some heraldic motifs. In the Mayan room he executed the architect's design for a complicated intertwining pattern of South American Indian motifs that give the area a great deal of character and interesting detail.

Willumsen also painted the ceilings in the Pauline Chapel and in Colorado College's Shove Chapel in addition to doing interior design work for many private homes.

Charley Tutt initiated and oversaw all of these developments with the assistance of three of his five children, whom he had assigned positions within the hotel and El Pomar Foundation. His second son, Thayer, became Vice President of the hotel in 1946, Russell, the third son, was given the post of Vice President of The Garden City Company in Kansas (one of El Pomar Foundation's holdings) and then joined Thayer in the Vice Presidency in 1956. Josephine took over the management of the stables, an appropriate choice given her passion for horses and exhibition events. Charley's first son Charles Leaming Tutt III and his fifth son John Wood Tutt by his second wife, Vesta, pursued other avenues of employment.

In December of 1944, after the Count and Countess had returned home to Belgium, Julie decided to leave El Pomar and came to live on the sixth floor of the Broadmoor Hotel. The house seemed too huge and empty to her now that she was alone, and by moving into the hotel itself she felt closer to Speck. The entire sixth floor was renovated and made into a private apartment with a dining room for entertaining, small kitchen, and sun room as well as numerous guest rooms. The suite was decorated with the antiques and fine art which had graced El Pomar. The house was donated to the Catholic Sisters of Charity, the organization that later owned and operated Penrose Hospital and Penrose Community Hospital. Shortly thereafter it became a retreat house for women. In 1991, the house was reacquired by El Pomar Foundation and transformed into a conference center for nonprofit groups. With the assistance of a historical preservationist, the Foundation renovated the structure and accumulated as many of the original furnishings as possible so that it looks as much as it did when the Penroses lived there.

General Doolittle in Broadmoor car with Charles Tutt. Doolittle was a war hero who led the 1942 air raid on Japan following the bombing of Pearl Harbor.

Broadmoor Historical Collection

During this, last, period of her life, Julie supplemented her duties on El Pomar and Broadmoor Hotel boards with cultural and charitable activities. When her friend, the architect Jan Ruhtenberg, moved to Colorado Springs in the early forties, she asked him to design a Carriage House Museum to house Penrose's collection of carriages and some of the other equestrian artifacts that he had collected. The museum opened in 1941 and since then has provided visitors with unusual visual perspectives both inside and out. Ruhtenberg was a Swede, of the Bauhaus school of architecture and furniture design, who had come to the States to teach in the architectural department of the Museum of Modern Art and Columbia University. In Sweden he had designed houses for King Gustav V and several other of the royal family as well as for Greta Garbo and Nelson Rockefeller in the United States.

In 1953, Ruhtenberg designed a private home for Julie where she could entertain her friends, or simply have some time away from the hotel. This house, which Julie called "The Shack" was built up on Cheyenne Mountain just a few hundred yards from Spencer's Cooking Club. She filled the house with oriental art works and antiques collected on her trips abroad. Julie also maintained a small home in Central City, where she helped to fund and support the revival of the annual summer opera festival. Her love of music and the arts did not wane in her later years, it seemed, rather, to be one of the things from which she derived the most solace.

In addition to her activities in Central City, she provided funds for several other organizations. Construction began on a new building for

ABOVE: Hood ornament of
Julie Penrose's Cadillac, housed
in the Carriage Museum.

Courtesy El Pomar Foundation
David Beightol photo

When her mother died Gladys
was too ill to leave Europe, but
her son-in-law, Baron M.
Francois de Selys Longchamps,
saw to it that the appropriate
social customs were observed.

Fountain Valley School

COUNTESS CORNET DE WAYS RUART

THE DAUGHTER OF MRS. SPENCER PENROSE

AND FAMILY

ACKNOWLEDGE WITH GRATEFUL APPRECIATION

YOUR KINDNESS AND SYMPATHY

St. Mary's High School in downtown Colorado
Springs in 1941. She endowed the Boys Club, continued to provide funding for the Fountain Valley
School and also constructed a parochial school—
the Pauline Memorial Catholic School—next to
the Pauline Chapel. The largest of her contributions was a 3.2 million dollar grant for the
building of the new Penrose Hospital. The funds
for these gifts came both from El Pomar Foundation and from her personal fortune.

Donations on such a grand scale, and her
increasing importance as a public figure, however, did not cause her to lose her charm or her
warmth on an individual level. All of those who
worked for her or whose life touched hers in some way remember her civility,
and her thoughtfulness. She made it possible for many of her employees,
or their children to attend
universities and helped them
in times of need. Despite the
many blows that life had
dealt her, she remained
serene, vivacious and cheerful until she entered the
hospital for exploratory surgery on December 26, 1956.
She died three weeks later
on January 23rd and was
buried next to Spencer in the Will Rogers Shrine of the Sun three days later.

In her later years, Julie Penrose was rarely without
her faithful companion PittyPat.

Courtesy Hermine Weber

The Tutts and the Modernization of the Broadmoor

ABOVE: Winter night shot of Broadmoor in the early 1940s.

Courtesy Joan Wyman

WITH THE PASSING OF Julie Penrose, the Broadmoor Hotel reached a turning point in its history. Julie had not wanted the hotel to change more than was absolutely necessary, but Charles Tutt, and especially his younger sons, realized that the era when a hotel could survive exclusively on tourist and summer occupancy was over. Times had changed in America and families no longer filled the resort for two or three months at a time during the summer. The Broadmoor Hotel needed a new vision that would carry it into the future and allow it to survive in a rapidly changing world.

The Broadmoor Ice Revue remains an annual tradition. The cast of this 1950 show includes Dick Button as well as Peter and Karol Kennedy (group of three in center of second row).

World Arena Pictorial Collection

BELOW: The Broadmoor World Arena's winning tradition carries on through the present. Jill Trenary of the Broadmoor Skating Club captured first place in the 1990 World Champion competition.

World Arena Pictorial Collection

After Julie's death, Charles Tutt assumed the presidency of El Pomar Investment Company and El Pomar Foundation. Shortly thereafter, he appointed his sons Wm. Thayer and Russell to the board of the Foundation, as well as to the boards of several other El Pomar-controlled companies. The Tutts began to make plans for a sweeping modernization of the entire property. These changes had actually begun before Julie's death, when Charles Tutt hired his son Thayer as Vice President of the hotel.

When Wm. Thayer Tutt first began working in the hotel's administration, he lost no time in expanding the Broadmoor's horizons. Like Penrose, he was interested in sports and realized both their intrinsic and promotional value, but he wished to elevate the Broadmoor facilities to international standards. The year after he became Vice President of the Broadmoor Hotel, 1947, he took a trip to New York and returned with the news that the Broadmoor Ice Palace would host not only the National Figure Skating Championships, but also the National Collegiate Ice Hockey Championship Play-Offs. This was only the beginning of Thayer's involvement in ice-oriented competition which led him all over the world and to his involvement with the United States Olympic Committee.[1]

The Pikes Peak Figure Skating Club (later the

_____

1. William Thayer Tutt was awarded the International Olympic Order in 1987 in recognition of his efforts and dedication to the promotion of international sporting competitions.

Broadmoor Skating Club) was organized in 1938 and from its humble beginnings as a small local skating club developed rapidly into a nationally known training ground for champion ice skaters. The Broadmoor Ice Palace was one of the few rinks in the country that remained open during the summer months and therefore the club attracted many skaters from all over the country who wished to be able to train all year round. A boarding house just north of the Broadmoor Hotel where many of the musicians in concert at the hotel also stayed became the skaters' "home away from home." The combination of lively young skaters and colorful musicians and singers made the Mayhurst boarding house a novel place to stay.

The club continued to grow in reputation and importance as the years progressed. When Carlo Fassi became Head Coach, Director of Skating and Ice Show Producer in 1961, his fame attracted students from many parts of the world. During the years of Fassi's directorship, there were as many as one hundred and fifty summer students at the Broadmoor. The skaters ranged in age from eight years to the late teens. The Broadmoor also attracted speed skaters who trained both at the rink and at Rosemont Reservoir, up in the foothills behind the hotel. Terry McDermott trained at Rosemont for several months prior to winning the only U.S. gold medal at the 1964 Olympics.

Many of these young athletes boarded with private families or stayed at the Mayhurst, but more accommodations were needed. In 1967, Wm. Thayer Tutt had a dormitory built which could accommodate up to forty-eight skaters. Beatty Hall, as the building was called, was named in honor of Henry M. Beatty, a World Judge and Referee who had long been a mem-

ABOVE: Peggy Fleming was one of the Broadmoor Skating Club's biggest stars. Here she skates on one of the frozen ponds at the Broadmoor after winning the gold medal at the 1968 winter Olympics in Grenoble.

Broadmoor Historical Collection

1971 World Cup Hockey game between USA and USSR.

Broadmoor Historical Collection

ABOVE: The Broadmoor International Center provides meeting and banquet space underneath the hyperbolic parabola of its ceiling.

Broadmoor Historical Collection, Bob McIntyre photo

ber of the Broadmoor Skating Club. The dormitory, run by Ursula and Joe Spiers, was booked for years in advance by skaters, hockey teams and members of the casts of visiting ice shows. Wm. Thayer Tutt, with initiatives like Beatty Hall, and all of the other activities that he undertook to support ice sports at the Broadmoor, managed to create a family-like, supportive atmosphere which created a number of world-class athletes and an extremely close-knit organization. Some of the most prominent members of the Broadmoor Skating Club include: Karol and Peter Kennedy, 1952 Olympic Silver Medalists in the pairs competition; Hayes Alan Jenkins, 1956 Olympic Men's Gold Medalist; David Jenkins, 1960 Olympic Men's Gold Medalist; Peggy Fleming, 1968 Olympic Ladies' Gold Medalist; Caryn Kadavy, 1987 Ladies' Bronze Medalist; Jill Trenary, 1990 Ladies' World Champion and Scott Davis, 1993 Champion of the United States.

The Ice Palace's name was changed to the "Broadmoor World Arena" in 1961 to reflect the facility's increasingly international status, and was enlarged to include locker rooms for the athletes, better seats and more retail services for spectators. The smaller, studio rink was added in 1968. The Arena has hosted athletes and events of major importance which are far too numerous to list here.[2] Many remember, however, the first time that Wm. Thayer Tutt brought the Soviet national team to the Broadmoor in 1958 for a number of demonstration games, and then the Walter A. Brown Memorial Tournament Series which began in 1964 with a game between the Denver University team and the Soviets. The game was broadcast on national television with commentator Bud Palmer and resulted in a surprising 4–4 tie. The tournament was held for four consecutive years and included more than twenty international teams. The Arena also hosted the hockey World Cup competitions several times during the seventies.

Wm. Thayer Tutt did not limit his promotional activities to the sporting arena, however. In 1949, the United States Government decided that the Air Force required an officer training academy and a commission was created to determine where it should be located. Communities across the country competed for the honor of having the Air Force Academy, and Colorado Springs maintained high visibility among the choices. The hospitality that the Broadmoor Hotel had extended to the armed services during the war had not gone unnoticed, and when the top brass of the Air Force

---

2. For a complete history, see *The Broadmoor World Arena Pictorial History Book* by Diane Lynn Betts and the staff of the Broadmoor World Arena, 1988.

convened for a discussion of air strike readiness in October of 1951, they chose the Broadmoor Hotel as their headquarters.

As late as 1954, still no decision had been made, but the list was narrowed down to three: Alton, Illinois; Lake Geneva, Wisconsin; and Colorado Springs, Colorado. Thayer Tutt and Russell Law, the co-chairmen of the Chamber of Commerce Military Affairs Committee, along with all of the other members lobbied long and hard to prove that Colorado Springs was the ideal site. This effort included a great deal of hospitality and entertainment of the selection committee at the Broadmoor Hotel, the Penrose Stadium, the Fine Arts Center and the Colorado College. In the end, the city's climate and location, the committee's persuasive powers and the cultural and economic legacy left by the Penroses convinced the members of the selection committee who voted four to one in favor of Colorado Springs.

As Charles L. Tutt Jr. reached the end of his life, he too could rest secure in the knowledge that he was passing the hotel on to capable hands. His son Thayer had already proved himself a successful promoter who, in just a few years, had projected the Broadmoor Hotel and its sports facilities onto the international scene. Russell, in a much quieter and reserved way, had been gaining expertise in the world of finance. Since 1946, he had been the Vice President and General Manager of the Garden City, Company (a vast real estate and sugar production company in Kansas) in addition to his other administrative duties at the hotel. When Charley Tutt died on November 1, 1961, his sons assumed the positions that he

Wm.Thayer and Russell Tutt survey the site of Robert Trent Jones Sr.'s new course. 1964.

Broadmoor Historical Collection.
Bob McIntyre photo

had held on the boards of El Pomar Foundation, El Pomar Investment Company and the Broadmoor Hotel. Charles' passing marked the end of the first generation of the Broadmoor and with the advent of the 1960s the next generation began its stewardship.

Wm. Thayer Tutt had already submitted plans for enlarging the Broadmoor Hotel to the board of the Foundation in 1959. He and Russell believed that expanding the hotel so that it could handle the booming convention trade was the only way for the Broadmoor to survive. The plans included the building of a new tower on the south side of the hotel which would provide an additional one hundred and forty-four guest rooms, meeting facilities, and a penthouse restaurant. The construction of this building entailed razing the Colonial Club building, the oldest edifice on the property. The wooded area that had surrounded the Colonial Club was made into a parking lot for the new complex. The Broadmoor South tower, designed by Carlisle Guy and Edwin Francis, is nine stories high. Each room has a dramatic view either east or west of the hotel. The restaurant at the top, named the Penrose Room, made it possible for guests to avail themselves of the most sophisticated cuisine to be found in the area while gazing out over the dramatic landscape that had inspired Palmer and Penrose.

With significantly more room for guests (upon completion of Broadmoor South the hotel's capacity grew from 248 rooms to 392) the hotel also required a large meeting hall. Thus, plans were made for the construction of the International Center, a building able to seat 2,400 spectators in auditorium style seating or serve circa 1,600 at a banquet. The International Center, built across Lake Circle from the hotel, was also designed by Guy and Francis. The building's plans called for a hyperbolic parabaloid, an architectural form much in vogue at the time. The structure's roof is an arched parabola which touches the ground at four points quite distant from each other. In this way, the open area within it is maximized without the interference of columns or other internal support systems. The conference space is extremely versatile and adapts itself easily to the needs of the many conventions that meet there. Although primarily planned for use by large conferences, after the International Center was completed it was used as an entertainment facility as well.

As these two major construction efforts were underway, Thayer and Russell Tutt hired the New York firm of W. & J. Sloane to redecorate the common rooms in the main building as well as to design the interiors for the two new buildings. Marshall Morin, a Colorado Springs interior designer, updated the decor of the older bedrooms and many other areas of the hotel. In Broadmoor South, the Sloanes created a regally formal interior reminiscent of European villas, with expanses of marble floors, rich fabrics and shining mirrors. The tapestry that hangs in the lobby and depicts Penrose in front of his accomplishments was commissioned by V'soske, as were all of the original carpets.

An unusual feature of the International Center is an English pub called the Golden Bee. The paneling and fixtures of an entire pub had been shipped from England in the 1800s and stored in a New York warehouse. The decorators, thinking that an authentic pub would be quite appropriate in a town once called "Little London," offered it to Thayer Tutt. Tutt decided to recreate the pub on the ground floor of the International Center, thus utilizing an otherwise wasted space. T.C. Willumsen, the artisan who did all of the new painting in the hotel's main building, removed more than twenty layers of varnish from the African mahogany interior and restored its original oil finish. The ceiling and furnishings were all carefully chosen to match the period and create the appropriate mood. The Hotel's administration was not delighted with the pub idea. They thought that the Bee was yet another of Wm. Thayer's extravagant ideas and he had to argue with board members at length to obtain the funds for its construction. After it was completed, a number of initiatives were implemented to publicize the Golden Bee including a ragtime piano player with a repertoire of sing-a-long songs and the Order of the Pewter Tankard, which made the Golden Bee an overwhelming success. The Order of the Pewter Tankard (members of which have a pewter tankard inscribed with their names on the walls of the pub to use as their own personal drinking vessel) has grown to such size that there is a waiting list to join. Visiting dignitaries at the Broadmoor Hotel who enjoyed the pub were formally inducted into the Royal Order of Rum-anian Fusel-Oil-Leers, and given a medal and tri-corner hat to wear in the Golden Bee. This prestigious group includes many prominent generals and military men, as well as guests such as Gerald Ford and John Wayne. The Golden Bee continues to offer an assortment of classic English ales and beers in the hotel's tradition of the finest in fermented beverages.

In this total reconception of the Broadmoor's interiors, the hotel lost the simple elegance that had been Julie's trademark, and adopted a much

more ornate appearance. The ceilings in the ballroom, mezzanine lounge and the golf club were painted in contrasting colors so that their intricate details would be more evident. The wallcoverings and furnishings went from Renaissance to Baroque in design. Progress always has a price, and for the Broadmoor, joining the ranks of the world's top resorts meant forfeiting some of its original simplicity and charm in exchange for worldliness and sophistication. The clientele continued to expand and encompass travelers and conventions from around the world and all over the United States. International fashion shows became yearly events. In 1960 the hotel hosted the officials of the "Chambre Syndicale de la Haute Couture Parisienne" whose meeting included a fashion show in the Broadmoor's ballroom where designs by Pierre Cardin, Hermes, and Nina Ricci, among others, were modeled. The success of these multi-national events was in large part due to the hotel's staff which included many foreign born experts in the hotel and restaurant business who catered to guests' every whim.

THE BROADMOOR GOLF Club continued to grow and expand over the years and also brought numerous luminaries to the hotel's door. Lewis B. Maytag replaced Charles L. Tutt, Jr. as President of the Golf Club when Tutt became the President of the hotel. Under Maytag's guidance, the club hosted tournaments of increasing importance. The Trans-Mississippi was held on the Broadmoor links six times, as were three National Collegiate Championships hosted by Colorado College. Lewis B. Maytag (heir to the Maytag Washer fortune) was an excellent golfer himself and actively promoted both tennis and golf at the Broadmoor.[3] He had the honor of presenting the winner's cup to "Babe" Didrikson Zaharias on the occasions of her winning the Broadmoor Women's Invitational Tournament in 1945, 1946 and 1947. Wm. Thayer Tutt replaced Bud Maytag as President in 1950.

Ed Dudley became the club's professional in 1941 and his contacts in the entertainment and professional world did a great deal for the promotion of the club. He toured the country with his friends Bing Crosby and Bob Hope playing golf matches to raise money for war bonds. On one of Crosby and Hope's frequent stays at the Broadmoor, Crosby was asked to donate a personal object to a traveling museum for American soldiers abroad. On the steps of the Broadmoor Golf Club, Bing took the shirt off his back and handed it to Fred Corcoran who took the collection to the troops in Europe. Dudley was also President of the Professional Golfers Association and thus furthered the national prominence of the Broadmoor

---

3. The Maytags had come to Colorado Springs from Newton, Iowa, so that L.B.'s sister Frieda could be treated by Dr. Webb for her lung ailment.

course.[4] One of his most famous pupils was Dwight D. Eisenhower, who often came to visit and play golf with his old teacher. After Ed Dudley died, the Broadmoor hired Dow Finsterwald, who had won a total of twelve PGA tour matches, including the Vardon Trophy, when he joined the Broadmoor Golf Club in 1963. He was a member of Ryder Cup teams for many years and was non-playing captain of the victorious 1977 team. He continues to play in Senior Tournaments and teaches on the Broadmoor course at the time of this writing.

In 1958 Robert Trent Jones Sr. was hired to design an additional nine-hole golf course. He also redesigned the original course so that nine holes remained together and then incorporated the other nine into a new eighteen-hole course. The smaller course, called the "Broadmoor Nine," was laid out so that club members and guests could play while tournaments were in progress on the championship eighteen. He was invited back in 1964 to expand the Nine into the hotel's second 18-hole golf course. This course, which lies to the west of the first eighteen, is considered even more challenging. Given that they are closer to the mountains, the greens have a steeper slope than the first eighteen. A more capacious hotel and the first 36-hole

ABOVE: Drawing of Broadmoor golf courses after Robert Trent Jones Sr. completed the second 18-hole golf course in 1965.

Broadmoor Historical Collection

---

4. Ed Dudley was the head professional at the Broadmoor Golf Club for twenty-two years. He died at Penrose Hospital in November of 1963 and was elected to the Golf Hall of Fame eleven months later.

ABOVE: Bing Crosby taking the shirt off his back on the steps of the Broadmoor Golf Club. Fred Corcoran, left, was collecting celebrity items to exhibit to American soldiers in Europe. Circa 1943.

Broadmoor Historical Collection,
T.O. Johnson photo

golf course in Colorado ensured that the club would host larger tournaments, the most significant of which include: the 1962 International Curtis Cup Match, 1967 U.S.G.A. Men's Amateur Championships, 1963 U.S.G.A. Women's Western Amateur Championships (won by Barbara McIntire of the Broadmoor Golf Club), and many others.

Several women members of the Broadmoor Golf Club have acquired national and international titles. Barbara McIntire won the U.S. Women's Amateur Championships in 1959 and 1964, as well as the British Amateur title in 1960. Judy Bell has been a member and captain of the U.S. Curtis Cup team and was the first woman member of the U.S. Golf Association. She is currently the only woman officer on the U.S.G.A. executive committee.

The first annual Seniors Golf Tournament was held at the Broadmoor in August of 1960. Chick Evans had nurtured the idea for formal Seniors play for years, and was finally able to make it a reality on a course that had always been an important part of his life. Chick Evans first played the Broadmoor course in 1918 when Penrose engaged him to play with Jim Barnes against Jock Hutchinson and Warren Wood in the course's first public tournament, and he had remained a faithful member since that time. Evans was the General Chairman for the Seniors Tourney, and the funds accumulated went to the Chick Evans Scholars Foundation. The Seniors Tournament has become an institution and is now an international competition which brings teams from over twenty-eight different countries to the Broadmoor each year.

Although the levels of play on the tennis courts did not reach those of the golf course, tennis pro Chet Murphy organized the Broadmoor Family Invitation Tennis Tournament which attracted many players from Colorado and around the country. The tournament, limited to doubles play, was sanctioned by the United States Lawn Tennis Association and was first held in 1954.[5]

The Broadmoor Hotel's transformation during this era included some radical changes in the hotel's interior organization and structure. The first floor of the hotel, half of which had been dedicated to the swimming pool, Turkish baths, massage and sauna rooms, was made into administrative and commercial areas. The swimming pool was closed and covered over. The lower portion became a storage area and a renovated drugstore which included a soda fountain and snack service was put in at the lobby level. De-

---

5. Chet Murphy was elected to the National Collegiate Tennis Hall of Fame in 1985 based on his performance as tennis coach for 25 years at the University of California at Berkeley (his occupation during the winter months). Murphy is considered one of the best teachers in the history of American tennis and has published numerous books on the subject. He taught at the Broadmoor from 1948 to 1987.

clining interest in riding and especially polo caused the hotel to dismantle the polo program and put less emphasis on the maintenance of the bridle paths.

To replace these sports, the slopes of Cheyenne Mountain were molded into a small ski resort, Ski Broadmoor, which provided a double chair lift, man-made snow to supplant the light snowfall in the Colorado Springs area, and a gentle lower slope which was perfect for beginning skiers. The upper part of Ski Broadmoor was designed as a racing slope for competition skiing, and was used as the training ground for the highly successful Broadmoor Ski Team. The slope hosted an Invitational International Slalom Derby in 1961 which featured skiers from seven European countries who had competed in the 1960 Olympics. This was not the Broadmoor's first attempt to provide skiing facilities for guests. Penrose had given financial and administrative support to Don Lawrie and the Pikes Peak Ski Club when they built a small ski resort and lodge at Glen Cove, on the slopes of Pikes Peak in the early 1940s. Although the resort was popular because it was so close to Colorado Springs, lack of adequate snowfall made it impossible to maintain. In 1991, Ski Broadmoor closed as well, due to escalating insurance and maintenance costs. The hotel is so close to Colorado's network of large and versatile ski resorts that maintaining such a limited facility at the hotel became unreasonable.

The skeet and trap shooting area, which had provided shooting facilities for guests since the 1920s, were

ABOVE: Broadmoor Golf Pro Ed Dudley gives his friend and student, Bob Hope, a few tips on his swing.

Broadmoor Historical Collection

The Broadmoor Golf Club was modified numerous times as the resort grew. When the Hawaiian Village closed, the roof terrace was used for air filtering and conditioning equipment.

Broadmoor Historical Collection

RIGHT: Synchronized divers at outdoor pool for promotional picture. Divers are Joan Wyman, Edgar McVehil and Doug Gregory. 1949.

Courtesy of Joan Wyman
photo Bob McIntyre

ABOVE: Abercrombie and Fitch, which opened a shop on the mezzanine level of the South Tower in 1961, managed the skeet shooting grounds for several years.

Courtesy of Siegfried Faller Jr.

rejuvenated and repositioned when the hotel's director of Sales and Conferences, Siegfried Faller, Jr. (an avid sportsman who was with the hotel for thirty years) updated the facility in 1974. When the new competition, Sporting Clays,[6] became popular in the eighties, the Hotel built a course which opened in 1986. The quality of the course was such that it quickly gained international renown and was chosen as the site for the Sporting Clays International Grand Prix in 1990 and the Pan-American Championships in 1991. Although several resort hotels now provide facilities for the sport, the Broadmoor was the first hotel to do so, and has added another range to the original one.

The expansion and modernization of the hotel's grounds, as well as increased emphasis on sales and marketing allowed the hotel to gradually increase its sales and to attain profitability as a business venture. This was due, in large part to Russell Tutt and Karl Eitel. Tutt took over the financial management of El Pomar Foundation and the Broadmoor Hotel upon his father's death and Karl Eitel was hired by Wm. Thayer as Resident Manager in 1961. Eitel's management of the hotel ensured that all of the newly constructed facilities of the hotel operated smoothly.

---

6. The sport requires that the competitors walk through a wooded trail and shoot clays which are projected in such a way as to simulate live birds.

Russell Tutt, who succeeded his brother as President of the Broadmoor Hotel in 1975, was a very quiet and reserved man, a counterweight to his brother's flamboyant, extroverted personality. The two brothers ran the Foundation and the Hotel for almost thirty years during which period their two characters balanced each other out. Thayer had creative, wild ideas for the promotion of the hotel and Russell assessed the plans to determine whether or not they were economically and practically feasible. The combination of the two personalities provided the hotel with a charismatic leader who attracted many clients and a sensible administrator who made choices which allowed the hotel to survive economically.

Russell was less involved in the Broadmoor Hotel than Thayer also because he devoted a great deal of time to El Pomar Foundation and to representing the Foundation in the community. The Broadmoor had always had an especially close relationship with Colorado College, a highly respected liberal arts college in downtown Colorado Springs. Over the years the college held most of its important social events on the Broadmoor mezzanine, its swimming events and competitions in the indoor pool, football games in the stadium and hockey games in the Ice Palace. Russell Tutt further cemented this relationship by becoming a trustee of Colorado College in 1957 (chairman of the board from 1966–84) and directing a great deal of money from El Pomar Foundation towards the promotion and development of the school. Russell Tutt also served on the board of the Fountain Valley School and participated in many other community and business organizations.

In the early 1970s it was clear that the hotel needed

ABOVE: Jack Nicklaus won the first major tournament of his career on the Broadmoor links in 1959. He is shown receiving the trophy for his U.S. Men's Amateur Championship victory and shaking hands with runner-up Charlie Coe (left).

Broadmoor Historical Collection, photo Bob McIntyre

L.B. Maytag presenting trophy to the winner of the Broadmoor Ladies Invitational Tournament, Babe Didrikson Zaharias (at right with handbag).

Broadmoor Historical Collection, T.O. Johnson photo

even more space for guests and for events. The stadium across the lake no longer served the needs of the hotel, or of its clientele, and the administration decided to move the arena to another location and build the Broadmoor West complex in its place. In 1973, plans were drawn up by Carlisle Guy for a four-story building that stretched across the west side of the lake and provided one hundred fifty-six additional rooms without obstructing the view of the mountains from the main hotel. The west complex, completed in 1976, has ample meeting areas, and another fine restaurant, Charles Court, which borders the lake.

For the first eight years of its existence, Charles Court was the domain of Chef Herbert J. Uerdingen, a master chef who had been hired in Germany in 1962 by Wm. Thayer Tutt. Uerdingen began his Broadmoor career in the Penrose Room, but upon completion of the West complex became chef and Maître d' of Charles Court. The menu listed over four dozen main courses, all developed or invented by Uerdingen. The range of dishes reflected his background in traditional Continental cuisine (for which the Penrose Room is justly famous), but in Charles Court he was able to concentrate on the dramatic tableside presentations and his inventive variations on classic themes which became the restaurant's trademark. After his retirement in 1983, the restaurant maintained its popularity although the menu is now more oriented towards American regional cooking so that guests have a range of dining options to choose from.

While the West complex was under construction, another eighteen-hole golf course was laid out, bringing the total number of championship 18-hole courses at the Broadmoor to three. This last course was designed by Ed Seay and Arnold Palmer and offers many technical challenges. The South clubhouse, perched on the lower slopes of Cheyenne Mountain offers

Charles Court combines innovative American cuisine with a lakeside panorama. When the trees are lit for the holidays, the atmosphere is magical.

David Beightol photo

The Broadmoor Golf Club's Barbara McIntyre (left) and Judy Bell (right) at the 1976 Broadmoor Ladies Invitational with Debbie Massey (holding cup), who defeated Nancy Lopez (2nd from right).

Broadmoor Historical Collection, photo Bob McIntyre

yet another dining opportunity at Spencer's restaurant as well as a unique view of the southern foothills. The golf course project was followed by the construction of Colorado Hall in 1982. This building, adjacent to the International Center, provides another 18,000 square feet of exhibition and convention space, which allows the Broadmoor Conference Center to meet the increasingly technological and specific demands of the conferences that meet there.

In July of 1988 El Pomar Foundation was obligated by the Federal Tax Reform Act of 1969 to sell controlling interest in the Broadmoor Hotel, Manitou & Pikes Peak Cog Railway and the Manitou Incline. Congress had determined that it was unfair for charitable foundations to run for-profit businesses and required that foundations divest themselves of fifty percent of these properties by the year 1989 and an additional fifteen percent by the year 2004. El Pomar Foundation fought the law at length, arguing that the Penrose legacy was a unique one, but failed to obtain an exemption.

Thus, having attained seventy years of age, the Broadmoor Hotel lost its patron and ventured out of its protected fold into the world. The new owner of the Broadmoor Hotel is planning an ambitious future for this grande dame of the resort industry. He, like Penrose, built a great fortune with his own two hands. And he, too, wants the Broadmoor Hotel to sparkle in its setting and attain the most glorious of reputations among other world-class hostelries.

Fascinating People

THE BROADMOOR HOTEL, like all great hotels, radiates an atmosphere of beauty and mystery which is strangely conducive to romance and attractive to those who have attained fame and fortune. The rooms and stages of the Broadmoor have hosted some of the best known and loved entertainers of their time as well as distinguished members of a wide range of professions. Penrose invited a number of celebrities to his hotel and then shamelessly exploited them for publicity purposes, but he saw to it that they were treated royally in exchange for their trouble and many came back for more. When Mr. William Gibbs McAdoo, former right-hand man to President Wilson, and his wife, the President's daughter, stayed at the Broadmoor for a week, Mr. McAdoo commented "And I want to say that I didn't realize that the Broadmoor was the beautiful institution that we found it to be. The men who founded it have a local patriotism that is remarkable, and they also had a vision of what travelers want. One seldom finds in hotels and resorts what he wants, but here we are perfectly contented."[1] As the hotel gained an increasingly fashionable reputation, people came to see and be seen, as well as to enjoy the Broadmoor itself.

While the Penroses were alive, the hotel was populated with prominent politicians, athletes and personalities who dutifully had their pictures taken at various scenic locations and then seriously devoted themselves to being entertained. John D. Rockefeller was the hotel's first celebrity. He attended the hotel's informal opening party on June 1, 1918. He and his wife had checked into their rooms the afternoon before the party, but the fumes from the wet paint were so strong that the couple finally had to move down to the Antlers Hotel for the night. The family returned again later, when the paint was dry, and managed to complete their vacation. On the

The wealthy, talented, beautiful and newsworthy who have passed through the Broadmoor left a trail of tantalizing stories.

AT LEFT: Jon and Vivian Williams tripped their heels with Fred Astaire prior to moving permanently to the Broadmoor.

Courtesy of Jon and Vivian Williams

---

1. As reported in the *Colorado Springs Evening Telegraph* May 18, 1920.

occasions of Will Rogers' visits, Penrose treated him like a king and provided him with every luxury the Broadmoor had to offer. When Spencer Tracy came to the Broadmoor in April of 1939, he agreed to participate in a well-publicized polo match. The team included Hollywood notables: Walter Wanger, Hal Roach(a famous actor/producer) and Peter Perkins. The referee was Jack Holt. Senator and Mrs. Coleman DuPont put the Broadmoor's name in the national media when they stayed at the hotel for several months in the period between Senator Coleman's election and his taking office in 1920. Penrose missed meeting Helen Keller by two years, for she stayed at the Broadmoor with her companion, Polly Thompson, in 1941.

In the cultural arena, Julie invited some of the world's top musicians and singers to perform at evening musical concerts and to relax in mountain splendor. The celebrated pianist, conductor and composer Igor Stravinsky gave a concert at the Broadmoor Hotel on March 3, 1935. He was accompanied by the violinist Samuel Dushkin, with whom he had collaborated for the previous five years. Prior to this event, Vladimir Horowitz and Serge Rachmaninoff had also performed at the hotel. Julie's passion, however, was the opera and by far the largest group of artists who came at her invitation were singers. Grace Moore, star of the Metropolitan opera, stage and screen, stayed at the Broadmoor for about a month from August to September of 1943. She gave a concert in Penrose Stadium and took lessons from golf pro Ed Dudley. The summer before Moore arrived, the Penrose Stadium had hosted four exceptional singers for a series of summer concerts. They were: Jeanette MacDonald, soprano of screen, radio and concert, Brazilian soprano Bidu Sayao, tenor James Melton of the Metropolitan Opera and Paul Robeson. In 1945, Metropolitan Opera star Anna Kaskas and Polly Grimes of Denver were guests at the Broadmoor before their concert at the City auditorium. Kaskas also sang at mass in the Pauline Chapel. Later that same year Helen Jepson, also of the Met, was Mrs. Penrose's guest.

Celebrities' visits were not without incident, and these were reported with great gusto in the society pages of the nation's newspapers. When the journalist, author, and columnist Lucius Beebe stayed at the hotel in 1945, he was researching short line railroads. This task necessitated the inspection of engines and other heavy equipment. When he arrived in the Broadmoor's main dining room for lunch he was refused entry due to the dusty condition of his clothes. The incident was reported in papers across the country because Beebe had recently been chosen as one of America's 10 best-dressed men. He returned later in an elegant suit and was permitted to dine. As the hotel's reputation grew, it earned a place in popular culture. The hotel was used as a location in several comic strips and in popular novels. In 1946 the "Wash Tubbs" comic strip depicted its characters in Colorado Springs at the Broadmoor Hotel, and going up Pikes Peak as part of the continuing plot.

Honeymooners flocked to the Broadmoor resort as it provided numerous romantic opportunities amidst beautiful scenery and remarkable luxury. The Cheyenne Mountain Lodge, until it was closed down shortly after Mrs. Penrose's death, was a popular destination for newlyweds as were the bridle trails, golf courses and swimming facilities. As early as 1921 Penrose had realized that honeymooners were a large potential client pool. Just in case newlyweds didn't think of going to the Broadmoor by themselves, Speck conjured up a little publicity stunt to encourage them.

Fred Parrish, the flying cameraman from the *Denver Fox News* who had filmed several of Penrose's splashiest openings, was planning to marry a young woman named Zoella Roschie, organist at the Rivoli Theater in Denver. Surrounded by reporters, the couple "eloped" to Colorado Springs by plane. They married at the airport and spent their honeymoon at the Broadmoor. Newlyweds did not take long to catch on, and the Broadmoor became

BELOW: Carriages from the Broadmoor's collection were used to transport celebrities to the stadium on the other side of the lake during the annual rodeo. Burl Ives is seated in the center of the front seat. The man helping the woman up is Washington photographer, Frank Turgeon.

Broadmoor Historical Collection, Bob McIntyre photo

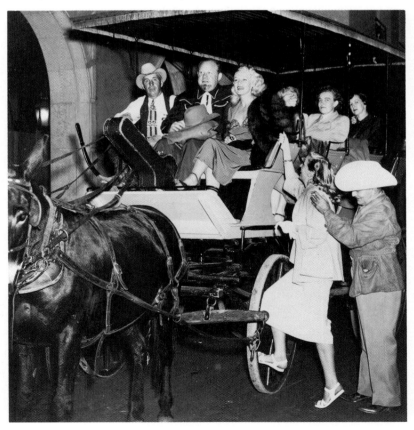

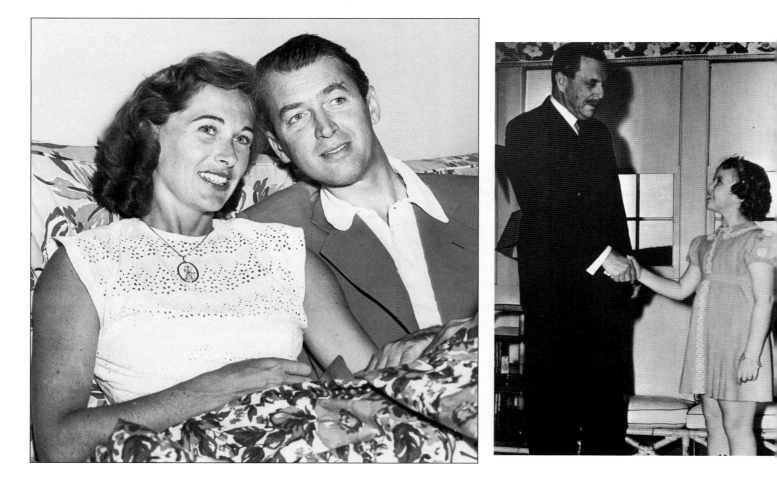

one of the preferred honeymoon locations in the country. At one time in 1948, thirty-six newlywed couples were staying at the hotel. Julie did her part as well. With her many connections among the European nobility, she managed to arrange numerous visits to the Broadmoor. In the summer of 1942, Count Court Haugwitz Reventlow married Mrs. Margaret Drayton (a member of the Astor family) in Colorado Springs. The wedding reception was held at the Penrose home, El Pomar, and the couple honeymooned at the Broadmoor.

Romance also flourished among the "beautiful people" who populated the hotel every summer or who were permanent residents. Mrs. Edgar B. Hatrick, who occupied an apartment on the first floor of Northeastmoor for many years, had a lovely daughter who became a protagonist in one of the Broadmoor's most colorful stories. One summer in the early 1940s, Miss Gloria Hatrick, a former Powers model was introduced to Ned McLean, a dashing young man from the East Coast who had purchased a ranch in Black Forest. Part of Ned's charm was the glittering family from which he came. His mother was Evelyn Walsh McLean, the daughter of Thomas F. Walsh, a Colorado prospector who had struck it rich and made millions. Evelyn Walsh married Edward B. McLean (of the McLeans who published the *Cincinnati Enquirer* and the *Washington Post*) who purchased

Dinah Shore, at the Broadmoor for the annual Dinah Shore/Junior Achievement Golf Tournament, poses with former Vice President of Marketing, Mike Dimond and Debra Cayler, Director of Public Relations.

Broadmoor Historical Collection, Bob McIntyre photo

Julie Penrose's acquaintances among the European nobility came to see her resort in Colorado. Count Court Haugwitz Reventlow and his newlywed bride Margaret (of the Astor family) honeymooned at the Broadmoor.

Broadmoor Historical Collection

Candice, when she accompanied her father, Edgar, to the Broadmoor in 1952.

Broadmoor Historical Collection

Edgar Bergen and Charlie on top of Pikes Peak in 1948. The comedy team, frequent visitors to the Hotel, did not miss any of the local sights.

Broadmoor Historical Collection, T.O. Johnson photo

the Hope diamond for her in 1912. She entertained at the Broadmoor Hotel and wore the diamond on several occasions at hotel functions. When her son was introduced to the glamorous Gloria during a party at the hotel, he lost his heart to her. Edward and Gloria married in 1943. The marriage was not a success, and they separated in 1948. Despite a first failure, however, neither the institution of marriage nor the Broadmoor lost their charm for the couple. Both remarried shortly after the divorce and both honeymooned at the Broadmoor. Ned McLean married Manuela Hudson Vanderbilt in 1948 and Gloria McLean married actor Jimmie Stewart in 1949. The Stewarts have since returned to the hotel many times with their two children.

Hollywood gave the Broadmoor Hotel some additional glitter when film stars Anne Baxter and John Hodiak came for their honeymoon in 1947. During their stay they met another Hollywood group: Peter Lawford, Lynn Bari and her husband Sid Luft who were also staying at the hotel. Many stars of stage and screen found their way to the Broadmoor either to vacation or to perform at the Hawaiian Village Nightclub and later the International Center (many combined work and play by including a period at the hotel with their families as part of their remuneration package).

The Hawaiian Village nightclub in the Golf Club became extremely popular during and after World War II. The second floor of the Golf Club building was a large room with a stage at the west end and a long bar which occupied most of the south wall. The room opened out onto the roof over the snack shop and porch on the first floor and guests could sit or dance under the moonlight. The interior decorations, grass thatched huts and Japanese lanterns which

looked so improbable in the light of day, created a magical atmosphere after dusk where hotel guests, Colorado Springs residents and officers from the local bases managed to forget their troubles for a time. Couples danced on the roof until dawn's first light to music provided by some of the country's most popular performers and had the opportunity to see shows that were also performed in Las Vegas and New York. Pat O'Brian, Dagmar, Edgar Bergen and Charlie McCarthy, Gordon McRae, Mickey Rooney, Carmen Miranda and Harry James and his orchestra among many others compressed their shows onto the Hawaiian Village's small stage. The incomparable Hildegarde thrilled the crowds (especially the men) with performances that involved a great deal of audience participation. Many guests at the hotel held private parties at the Hawaiian Village and strove to outdo each other with extravagant food and decorations. It was a place that many remember with great fondness, but as time went on and renovations in other areas of the hotel progressed, it became clear that the area was too small.

When the International Center was completed in 1961, a much larger space was available for entertainers and for audiences. The Hawaiian Village was closed and made into

ABOVE: Marlene Dietrich at a press conference in the Broadmoor. 1969.

Broadmoor Historical Collection,
Bob McIntyre photo

ABOVE LEFT: Carol Channing on vacation at the Broadmoor with her husband and son.

Broadmoor Historical Collection

BOTTOM LEFT: Liberace, who performed often in the International Center, occasionally sat at the piano in the Lake Terrace Lounge to please his fans among hotel guests and staff.

Broadmoor Historical Collection,
Bob McIntyre photo

the Oval and Copper Rooms, which were used as meeting spaces. The International Center opened with Harry Belafonte and his twenty-two member orchestra. Belafonte was the first in a long string of fine entertainers who appeared at the Broadmoor International Center from the early sixties to the late seventies. During the two decades that the shows went on, Colorado Springs' audiences were given the opportunity to enjoy a wide range of styles and types of music, comedy and drama, chosen by the Broadmoor's booking agent, Carol Truax.

Featured performers included several who came almost every year and became familiar figures around the hotel: Victor Borge, Liberace, The Preservation Hall Jazz Band and pianists Ferrante and Teicher. The rock band, Jefferson Airplane, made a one-time appearance in 1967, the same year that Jack Benny and Sid Caesar were on the playbill.

Marlene Dietrich appeared in 1961 and again in 1969 and was such a difficult guest that she has a permanent place in the memories of some of the older staff members. The majority of the star performers, however, were extremely well-mannered and made the experience of working at the Broadmoor Hotel a very exciting one.

Carol Truax's bookings ensured that Colorado Springs' audiences would be exposed to musicians from all over the globe. Miriam Makeba (an exile from South Africa) brought African music to the Broadmoor stage in 1963. Spanish pianist Alicia de Larrocha, and Flamenco guitarist Carlos Montoya were among the musical appearances in 1971, followed by Los Indios Tabajaras from Brazil in 1972. British and American music, ranging from the mundane to the marvelous, was represented as well. Commander Cody and His Lost Planet Airmen, Petula Clark, Nelson Eddy, Gladys Knight and the Pips and Chuck Mangione among many others, made their way to the Broadmoor and Colorado Springs.

Comedians and dramatic artists included the teams of Rowan and
Martin and the Smothers Brothers who came on several occasions, Carol
Channing in 1961, Phyllis Diller in 1964, Bob Newhart and Maurice
Chevalier in 1965 and Goldie Hawn in 1973. Hal Holbrook interpreted
Mark Twain and Cornelia Otis Skinner was herself. The world of modern
dance was represented by Hanya Holm in 1961, Joan Toliver in 1963 and
the American Ballet Theater in 1965. Some of the most popular shows
at the International Center were the big bands and jazz performers who
encouraged the audience to push back their chairs and dance. Herb Alpert
and the Tijuana Brass, Buddy Morrow and the Tommy Dorsey Orchestra,
Wayne King and his Orchestra, Jimmy Hendricks and the Glenn Miller
Orchestra and the legendary Duke Ellington and orchestra set many feet
to tapping. The hotel has maintained the big band tradition over the years.

Guy Lombardo and the Royal Canadians played
at the Gala Opening of Broadmoor West in 1976.

Dancing has always been a major part of
the Broadmoor's entertainment offerings. Ever
since the hotel opened, every summer season featured either a single male or female dance instructor or a couple, usually from the Arthur Murray
studios, who held dance lessons in the ballroom
during the afternoons, opened shows in the
Hawaiian Village and did demonstration dances

Henry Fonda and wife Shirley during a 1966 visit.

Broadmoor Historical Collection, Bob McIntyre photo

at major functions. In 1950 the Broadmoor hired a couple by the name of Jon and Vivian Williams who worked for Fred Astaire and were assisting him in setting up Fred Astaire Dance Studios across the country. Jon and Vivian liked Colorado Springs and the Broadmoor Hotel so much that they decided to leave the Astaire Studios and set up permanently at the Hotel. In 1953 they began cotillion classes for children in the Broadmoor ballroom where myriads of young locals learned to bow, curtsey and fox-trot. Although times have changed and they teach many more recent dances as well, the Jon D. Williams Cotillion still instructs budding socialites in the same location.

The charm and romance of the Broadmoor hotel has attracted a wide range of fascinating and talented people over the years. Some of them did not come entirely of their own volition. Buddy Rogers, a 1930s motion picture producer and actor, was forced to land at Peterson field by a snowstorm that interrupted his cross country trip. He was, however, happy to have the opportunity to stay at the Broadmoor and to take a break from his country-wide recruitment campaign for the Navy. The Broadmoor's location, its world-class sporting venues, and its proximity to the Air Force Academy and other major military bases have attracted a constellation of stars from many fields of endeavor. After the North American Air Defense Command was organized in 1958 at Ent Air Force Base, and then moved to a secured installation built inside of the southern portion of Cheyenne Mountain in 1965, statesmen, royalty and prominent military officials visited with even greater frequency.

RIGHT: Jack Benny gave an impromptu performance in the dining room in 1946, with the Broadmoor's bandleader, Bob McGrew.

Broadmoor Historical Collection

Protagonists of Screen and Stage

THE BEAUTY, GLAMOUR and glitter of the Broadmoor Hotel are especially attractive to those who already have a following among the public and want to stay in a resort that is as famous as they are. As you walk through the lobby, mezzanine and halls of the Broadmoor Hotel you are following the shadows of many noted artists from a number of media. Clark Gable, while a first lieutenant in the Army Air Force stationed in Pueblo, was a frequent visitor at the Broadmoor when he had overnight passes. He played golf, went skating and drove the women wild in the Hawaiian Village nightclub. The post-war era was a time of relief, relaxation, and an opportunity to take vacations that had been postponed for some time. Film and radio comedian Danny Kaye vacationed at the Broadmoor in 1946 as did Alex Dreier, famous radio personality and friend of Wm. Thayer's. Tutt convinced Dreier to combine business with pleasure and his trips often became opportunities to publicize the Broadmoor on his radio show. Dreier later became a broadcast journalist and news analyst for CBS, but continued to appear at the Broadmoor for important events. On the occasion of the installation of the new Cadillac engine for the Broadmoor's Cog Train to the zoo, he drove the train and dedicated a broadcast to the event. When General Doolittle held the Annual Reunion of the Tokyo

Left: Reba McIntyre in her Broadmoor suite prior to her concert at the U.S. Air Force Academy. 1992.

Broadmoor Historical Collection,
Bob McIntyre photo

MIDDLE: Jackie Gleason in his classic pose, on the Broadmoor links. 1962.

Broadmoor Historical Collection,
Bob McIntyre photo

RIGHT: Jonathan Winters at the Broadmoor in 1981.

Broadmoor Historical Collection,
Bob McIntyre photo

Raiders in 1960, Dreier was Master of Ceremonies. To thank him for his assistance over the years Wm. Thayer Tutt had a racy sports car built in the Broadmoor Garage and presented it to him on behalf of the hotel.

Jack Benny also arrived at the Broadmoor in the years following the war. In 1945 he booked rooms at the Colonial Club (the least expensive rooms at the Broadmoor) in order to maintain his reputation as a skinflint. In 1946, however, he occupied a seventh floor suite with his traveling companion Leo Durocher, Manager of the Brooklyn Dodgers. They came to try out the Broadmoor golf course and see the sights. Benny returned to perform at the International Center on several occasions in the sixties and seventies. When Benny appeared one night on the *Tonight Show* Johnny Carson asked him where he was going to spend the summer. Benny replied that he was going to stay and perform at the Broadmoor Hotel which he really enjoyed despite the fact that the hotel didn't pay him anywhere near enough money. When he arrived at the Broadmoor, Russ Freymuth (employee of the Broadmoor Hotel for forty-seven years and Assistant Manager at the time), who had seen the show, laid out a red carpet in front of the Broadmoor South tower so that Jack Benny would know that he was appreciated symbolically, if not monetarily.

The annual rodeo held in the stadium at the Broadmoor until 1973 when it was moved so that Broadmoor West could be built, featured many well-known names. Gene Autry, cowboy star of radio, screen and television was the featured star at the 1952 and 1953 rodeos. He thrilled the crowds, especially his younger fans with his blindingly white, bejeweled cowboy suit. In 1964, "Doc" Adams and Festus of *Gunsmoke*, Milburn Stone and Ken Curtis in real life, were the featured performers.

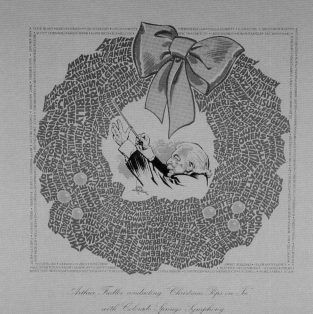

The Cheyenne Mountain Zoo offered celebrities photo opportunities as well. In 1956 Marlin Perkins, the star of *Zoo Parade* on NBC, filmed an episode of his show at the Cheyenne Mountain Zoo. He later became the host of the popular wildlife show *Mutual of Omaha's Wild Kingdom*. Victor Borge played an impromptu concert at the zoo during one of his visits and was accompanied by some of the more musical animals.

The fifties too provided their share of illustrious visitors. Alfred N. Steele, Chief Executive Officer of Pepsi Cola, and his wife, actress Joan Crawford, stayed at the hotel in March 1959. Steele was at the hotel for a Pepsi Cola promotional conference to kick-off the company's new colorless soda, Slice. The couple was photographed offering a drink of Pepsi to a baby tiger at the zoo, but the staff of the hotel did not require a photograph to have Crawford's visit incised on their memories. Prior to her arrival the hotel received a list with several pages of instructions on the proper way to treat a person of Ms. Crawford's stature. Other captains of industry, such as H.L. Hunt and J.C. Penney came in years following. Fred Mac-Murray, movie and television star vacationed at the hotel with his wife in 1950. Actress Agnes Moorehead stopped at the Broadmoor in 1958 just after she had completed filming *Night of the Quartermoon* for MGM. She was on her way East to appear on Shirley Temple's television program.

Distinguished members of the press who came to the hotel both to gather stories and to escape from gathering stories included Walter Cronkite, CBS news correspondent, who stayed at the hotel while filming a *Twentieth*

Century broadcast in Colorado Springs and newscaster Paul Harvey, who visited in the summer of 1964. Andy Rooney of *Sixty Minutes* arrived in 1981 to address a local organization and surprised those who met him by acting just as cynical as he does on television.

The Air Force Academy is responsible for bringing a number of talented people to the Colorado Springs area, either as guests or entertainers. Charlton Heston stayed at the Broadmoor in 1981 when he came to town to address the Most Outstanding Cadet Squadron at the annual Air Force Academy banquet held in the International Center. Tennessee Ernie Ford, radio and television personality, had been invited as speaker for this event several times prior to Heston's engagement. Ford was a popular speaker at the Broadmoor because after his official appearances he thrilled audiences at the Golden Bee with renditions of his songs, especially his most popular hit "Sixteen Tons."

Although many comedians came to perform at the Broadmoor, a number came purely for relaxation. These include the likes of Art Linkletter, the host of the radio talk show, *People are Funny* who first visited the Broadmoor in 1949 and returned several times afterwards; Jackie Gleason who stayed at the hotel in 1962 and played golf with Ed Dudley, Buddy Hackett, Jonathan Winters, and Flip Wilson.

The Broadmoor's proximity to the Wild West has made it a haven for Hollywood stars who need a break in the process of filming movies on the dusty prairies. Charles Bronson, for example, came up to the Tavern for lunch while filming the movie *White Buffalo* in Canon City. John Wayne was a frequent visitor, but perhaps his most memorable visit was when he decided to take a break from filming a movie in Durango and come to the Broadmoor for a few days. When his manager called to book him a room, the desk clerk who

ABOVE: Maurice Chevalier, the epitome of elegance and charm, at the Broadmoor in 1965.

Broadmoor Historical Collection, Bob McIntyre photo

BELOW: Jane Fonda and Ted Turner were guests at the hotel while attending the Olympic Congress. 1992.

Broadmoor Historical Collection, Bob McIntyre photo

took the call (who had not been at the hotel very long) thought it was a prank and did not make a reservation. When John Wayne walked through the lobby doors later that evening the same clerk became extremely flustered and in his confusion assigned him and his manager a honeymoon suite with one, king-size bed. After going up to his room, John Wayne telephoned the desk and said "I like my manager a hell of a lot, but I'll be damned if I'm going to sleep with him!" He was quickly given more appropriate accommodations. [2] Other Hollywood celebrities stayed at the hotel during the Rocky Mountain Motion Picture Association awards ceremony in 1967: Rock Hudson, Robert Conrad, John Saxon, Slim Pickins, Sherry Jackson and Robert Lansing.

The list of the famous and talented who have graced the halls of the Broadmoor is very long, but in closing it is necessary to mention a last few who represent the very best of American talent. Ethel Merman, Broadway star, and her husband Robert Six (President of Continental Airlines) stayed at the hotel quite often, as did Lucille Ball and her husband who came with absolutely no acknowledgment to the press. Mr. and Mrs. Walt Disney and opera singer Lily Pons used to stay at the Garden of the Gods Club (an establishment founded by Al Hill, another prominent Broadmoor guest) where it was easier to find private lodgings during the extremely busy summer season at the hotel. They did, however, frequently dine in the Penrose Room as well as enjoying other aspects of the resort. Shortly before his death, Arthur Fiedler conducted the Colorado Springs Symphony Orchestra for the first Christmas Pops on Ice in December of 1978.

Princess Anne of England passes through the lobby of the South tower.

Broadmoor Historical Collection, Bob McIntyre photo

Kings, Queens, Regents and Nobility

THE BROADMOOR'S PROMINENCE on the international scene and its proximity to military bases vital to the national defense have made it an obligatory destination for some of the world's titled heads of state and royal families. The Emir Abdul Ilah, prince regent of Iraq stayed at the Broadmoor in June of 1945. He greatly enjoyed the scenery, but was made quite nervous by the presence of so many uncovered women at the hotel. The prince was accompanied by an entourage of fifty men including Raymond Muir from the United States Department of State. His Majesty King Hussein of Jordan was an honored guest on two occasions. The Duke of Sparta, Crown Prince Constantine of Greece, occupied the sixth floor of the hotel while touring American military installations with the Secretary

2. This story was recounted by Russell Freymuth, a long-time employee of the Broadmoor who was in charge of the front desk at the time and later became General Manager.

TOP LEFT: John F. Kennedy stopped at the hotel briefly as a Senator, but came back to Colorado Springs in 1963 to tour NORAD in its first location at Ent Air Force Base.

Bob McIntyre photo

TOP RIGHT: Margaret Thatcher is welcomed by hotel manager Douglas Cogswell.

Broadmoor Historical Collection, Bob McIntyre photo

RIGHT: Seated in front of the Broadmoor Golf Clubhouse are, from the right: Ed Dudley, Dwight D. Eisenhower and L.B. Maytag.

Broadmoor Historical Collection, Bob McIntyre photo

of Defense in 1959. The king and queen of Thailand stayed at the Broadmoor in July of 1960. His majesty Bhumibol Adulyadej and Her majesty Queen Sirikit skated at the Ice Palace. The king joined an impromptu jazz session with Major Mark Azzolina and the NORAD dance band. The Crown Prince of the United Kingdom of Libya, Hasan al-Rida al Sausi stayed at the Broadmoor Hotel in 1962 while touring the Air Force Academy and NORAD facilities. Princess Anne of England attended a luncheon reception at the Penrose Room in the fall of 1982. The Grand Duke and Duchess of Luxembourg were guests at a dinner in the Penrose Room in their honor hosted by Colorado Governor Dick Lamm and his wife in January of 1984. The royal couple were in Colorado Springs to participate in a Fort Carson ceremony commemorating the participation of the 4th Infantry Division in the liberation of Luxembourg in September of 1944. Prince Michael Ajose of Nigeria was a guest in 1980.

Presidents and Politicians

P RESIDENTS, FORMER PRESIDENTS and presidential hopefuls have gravitated to the Broadmoor Hotel on many occasions. The resort gave them the opportunity to combine politics with golf, hunting, fishing and other amusements. Penrose was very politically opinionated and gave the hotel a decidedly Republican tilt, but he was not unwilling to associate with Democrats when they did sensible things like repeal Prohibition. His intolerance for Roosevelt's New Deal policies, however, was such that he left town when F.D.R. came to stay at the hotel. Herbert Hoover's visit in 1939 was much more palatable. Former President Hoover gave an informal talk to four hundred Colorado Republicans at the Broadmoor Hotel on August 5, 1939. He had gone fishing on the Gunnison river and stopped in Colorado Springs on his return.

In 1940, Wendell Wilkie made the Broadmoor Hotel into a temporary campaign headquarters when he was the Republican presidential nominee. He stayed at the Broadmoor Hotel for a three-week period in July and utilized the rodeo and other events to give his campaign some American West patriotic flair. President Dwight D. Eisenhower's summer White House was located in Denver because his wife's mother lived there. Although Eisenhower did not sleep at the Broadmoor, he frequently came down to play golf and for social functions and was always given a suite at the hotel for the duration of his stay. Jack Kennedy came to the Broadmoor on a brief visit when he was Senator to address the graduating class at the Air Force

Academy. He returned to Colorado Springs to tour NORAD as President of the United States.

The political and societal upheaval of the sixties did not seem to have much effect on the Broadmoor. Prominent politicians attended functions and vacationed at the hotel undisturbed. Senator Barry Goldwater came to the Broadmoor Hotel on numerous occasions while carrying out his duties as a member of the Air Force Academy Board of Visitors. Richard M. Nixon stayed at the Broadmoor Hotel on several occasions. The first was in the fall of 1956 during the presidential campaign, then as Vice President in 1958. He addressed the Governor's Convention in 1969 as President of the United States; the convention included Ronald Reagan of California and Nelson Rockefeller of New York.

Other visiting dignitaries include the former Secretary of State Henry Kissinger, who stayed at the hotel several times. Former President Gerald Ford who came both to give speeches at Colorado College and other organizations and to participate in the World Seniors Golf Tournament. Walter F. Mondale, former Vice President, has visited the Broadmoor as has Canadian Prime Minister Pierre Trudeau.

In more recent times, the Broadmoor has seen a great deal of the last two Republican presidents. President Reagan stayed at the Hotel on the

occasion of his speech to the U.S. Air Force Academy in 1984. Reagan returned to the hotel on October 29, 1986, when he campaigned for Ken Kramer. George Bush first came to the Broadmoor in 1978. He returned as Vice President on September 19, 1986, then as President in 1989 to address the Junior Achievement Business Hall of Fame dinner during the four-day Junior Achievement Convention which was emceed by Dinah Shore. His final visit as President of the United States was in August of 1992.

Russell Tutt and Henry Kissinger take a stroll in front of the Broadmoor International Center.

The Military

MILITARY MEN WERE always well-represented among the guests at the Broadmoor. Penrose involved a number of military teams in polo matches on the Broadmoor field, and held numerous events, such as the Remount endurance races and air shows, which involved the U.S. Army. During and after the installation of Camp (later Fort) Carson, Peterson Air Force Base, the U.S. Air Force Academy and NORAD the hotel hosted an ever-increasing number of prominent military officers and functions. Many of the nation's top generals have been and continue to be frequent visitors at the hotel.

General Hoyt Vandenberg, Chief of Staff of the Air Force during and after World War II was invited to spend a summer at the Broadmoor by Wm. Thayer and Russell Tutt after he had undergone surgery for cancer. When the Vandenberg's were ready to return home after their stay they were collected by the first Air Force One jet (before it was given to the President). Bill Roub, one of the two waiters who had served the convalescing General three meals a day for three months and who later became the hotel's Food and Beverage Director, remembers that when the military limousine arrived to transport the General and his wife to the airport, the couple insisted that the two waiters ride in it to the airport so that they could see the famous jet. At the airport, unknown to General and Mrs. Vandenberg, was a receiving line and a band. After they had passed through the receiving line, Mrs. Vandenberg called the two young men up the gangway and gave them a tour of the plane much to the surprise of the officials and dignitaries in the receiving line.

Athletes

PENROSE'S PASSION FOR athletes as promotional vehicles began a long and glorious tradition of athletes as guests at the hotel. In Penrose's lifetime, boxers Jack Dempsey and Max Baer made regular appearances, as did tennis players Bill Tilden and Helen Wills Moody among others. Will Rogers, although best known for his cowboy acting skills, was an excellent polo player and was to be seen on the Broadmoor field during his visits. Sonja Henie, the woman who had inspired the Ice Palace, came to the Broadmoor Hotel to watch the National Figure Skating Competition in 1948. She was accompanied by instructor Howard Nicholson and her skating partner, Michael Kirby. She later selected some members of the Broadmoor Skating Club to join her show.

The Broadmoor Ice Palace has hosted almost all of the great names in skating at one time or another in the course of the many United States and international championships that were held there. The same is true for the Broadmoor Golf Links. From other sports, athletes have come to avail themselves of high-altitude practice facilities, such as the New York Rangers, who held a three-day practice at the Broadmoor on their way West in 1974. Many others came simply to vacation: Joe DiMaggio; "Sugar" Ray Leonard, World Welterweight boxing champion; quarterbacks Roger Staubach, John Brodie, John Elway and Terry Bradshaw, among others, and track star Jackie Joyner-Kersee.

Wm. Thayer Tutt's involvement with sports and international sports organizations culminated when he and top officials of the United States Olympic Committee (Bob Kane, Don Miller and Phil Krum) began discussing the possibility of transferring the Olympic headquarters to Colorado Springs. Wm. Thayer and his nephew Bill Tutt negotiated at length with City officials and committee members and succeeded in coming up with a solution satisfactory to all parties. In 1977 the USOC transferred its offices to an area close to the center of Colorado Springs. Since then, a number of Olympic training facilities have been built on the site and numerous individual sporting associations have also moved their offices to Colorado Springs.[3] The presence of the Olympic Committee in Colorado Springs has resulted in the Broadmoor's hosting of a number of administrators and athletes both from the United States and abroad.

ABOVE LEFT: 1956 Men's Olympic Gold Medalist, Hayes Alan Jenkins, practicing at the World Arena.

Broadmoor Historical Collection

ABOVE RIGHT: President George Bush is greeted by Broadmoor President, Steve Bartolin, upon his arrival at the hotel. 1990.

Broadmoor Historical Collection, Bob McIntyre photo

BOTTOM RIGHT: Dorothy Hamill during a figure skating competition at the Broadmoor World Arena.

Broadmoor Historical Collection

---

3. The site was chosen for the Olympic facility was originally Ent Air Force Base, named after General Ent who was a guest at the Broadmoor facility for many months during his convalescence. The base was closed when operations were consolidated at Peterson Air Force base farther east of the city.

The Animals

ANIMALS HAVE ALWAYS had a special place in the history of the Broadmoor. From the cows that Pourtales encouraged to eat the best alfalfa and produce the richest butter for the Broadmoor Dairy, to the rare Okapi antelope at the zoo, animals figure largely in the area's past and present. Few animals have actually been guests of the Broadmoor Hotel, but some succeeded in prolonging their residence for some time. In 1952 a pair of young sea lions were put into the lake to deal with the problem of fish overpopulation. The lions consumed the fish in short order and then began barking loudly for their breakfasts rather early in the morning, to the dismay of sleeping guests. The sea lions also took a number of scenic walks, one ending up as far away as the Carriage Museum and another waddled down the stairs to the front entrance of the hotel. They were removed from the lake

AT RIGHT: At the 1969 Governors Conference, Ronald Reagan attended as the Governor of California.

Broadmoor Historical Collection, Bob McIntyre photo

Mr. & Mrs. Arnold Palmer and Mr. & Mrs. Dow Finsterwald pose in the Golf Club.

Broadmoor Historical Collection, Bob McIntyre photo

when their presence had become more of a hindrance than an attraction.

When the Garden Room in the Tavern first opened, it was populated with small singing birds from the zoo and two large pink flamingos in the wading pool at the far end. Diners were delighted with the picturesque scene until the birds began depositing their droppings in overhead flight and the flamingos insisted on taking walks between the tables. The Tavern is now tastefully decorated with live plants, but birds and other living creatures can be seen on the other side of the greenhouse roof. Two orangutans Maggie and Jiggs from the zoo were also used for promotional stunts at the hotel.

Literature and Literati

AUTHORS AND playwrights seek out places of interest to write about and to write in. Over the years, several have stayed at the Broadmoor Hotel. Edna Ferber stayed at the hotel during a tour gathering information for a new novel in June of 1928. Cornelia Otis Skinner visited on several occasions, including when she performed at the International Center. Truman Capote stayed at the Broadmoor and often dined here while filming *In Cold Blood* at the prison in Canon City. He brought the principal members of the cast to dinner at the Penrose Room. He returned in 1974 to work on a new manuscript. Harper Lee, author of *To Kill A Mockingbird*, vacationed at the Broadmoor in 1963, as did Erica Jong in the early eighties.

TOP: Mr. and Mrs. Bob Hope have returned to the Broadmoor numerous times over the years. Here they are pictured with Edward L. Gaylord, CEO of The Oklahoma Publishing Company.

Broadmoor Historical Collection, Bob McIntyre photo

BOTTOM: Author Truman Capote, standing before the Hotel's south face with race car driver Ken Wood Egar (who managed the Broadmoor's Abercrombie & Fitch store). 1974.

Broadmoor Historical Collection, Bob McIntyre photo

Conventions of Note

ALTHOUGH THE BROADMOOR Hotel was conceptualized and designed to provide the finest possible accommodations for individuals and families, conventions and conferences have always made up a portion of the clientele. The hotel did not make any serious effort to attract such groups until the early sixties, but many organizations had discovered that the Broadmoor was an extremely attractive place to do business long before. Groups ranged from the Colorado Springs Telegraph carrier boys, who were invited for a tour and dinner in 1922, to the National Governors' Conferences which were held at the Broadmoor several times. Many groups made the Broadmoor their traditional meeting place and the interlude at the hotel has become an integral part of their organizational history. The Broadmoor has hosted a number of unusual conventions with remarkable participants, some of which caused the hotel to transform itself, if only for a day, into a different sort of place. During the Edison Companies Convention in September of 1927, guests wandered about in the Broadmoor's gardens which were illuminated without any visible light source. The gardens had actually been floodlit with ultraviolet lights, while plants and objects had been painted with a reflective paint which caused them to glow. In 1946, the Women's National Aeronautic Association convened at the Broadmoor Hotel in April and May. The convention hosted some of the most famous women pilots of the time: Blanche Noyes and Eunice McCaskay among others. These women, many of whom had been in the military during the war, discussed the introduction of women into professional civilian and military flying corps, a process which is still going on today.

During the 1949 Governor's Conference every effort was made to see to the comfort and entertainment of the governors and their staffs. The Colorado State Patrol assigned sixty of its finest to make up the Colorado Courtesy Patrol who drove the governors in a fleet of sixty Columbine-blue Ford cars. The cars made quite a picture as they lined both sides of Lake Avenue in front the hotel.

One of the hotel's most prestigious conferences was the North Atlantic Treaty Organization conference in 1982. European Defense Ministers and Ambassadors from all NATO countries attended the conference which was directed by Secretary of Defense, Casper Weinberger. The hotel was virtually taken over with participants and their attendant staffs, press from all over the world, and numerous translators. The convention demanded extremely high levels of security and steel-helmeted officers were everywhere.

After World War II, Americans slowly lost the habit of spending long periods of time in luxury resorts and many great hotels discovered that

in order to survive they had to adapt to a changing society. Reluctant to alter the hotel's traditional mode of operations, the Broadmoor delayed its conversion to a hotel with adequate facilities to provide for larger and more sophisticated groups until the 1960s. But the reality of the change in clientele proved to be less stressful than imagined. In an increasingly harried and stressful world where men and women attempt to organize their lives in the midst of a myriad of demands upon their time, a professional convention in a luxury resort hotel is a welcome respite from day-to-day life. Since the sixties, the Broadmoor has been in the process of transforming itself into a hotel which can satisfy the increasingly sophisticated demands of modern clients, both convention guests and individuals, who come to soak themselves in the beauty and romance of a hotel with a past, which can also provide them with all of the amenities of the present.

ABOVE: The banquets for the 1949 Governor's Conference filled the dining rooms to capacity.

Broadmoor Historical Collection,
Bob McIntyre photo

Prospectus for the Future

WHEN EDWARD L. GAYLORD purchased a controlling interest in the Broadmoor Hotel in 1988, he brought to it his own personal vision; a vision born of his own experiences within the hotel's walls and his hopes for its future. Although the Broadmoor's past is a rich one, Ed Gaylord wants its future to be as glorious, so the resort must continue to grow and evolve. Oklahoma Publishing Company, the parent company which represents Gaylord's interests, has rejuvenated the hotel with intensive capital investments in property improvement and sophisticated marketing campaigns while maintaining the hotel's character and charm. Although Gaylord acquired the Broadmoor as an investment, his intent was also to preserve and maintain one of the landmark historic resorts in the United States. His own family's past is intertwined with the Pikes Peak region and ownership of this great hotel gives him a link to his own personal history.

Interestingly enough, there are a number of parallels between the founder of the Broadmoor Hotel and its new owner. Both are extremely successful businessmen, on the conservative end of the political spectrum and protective of their privacy. Both were born into families of substantial means, but went on to attain fortunes and fame much greater than that envisioned by their fathers, due primarily to their business acumen, vision and willingness to take risks. And, most importantly, both love the Broadmoor Hotel.

Edward L. Gaylord's father, Edward King Gaylord was born in 1873 on the family's farm near Muscotah, Kansas. E.K. Gaylord's father had served as a Captain in the Union Army and married Eunice Edwards of Massachusetts. The couple left the East Coast after the end of the Civil War seeking a better life, but found only drought and grasshoppers on their Kansas homestead. When Edward was six years old, his parents and older brother Lewis left Kansas and came to Denver, Colorado. Leaving

Majority partner Edward L. Gaylord and The Oklahoma Publishing Company join with El Pomar Foundation and the Broadmoor's future glows with promise.

OPPOSITE: Portrait of Edward L. Gaylord, President and Publisher, The Oklahoma Publishing Company; Chairman, Broadmoor Hotel, Inc.; Chairman, Gaylord Entertainment Co.

Oil painting by C.J. Fox
Courtesy Edward L. Gaylord

Denver, they crossed the mountains and finally settled in Grand Junction, Colorado. Edward was first employed outside the home at the age of eleven, and worked at a number of odd jobs, but he shared his mother's dream of higher education. At the age of eighteen, the family's pastor loaned him enough money to leave home and establish himself at an institution of higher education.

In 1891 Edward came to Colorado Springs with seventeen dollars in his pocket. He enrolled in Cutler Academy, a college preparatory school for prospective Colorado College students. E.K. lived in a boarding house at 1327 North Nevada Avenue and worked as a handyman to support himself while he completed his education at Cutler Academy and The Colorado College. Prior to leaving the College in 1897, he had served as President of the student YMCA, the Oratorical Association, and the Apollonian Club as well as editor and business manager of the *Colorado Collegian* (the college newspaper).

While E.K. was pursuing his academic career, his brother Lewis came to Colorado Springs and the two managed to put together enough money to purchase a controlling interest in the *Colorado Springs Evening Telegraph*. But this first venture in journalism did not prove to be successful enough for either of them. Lewis moved to St. Joseph, Missouri, where he purchased the *Daily Gazette* and E.K. accepted a position as Deputy Court Clerk in Colorado Springs and was then sent to Cripple Creek as Chief Deputy Court Clerk of the newly formed county. (This was the same period that Pourtales and Penrose were investing in Cripple Creek.) Although he enjoyed his work in Cripple Creek and had decided to continue his studies in the field of law, E.K. felt that his future lay in journalism. In 1900 he left Colorado Springs and joined his brother in St. Joseph, Missouri. After accumulating enough expertise in the field of journalism to believe that he could make it on his own, he set out once again and roamed the frontier seeking a propitious spot to establish his own newspaper.

Having visited several towns in Kansas, Texas, and the Territories he chose Oklahoma City, a lively little prairie town with several failing newspapers and a great deal of potential. E.K. convinced the owner of the *Daily Oklahoman* that he could revitalize the newspaper and shortly thereafter became partners with Roy E. Stafford who had founded it in 1894. E.K. borrowed the $5,000 that he needed to invest in the paper from the parents of Ray Dickinson, a classmate from Colorado College.[1] Gaylord's initiatives not only brought the newspaper back to life, but were the beginning of an empire. As the paper's circulation increased, so did E.K.'s power to affect events. He strove, however, to exercise his influence wisely and to maintain the highest professional standards in the field of journalism. He made the following statement to Ruth Anderson Lewis which she cited in her article "Romances of American Journalism," *Editor & Publisher of the Fourth Estate*, March 10, 1928.

Always we aim for cleanliness. We are becoming increasingly critical of our news columns, sensationalism is played down, crime news reduced to a minimum and features scrutinized carefully to the end that nothing unwholesome shall be presented. At the same time we desire to maintain the open mind. Narrowness would be a flimsy foundation upon which to build the influence that we aspire to wield.

E.K. Gaylord was one of the driving forces behind the consolidation of the Oklahoma Territory and Indian Territory into the state of Oklahoma in 1907, and then managed to have the state's capital moved from Guthrie to Oklahoma City, the city that he had chosen as his own. After building the *Daily Oklahoman* into a successful venture he bought out Stafford and founded the Oklahoma Publishing Company, which continued to grow as Gaylord's financial and political strength increased. E.K. himself never occupied a political office, but his frequently vitriolic front page editorials had a major effect on public policy decisions in the state of Oklahoma.

E.K. Gaylord was fascinated by science and technology and supported

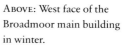

ABOVE: West face of the Broadmoor main building in winter.

Bob McIntyre photo

AT RIGHT: View of the resort from the south.

---

1. To this day, the Dickinson family remains in partnership with the Gaylords and are stockholders in the Oklahoma Publishing Company and the Gaylord Entertainment Company.

many charitable initiatives to promote education and progress in these fields. He was remarkably well-informed about the latest innovations and used his knowledge to multiply his profits. His early successes in journalism were based on his ability to obtain and print information before his competitors did. As his empire grew, so did the level of technology that he used to maintain it. His printing presses and distribution networks utilized the most sophisticated machinery available and repeatedly chalked up "firsts" in the publishing world for inventive uses of technology. He recognized the changing trends in the media industry and founded the first radio station west of the Mississippi and the first television station in Oklahoma. When E.K. Gaylord died at the age of 101 in 1974, the Oklahoma Publishing Company controlled numerous publications, radio and television stations, transportation networks and even an oil company. These accomplishments pale, however, compared to the heights attained by his son Edward.

ABOVE: The Oklahoma Publishing Company headquarters in Oklahoma City. The building, designed by the architects of The Benham Group, was completed in 1991.

Courtesy The Oklahoma Publishing Company

Due to his father's extraordinary vitality and rigorous work ethic (he worked a full day in the office the day he died) Edward L. Gaylord did not take over the family business until he was fifty-five years old, but the intervening years were not spent in vain. Edward L. was born in Denver, Colorado, in 1919. His mother, Inez Kinney Gaylord, bore three children: Edith, Edward and Virginia. Inez Gaylord came to Colorado before Edward's birth to spare herself and her newborn child the oppressive Oklahoma summer heat. Coming to Colorado for the summer became a Gaylord family tradition, particularly after E.K. built a summer cottage in Estes Park in 1920.

Inez Gaylord had worked in Paris for the YWCA prior to marrying E.K. and she wanted her children to have an understanding of the world outside of Oklahoma. They traveled through Europe on several occasions and the children even attended school in Lausanne, Switzerland, for six months. The Gaylord children pursued studies and interests in various parts of the country to further broaden their educations.

After attending public schools in Oklahoma City through the eleventh grade, Edward L. was sent to the Ashville School in North Carolina where he excelled at his studies. He subsequently attended Stanford University, unlike his sister Edith who followed her father's example and attended Colorado College. Edward attended the Harvard School of Business and then began his career at the Oklahoma Publishing Company on June 1, 1936. Prior to leaving for service in World War II, he worked summers in the transportation division and the circulation and advertising departments.

From 1942 to 1946 Gaylord served in the U.S. Army, primarily in Panama. When he returned from the war he lost his heart to Thelma Feragen, a warm and generous woman who, since 1950, has shared his life and given him four children. His son, Edward K. II (who married

Left: Sun Lounge, 1992.

Courtesy Wilson & Associates

Above Left: The Penrose Suite, on the sixth floor of the main building. 1992.

Courtesy Wilson & Associates

Above Right: Julie's gift to the Tavern, a Toulouse-Lautrec entitled "Jane Avril," hangs near the bar.

Broadmoor Historical Collection

Above: A sumptuous bathroom, 1992.

Courtesy Wilson & Associates

Natalie Smith at the Broadmoor Hotel in 1991) works with his father and maintains a ranch and rodeo facility. Daughters, Christy, an amatuer golfer and board member of OPUBCO; Mary, an avid horsewoman and breeder of Kentucky saddlebreds and hackney ponies; and Louise, a civic-minded Oklahoma City resident, pursue their individual interests and raise Gaylord's five grandchildren. The Gaylord children share in their father's love of Colorado and make frequent visits to the Broadmoor.

Following the war, Edward L. rejoined OPUBCO and was trained in all aspects of the business. In E.K.'s later years, he occupied himself primarily with the newsroom and the paper's editorial policy as well as his many projects in the larger community. As Executive Vice President, Edward L. ran all of the business aspects of the company. When the oil boom swept Oklahoma he founded Publisher's Petroleum and later began to invest in real estate in several western states with OPUBCO Resources. This real estate company has assets in Texas and Arizona as well as large tracts in Colorado. Edward continued to assist his father until E.K.'s death in 1974, when he took over the Oklahoma Publishing Company and made it into an international media conglomerate.

After assuming the Presidency of the Oklahoma Publishing Company, Edward L. maintained the legacy left to him by his father, but has since made a series of bold acquisitions which have moved his companies to the cutting edge of the media industry. Gaylord Entertainment Company, of which he is chairman, owns a range of companies in the entertainment industry based in Nashville, Tennessee: *The Grand Ole Opry*, the Opryland Hotel, three country music cable networks (The Nashville Network, Country Music Television and Country Music Television, Europe) as well as a number of television and radio stations in several Western states. The Opryland Music Company's Acuff-Rose music publishing house is one of the largest in the industry. The Opryland theme park as well as the

General Jackson showboat are offshoots of the company's country music successes. Although the entertainment company went public in 1991, Ed Gaylord kept the original family business among his private holdings. The Oklahoma Publishing Company controls the prestigious *Daily Oklahoman* newspaper, The Broadmoor, the Manitou and Pikes Peak Cog Railway, Sun Resources, the Greenland Ranch and American City Business Journals.

Ed Gaylord's interest in the Broadmoor stems from his family's continuing involvement in Colorado Springs and the state of Colorado. His father maintained his ties with the city in a number of ways. E.K. was a trustee of Colorado College from 1957 to 1970 (Edith Gaylord Harper, his daughter, is currently a trustee) and was a major contributor to the College. He was, therefore a frequent visitor to the city and its most prestigious hotel, the Broadmoor.

As a child, Ed Gaylord accompanied his family on the annual summer trek from Oklahoma City to Estes Park, which frequently included a stop at the Broadmoor Hotel. He was delighted by the sophisticated clientele and service as well as the numerous opportunities for entertainment. As a businessman, Gaylord wanted to maintain both his emotional and financial connections to the state of Colorado. Colorado is his birthplace and second home and Colorado Springs is the city that first fostered his father's ambitions.

In 1977, seeking quality investments in the state, the Oklahoma Publishing Company bought the Greenland Ranch, a 22,000-acre working ranch north of Colorado Springs. At that time, Ed Gaylord said he had turned down an offer to buy the *Denver Post* because he thought the ranch would be more valuable than the *Post*. A year later he purchased the Colorado Springs *Sun* newspaper, which competed with the Colorado Springs *Gazette Telegraph*.

The *Sun*, originally titled the *Free Press*[2] was a smaller paper than the *Gazette* with a fiercely loyal readership. The paper maintained a combative relationship with the *Gazette* which resulted in a higher standard of journalism for both papers. The *Sun* was deeply involved in community issues and stressed coverage of local and regional news with particular emphasis on alternative viewpoints. Under the Oklahoma Publishing Company

---

2. The *Free Press* newspaper was founded in 1947 when the *Gazette* locked out striking International Typographical Workers. The ITU sold the newspaper to H.M. Greensun in 1970 who changed the name.

management the newspaper won numerous national awards including the best sports pages in its circulation class in 1984 and 1985. Circulation and advertising revenues increased and the paper was well-respected, but there wasn't enough room for two newspapers in Colorado Springs. In 1986 Gaylord sold the newspaper for thirty million dollars to Freedom Newspapers Inc. which owned the *Gazette*, thus ending the notorious newspaper war. The *Sun*'s quality journalism, photography and pungent editorials are remembered fondly by many Colorado Springs residents.

When, in 1988, Ed Gaylord learned of the opportunity to invest in the cornerstone of the city, The Broadmoor, he contacted El Pomar Foundation. Russell Tutt and E.K. Gaylord had been appointed to the Governing Board of Colorado College at the same time in 1957, so Ed Gaylord had many acquaintances on the board of El Pomar Foundation. Given that the two parties shared an interest in the well-being of Colorado Springs and an enduring respect for the Broadmoor's traditions and history, the two were able to reach an agreement which was formalized in August of 1988.

The acquisition of eighty percent of the Broadmoor Hotel was a source of great personal pleasure for Ed Gaylord. It gives him much satisfaction to be part of the Hotel's restoration and regeneration and to partake in its glittering destiny. The Oklahoma Publishing Company's considerable financial resources give the Broadmoor a stable base upon which to grow and prosper in the years to come. Gaylord's relationship with his partner, El Pomar Foundation, is an excellent one given that both parties share common goals.

As of 1990, El Pomar Foundation, of which William J. Hybl is C.E.O., retains twenty percent of the Broadmoor Hotel. Bill Hybl has been involved in the Broadmoor enterprises since 1972 when he was hired as legal counsel for El Pomar Foundation and the Broadmoor Hotel. Following the Foundation's partnership with the Oklahoma Publishing Company, Hybl's position within the Broadmoor is that of Vice Chairman.

Ironically, one of Hybl's most significant efforts in the last two decades was his involvement in the Foundation's attempt to keep the Broadmoor Hotel under the umbrella of El Pomar Foundation after the Federal Tax Reform Act was passed in 1969. This law, which required that charitable foundations divest themselves of at least fifty percent of their for-profit business holdings by 1989, meant that Penrose's dream of keeping the Broadmoor Hotel associated with his own fortune would be shattered. For eight years, Bill Hybl prepared briefs and presented the hotel's case for an exemption, time and time again before Congressional committees and other departments within the Executive branch. The United States Senate passed legislation on three separate occasions which would have spared the Foundation, but the House of Representatives never approved it. In 1988, just a year before the twenty-year grace period ended, the trustees of the Foundation conceded and began to search for a partner who would be respect-

ABOVE: Ceiling detail from the Main Mezzanine. Note the male dancer's two right feet. 1993.

David Beightol photo

OPPOSITE: Ceiling detail from the Main Ballroom. 1993.

David Beightol photo

ful and protective of the Broadmoor Hotel's past while sharing their hopes for its future.

After negotiating with several potential buyers, El Pomar Foundation was able to reach a satisfactory agreement with Edward L. Gaylord and the Oklahoma Publishing Company. The Foundation's decision was influenced in part by the Gaylord family's involvement in the Colorado Springs community. The Broadmoor plays such an integral role in Colorado Springs' economy and culture that its owners must combine a commitment to the city's well-being with their interest in the resort. Gaylord purchased sixty-five percent of the Broadmoor in August of 1988 and then an additional fifteen percent in January of 1990. With the advent of majority ownership by the Oklahoma Publishing Company, the Broadmoor Hotel stepped out of the Foundation's protective shadow into the highly competitive resort market of the 1990s. Although the

trustees of El Pomar Foundation relinquished control of the Broadmoor Hotel with regret, they have joined with Gaylord to form a dynamic and creative partnership.

Edward Gaylord's purchase of the Broadmoor came at a critical time in the hotel's history. The number of elite resort hotels in the United States increased ten-fold during the 1980s. In order to keep pace with this rapidly changing and evolving industry, the Broadmoor had to radically update its facilities and services. The man chosen to head this transition was Stephen Bartolin Jr., who came to the Broadmoor from the Greenbrier in White Sulphur Springs, West Virginia. Bartolin's experience managing one of the few remaining outstanding historic properties in the United States made him particularly well-suited for the Presidency of the Broadmoor.

Steve Bartolin's plan for the Broadmoor resort is an ambitious one. It entails the restoration and preservation of the unique historical heritage of the hotel, modernization and improvement of existing facilities, and a multi million-dollar expansion of the hotel's offerings in order to make the property competitive in the twenty-first century. The renovation and redecoration of the main and auxiliary buildings' interiors commenced in 1988, when Wilson and Associates of Dallas were hired. The mezzanine, lobby and bedrooms of the main building recaptured the simple elegance of the Julie Penrose era with an emphasis on classically beautiful fabrics, patterns and furniture design. The frescos and architectural details on both the interior and exterior of the building were restored and cleaned and some of the more intrusive decorations of the sixties, such as the painted curtains in the Pompeiian Room, were removed.

ABOVE: These two plaques commemorating quotes from E.K. and E.L. Gaylord hang in the lobby of OPUBCO headquarters and demonstrate the company's commitment to high standards and the greater community.

Courtesy The Oklahoma Publishing Company

ABOVE: View of Broadmoor
West from the lake.

Photographs, written materials and artifacts which relate to the Penroses' and the Broadmoor Hotel's history are being accumulated and catalogued. As collection of these items progresses, they will be organized into a small archives and museum for the benefit of guests and visitors. These efforts will further preserve and protect the hotel's past, one of Bartolin's main concerns. In this way, many of the aspects of the Broadmoor Hotel that were available to its guests when it opened in 1918 will once again be part of the hotel's offerings.

Evolution and Progression

THE HISTORY OF THE Broadmoor records the hotel's long and colorful past, but no organization can afford to rest on its laurels. The resort's owners and administrators have taken up the challenge of carrying the Broadmoor into the next century. The hotel and resort market has changed radically since Penrose first conceived of the world's most unique hostelry at the base of Cheyenne Mountain, and the Broadmoor must grow and thrive in a world that offers many more resort opportunities than existed in the past.

The philosophical foundation that underlies this plan for the future, includes many of the elements which made up Spencer Penrose's concept for a first-class resort hotel in the early 1900s, as well as numerous adaptations for a future which he could not have foreseen. The Broadmoor will continue to provide the best in accommodations, service and dining, but will also provide a more complete experience of Colorado and the unique environment which surrounds the resort. Horseback riding, carriage and stagecoach excursions and the opportunity to utilize the extensive network of trails up Cheyenne Mountain and Cheyenne Canon have already been reintroduced.

William J. Hybl (right foreground), Vice Chairman of the Broadmoor Hotel and C.E.O. of El Pomar Foundation, leading the United States delegation during the opening ceremonies of the 1992 Summer Olympics in Barcelona in his role as President of the United States Olympic Committee.

Courtesy, United States Olympic Committee Archives

Plans are being executed for a new golf clubhouse, which include a fitness center and a European-style spa. General Palmer first decided to build the City of Colorado Springs while bathing in the mineral springs just a few miles from the Broadmoor, and the city's reputation was built on the promise of those health-giving waters and rarefied mountain air. The Broadmoor Spa makes these quintessentially Colorado resources available once again, utilizing techniques that have been perfected in the watering places of Europe. Mineral water baths, aromatherapy utilizing Rocky Mountain products and an array of services including massage and hydrotherapy are all part of the Spa's offerings.

The fitness center, golf clubhouse and new tennis complex will maximize guest and member opportunities for attaining physical well-being in a beautiful and inspirational setting. The hotel will, once again, include an indoor pool with Turkish baths, saunas and massage facilities. The center will provide aerobics areas, cardio-vascular and resistance training equipment as well as board-certified instructors and personal trainers. Clay tennis courts will be added, including a recessed stadium court for tournament play. The golf links will continue to be maintained at championship levels, and the improved golf club will make it easier to enjoy them.

A new complex of deluxe rooms will rise on the west side of the lake in the mid-1990s. The suites, whose windows look out upon the dramatic panoramas of the mountains or the lake, encircle a lakeside terrace. A ballroom occupies the western end of the ground floor which, in addition to those meeting spaces already extant on the property, provides an unparalleled amount of space for social and business-related events.

Architect Tag Galyean, an experienced resort planner and spa designer, and Ron Lustig of Earl Swensson Associates designed buildings in accord with the same principles that governed the design of the main building by Warren and Wetmore in 1917 — buildings that incorporate beauty and utility

ABOVE: Detail from domed ceiling over the spiral staircase. 1993.

David Beightol photo

while blending into the hotel's dramatic surroundings. The new structures utilize design elements from the original hotel, thereby recalling the eccentric vision of the hotel's founder, Spencer Penrose. When the design team was assembled, Bartolin instructed them to be passionate about building upon the architecture of the original hotel and creating new structures that look as if they had been on the property since 1918. In this way, the designers succeeded in recapturing the continuum which Penrose began. The architectural plans were developed in conjunction with landscape designers and horticulturalists to ensure that the different aspects of the expansion create a harmonious environment for the entire resort.

The landscaping changes, which will take place from 1993 to 1995, are the most radical since the Olmstead Brothers of Brookline, Massachusetts, laid out the grounds prior to the hotel's opening. At the time, American hotels wanted to emulate European ones and the gardens and grounds were laid out in ornate patterns utilizing plants which were not native to the area. In the intervening years, Americans have developed a sense of appreciation for their own plant culture and ecosystems. The new landscaping for the Broadmoor concentrates on species that are native to the area, fit in well with the surrounding slopes and do not overly tax the water supply. Paths and vistas will be laid out so that those interested in walking and viewing native plant and animal species will be able to do so without having to leave the hotel grounds.

The plan includes a bridge that links the two sides of Cheyenne Lake by extending the lakeside terrace of the main building westward and creating a similar terrace on the opposite bank. Although a tour of the lake's perimeter is a uniquely beautiful walking or jogging experience, its length can be an inconvenience. The bridge provides a shorter pathway between the two main portions of the hotel. It is not entirely utilitarian, however, in its center is a tile-roofed gazebo for small parties, weddings, or simply enjoyment of the surroundings.

These plans for the evolution of the hotel involve, as progress often does, the destruction of two older buildings. The original Broadmoor Golf Clubhouse (which was the second Broadmoor Casino) and the Broadmoor World Arena (originally the Broadmoor Riding Arena) have to be torn down to make way for the new structures. These two building have served many purposes during the course of their existence and been modified innumerable times so that they could fit into the fabric of the hotel's needs. It was no longer possible to adapt them so that they could meet the standards of excellence that must be maintained at the Broadmoor. It is with great regret, however, that they are razed. The beautiful windows, columns and tilework of the Clubhouse, as well as other fixtures, were preserved and incorporated into the new building.

Staff Par Excellance

At the time of this writing, the Broadmoor Hotel is celebrating its seventy-fifth anniversary. Part of the hotel's unusual history is the constancy and dedication of its staff. Over the years, many employees have spent their entire working careers as part of the Broadmoor. To them, the Broadmoor is more than just a hotel, it is a way of life and an opportunity to creatively express their estimable talents to a world-class clientele. In its seventy-five year history the hotel has had only four Executive Chefs and six Presidents; this data is, in and of itself, a tribute to employees' dedication and affection for the hotel.

Louis Stratta, Executive Chef (1917-1976)

Louis Stratta was hired by Spencer Penrose in 1917, a year before the Broadmoor opened its doors to the public. During the construction of the hotel he ran a camp kitchen on the premises and saw to the feeding of the construction crews. When the hotel formally opened on June 29, 1918, he offered the menu on the right, which he prepared a second time for the hotel's fiftieth anniversary in 1968.

Louis Stratta was born in Ivrea, Italy, in 1887 and spent his formative years there, learning the profession that was to become his life's work in

---

Menu

FAVORITES MONDAINE

VELOUTE DE VOLAILE, ISOLINE
Celery Ripe Olives Salted Almonds

BROADMOOR TROUT AU BLEU
Sauce Exquisite

BRAISED SWEETBREADS AUX PERLES DU PERIGORD
Petits Pois Nouveaux a la Francaise

BONELESS ROYAL SQUAB,

ROTI
Potatoes Pasqualine   Guava Jelly

SALADE DE ROMAINE ET CERISES

SOUFFLE GLACE, COMTESSE DE CORNET
Friandises

CAFE FILTRE

Group of legendary Broadmoor employees assembled in the Dining Room. From the left: Dining Room Captain, Jumbo Flynn; Chef Louis Stratta; Bill Roub (later Director of Food and Beverage); Chef Georges Ferrand; Maître d'hôtel, John Altrichter.

Courtesy William Roub

ABOVE: Changing of the guard; retiring Chef Hank Trujillo (right) leaves Chef Siegfried Eisenberger in charge.

Broadmoor Historical Collection, Bob McIntyre photo

restaurants in Torino. To broaden his horizons, he went to Manchester, England, where he was discovered by a representative from Palmer's Antlers Hotel and brought to America. When Penrose discussed his idea for the world's finest hotel with the twenty-nine year-old chef, he agreed to leave the Antlers and take on the position of Executive Chef at the new Broadmoor Hotel.

Chef Stratta served the hotel well for fifty-nine years and is remembered by many as the person who brought international haute cuisine to Colorado. He provided inspiration for numerous budding chefs whom he helped to sponsor during the course of his long life. Those who worked for him recall his autocratic rule of the kitchens and his skill in the aging of meat. In his prime, he stood on a podium in the center of the Broadmoor's main kitchen with a large chef's knife and orchestrated the operations of all the sous chefs and wait staff. Every plate that left the kitchen had to be perfect in appearance and in content. In Chef Stratta's kitchens all of the preparations were done by hand, with few or no concessions to modern appliances and techniques. Louis Stratta personally ensured that the standards which Penrose had insisted on continued to be maintained until his own death in 1976.

GEORGE FERRAND, EXECUTIVE CHEF (1976-1981)

Chef Ferrand initially came to the Broadmoor for a vacation when he needed a respite from his position as Executive Chef at a hotel in Texas and later in St. Louis. Ferrand came to the Broadmoor as an employee in 1962 and worked under Chef Stratta until his death, when Ferrand assumed the position of Executive Chef. Chef Ferrand continued the Broadmoor's tradition of the finest in French cuisine. He was born in Monte Carlo and trained in fine hotels in both France and England before coming to the United

States under the auspices of the U.S. Army. Chef Ferrand retired in 1981, after serving as Executive Chef for five years.

HENRY J. TRUJILLO, EXECUTIVE CHEF (1981-1992)

Henry (Hank) Trujillo came to the Broadmoor for the first time as an eighteen year-old. While in the Navy he went to cooks' and bakers' school and was employed by the Broadmoor immediately after his discharge. He started in 1956 as Saucier then moved up to Garde Manger (preparing and designing cold foods, specializing in presentation) then continued his apprenticeships in all of the different areas of the kitchen. He worked for

the Broadmoor in one capacity or another for thirty-seven years, but as Executive Chef from the time of Chef Ferrand's departure until 1992.

Chef Trujillo is of Native American and Hispanic descent and never trained in Europe, but he attained an extremely high level of professionalism (as well as a working knowledge of French, Italian and German) under the tutelage of Chefs Stratta and Ferrand as well as the many other foreign chefs who worked in the hotel's kitchens. He retired in 1992, and handed the baton on to Chef Eisenberger.

The innovative menu in Charles Court includes "Medallions of Free Range Black Buck Antelope" pictured below and desserts such as this luscious raspberry mousse (left) in a chocolate dipped biscuit bowl designed by pastry chef Jean Spielmann. 1993

David Beightol photo

SIEGFRIED W. EISENBERGER, EXECUTIVE CHEF (1992-)

Chef Eisenberger was born in Frohnleiten, Austria, where he received his early training in the culinary arts. He emigrated to the United States in 1975 and directed kitchens in several prestigious American hotels and restaurants. He has received numerous awards and honors and led the American teams to an unprecedented number of medals at the 1984 and 1988 Culinary Olympics. Like the chefs that came before him, he is committed to providing guests with the best in Continental and traditional American cuisine.

This alone, however, is not enough for Chef Sigi. American chefs have developed exciting new interpretations of traditional foods, as well as a range of dishes which utilize exclusively American ingredients and techniques. While the Penrose Room and the

Tavern will always provide guests with excellent traditional cuisine, Charles Court allows guests to venture into the innovative and sample what's new on the cooking scene.

Presidents

ABOVE: Stephen Bartolin Jr. (center), President of the Broadmoor Hotel, accepts the 1993 AAA Five Diamond Award on behalf of the hotel.

AT RIGHT: Karl Eitel, President of the Broadmoor Golf Club, and former U.S. President Gerald Ford under the loggia at the front entrance.

Broadmoor Historical Collection, Bob McIntyre photo

THE STORY OF THE Presidents of the Broadmoor has in great part, already been told as part of the history of the hotel itself. Spencer Penrose, was president until his death in 1939. Julie Penrose held the office very briefly before hiring Charles L. Tutt Jr. in 1940. Charles died in 1961 and was replaced by his son Wm. Thayer, President until 1977 when his brother Russell took office until 1982. In 1982, Karl Eitel, who had been employed at the Broadmoor as Resident and General Manager since 1961, was appointed President of the Broadmoor Hotel.

Karl Eitel was the first hotel professional to be President of the Broadmoor. He came to the hotel when Broadmoor South and the International Center had just been completed and oversaw the Broadmoor's development into a resort which could cater to the needs of large conventions and meetings. As General Manager Eitel established the Broadmoor's first organized Sales and Conventions offices and instituted formal marketing campaigns. He also supervised the planning and construction of Broadmoor West. Although Karl Eitel retired from the Presidency on September 1, 1990, he remains quite active in his role on the board

of El Pomar Foundation and as President of the Broadmoor Golf Club.

The sixth President, Stephen Bartolin, has taken on the formidable task of overseeing the Broadmoor's latest transformation. The Broadmoor's staff and facilities must keep up with the levels of service and sophistication demanded by the modern traveler without losing the character and atmosphere which make the Broadmoor unique. Bartolin's goal is to ensure that the Broadmoor retains its standing among the world's finest resorts while maintaining its historical integrity.

THIS HISTORY OF THE Broadmoor draws to a close, after recording the glories and vagaries of times past, for readers of the present and future to ponder. The Broadmoor itself moves onward, with history being made each day within its venerable walls and stored up to be savored by future generations. In a country which glorifies progress and is beguiled by the attraction of the new, few institutions can claim to fulfill their original function in their original structure. The Broadmoor's promise to its patrons is that they will be immersed in the finest traditions of the past while benefiting from the amenities of the present in a setting that has always been and will continue to be absolutely stunning.

When the Broadmoor was built, it stood alone on the mesa at the base of Cheyenne Mountain; the unlikely offspring of a mining millionaire and a patroness of the arts. Spencer and Julie Penrose combined their notable talents to build not just a hotel, but an experience. The resort's staff and administrators are committed to providing guests with that same incomparable "feeling" every time they come to the Broadmoor. Beauty, Julie's guiding principle, surrounds the guest at every juncture, both within the hotel's walls and all about its grounds. The levels of service and quality of food and drink match or exceed those established under Speck's punctilious management.

BELOW: Afternoon light on tower.

The Penroses' successors, El Pomar Foundation and the Oklahoma Publishing Company, have done much to widen the Broadmoor's scope and renown throughout the world. The resort now offers an unparalleled range of services and opportunities for entertainment in the same environment that has attracted visitors since humans first set eyes upon it. Although the Broadmoor has grown and evolved with the times, its fundamental nature and purpose remain the same. The cragged "horns" of Cheyenne Mountain and the verdant foothills below continue to act as a beacon to those seeking health, divertissement, and conviviality in the opulent surroundings of the Broadmoor.

Main mezzanine, 1992. Courtesy Wilson & Associates

Acknowledgements

M Y THANKS TO ALL of the people who allowed me to interview them in the process of collecting information for this book and those who lent artifacts, photographs and ephemera from their collections. I wish to thank the staffs of the Local History Collection at Penrose Library, Special Collections at Colorado College Library and especially Sharron Uhler and David Ryan at the Colorado Springs Pioneers Museum. Tracy Felix introduced me to numerous Oral History candidates and assisted with the collection of art for the book. El Pomar Foundation allowed me to use their scrapbook collection and Beverly Mason unlocked the doors with unflagging patience. Photographers Richard Stites, Bill Bowers, John Gair, Bob McIntyre and David Beightol went out of their way to shoot and produce the visual materials in this book, sometimes under rather difficult conditions. Paolo Villa, Debra Cayler, Dennis Lesko, Sally Mayo and Steve Bartolin edited the text and reviewed the photographs. Susan Ridley provided moral support and practical assistance on an almost daily basis. I wish also to express my admiration for Steve Bartolin who commissioned this book, and whose committment to the preservation of the Broadmoor's past gives me great hope for its future.

Bibliography

E XTENSIVE USE WAS made of articles about the Broadmoor Hotel and the Penroses contained in the Broadmoor Hotel scrapbook collection which has been maintained since 1917. Given that the articles pasted in these books frequently omit the name of the newspaper, they cannot be cited individually.

WRITTEN MATERIAL

Abbott, Morris W. *Pike's Peak Cog Road, The.* Pulpit Rock Press, Colorado Springs, Colorado. 1972

Betts, Diane Lynn et. al. *Broadmoor World Arena Pictorial History Book.* Copyright, 1988, Broadmoor World Arena

Broadmoor Bonanza, Broadmoor Hotel publication, 1943–1992.

Broadmoor Polo Association. *The Polo Annual*, 1925; Broadmoor Hotel Print Shop, 1925

Buzzin' Bee, The. Broadmoor Hotel publication, 1962–1993

Browning, Boo, "The Wizard of Fourth and Broadway," *Oklahoma Monthly*, November, 1978

Carlton, Carol Ann, "Broadmoor Art Pottery," article in the *Antique Trader Weekly*, April 4, 1990.

Carlton, Jim and Carol. Letter to the author including information on the Broadmoor Pottery, October 1, 1992.

Chapman Publishing Company, *Portrait and Biographical Record of the State of Colorado.* Chicago, 1899

Clapesattle, Helen. *Dr. Webb of Colorado Springs, Colorado.* Associated University Press, Boulder, Colorado. 1984

Colorado Springs Fine Arts Center. *Pikes Peak Vision: The Broadmoor Art Academy, 1919–1945*, privately printed, 1989

Conte, Robert S. *The History of the Greenbrier: America's Resort.* Pictorial Histories Publishing Co., Charleston, West Virginia. Copyright 1989 The Greenbrier

Cooking Club, The. (pamphlet) privately printed, April, 1990

Cuff Stuff, Volume 25, Number 2, The Oklahoma Publishing Company, Oklahoma City, OK, 1963

Daily Oklahoman, The, Oklahoma City, OK, January 17, 1974

DeGeer, Stanley. *Pikes Peak is Unser Mountain.* Peak Publishing Co., Albuquerque, NM, 1990

Ellis, Amanda. *The Colorado Springs Story.* (pamphlet), The Dentan Printing Co., Colorado Springs, Colorado, 1954

Frost, Hunter S. *Art, Artifacts, Architecture, Fountain Valley School.* Privately published, Tiverton Press, Colorado Springs, CO, 1990

Gaylord, E.K. *The Frontiers Ahead.* Paper read by author at The Colorado College Invitational Seminar for High School Science Teachers, privately printed, 1956

Gaylord, E.K. *The Oklahoma Publishing Company, The Newcomen Society in North America,* Princeton University Press, New York and Princeton, 1971

Geiger, Helen. *The Broadmoor Story.* (pamphlet), privately printed, 1968, revised 1985

Giggey, Roland. *Recapitulation,* unpublished autobiography and history of events at the Broadmoor during his period of employment, 1983

Goodyear, George F. *Goodyear Family History.* Privately printed, Buffalo, New York, 1976.

Hagerman, Percy. *The Cheyenne Mountain Country Club: The First Twenty-five Years.* (pamphlet), privately printed, 1947

Hyde, Anne Farrar. *An American Vision: Far Western Landscape and National Culture, 1820–1920.* New York University Press, New York. 1990

James, Pat. "Gaylord, Colorado College reach centennial year Alumnus Centenarian makes good in Oklahoma City." The Colorado College *Catalyst,* May 11, 1973

Johns, Gilbert. "A Gastronomic Era," article in the Colorado Springs *Gazette Telegraph Leisuretime Magazine,* December 17, 1983

Lee, Mabel, Barbee. *Cripple Creek Days.* Doubleday & Company Inc., Garden City, New York. 1958

Lewis, Ruth Anderson. "Romances of American Journalism," article in the *Editor & Publisher of The Fourth Estate.* March 10, 1928

Morin, Marshall. *Broadmoor History.* unpublished manuscript, sine datum. (Marshall Morin was the interior decorator for the Broadmoor Hotel for many years)

Ormes, Manley Dayton & Eleanor. *The Book of Colorado Springs.* Denton Printing Co., Colorado Springs, Colorado, 1933

O'Toole, Charles. *Adventures of an Innkeeper.* privately printed, 1989.

Parkhill, Forbes. "The Last of the Penroses." Article published in the *Saturday Evening Post,* 1937

Peknik, George. *The Cheyenne Canon and Broadmoor Guidebook and Almanac.* Hoopoe Publications, Colorado Springs, Colorado, 1992

Phillips, Dr. Glenn A. *Three Studies in Fountain Valley Biography.* Unpublished Manuscript, 1991

Pourtales, James. *Lessons Learned from Experience.* Translated from the German by Margaret Woodbridge Jackson, Ph.D., printed by W.H. Kistler Stationery Co., Denver, Colorado, Copyright, Colorado College, 1955

Ruhtenberg, Jan. Curriculum Vitae, unpublished, courtesy of stepdaughter Shirley Dearing of Colorado Springs

Sprague, Marshall. *Newport in the Rockies: The Life and Good Times of Colorado Springs.* Sage Books, Denver, Colorado, 1961

Sprague, Marshall. *Money Mountain.* Little, Brown and Company, Boston, Massachusetts. 1953

Time Magazine, "Publishers—Survival of the Fittest," May 3, 1968

Tutt, Russell T. II. *The Tutt Family of Virginia, Philadelphia and Colorado Springs.* (pamphlet) privately printed, June 1984

Willumsen, Henry C., letter to the author including biographical information on Thorvald Christian Willumsen, unpublished. August 9, 1992.

Woodward, David. *History of the Broadmoor Greenhouse,* unpublished manuscript, sine datum

ORAL HISTORIES CONDUCTED BY ELENA BERTOZZI-VILLA

Bartolin, Stephen Jr., President, Broadmoor Hotel; interviewed 4/16/1993

Brown, F. Martin, Professor, Fountain Valley School and associate of Spencer Penrose; interviewed 8/20/1992

Calder, John and Catherine, daughter and son-in-law of Robert Menary; interviewed 2/26/1993

Coleman, Norman A., interviewed 9/22/1992

Eisenberger, Siegfried, Executive Chef, Broadmoor Hotel; interviewed 4/26/1993.

Eitel, Karl E., former President, Broadmoor Hotel; interviewed 3/17/1993

Faller, Siegfried Jr., former Director of Convention Services, Broadmoor Hotel; interviewed 2/24/1993

Freymuth, G. Russell, former General Manager, Broadmoor Hotel; interviewed 8/25/1992 and numerous consecutive occasions

Gaylord, Edward L., Chief Executive Officer, Oklahoma Publishing Company, interviewed August 30, 1993.

Harper, Edith Gaylord, daughter of E.K. Gaylord, member of the Board of Directors of the Broadmoor Hotel Inc., interviewed June 14, 1993

Hybl, William J., Chief Executive Officer, El Pomar Foundation; interviewed 4/21/1993

Lawrie, Don, former employee of Spencer Penrose, Pikes Peak Highway and Broadmoor Hotel, also President, Pikes Peak Ski Club; interviewed 3/15/1993

McDermott, Lillian Sousa, former secretary to Roland Giggey (Julie Penrose's personal secretary); interviewed 8/26/1992

Michael, Mary Eleanor Giggey, daughter of Roland Giggey; interviewed on numerous occasions

Might, Jack, former skater and member of the Broadmoor Skating Club; interviewed 12/3/1992

Roub, William L., former Food and Beverage Director, Broadmoor Hotel; interviewed 8/24/1992 and numerous consecutive occasions

Slothower, L.C. Jr., longtime resident of the Broadmoor area; interviewed 8/30/93

Spiers, Joseph and Ursula, former Managers of Beatty Hall, Broadmoor Hotel; interviewed, 2/24/1993

Stewart, Marka Webb, daughter of Dr. Gerald Webb; interviewed 9/25/1992 and numerous consecutive occasions.

Trujillo, Henry J., former Executive Chef, Broadmoor Hotel; interviewed 3/23/1993

Tutt, R. Thayer Jr., President, El Pomar Foundation (son of Russell Tutt); interviewed 3/3/1993

Tutt, William Bullard, former Executive Vice President, Broadmoor Hotel; interviewed 3/23/1993

Wyman, Joan P., former Aquatics Director, Broadmoor Hotel; interviewed 8/25/1992

Zinky, Kay, worked with Julie Penrose in Broadmoor Sports Shop and married to Ray Zinky, Purchasing Director for the Broadmoor; interviewed 10/5/1992

The Broadmoor rises out of the plain under an autumn sky.

This book was designed by Bill Vaughn,

and typeset in Sabon by Kitty Herrin

of Arrow Graphics, Missoula, Montana.